Connecting the Dots: A Handbook of Bible Prophecy

Ron Graff and Lambert Dolphin

Revised and updated from the popular Internet book,
Thy Kingdom Come, Thy Will Be Done…
The Prayer Offered Most Often Is About To Be Answered!

xulon PRESS

Connecting the Dots: A Handbook of Bible Prophecy
by Ron Graff and Lambert Dolphin

Printed in the United States of America

ISBN 9781609579784

www.xulonpress.com

Introduction

How the world has changed in the past decade! During the last 13 years the original
version of this book has been the standard Internet reference work for the broad
subject of the coming days in biblical prophecy. Hundreds of thousands of visitors have
accessed the book or downloaded it to guide them in their study of this great subject.
September 11th of 2001 changed the way that everyone looked at the world and at the subject of prophecy. In spite of this, the classic outline of future events given in the book has
not needed to be changed. What is needed now is an update of the material to include the
new reality of terrorism, which explains many of the details of the End Times predictions.
It is also time to consider the shifting alliances of nations in the light of prophecy and to
note the incredible advancements in technology that make it easy to believe that we are
getting closer than ever to the fulfillment of the events prescribed in the Bible for the last
generation of this age.

This revised version may serve as a handbook of biblical prophecy, helping sincere
students of God's Word stay on course in their thinking and their teaching of the subject.
It is not a collection of wild imaginations about how things might be, but a careful outline
of basic truth about revealed future events and how the current world situation relates to
that outline.

In some of the appendices, *Yeshua*, the transliteration of the Hebrew word for Jesus
is used. Also, *Yahweh*, the transliteration of the Hebrew word for Jehovah is sometimes
used.

As you will discover, both of the authors are indebted to the scholarship and spirit of
the late Ray Stedman. We quote him often, with kind permission of the Stedman family. In
a sense, he is a third author of this work.

We are also grateful to Gary Kah for providing much of the information used in Chapter 5 -
Satan's Final Empire: Global Governance and Religion. The quotations and references to his
work are used with his permission.

Special thanks are due to Ron's wife, Barbara Graff, for her encouragement and assistance in this project. We are also indebted to Denise Schubert and Neville Trindade for proof-reading and critiquing the manuscript.

There are variant translations of names, especially from Hebrew and Arabic. In most cases we have chosen what we believe is the most prevalent spelling of words like Al-Qaeda, Al-Aqsa, and Qur'an.

The contents of this book will be a framework into which you can fit the endless flow of current events that relate to prophecy. For current information and relevant news, please visit the authors' websites:

Prophecy Central, http://www.Bible-prophecy.com
Lambert Dolphin's Resource Files, http://ldolphin.org
The Temple Mount in Jerusalem, http://templemount.org
Apologetics Central, http://www.apologetics-central.com
Connecting the Dots, http://www.connectingthedotsprophecy.com

Table of Contents

Part II - The Church: A Mystery Revealed

Chapter 3 - The Mystery of the Church . . . 52

Chapter 4 - Church History . . . 65

Chapter 5 - Satan's Final Empire: Global Governance and Religion . . . 75

Chapter 6 - The Rapture of the Church . . . 96

Part III - Tribulation Saints
The Destiny of Believers during the Coming Tribulation

Chapter 8 - Believers during the Tribulation . . . 126

Chapter 9 - The First Half of the Tribulation . . . 136

Chapter 10 - The Rebuilt Temple . . . 147

Chapter 15 - Coming of the King of Kings . . . 212

Part IV - After the Tribulation

Chapter 16 - The Millennium and Beyond . . . 226

Appendices

Part I - Are These the End Times?

Chapter 1
What In The World Is Happening?
An Overview of Things to Come

Approximately one-third of the Bible contains prophecies. The book of Revelation is devoted entirely to the subject. It is amazing that so little attention is paid to the great prophetic passages in the Bible from many of the pulpits of the land. The aim of the prophets is to enlighten, to awaken hope, and to turn people from their destructive ways so God may bless them. Knowledge of what the future holds is the best way to prepare us to be ready.

Because of all the problems that threaten the world today, there is intense interest in this subject. A new poll from the Pew Research Center indicated that 41% of Americans expect Christ to return by the year 2050.[1] What an amazing fact! Undoubtedly the influence of the "Left Behind" series a few years ago can take some credit for this high percentage.

The subject of biblical prophecy is very interesting to most people for a number of reasons. The Bible has been shown to be the only book in history to predict the future with one hundred percent accuracy. In a world full of wrong answers and laughable predictions on every side, an accurate, reliable source of infallible information should be welcome news.

Undoubtedly, there is also interest in prophecy because of the constant barrage of bad news that this generation has suffered. Here is a short list of the troubling issues of our time.

First, there is the breakdown of family values. This has led to divorce, fatherless families, poor discipline, homosexuality, promiscuity, and other family problems.

Then there is apostasy and deception in the Church. This is a "falling away" of believers from a close relationship with The Lord and from a vital life-changing faith that draws other people to Christ and sets a high moral standard for society.

Corruption in government and greed in big business has caused the worst recession since the Great Depression, and has raised questions about how the country's mushrooming debt can ever be repaid. By some calculations, nearly 20% of the workforce is unemployed, resulting in unprecedented bankruptcies, foreclosures, and other financial calamities.

These conditions make the concept of a world government more desirable to some people. Shrinking borders, immigration problems, loss of national sovereignty, the apparent need for a world police force, common trade areas, and international banks and currency all push us toward a socialistic globalism.

Ignorance about the ideals of our Founding Fathers is causing many to wonder if our freedoms and Christian beliefs will soon be lost. Our history has been rewritten for school textbooks to downplay the importance of Christianity in our nation.

Unprecedented disasters, like the tsunami in 2004, the AIDS epidemic, drug-resistant superbugs, massive storms like Hurricane Katrina, and the BP oil spill in the Gulf of Mexico remind us of our inability to cope with the natural and man-made catastrophes.

And, of greatest concern, is what Jesus' foretold about "wars and rumors of wars" in the End Times. The threat of major wars, even world wars is greater now because of the existence of weapons of mass destruction (WMD).

The 9/11 attacks on New York and Washington D.C. literally changed the way we see our world because of the new threat of Islamic terrorism. This growing ugly reality seems to have no means of control.

Furthermore, the fountainhead of terrorism is the festering tensions in the Middle East. The whole world hopes for peace in that region so that there might be peace in the rest of the world.

There have been many years of negotiations, and numerous different peace plans and promoters, trying to bring peace to Israel and her neighbors. But tensions have just continued to grow, and now Iran is on the brink of deploying nuclear weapons. That country's president, Mahmoud Ahmadinejad, wants to destroy Israel and bring about the Islamic version of the Apocalypse in order to prepare the way for their messiah, the Twelfth Imam.

We will discuss this issue more fully later in the light of Bible prophecies about the rebirth of Israel, the rapture of the Church, and the coming Tribulation.

There is a peculiar development in our generation. In spite of the interest in prophecy by the public, there is a lack of teaching about prophecy in the pulpits. This may be caused in part by disappointments in the past. After becoming excited about Jesus' soon coming, many have reacted to the fact that he hasn't come yet. For other pastors this lack of end-times interest may be a result of false teaching that the Church has replaced Israel. But more likely, it is part of the reluctance by today's pastors to engage in any controversial subject, whether it is a moral issue or a difficult passage of Scripture. We fear for the average pastor of our age when he faces his Lord and has to explain why he did not teach the whole Bible! (Acts 20:26-27)

In his farewell address, "The Whole Counsel of God," evangelist C.G. Finney said,

But see the unfaithful minister in the Day of Judgment, he comes on to his trial, but he cannot look up. Those who sat under his ministry have caught sight of him, and they say to each other that is our minister; you remember his pretty tastes, his dazzling oratory, his graceful amblings, and his captivating blandishments; you remember about his pretty sermons, and you recollect how afraid he was to say hell, or let us know there was such a place; you recollect how he trimmed and truckled, how opposed to this thing and that thing, because it was not genteel, and was against all reform or progress in religion—do you remember all that: well that was our minister; see him looking down: he is speaking, what does he say? What does he say? See the eye of the judge looking through and through that unfaithful minister, that man who pretended to preach the gospel, and dealt deceitfully with souls. How much guilt there is upon him! What an awful thing that must be! How dreadful his position.[2]

The Wonder of Fulfilled Prophecy
Coming of Messiah as Savior

Unlike all other claims of foretelling the future, biblical prophecy is 100% accurate in all of the events that should have already come to pass. Josh McDowell, in his classic book, *Evidence That Demands a Verdict*, lists sixty-one categories of fulfilled prophecies about the coming of Messiah. All of them were fulfilled by the life of Jesus Christ. He quotes figures from Peter Stoner's earlier book, *Science Speaks*, to demonstrate the astronomical odds against just eight of these prophecies being fulfilled by coincidence.

Stoner wrote, "We find that the chance that any man might have lived down to the present time and fulfilled all eight prophecies is 1 in 10^{17}." To illustrate that number, Stoner then suggested that the reader visualize that many silver dollars spread across the whole state of Texas. They would cover the state 2 feet deep. Then, if one silver dollar were marked and buried, the chances of a blindfolded man picking that one marked silver dollar with his first attempt would be the same chance that the prophets would have had of writing these eight prophecies down and then having them all come true in one person.[3]

Now, since the prophecies of Jesus' first advent were fulfilled perfectly, we can expect the ones that still await fulfillment to also come true.

Major Prophetic Events Yet To Be Fulfilled
Restoration of Israel

Restoration of the scattered Israelites was a common theme among the Bible's prophets. In Ezekiel 36 and 37 we read detailed predictions about the Lord's plans to regather his dispersed people from all over the world, and bring them back to the mountains of Israel. At long last, they would have control of their own nation again. Please refer to Appendix C - *Harmony of Prophecy Chart* as you continue this overview of prophecy.

These prophecies were partially fulfilled in 1948. After <u>one-half of all Jewish people</u> <u>were killed in the prison camps of World War II,</u> most of the nations of the world recognized the right of Jewish immigrants to the Holy Land to declare their independence.

Ezekiel's prophecies had depicted the event as a valley of dry bones. The bones started shaking and joining together into a skeleton. Then the skeleton was covered by muscles and skin. The rebirth of the nation of Israel is a stark fulfillment of this vision.

However, the last part of that vision has not yet been fulfilled. Just as God had first formed Adam and then breathed life into him, in Ezekiel's vision, God also breathes new life into Israel, and gives her a new heart. These are pictures of spiritual birth, but most of the people of Israel have not yet experienced this spiritual transformation. It will happen in time, according to this and other prophecies about God's Chosen People. Multitudes of Jewish people have already turned to Jesus as their Messiah in our generation!

Emergence of a Final Evil World Empire - *feet of iron & clay*

In any overview of prophecy it is necessary to review the Bible's predictions about future world empires, leading to a final evil world government just before Christ returns to Earth as King of Kings.

These world kingdoms are depicted in a series of dreams and visions in the Book of Daniel. King Nebuchadnezzar had a dream about a giant statue (Daniel 2). He asked his wise men to interpret the dream, but they could not. However, Daniel, a devout young Hebrew captive, was given the ability to declare the dream and its interpretation to the king. The statue had a head of gold that represented the Babylonian Empire and King Nebuchadnezzar.

The chest and arms were silver, and stood for the next world empire, which would have two parts. This was fulfilled by the Medo-Persian Empire that eventually conquered Babylon.

A bronze waist and thighs stood for another powerful empire that would arise. This was a preview of Greece.

The legs were of iron, stronger than the other metals, and they symbolized <u>Rome, the</u> strongest of all empires, and <u>the last world empire </u>to reign over the known world.

The final aspect of the statue was the composition of the feet. They were partly of iron, and partly of clay. Then a rock fell from heaven, symbolizing the coming of Messiah to reign, and broke the feet, causing the whole statue to fall and break apart. The <u>rock</u> then <u>grew into a great mountain, representing the coming righteous reign of Christ </u>(Messiah). This subject will be developed more thoroughly in Chapter 8.

Several other portions of Daniel's prophecies (Daniel Chapters 7-9) and the Book of Revelation (Revelation Chapters 12-18) predict the same drama. The end result is the destruction of the final evil empire by the coming of Jesus to reign as King of King and Lord of Lords.

Time of Jacob's Trouble/ Tribulation

The Prophet Jeremiah gave a strong warning about a terrible time in the future for Israel.

These are the words the LORD spoke concerning Israel and Judah: [5] "This is what the LORD says:

"'Cries of fear are heard—
terror, not peace.
[6] Ask and see:
Can a man bear children?
Then why do I see every strong man
with his hands on his stomach like a woman in labor,
every face turned deathly pale?
[7] How awful that day will be!
None will be like it.
It will be a time of trouble for Jacob,
but he will be saved out of it." - Jeremiah 30:4-7

This Tribulation is described in the book of Daniel as one "week" or seven-year period of time in the future, following 69 "weeks" or 483 years leading to the time that Messiah would be cut off (Daniel 9:24-27). Between the 69 "weeks" and the 70th "week" there would evidently be an indeterminate period of time. We now know that this interval is the period of the Church Age in which we are now living. The Apostle Paul called it a "mystery". The Church Age and this mystery are explained more fully in Chapter 3.

The time of trouble begin with a seven-year peace treaty from the future prince, whom most prophecy scholars expect will be the end-times dictator.

In the middle of the seven-year peace treaty the dictator will break the agreement by setting up a statue of himself in the newly-rebuilt Temple (Daniel 9:27; Matthew 24:15; 2 Thessalonians 2:4; Revelation 13). His associate, The False Prophet will require people to worship the image, and will impose a financial dictatorship on people everywhere, requiring them to receive the "Mark of the Beast" (Revelation 13). Chapter 11 develops this aspect of the Great Tribulation.

Coming of Messiah as King

At the end of the seven years of the Tribulation, the Beast will gather his forces from all over the earth to do battle against The Lord. This will be the dreaded Battle of Armageddon (Revelation 19:11-21). Jesus will appear as a rider on a white horse, followed by the armies of heaven. But he will do all the fighting, by use of his powerful words. He will come as King of Kings and Lord of Lords.

Heb 1:3 "Word of His power"

The Old Testament is full of visions of this great day and of the restored Earth over which Messiah will reign. In addition to these passages in the Major Prophets, we have other pictures of the event as well. As mentioned earlier, Christ's coming is depicted by Daniel 2:44-45 as a rock from heaven, landing on the brittle feet representing the final evil world empire, smashing the image, and then growing into a great mountain.

In Jeremiah 30:8-11, after the "Time of Jacob's Trouble," there is a promise of freedom and happiness. God's people will be brought back from distant places and will live in peace and security.

From Jesus' own teaching in Matthew 24:29-31, there is a promise of his return in power and great glory, gathering the faithful together to enjoy His restored kingdom.

Finally, in the last several chapters of the Bible (Revelation Chapters 19-22), details are given about how Jesus will return with His saints to win the Battle of Armageddon and deal with Satan, the Beast, and the False Prophet. Jesus will reign over the restored Earth for 1000 wonderful years, and then usher in the New Heaven and the New Earth, where there will be no tears or sorrow forever!

Jesus' Own Outline of the Future - The Olivet Discourse
Four Periods of Time - Matthew 24:9-14

We mention this key passage here even though some of the same information has already been given above. It holds special importance because it was Jesus' own explanation of things to come.

Beginning of Birth Pains (Matthew 24:4-8) - Jesus warns about false messiahs, predicts an increase in wars and rumors of wars, as well as famines and earthquakes before the beginning of the Tribulation. The list of signs given in the parallel passage in Luke's Gospel includes plagues, fearful events, and signs in the heavens (Luke 21:9-11).

In the later writings of the Apostle Paul, after the mystery of the Church Age had been revealed, he added another facet of the final days. He said the times would be characterized by apostasy, the "falling away" of the Church from its devotion to the Lord and to its commitment to biblical principles. As a result of the Church's failure to be the champion of morality, the culture will slip into greater sin (1 Timothy 4:1-4; 2 Timothy 3:1-8; 2 Thessalonians 2:3, 6-7; 2 Timothy 3:1-8). The Revelation given to the Apostle John agrees that the Church at the end of the Church Age—the Laodicean Church—will be "lukewarm" and ineffective (Revelation 3:12-22).

The apostasy in so many churches in the past 50 years is shocking. In many cases it appears that only a small remnant is aware of what God is doing in history. This was the state of affairs in Israel when the Lord came the first time. There are many more false teachers running around now, and wilder legends and folklore are being taken seriously— as the fabric of our civilization collapses and as all truth appears to be relative. Breakouts of anarchy and revolt in the world are easier to understand when the things men once believed disappear. True Christianity is increasingly marginalized and a false world religion appears necessary to help hold the fragile world culture together.

The Tribulation (Matthew 24:9-14) - The first half of the seven years of turmoil will be characterized by a growing polarization between good and evil, with believers being severely persecuted. You might notice that Jesus does not explain the rapture of the Church because the subject of the Church was a mystery not revealed in the Old Testament. It was gradually explained by Jesus and his Apostles in the days to come. Several chapters are devoted later to the explanation of the Mystery of the Church, its history and the rapture (See Chapters 3 through 6).

The Great Tribulation (Matthew 24:15-28) - Jesus gave a preview of the horrifying events at the middle of the seven years of the peace treaty. According to the Book of Revelation, the first half would have already been a time of distress since true believers would have been persecuted and driven underground or killed. But then, the Beast will have an image of himself set up in the "Holy Place" in the newly rebuilt Temple in Jerusalem. This is the "Abomination of Desolation" predicted by Daniel, and it will lead to the institution of a world-wide economic dictatorship and the dreaded "Mark of the Beast." *See Chapter 11 - The Great Tribulation.*

As mentioned above, there is a promise of Jesus' return in power and great glory, gathering the faithful together to enjoy His restored kingdom.

Are We There Yet?
Where is the Promise of His Coming?

First of all, you must understand that in the last days scoffers will come, scoffing and following their own evil desires. [4]They will say, "Where is this 'coming' he promised? Ever since our fathers died, everything goes on as it has since the beginning of creation." - 2 Peter 3:3-4

Skeptics in our day are already saying this. "Where is the coming he promised?" In the following verses Peter explains that it is like it was in Noah's days. A flood had not come during the hundred years it took for Noah to build the ark. They mocked him for believing in a flood. But, as Peter says, to the Lord, "One day is like a thousand years and a thousand years is like a day." And besides, he doesn't want people to perish if they would believe, so he is giving them every opportunity to repent (1 Peter 3:5-8).

Here are some of Jesus' answers to the problem of doubt about prophecy...

Jesus' Guidelines
- We should be able to interpret the signs of the times.

Jesus said that His listeners should be able to recognize the obvious signs of the times. There is something wrong with them if they miss the obvious proofs that the end of this age is near.

> The Pharisees and Sadducees came to Jesus and tested him by asking him to show them a sign from heaven.
> [2]He replied, "When evening comes, you say, 'It will be fair weather, for the sky is red,' [3]and in the morning, 'Today it will be stormy, for the sky is red and overcast.' You know how to interpret the appearance of the sky, but you cannot interpret the signs of the times."
> - Matthew 16:1-3

- It is futile to try to pin down exact dates and details about how the prophecies will be fulfilled.

About date-setting, Jesus simply said, "No one knows about that day or hour, not even the angels in heaven, nor the Son, but only the Father" (Matthew 24:36).

This makes a great deal of sense if you think about his first coming into the world. Even though some sixty different categories of prophecy were fulfilled by his birth and life, it would not have been possible for even the strongest believer and best student of prophecy to have written His Story in advance. Every detail matches the prophecy, but no one could have imagined all the richness of his story, including exact dates of his advent or of his death.

-Most people will ignore the facts until it is too late for them.

> [3]As it was in the days of Noah, so it will be at the coming of the Son of Man. [38]For in the days before the flood, people were eating and drinking, marrying and giving in marriage, up to the day Noah entered the ark; [39]and they knew nothing about what would happen until the flood came and took them all away. - Matthew 24:37-39

The amazing thing about Noah's days is that, in spite of his work on the Ark, and his preaching to people for 100 years, his generation did not want to hear the truth until it was too late! In our days, many, even of the 41% who expect Jesus to return by the year 2050 still do not live like they believe it is true.

-The Lesson of Fig Tree shows that we are living in the last generation.

Could this really be the last generation before the end of this age? Look at what Jesus said:

"Now learn this lesson from the fig tree: As soon as its twigs get tender and its leaves come out, you know that summer is near. [33]Even so, when you see all these things, you know that it is near, right at the door. [34]I tell you the truth, this generation will certainly not pass away until all these things have happened. [35]Heaven and earth will pass away, but my words will never pass away." - Matthew 24:32-35

The word for "generation" (Gr. *genea*), can have several meanings. Some think it means the Jewish people will not become extinct before these prophecies are fulfilled.

However, the most obvious meaning is the generation of people who are living when these events begin to come to pass in startling succession. The first and most amazing fulfillment is the rebirth of the nation of Israel. The fig tree is one of the symbols of Israel.

Since Israel became a nation in 1948, we have every right to consider ourselves the last generation of this age. But how long is a generation? Thirty-five years? Forty years? There are various biblical possibilities. It has now been more than 60 years since this great event. But notice that Jesus said this generation will not *pass away* until all these things have happened! If the rebirth of Israel is the starting point, this generation will not have passed away until the last person living at that time has died. That gives another 60 years or so! But we can seriously expect His return any day. Some of us have believed this for many years now, but in any case, his return is nearer now than it ever was before!

Now let's take a quick look at the violence in the Middle East that is top news day after day. This information will be expanded in *Chapter 7 - Historical Developments*.

War and Peace in the Middle East
Current Events

This is the word of the LORD concerning Israel. The LORD, who stretches out the heavens, who lays the foundation of the earth, and who forms the spirit of man within him, declares: [2]"I am going to make Jerusalem a cup that sends all the surrounding peoples reeling. Judah will be besieged as well as Jerusalem. [3]On that day, when all the nations of the earth are gathered against her, I will make Jerusalem an immovable rock for all the nations. All who try to move it will injure themselves." - Zechariah 12:1-3

Various versions of this passage translate the expression about the cup as "a cup of reeling," "a cup of staggering," or "an intoxicating drink." There are other prophecies in the Bible that compare God's wrath to the stupefying effects of drunkenness (Psalm 75:8; Isaiah 51:22). It is a fitting picture of the confusion that faces world leaders today over the tensions in the Middle East.

Israel and Her Neighbors - Multiple Wars

On May 14, 1948, Israel declared her independence. For more than 50 years before that date Jewish people had been moving back to their homeland. This area, known as Israel in the Bible, had been subject to foreign control since before Jesus was born. In later years the Romans called the land "Palestine" (from the Philistines, who were earlier enemies of Israel). This was an insult to the Jewish people who had been driven away from their God-given land.

The land was sparsely occupied by mostly Arab settlers, who were called "Palestinians" by virtue of living in Palestine.

After the horrors of World War II, and the death camps of the Nazis, which destroyed 6 million Jews, the sympathy of much of the world was with them when they declared their rebirth as the nation of Israel in 1948.

The big problem was that this act displaced many of the Palestinians who had lived there. Actually, the Palestinians were given the choice of staying and becoming Israeli citizens. Or they could move to the Gaza or West Bank areas. Some of them tried to move to nearby Arab countries, but were not permitted to do so. Therefore, they found themselves living in the difficult environment of refugee camps.

On the very day that Israel declared their independence they were attacked by all of their neighboring countries. Miraculously, by God's grace, they won that war. Since then they have had to fight several other wars to retain their existence.

During the Six-Day war in 1967 Israel acquired additional areas, including the Golan Heights, the West Bank, and parts of the Sinai Peninsula.

The Islamic Revolution - Iran 1979

In 1979 Iran experienced a revolution, exiling the reigning leader, the Shah, and installing an Islamic government. This, in fact, became the Islamic Revolution. It was a reaction to the successes of the new nation of Israel, and signaled a rebirth of Islamic aspirations to rule the world that had been stopped by World War I.

The Islamic Revolution also provided the environment that eventually gave rise to modern terrorism all over the world. Iran itself has not produced many terrorists, but the government of Iran encourages and sponsors terrorist groups like Hezbollah and Hamas.

It must be noted that not all Muslims agree with this radical, militant view of Islam. It is generally claimed that only about 10% of them hold this position, but the majority do little or nothing to stop the rise of this dangerous trend.

Iranians are not generally Arabs. They are mostly of Persian descent and are proud of their ancient history.

These deep enmities go all the way back to Old Testament times. Modern nations that are descendants of Israel's ancient enemies are at the heart of this struggle. There has always been tension between the descendants of Abraham's older son, Ishmael and his younger son, Isaac. Isaac, of course, was the father of Jacob, the father of the twelve tribes of Israel. Ishmael's large family became a significant portion of the Arabs—inhabitants of the Arabian Peninsula. Joktan and Esau became patriarchs of many other Arab tribes in the same area (Genesis 10:25-30; 25:1-34).

9/11 and Islamic Terrorism

Islamic terrorism shook the United States unexpectedly on September 11, 2001, when three hijacked airliners executed simultaneous attacks on the World Trade Center in New York and the Pentagon in Washington DC. A fourth plane, heading for either the Capital Building or the White House was forced to crash by the brave passengers aboard.

Afghanistan and Iraq

The sneak attack was planned by a fringe group of Islamic terrorists called Al-Qaeda, who were led by a Saudi Arabian zealot named Osama bin Laden. Bin Laden's group was in Afghanistan, so the U.S. soon invaded that country.

During this time Saddam Hussein, the dictator of Iraq (the ancient land of Babylon and Assyria), ignored numerous United Nations resolutions to stop development of nuclear weapons. It is still debated today whether or not they actually had nuclear weapons, it was known that they had and used other weapons of mass destruction to destroy their own Kurdish countrymen.

After much debate, the U.S. invaded Iraq in 2003 and is still there today, having high hopes of producing a free democratic nation in the area.

Threat from Iran

Now, again, a Middle Eastern nation is developing nuclear weapons, and doing so against the various resolutions that have been made by the United Nations. Iran's president, Mahmoud Ahmadinejad, has engaged in the most hateful rhetoric against Israel, claiming they have no right to exist, and vowing to destroy them. And in his case, if they really do obtain nuclear weapons, they will probably use them, because he believes he is the forerunner of the Islamic Messiah, whom they call The Twelfth Imam. According to their worldview there must be an apocalypse first, and then their messiah can step forward to restore order.

The Quest for Peace

During the past several decades, terrorism has become a major problem in Israel and the surrounding nations. American Presidents and many other world leaders have taken the initiative of proposing various peace plans that would hopefully settle the tensions between Israel and the Palestinians that is at the heart of the problem.

The whole world is eager to see peace in the Middle East because only then can they hope to see the decline of world-wide terrorism.

One after another these various plans have failed to bring agreement and/or implementation.

A Two-State Solution?

Peace talks continue from year to year. One proposed solution is to establish a separate Palestinian state existing beside Israel in harmony. The Palestinians want all of the land they lost in the 1967 war, but Israel feels that those exact boundaries would leave them vulnerable to future attacks. For that reason they have established numerous Jewish settlements, presumably with the idea in mind that when a peace proposal is accepted, some settlements would be kept for security reasons and others could be traded with the Palestinians for certain areas necessary to Israel's defense.

There is also the question of whether or not to allow displaced Palestinians to return to Israel. The Palestinians insist on "the right of return." Israel's position has been that this is not negotiable because it would alter its Jewish character. So far the Palestinians have not been willing to recognize Israel as a Jewish state.

What about Jerusalem and the Temple Mount?

Of greatest importance to both Israel and the Palestinians are the issues of Jerusalem and the Temple Mount. Both countries would want their capitals in Jerusalem. This might be accomplished by a division of the city, but numerous Israeli leaders have promised their people they would not give up any of Jerusalem in the future. However, there are indications that they might be willing to give up portions of East Jerusalem, which is populated primarily by Palestinians.

The Temple Mount is sacred to both Jewish and Muslim people. This is undoubtedly the most difficult aspect of the peace process. A new Temple could be built for Jews without destroying the existing Islamic shrines there, but would either side ever agree to such a thing? *See Chapter 10 - The Rebuilt Temple.*

A Temporary Peace

Everyone is hopeful that a peace agreement can eventually be hammered out between the Israelis and the Palestinians. It should be added here that there could be more than one peace agreement before people would proclaim that "peace and safety" have finally prevailed. But when that effective agreement has been signed, it will be a shaky peace.

> While people are saying, "Peace and safety," destruction will come on them suddenly, as labor pains on a pregnant woman, and they will not escape. - 1 Thessalonians 5:3

The scene will then be set for the opening acts of the Tribulation, according to Revelation Chapter 6. Without being dogmatic about the details, here is one possible sequence that could lead from the signing of a peace agreement to the events of the Tribulation.

The first major development of the Tribulation is the opening of the First Seal.

> I watched as the Lamb opened the first of the seven seals. Then I heard one of the four living creatures say in a voice like thunder, "Come!" ²I looked, and there before me was a white horse! Its rider held a bow, and he was given a crown, and he rode out as a conqueror bent on conquest. - Revelation 6:1-2

The rider will be the coming world dictator, though he may not be recognized as such at the beginning. Riding a white horse symbolizes the fact that he will be accepted as some kind of messiah. (Jesus, the true Messiah will come on a white horse at the end of the Tribulation - Revelation 19.)

As a military victor, this rider of the white horse may be the one who facilitates the peace process. But even if he does, this will probably not yet be the seven-year covenant predicted in Daniel 9:27. The reason for this is shown by the event that takes place when the Second Seal is opened.

> When the Lamb opened the second seal, I heard the second living creature say, "Come!" ⁴Then another horse came out, a fiery red one. Its rider was given power to take peace from the earth and to make men slay each other. To him was given a large sword. - Revelation 6:3-4

This war takes peace from the earth. It is a world war. But it is not the Battle of Armageddon, which comes at the end of the Tribulation. This war is at the beginning of the Tribulation, and is different than the Battle of Armageddon in many ways. Many prophecy scholars relate this war to the one described in Ezekiel, Chapters 38 and 39. That war is said to begin after Israel has been supernaturally restored as a nation (Ezekiel Chapters 36 and 37). It will take place at a time when it could be said, of Israel that it is, "a land of unwalled villages," and "a peaceful and unsuspecting people" (Ezekiel 38:11).

The battle itself involves nations from many places. It is over quickly because The Lord intervenes by sending "fire and brimstone," which could be literally the same as what happened to Sodom, or it could describe a nuclear war. Great wars are normally ended by a peace treaty, and since Israel is the object of the war, the treaty would be between Israel and her enemies. That might very well be the seven-year pact of Daniel's vision.

Before or After the Rapture?

Will this temporary peace be before or after the rapture? The rapture might come before or after the signing of a peace agreement. This is one reason we live in any-moment anticipation of the rapture. There is no exact sign that accompanies this great event. It comes suddenly, so we should always be ready for it (1 Thessalonians 4:13-5:10; 1 Corinthians 15:50-58).

Understanding the Times

What we need now is to be people like the men of Issachar," who understood the times and knew what Israel should do" (1 Chronicles 12:32).

You might wonder if a person can really hope to know the meaning of the prophecies. The Wise Men found the Newborn King because of the accuracy of prophecy that he would be born in Bethlehem (Micah 5:2; Matthew 2:4-5); and those who followed The Messiah did so because they recognized that his life and message were the fulfillment of specific prophecies (Matthew 1:22-23; 8:17; John 1:41; 7:41-42; Acts 9:22). God is always eager to teach his children, to shine new light on his Word, and to help them sort out the relevance of events in the modern world. He does not want us to be ignorant but well-informed.

Other Prophecies

This book is about biblical prophecy. Little notice is taken of prophecies that were not recorded in God's Word. Biblical prophecies were spoken by inspiration of the Holy Spirit (2 Peter 1:21; Hebrews 1:1-2). The Old Testament penalty for giving a false prophecy was death (Deuteronomy 18:18-20). Jesus himself warned that there would be false prophets in the End Times (Matthew 24:10-13, 24).

There is, however a "gift of prophecy," described in the Bible. This is the supernatural ability that is given to some people at certain times to reveal God's will or to predict future events. It is explained by the Apostle Paul in 1 Corinthians chapters 12 through 14 as one of the ways that the various members of the body of Christ work together for the benefit of the whole Church. Strict rules are given about the use of this gift so that it is not abused. One of the main restrictions is that any prophetic statement should be approved by the others in the group who also had that spiritual gift (1 Corinthians 14:32-33).

It is not the purpose of this book to consider these "other" prophecies. Individual Christian groups should weigh such utterances carefully and not tolerate any abuse of this gift.

Astrology and Fortune-telling

There are many other non-biblical prophecies that can not be taken seriously, and are therefore not considered at length in these pages. Astrology is probably the most obvious of these non-biblical methods of telling the future. Astrology is an occult perversion of the true science of Astronomy. Astrology is strictly forbidden by the Scriptures (2 Kings 17:16-17; 23:5; Psalm 81:12; Isaiah 47:13; Jeremiah 10:1-2; Daniel 1:20, 2:27; 4:7; 5:7).

However, the Bible does say that the lights in the heavens were to be used for signs and seasons (Genesis 1:14), and it indicates that God, who created them, calls the stars by name (Isaiah 40:26; Psalm 147:4). Psalm 19:1-6 says that the heavens tell of the glory of God. According to John 1:14, Jesus revealed the glory of God. Therefore, this could mean that the heavens foretell the coming of Christ.

Some respected Bible scholars believe that, before there were written Scriptures, God may have used the clustering of stars that we call constellations as object lessons about his future plans for salvation and other prophetic subjects. This theory is sometimes called, "The Gospel in the Stars."[4] There is a fascinating correlation between these cosmic images and the biblical story of the birth, life, and work of Christ. This theory has merit because it relates only to biblical prophecies, and gives a more meaningful and coherent story than the mythological imaginations of astrology. There is no connection between this concept and the modern attempt by astrologers to predict the course of events of living individuals.

Fortune-telling and occult practices of predicting the future are usually phony theatrics to separate gullible people from their money. Worse yet, they may be evil messages, sometimes containing half-truths, revealed by demonic mind-control. Séances, use of Ouija boards, Tarot cards and other methods of telling the future apart from the Bible should be avoided at all costs.

Some new age writers claim that their messages are "channeled" by supposed "ascended masters", or avatars. If these spirits really exist, they too must be demons.

Nostradamus and Other Psychics
Michel de Nostredame (Nostradamus) was a French chemist who wrote a book of prophecies. His "quatrains" contained mysterious and apocalyptic elements that have frequently been cited after some important historical event as proof that he could foretell the future. One example of this is a hoax spread on the Internet that he had prophesied the destruction of the World Trade Center. The truth is that his prophecies were too vague, and could be twisted to mean almost anything after the fact. None of his prophecies have been used to accurately predict something important before it happens.

Edgar Cayce and Jean Dixon claimed to be psychics. They often made predictions about near future events, and were sometimes right; the same way a good political analyst could list probable world developments, and sometimes be correct. Benjamin Creme has been predicting the imminent appearance of Maitreya, a supposed messiah who has been living secretly in London since 1977. These and many other psychics of our generation were predicted by Jesus:

At that time many will turn away from the faith and will betray and hate each other, [11]and many false prophets will appear and deceive many people. [12]Because of the increase of wickedness, the love of most will grow cold. - Matthew 24:10-12

Mayan Prophecies and the Year 2012

Students of Mayan culture in South America have always known that the unique dating technology of the Mayans included a "Long Count" calendar that ends on Dec. 21, of the year 2012. It is doubtful that the Mayans themselves thought that this end would bring great disasters. Mayan scholars think they just expected a new beginning. But later speculation, New Age teaching, and some prophecies have led to unrealistic claims about the destruction of the earth in 2010. Without scientific evidence, some have claimed that the magnetic poles of the earth will reverse at that time. This, of course, could cause unimaginable consequences, but we need much more scientific proof before believing this will happen.

In 2009 Sony Pictures released "2012," a major movie, with a production budget of $150,000,000. In the movie, neutrinos from a massive solar flare cause the earth's core to overheat, triggering a catastrophic chain of natural disasters. Ironically, the movie chose to portray the survival of some 400,000 people aboard huge "arks." that could survive the cataclysm and allow the human race to start over. See the discussion of coronal mass eruptions in Chapter 13 – *The Plot Thickens.*

Many New Age devotees see this date as the beginning of their "golden age," or "the Age of Aquarius. A Google search returns millions of matches for a Google search of "new age" and 2012. One site claims to channel a message from "Master Quetzalcoatl" claiming that this date will mark the official return of the Christ / Imam Mahdi / Buddha Maitreya and other ascended masters. This interest in the year 2012 is a windfall for New Age authors, who have many different ideas about the importance of the coming date. See the discussion of New Age spirituality and the Age of Aquarius in Chapter 5 - *Satan's Final Empire: Global Governance and Religion.*

Bible students can agree that there are dreadful events ahead, but there is no logical or biblical connection between the prophesied disasters of the Tribulation and the imagined events of 2012.

Islamic Prophecies

Islam has a highly-developed belief in End Times events. To the surprise of many Christians, there are important correlations between their prophecies and our own biblical revelations. For example, they believe in an end-times battle between good and evil, and Jesus (Isa) will return to help Muslims overthrow the false messiah (Dajjal).[5] But it must be remembered that Mohammed lived hundreds of years after Christianity had become a major influence in the world. He had access to the Jewish Scriptures (Old Testament) and the Christian Scriptures (New Testament). He and his later followers could borrow freely from these sources, changing things as necessary to predict a favorable outcome for Islam.

Some Muslims claim that prophecies from the Qur'an (Koran) and the Hadith have come to pass. Examples include the invention of the light bulb and the establishment of Israel, but on close examination they fail to be convincing.[6] David Reagan, from lamblion.com lists 18 end-times prophecies that are generally taught by Islam. They are mostly variations of biblical prophecies.

In the Shiite branch of Islam there is a prophecy about a coming messiah. According to their history, "The Twelfth Imam," Muhammad al-Mahdi, was hidden by Allah until the end of time. They believe that he will return to save the world when it is in a state of chaos.[7] See "Nuclear Iran" in *Chapter 7 - Historical Developments*.

About the Name "Antichrist"

It is common practice in today's end-times literature to identify an "unholy trinity" of Satan, Antichrist, and the False Prophet. This evil trinity does exist in Revelation chapters 12 and 13. In chapter 12 the devil, or Satan, is symbolized by a red seven-headed dragon that persecutes Israel. In chapter 13 there are two other beasts. One of these is the second person of the "unholy trinity." He is a seven-headed beast from the sea. He receives his power from the dragon, and becomes a global military dictator. The other beast has two horns like a lamb, symbolizing his religious nature, but he speaks like a dragon. This third person of the ungodly threesome is called "the false prophet" (Revelation 16:13; 19:20; and 20:10).

In Revelation 16 the three entities are all mentioned together, but the name "Antichrist" is not applied here or anywhere else to any of them.

> [13]Then I saw three evil spirits that looked like frogs; they came out of the mouth of the dragon, out of the mouth of the beast and out of the mouth of the false prophet. [14]They are spirits of demons performing miraculous signs, and they go out to the kings of the whole world, to gather them for the battle on the great day of God Almighty. - Revelation 16:13-14

In his epistles, the Apostle John writes that there are already many antichrists. To him this word signifies deceivers who deny that Jesus is from God (1 John 2:18; 1 John 4:3 and 2 John 7). But in writing the Revelation, he does not use the word "antichrist" at all. Instead, he uses the expression "the beast" regularly from Revelation chapter 13 through 20.

There are many other biblical names for "the beast." In Daniel 7:8 he is called another (eleventh) horn that speaks boastfully. In Daniel 9:26 he is referred to as "the ruler who will come." In Daniel 11:21 he is described as "a contemptible person." In 2 Thessalonians

2:1-12 the Apostle Paul labeled him "the man of lawlessness," and "the lawless one." And in Revelation 6:1-2 he is seen as the rider on the white horse.

Everything considered, the person most prophecy writers call "Antichrist" is "the beast." But from John's perspective "the false prophet" would also be an antichrist. So, for the sake of accuracy, we have usually called this end-times dictator "the Beast" in this book.

In the next chapters we will consider biblical teaching about Israel and the Church. Unless we understand them we will not be able to make sense of the great prophecies that are yet to be fulfilled.

Chapter 2
The Chosen People

The Bible is the revelation of God's will to man. It is a self-disclosure by God, giving us information we could not gain from any other source. It begins with the book of Genesis, explaining in just a few chapters, how the human race was brought into existence by the personal activity of the God who created the universe. It shows that the first man and woman were the objects of his love and special attention. They were created "in his image" (Genesis 1:26-27), and were given the privilege of regular communication with him (Genesis 2:15-17; 3:8). One man and one woman were appointed, not only as the progenitors of our race, but also as God's stewards, his custodians and caretakers over the creation. They were created with the characteristics of mind, emotions, personality, and will. They were made creative, imaginative, inventive, artistic, capable of loving and being loved—and above all, able to worship.

As the account of Genesis continued, the problem of evil surfaced. Even though Adam and Eve had been created perfect, they had also been created with the ability to choose, or reject, God's will for them. In theory, they could have chosen to obey God completely. Instead, being tempted by Satan, they partook of the forbidden fruit (Genesis 3). Evil did not begin with man but with a rebellion among the angels. The angelic rebellion damaged the created universe and its invisible angelic government (Isaiah 14:12ff. Ezekiel 28:12ff.). It also brought about the possibility that man, too, could choose a course of action contrary to the perfect ways of God. This first human sin alienated our original parents from their creator. Instead of looking forward to walking with him in the garden, they hid themselves from him (Genesis 3:8-10).

The separation from God that is the result of sin is the greatest of all problems for the human race. God had warned Adam that if he disobeyed, "you will surely die" (Genesis 2:17). Adam did not die immediately in a physical sense, although the process of aging and eventual death was triggered by this event of rebellion. But Adam died spiritually (Romans 5:12). The word "death" in the Bible actually means "separation." Thus, when a person dies physically, there is a separation between the physical and the non-physical aspects of his being: his Soul and Spirit. The body is laid to rest where it will return to dust (Genesis 3:19), while the immaterial part of man goes on to wait the judgment, and the eventual destination of heaven or hell (Luke 16:19-31). There is also a spiritual death separation of man's spirit from the spirit of his Creator. This is what the Apostle Paul had in mind when he declared,

> As for you, you were dead in your transgressions and sins, ²in which you used to live when you followed the ways of this world and of the ruler of the kingdom of the air, the spirit who is now at work in those who are disobedient. - Ephesians 2:1-2

Sin, therefore, poses the greatest of all threats to the well-being of our race. Man's fall resulted in his spiritual death. His body was genetically damaged so that all men are mortal because of the sin of Adam. Men cut off from the source of life have no hope—and God IS Life! All life, all forms of life, come from God. Being disconnected from the source of life (for any reason) means an organism will begin to die, and continue to die. Men begin to die as soon as they are born, but God in his love for us did not abandon us in our plight. A god who was simply good might have declared the human experiment a failure, and would have left us to suffer the consequences of our rebellion, or, perhaps, would have put us out of our misery, snuffing out the planet with a momentary explosion, in order to preserve the rest of his creation from possible contamination. A god who was simply just could have easily allowed anarchists and rebels to perish. After all it is his universe not ours.

But God is not simply good, nor simply just. Above all he is holy, and he is a God of love. His very nature is love (1 John 4:8). In his love, he sought to reestablish a relationship with Adam and Eve by seeking them out. When they hid from him, the Lord found them and offered a way back, a way of restoration. That restoration involved wearing the skins of an animal sacrifice. An animal sacrificed by God himself was the first creature to die. The death of the animal was symbolic of the physical death they deserved to die. It demonstrated a great principle of Scripture that "without the shedding of blood there is no remission (removal) of sin." The concept of a substitutionary atoning sacrifice was introduced. Before they received this gift from God, they were in a state of being spiritually dead-cut off from him. But when they received it and wore it, they were in effect confessing their sin and their inability to solve the problem for themselves. The death of that first animal on their behalf became a "covering" for their sin (Genesis 3:21). Fig leaves and other forms of clothing would come to be symbols of man's self-righteousness. Sin causes man to lose his own righteousness as the prophets tell us, "All of us have become like one who is unclean, and all our righteous acts are like filthy rags" (Isaiah 64:6). This would later be the basis for the institution of the system of animal sacrifices and would teach us about "imputed righteousness"—that inherent goodness of Christ with which we are clothed when we place our faith in him. And the animal sacrifices, in turn, point to a future final sacrifice by the Messiah. That is why Paul continued the explanation in Ephesians this way:

> But because of his great love for us, God, who is rich in mercy, [5]made us alive with Christ even when we were dead in transgressions—it is by grace you have been saved. - Ephesians 2:4-5

The next few chapters of Genesis trace the spread of the human race and its eventual corruption—within less than 2000 years—to the point that God needed to send a flood to destroy the evil. Again, he did not destroy the entire planet, but, in love and grace, God preserved the eight persons who still trusted in him. Therefore, Noah and his family were saved (Genesis 6-10).

After the Flood, God told men to "be fruitful and increase in number and fill the earth" (Genesis 9:1). This would require them to gradually migrate in all directions. Some were undoubtedly obedient to God's will, but many of them decided to rebel. They built a city and a tower at Babylon, and established there a false religious system in an effort to disobey God and stay together on their own terms. God confused their languages so they could no longer work together (Genesis 11).

Chosen to Share the Truth

Several hundred years later people had established cultures in many places. There were some who still retained the truth passed down to them by their fathers from the time of Noah, but there were many who had abandoned that truth. God picked out one man, from the city of Ur of the Chaldees, a place where most people no longer believed in him. He called Abram (later named Abraham) with these words:

> The LORD had said to Abram, "Leave your country, your people and your father's household and go to the land I will show you.
> [2] "I will make you into a great nation
> and I will bless you;
> I will make your name great,
> and you will be a blessing." - Genesis 12:1-2

The Covenants

God does not act whimsically or arbitrarily, but deals with individuals and nations on the basis of great contracts or covenants that he himself initiates. The very name Yahweh is known as the "covenant name" of God. Yahweh is related to the Hebrew verb "to be" and indicates that God is a living Person who enters into personal relationships with individuals and with groups of individuals. Everything God has done in regards to our salvation is based on one or more of the covenants God has made in the past. None of these has been abrogated or annulled.

Even before Abraham's time God had made a covenant with Noah on behalf of the whole human race. That covenant was a promise never again to destroy the earth with a flood. (Genesis 9:8-17)

There are groups of churches today that stress what they call "covenantal theology." We do not disagree with this emphasis on the ways God has chosen to enter into contracts with his peoples. However many of the "covenant churches" would not necessarily agree with our eschatology. The subject of covenants in the Bible is important and complex. Appendix E - *Notes on the Covenants in the Bible*, introduces this subject for the serious student.

Five principle covenants—*all still in effect*—apply to the nation of Israel. These include the Abrahamic Covenant (later confirmed to Isaac and Jacob), The Mosaic Covenant, the Covenant of The Land, the Davidic Covenant, and the New Covenant.

The Purpose of a "Chosen People": Blessing of All Nations

The Abrahamic Covenant was the promise of a special blessing for Abraham's descendants: a "chosen" people. But it is obviously not for their benefit alone, but that, through them, all people would be blessed!

> "I will bless those who bless you,
> and whoever curses you I will curse;
> and all peoples on earth
> will be blessed through you." - Genesis 12:3

The promised benefit to the whole human race was later revealed as the Messiah - - the Deliverer from the penalty of sin. That is, the promise to Abraham was really the promise of one unique seed, Messiah, in whom all the covenants would find their fulfillment (Galatians 3:16). The theological term "eternal covenant" refers to an agreement within the Godhead, made before the foundation of the world, out of which all the covenants with mankind would later flow.

The Promised Land

An important part of the promise to Abraham was that he would be led to a land that God would show him.

Canaan

At the time of Abraham's journey, the land was occupied by various Canaanite tribes, and was therefore known as the land of Canaan. Canaan was the son of Ham, and the grandson of Noah. Following the flood, the descendants of Canaan traveled to the area and settled there. Canaan's sons became the heads of what would become the tribes of Canaan. When Noah accidentally became drunk, his grandson Canaan had evidently participated in his father's sin of mocking and dishonoring Noah (Genesis 9:21-26). Canaan manifested the same moral weakness his father had, but to a greater degree. His descendants, resisting God's grace, became more and more decadent and ungodly as their history unfolded. Eventually these idolatrous peoples were to be deprived of their land (Deuteronomy 7:1-10).

Israel

Following a long series of conquests of the Canaanite tribes (See the Book of Joshua), the twelve tribes of Israel finally owned a large portion of the land originally promised to Abraham. In the days of David the land was renamed "Israel," meaning *Prince with God*, This was the new name God had given the patriarch Jacob. Jacob's twelve sons were the heads of the twelve tribes of Israel. The tribes were united in one great kingdom until after the reign of David's son Solomon. After Solomon died a power struggle ensued, resulting in a division of the people. The northern ten tribes were still called Israel, but the southern two tribes, and their land, was called Judea, after the name of the larger of the two tribes, Judah. This is the name from which the words "Jew" and "Jewish" were derived.

Palestine

The name "Palestine" is not found in the Bible. It has had a variety of meanings. Nelson's Bible Dictionary tells us how the word was first used:

> "The word itself originally identified the region as "the land of the Philistines," a war-like tribe that inhabited much of the region alongside the Hebrew people. But the older name for Palestine was CANAAN, the term most frequently used in the Old Testament...
> "The term Palestine as a name for the entire land of Canaan, beyond the coastal plains of the Phoenicians, was first used by the fifth century B. C. historian Herodotus. After the Jewish revolt of A. D. 135, the Romans replaced the Latin name Judea with the Latin Palaestina as their name for this province."[8]

As you can see, the name is actually an insult to the Jewish people, denying the name Israel, which it once had, and going back to the Philistines, their earlier opponents.

Before the rebirth of the Nation of Israel in 1948, the name Palestine was virtually synonymous with "The Holy Land." Most writers from the time printed books were first introduced until this generation used the term in a non-political sense for the entire region of the Bible lands. Palestine was a well defined area at the end of World War II. The modern nation of Jordan was carved out of the larger portion of Palestine, and the remainder was the area now known once again as the nation of Israel.

Today the name "Palestine" has a different meaning with highly political connotations. This will be described later in the section on "Modern Israel."

Conditional Nature of the Promise for the Land

Covenants can be conditional or unconditional. As it turns out, only one of the covenants applicable to Israel is conditional—the right of the Jews to live in the Promised Land.

This partly conditional covenant has several elements: (1) dispersion of the Jews was to be a consequence of disobedience. (2) Future repentance will be accomplished by God. (3) God will regather his scattered people and restore them to the land. (4) The people of Israel will be brought to the Lord as a nation. (5) The enemies and oppressors of Israel will be punished. (6) Future national prosperity and preeminence is guaranteed (See also Deuteronomy, chapters 28, 29). Because of this covenant, the right of the Jews to live in the land is conditional upon their behavior.

> See, I set before you today life and prosperity, death and destruction. [16] For I command you today to love the LORD your God, to walk in his ways, and to keep his commands, decrees and laws; then you will live and increase, and the LORD your God will bless you in the land you are entering to possess.
> [17] But if your heart turns away and you are not obedient, and if you are drawn away to bow down to other gods and worship them, [18] I declare to you this day that you will certainly be destroyed. You will not live long in the land you are crossing the Jordan to enter and possess. - Deuteronomy 30:15-18

The Disobedience and Restoration of Israel
Disobedience and Discipline

Second Kings, Chapter 17, documents God's reasons for his temporarily removing the ten Northern tribes from the Land. The Lord indicates that the approaching 70 year Babylonian captivity would allow the Land to enjoy its seventh-year Sabbath rests that had been ignored by the Jews since their entry into the land under the leadership of Joshua.

Moses had given Israel this warning about what would happen if they forsook the Lord:

> I will scatter you among the nations and will draw out my sword and pursue you. Your land will be laid waste, and your cities will lie in ruins. [34] Then the land will enjoy its sabbath years all the time that it lies desolate and you are in the country of your enemies; then the

land will rest and enjoy its sabbaths. [35] All the time that it lies desolate, the land will have the rest it did not have during the sabbaths you lived in it. -Leviticus 26:33-35

Second Chronicles records the result of their disobedience:

He carried into exile to Babylon the remnant, who escaped from the sword, and they became servants to him and his sons until the kingdom of Persia came to power. [21] The land enjoyed its sabbath rests; all the time of its desolation it rested, until the seventy years were completed in fulfillment of the word of the LORD spoken by Jeremiah. - 2 Chronicles 36:20-21

Repentance

Daniel, who had been among the young men taken captive to Babylon, expressed the repentance that the exiles felt after years of captivity. He had lived out a long and useful life in Babylon serving a succession of governments and administrations, but as an old man he realized the time of the captivity there was about to end when he happened to be reading the scroll of his immediate predecessor Jeremiah:

I prayed to the LORD my God and confessed:
"O Lord, the great and awesome God, who keeps his covenant of love with all who love him and obey his commands, [5] we have sinned and done wrong. We have been wicked and have rebelled; we have turned away from your commands and laws. [6] We have not listened to your servants the prophets, who spoke in your name to our kings, our princes and our fathers, and to all the people of the land.
[7] "Lord, you are righteous, but this day we are covered with shame—the men of Judah and people of Jerusalem and all Israel, both near and far, in all the countries where you have scattered us because of our unfaithfulness to you. [8] O LORD, we and our kings, our princes and our fathers are covered with shame because we have sinned against you." -Daniel 9:4-8 (Also see Daniel 9:15-19).

Rebuilding - Ezra, Nehemiah

The books of Ezra and Nehemiah describe the leadership of Zerubbabel and Nehemiah, who led small numbers of Jews back to the Land at the end of the appointed 70 years in Babylon. A modest Second Temple was constructed and the city walls were rebuilt in answer to Daniel's prayer of intercession (Daniel 9:1-19). The land from that time until now was under Gentile dominion, however. Jesus would later affirm that Israel's subservience to Gentile powers would continue until he returned (Luke 21:24). This did not change in 1948 when Israel achieved national independence—Jerusalem is to be overrun and destroyed by foreign armies at least one more time (Zechariah 14:1-3).

Coming of the Messiah

The Gospel of Matthew was written primarily for Jewish readers. It constantly refers to the Messianic prophecies fulfilled by Jesus as the rightful King of the Jews. Among these striking fulfillments, Matthew cited Jesus' virgin birth (Matthew 1:22-23 / Isaiah 7:14), the place of his birth in Bethlehem (Matthew 2:5-6 / Micah 5:2), the flight of his parents to Egypt to spare him from Herod's slaughter of children (Matthew 2:14-15 / Hosea 11:1), the beginnings of his public ministry in the area of Galilee (Matthew 4:13-16 / Isaiah 9:1-2), his miraculous healing ministry (Matthew 8:14-17; 12:17-21 / Isaiah 35:5-6), his rejection by non-believers (Matthew 13:13-15 / Isaiah 53;3), his entrance into Jerusalem on a donkey (Matthew 21:1-5 / Zechariah 9:9), and his betrayal for thirty pieces of silver (Matthew 27:3-10 / Zechariah 11:12-13).

His agony in the garden, illegal trial in the middle of the night, crucifixion, burial and resurrection are vividly described (Matthew chapters 26-28 / Psalm 22; Isaiah 53). The other three gospels give complementary details.

Fulfillment of Prophecy

A comparison of all the Gospels with the Old Testament record results in over sixty different prophecies fulfilled in Jesus' birth, life and death. The odds against any person coincidentally fulfilling these prophecies are astronomical! It was this fact that convinced his followers that he truly was the long-awaited Messiah. Here are some examples of this fact:

The first thing Andrew did was to find his brother Simon and tell him, "We have found the Messiah" (that is, the Christ). - John 1:41

When Jesus spoke with the Samaritan woman at the well, he revealed to her that he was the Messiah.

The woman said, "I know that Messiah" (called Christ) "is coming. When he comes, he will explain everything to us."
[26]Then Jesus declared, "I who speak to you am he." - John 4:25-26

The Believing Minority: Apostles and Early Christians

It should always be remembered that the entire first church was Jewish. All of the Twelve Apostles were Jewish. Their first assignment was to preach to "the lost sheep of Israel" (Matthew 10:6). Jesus was reluctant at first to even share the Gospel with the Canaanite woman who asked for his help because his focus was on the Jewish people (Matthew 25:22-28).

As the nation began to reject their promised King and Messiah (Matthew 12:14-21), Jesus began to conceal truth from the nation, by speaking in parables (Matthew 13). He focused on training his disciples for the age that would follow, and on his primary mission of arriving in Jerusalem at the time appointed for his crucifixion. God's plan for ultimate blessings promised to the Gentiles came more into view.

On the night of his betrayal at the "Last Supper," after Judas had left to finalize his plot to betray the Lord, Jesus brought the 11 disciples, as representatives of true, believing Israel into the "New Covenant" that had been promised to Israel hundreds of years earlier by the prophets Jeremiah, Ezekiel and Isaiah. This New Covenant was to be the basis of the spread of the gospel message of Jesus by these same men, after they were made Apostles of the Church. The nation of Israel was to be brought back to God under the terms of this New Covenant. For a period of time Israel would be set aside because of their rejection of Jesus as Messiah.

Jesus' official rejection of Israel and his plan for the calling out of a church was announced at Caesarea Philippi (Matthew 16:17-19). A few months later, during his final week in Jerusalem, he announced to the nation and its leaders,

> Jesus said to them, "Have you never read in the Scriptures:
> 'The stone the builders rejected
> has become the capstone;
> the Lord has done this,
> and it is marvelous in our eyes'?
> [43]"Therefore I tell you that the kingdom of God will be taken away from you and given to a people who will produce its fruit. [44]He who falls on this stone will be broken to pieces, but he on whom it falls will be crushed." - Matthew 21:42-44

Jesus wept over Jerusalem as he realized the terrible fate that would come upon the nation because of their rejection of him. For the second time the conditional provisions of the Covenant of the Land were to be enforced. This time their exile ("Diaspora") was to last not 70 years but 2000!

> "O Jerusalem, Jerusalem, you who kill the prophets and stone those sent to you, how often I have longed to gather your children together, as a hen gathers her chicks under her wings, but you were not willing." - Matthew 23:37

The resurrection of Jesus and his appearances to friends and disciples over the next 40 days, reassured them considerably—for they had all forsaken him when he died (Matthew 26:31). Promising to send them "Another Strengthener" (John 14:15-16), he told his followers to wait ten more days.

Gathering in Jerusalem on the appointed day—the Feast of Pentecost following Passover—the Jewish followers of Jesus were empowered by the Spirit of God and baptized into a new community of believers known as the Church—the Body of Christ (Ephesians 3:1-21).

All of those who first heard the Gospel on the Day of Pentecost (Acts 2) were Jewish (including converts and those dispersed to other countries).

It was only after the persecution of the early church by the Jewish enemies of Jesus in Jerusalem that they were scattered from there, and began to take the message to the rest of Judea and Samaria, and eventually, to Gentiles living in Israel, and even to other nations (Acts 8:1; 10:1-48; 13:1-4).

Even when Paul, the "Apostle to The Gentiles" would go to any new place, he would first seek out the Jewish people and proclaim the Gospel to them (Acts 13:5; 14; 14:1-5; 17:1-5; 18:1-6). Typically, some of the Jews would believe and the rest would not. Only then would he begin to preach to the Gentiles. Here is an example from the visit to Antioch in Pisidia:

> As Paul and Barnabas were leaving the synagogue, the people invited them to speak further about these things on the next Sabbath. [43]When the congregation was dismissed, many of the Jews and devout converts to Judaism followed Paul and Barnabas, who talked with them and urged them to continue in the grace of God.
> [44]On the next Sabbath almost the whole city gathered to hear the word of the Lord. [45]When the Jews saw the crowds, they were filled with jealousy and talked abusively against what Paul was saying.
> [46]Then Paul and Barnabas answered them boldly: "We had to speak the word of God to you first. Since you reject it and do not consider yourselves worthy of eternal life, we now turn to the Gentiles. [47]For this is what the Lord has commanded us:
>   "'I have made you a light for the Gentiles,
>   that you may bring salvation to the ends of the earth.'"
> [48]When the Gentiles heard this, they were glad and honored the word of the Lord; and all who were appointed for eternal life believed. - Acts 13:42-48

Paul summarized his God-given method in Romans 1:16 where he stated, "I am not ashamed of the gospel, because it is the power of God for the salvation of everyone who believes: first for the Jew, then for the Gentile."

Israel's Unbelief
Rejection of Messiah
The second violation of the conditional provisions of the Covenant Of The Land occurred when Israel as a nation rejected her rightful Messiah, Jesus, when he came riding into Jerusalem on a donkey as legitimate King of Israel (exactly fulfilling Zechariah 9:9).

When he came near the place where the road goes down the Mount of Olives, the whole crowd of disciples began joyfully to praise God in loud voices for all the miracles they had seen:

[38]"Blessed is the king who comes in the name of the Lord!"

"Peace in heaven and glory in the highest!"

[39]Some of the Pharisees in the crowd said to Jesus, "Teacher, rebuke your disciples!"

[40]"I tell you," he replied, "if they keep quiet, the stones will cry out."

[41]As he approached Jerusalem and saw the city, he wept over it [42]and said, "If you, even you, had only known on this day what would bring you peace—but now it is hidden from your eyes. [43]The days will come upon you when your enemies will build an embankment against you and encircle you and hem you in on every side. [44]They will dash you to the ground, you and the children within your walls. They will not leave one stone on another, because you did not recognize the time of God's coming to you." - Luke 19:37-44

One might have thought that during the 400 years following the close of the Old Testament (after the book of Malachi was written) the nation would have learned its lessons from history and been ready for the coming of the Promised One. But the priesthood had become thoroughly corrupt and the bulk of the populace wanted relief from Roman Oppression—not release from inner evil, sin and spiritual death. Messiah's rejection as rightful King in the line of David was followed within a few days by his betrayal and execution. When Jesus stood before Pontius Pilate the assembled crowd of Jews was given an opportunity to free Jesus who was completely innocent, or to release a known criminal. In the ensuing clamor the people asked instead for the release of Barabbas (Matthew 27:15-25).

It is wrong for us to label Jews as "Christ-killers" because quite clearly all mankind is involved in the conspiracy that put Jesus to death. Representatives of each of the sons of Noah: Shem, Ham, and Japheth had a responsible role in putting Messiah to death. Had the Son of God been born in any other country, in any other time, the results would have been the same.

The resurrection of Jesus three days after his death and the sudden and dramatic formation of the Church of Jesus Christ in Jerusalem on the Day of Pentecost (50 days after the resurrection) did not turn the heart of the nation to their Messiah. It was only a matter of time until the Jewish followers of Jesus, some thousands in number, were forced to flee Jerusalem. Soon the unbelieving Jews, in their continuing revolt against Rome, provoked the Romans to remove them from the land. As a consequence, the provisional terms of the Covenant of The Land were invoked for the second time by the Owner of the Land.

After this second dispersion, lasting nearly 2000 years, God allowed his chosen people to return to their land again. The exciting history of the regathering of the Jews from all lands began more than one hundred years ago—culminating in the rebirth of the State of Israel in 1948 and the tiny nation's rise to power and a restored place of influence as a modern progressive democracy. Thankfully, God is faithful to his promises in spite our unbelief!

The drama of the Jewish people during their Diaspora is little known to most Christians. It is fascinating reading because it demonstrates that God has in fact protected the Jewish people, their religion, values and culture against great pressures to assimilate; against almost constant terrible anti-Semitism; against horrendous persecution down through the ages. The very existence of the Jews today, the recovery of their language, their regathering to the land of their fathers, and the clear signs of their Messianic expectations, are surely among the greatest miracles one can find on the pages of human history.

Hardening and Blindness - Romans 11

In the early years when God had moved to call out a church to his name, and because the majority of Jewish people did not accept Jesus as Messiah, the Apostle Paul explained that they had become spiritually blind. The same thing happens to any people anywhere in any age who hear truth from God and ignore it. The Jews are representative—not unique—in their demonstration of all of mankind's rebellion against God down through the ages.

> I do not want you to be ignorant of this mystery, brothers, so that you may not be conceited: Israel has experienced a hardening in part until the full number of the Gentiles has come in. - Romans 11:25

One might ask if the past hundred years of great economic development, prosperity, and overwhelming military victories against enormous odds, has brought the Jews to a place of contrition and repentance and humility as far as their God is concerned—especially since the restoration of the State of Israel was born out of terrible persecution and hardship.

It is quite true that many thousands of Jews from all over the world have become believers in Jesus over the past 2000 years, and these have been added to the Church. (See Ephesians 2:11-3:12 for God's purposes in this present age.) It is also true that there is a small remnant of some thousands of believing Jews now resident in the Land of Israel (Romans 11:5). Yet for the most part Israel is a secular state. Most of her citizens are not only indifferent to the God of their Fathers, but openly hostile to any notions that the God of the Land is anything more than an interesting mythological character now outgrown and to be discarded.

People who live in Israel cannot help but be reminded of their past because the Sabbath is observed, and the major biblical feasts are kept by many. Furthermore, archaeology is the national pastime, so there are reminders of early history in the news every day. At the present time about half of the Jews living in the land are "Sabras"—that is, they were born in the land and not immigrants. This younger generation is especially involved in a quest for their roots and identity, and from among the young men of this generation, well over 100,000 are already diligently studying the Torah in the many yeshivas of the land.

Although God is known for his great patience and long-suffering, it is appropriate to ask how much longer the Holy God of the Covenants will tolerate the present indifference, rebellion and disregard for his Person that typifies the Israel of the past hundred years. Of course we cannot speak much more favorably about the disregard for God in our own country these days, especially since most Americans have already heard the truth about God, but never taken it seriously.

Sadly, we have further indications from the New Testament that tell us that not only will Israel continue in its denial of Jesus as Messiah—they will in fact readily embrace a counterfeit Messiah. Jesus warned his people when he was with them,

> "You diligently study the Scriptures because you think that by them you possess eternal life. These are the Scriptures that testify about me, [40]yet you refuse to come to me to have life.
> [41]"I do not accept praise from men, [42]but I know you. I know that you do not have the love of God in your hearts. [43]I have come in my Father's name, and you do not accept me; but if someone else comes in his own name, you will accept him. [44]How can you believe if you accept praise from one another, yet make no effort to obtain the praise that comes from the only God?" - John 5:39-44

Israel is God's model nation, yet in spite of the fact that Israel's history of repeated failure is on public display in the Bible for all to read, God has neither abandoned nor rejected his chosen people. When all the final scores are in concerning all the nations, with their animosity and hatred of the one true God, no one will have any cause for boasting. In fact God will judge all the other nations of the world by how they have treated the Jews (Joel 3:1-21).

Decades of God's grace, kindness, mercy and favor have not turned the nation of Israel towards faith in their God. Nor are they any closer to accepting their true Messiah. Will then God banish the Jews from the land again, perhaps this time permanently?

The answer from Scripture is clear. Israel's final testing will occur in their land and involve the destruction of a majority of the populace, a time of trial compared to which the Nazi holocaust will pale in insignificance.

Modern Israel

As discussed in chapter 1, Ezekiel plainly predicted that the Chosen People would one day be regathered from the various nations of the world, back to their own land, Israel (Ezekiel chapters 38 and 39). The Prophet saw a vision of a valley full of dry bones, shaking and coming back together. Once the skeleton was formed, muscles appeared. Then skin covered the reconstructed body, which is symbolic of the rebirth of Israel.

The modern nation of Israel came into existence on May 14, 1948, when the British, who had controlled the area of Palestine since the end of World War II, withdrew their forces and ended their occupation of the land.

War and Peace

However, all of the nations immediately surrounding the little sliver of land were opposed to the formation of a Jewish state, so, on the very first day of Israel's independence, all of Israel's neighbors declared war against them. Israel miraculously won that war—and four more that have been waged against them during their first fifty years of existence.

Chapter 1 shows the ongoing military struggle in Israel and the current threat of annihilation. A peace process should eventually result in a short period of peace between Israel and her neighbors, followed by a great war seen by the prophet (Ezekiel 38-39).

Israel's Glorious Future

After the Church Age is completed, God will turn again to Israel as a nation and focus his activities once again from his unseen headquarters in Jerusalem.

Simon has described to us how God at first showed his concern by taking from the Gentiles a people for himself. [15]The words of the prophets are in agreement with this, as it is written:
[16]" 'After this I will return
        and rebuild David's fallen tent.
Its ruins I will rebuild,
        and I will restore it,
[17]that the remnant of men may seek the Lord,
        and all the Gentiles who bear my name,
        says the Lord, who does these things'
[18]that have been known for ages." - Acts 15:14-18 (The quote is from Amos 9:11-12.)

In his great discourse on Israel's future the Apostle Paul assures us,

I do not want you to be ignorant of this mystery, brothers, so that you may not be conceited: Israel has experienced a hardening in part until the full number of the Gentiles has come in.
[26]And so all Israel will be saved, as it is written:
        "The deliverer will come from Zion;
        he will turn godlessness away from Jacob.
[27]And this is my covenant with them
        when I take away their sins." - Romans 11:25-27

The Old Testament books of prophecy are full of promises of the future blessing of Israel. This will be developed later in the last chapter on the Millennial Reign of Christ and beyond.

Next, we must turn our attention to the Church Age. The Church is also a chosen and blessed people to whom the task of evangelizing the world has been given. But there is a definite beginning and end of this period of time. Those who do not distinguish between Israel and the Church cannot understand prophecy.

Part II - The Church: A Mystery Revealed

Chapter 3
The Mystery of the Church

Announcement by Jesus

Toward the end of his public ministry Jesus made an announcement to his disciples about the formation of his "church."

> When Jesus came to the region of Caesarea Philippi, he asked his disciples, "Who do people say the Son of Man is?"
> [14]They replied, "Some say John the Baptist; others say Elijah; and still others, Jeremiah or one of the prophets."
> [15]"But what about you?" he asked. "Who do you say I am?"
> [16]Simon Peter answered, "You are the Christ, the Son of the living God."
> [17]Jesus replied, "Blessed are you, Simon son of Jonah, for this was not revealed to you by man, but by my Father in heaven. [18]And I tell you that you are Peter, and on this rock I will build my church and the gates of Hades will not overcome it. - Matthew 16:13-18

The word "church," was the normal Greek word for "assembly." Literally, it meant to "call out," as when the people of the city would be called together for a town meeting. Later the concept of being "called out" would take on special meaning. It would come to mean that the followers of Jesus should consider themselves no longer members of the old fallen world system (*cosmos*), but they are now citizens of a heavenly country, ambassadors from a far country serving in the world as sojourners and aliens. Down through history every generation of Christians has had to rediscover this pilgrim-nature of our calling.

Like many important teachings of Christ, the Disciples did not understand what Jesus meant at the time when he said that he would build a church that would assault and ultimately conquer the very strongholds of evil (Matthew 16:18). In fact, in the same chapter

Jesus also revealed that he would soon die and be raised again on the third day. Peter actually argued with him about that! (Matthew 16:21-23). It was only after Jesus' resurrection that they remembered his teaching (Luke 24:7-8).

The fact that the Church was not described by Christ at this time is significant in the light of his teachings, sometime later, about future things. In his great discourse on the future, known as "The Olivet Discourse" (because it was delivered on The Mount of Olives), he spoke of Israel's future trials, but made no reference to the Church. That is why the events of the future seem to be imminent. The entire church period, including the rapture of the Church, was still a mystery, not yet revealed. This vast new body of revealed information was later made known to the Apostles (including Paul). It would have only have confused his disciples had it been given to them in the tumultuous transitional period toward the end of Jesus' earthly life. It would take time for them to comprehend the important differences between Israel and Jesus' new Church.

Beginnings at Pentecost

It is interesting that even during the last week before his crucifixion, while Jesus was giving many important instructions; the subject of the Church was not specifically addressed. Everything he taught would later be *applicable to* the Church, but it was not *about* the Church *per se*. This, again, was because the nature of the Church had not yet been revealed.

During the forty days Jesus spent with the Disciples, between the time of his resurrection and the time of his ascension into Heaven, he still did not give details about the Church. But he did tell them to wait for a special gift from the Father.

> "Men of Galilee," they said, "why do you stand here looking into the sky? This same Jesus, who has been taken from you into heaven, will come back in the same way you have seen him go into heaven." - Acts 1:11

This, incidentally, corresponds exactly to the Old Testament prophecy of the coming of Messiah at the end of the age. Jesus will return to the same Mount of Olives from which he departed almost 2000 years ago.

> On that day his feet will stand on the Mount of Olives, east of Jerusalem, and the Mount of Olives will be split in two from east to west, forming a great valley, with half of the mountain moving north and half moving south. - Zechariah 14:4

In obedience to the parting words of their Lord, the fearful, powerless little band of about 120 Jewish followers of Jesus gathered in the Upper Room. They waited there for about one week until the Day of Pentecost, a Sunday morning. It was part of a time period on the calendar known as the Feast of Weeks and the Feast of Harvest. This was one of the major events of the year for which Jewish men were expected to travel to Jerusalem. Because of this, the city was full of Jewish believers from all over the known world on this great day.

The Book of Acts describes the amazing "gift" from the Father for which the Disciples had been waiting.

> When the day of Pentecost came, they were all together in one place. ²Suddenly a sound like the blowing of a violent wind came from heaven and filled the whole house where they were sitting. ³They saw what seemed to be tongues of fire that separated and came to rest on each of them. ⁴All of them were filled with the Holy Spirit and began to speak in other tongues as the Spirit enabled them.
> ⁵Now there were staying in Jerusalem God-fearing Jews from every nation under heaven. ⁶When they heard this sound, a crowd came together in bewilderment, because each one heard them speaking in his own language. - Acts 2:1-6

This filling with the Holy Spirit was followed by a powerful message by Peter to the crowds that had gathered. He made many references to the Hebrew Scriptures, and showed how Jesus was indeed the long-awaited Messiah (Acts 2:14-40). Three thousand out of the gathered crowd became believers that day and were all baptized immediately (Acts 2:41).

This was the beginning of the Church. As mentioned before, all the first believers were Jewish, and all of them understood that what they were doing was totally compatible with their Jewish history and Scriptures.

The word "church" is very similar to the word "synagogue." The Greek word for church was *ekklesia*, which means "called out," "an assembly." The Greek for synagogue is *sunagoge*, meaning "gathering together." Neither of these words are used in the Book of Acts until a little later ("church" in Acts 5:11 and "synagogue"—implied in Acts 6:9, and actually used in Acts 13:14). When the words were used, it was always clear that the Church referred to the new sect of Christians, while the synagogue referred to traditional Jewish groups.

Therefore, there are both similarities and differences between the new "church" and the old "synagogue." The differences were not contradictory. The new group saw itself as a continuation of the old, believing that Jesus was the fulfillment of the promise of a Messiah.

The Feasts and Fulfilled Prophecy

Since the Holy Spirit was given on the Day of Pentecost, and this is considered the birthday of the Church, it is helpful to study the connection between other major Feasts of Israel and God's prophetic timetable.

Leviticus 23 -is the key passage that describes the original seven feasts.
- **The Passover Supper (Pesach)** - Leviticus 23:4-5
- **The Feast of Unleavened Bread** - Leviticus 23:6-8
- **The Feast of Firstfruits** - Exodus 23:19; Leviticus 23:9-14
- **The Feast of Weeks** - Leviticus 23:16-21
  (Also called Pentecost- meaning 50 days after Feast of Firstfruits)
  (Also called The Feast of Harvest)
- **Rosh Hashanah** - New Year's Day - Leviticus 23:23-24
  (Also called The Feast of Trumpets)
- **Yom Kippur** - The Day of Atonement - Leviticus 23:26-32
- **The Feast of Tabernacles (Sukkot)** - Leviticus 23:33-34, 42-43
  (Also called The Feast of Booths and The Feast of Ingathering)

Since that time several others have been added. These include:
- **Purim**
- **Feast of Lights (Hanukkah)**

These holy days were symbolic of things to come.

Therefore do not let anyone judge you by what you eat or drink, or with regard to a religious festival, a New Moon celebration or a Sabbath day. [17]These are a shadow of the things that were to come; the reality, however, is found in Christ. - Colossians 2:16-17

It is surprising how many of the most important events in Jewish and Christian history have occurred on one of these dates, especially when one notices the correlation between the events and what the corresponding feast originally signified. Grant Jeffrey points out that all of the feasts and fasts of Israel have had significant historical events occur on their anniversaries.

Of the seven prescribed feasts of Moses, the first three all have something to do with the First Coming of Christ, the last three have to do with the Second Coming, and the one in the middle, Pentecost, is the birth date of the Church. Let us look at them more closely:

The Passover Supper (Pesach) — Fourteenth of Nisan
Leviticus 23:4-5

The event known as the "Last Supper" was actually the observance of Passover. Jesus told his disciples, "I have eagerly desired to eat this Passover with you before I suffer" (Luke 22:15).

Instructions for the first Passover were given to Moses just before the Israelites left the land of Egypt. Each family was to kill a year-old male lamb or goat without defect and paint some of its blood on the sides and the tops of the door frames of their homes. Then they were to roast the animal and eat it with bitter herbs and unleavened bread. That night the tenth plague was visited upon Egypt. The Lord killed all of the firstborn males in the land that night except where He saw the blood on the believers' houses. He passed over those homes, sparing them from the terrible plague. And they were told to observe this event as a "festival to the LORD—a lasting ordinance (Exodus 12:5-14).

This feast was a reminder of their deliverance from slavery in Egypt. It was mentioned often in their literature, and was to be commemorated yearly forever. It became the perfect occasion for education of the young about the story of their sojourn in Egypt, the Ten Plagues, the Exodus, and their Wilderness experience.

The central issue of the feast is the death of the lamb in the place of the firstborn. When John the Baptist first saw Jesus, he cried out, "Look, the Lamb of God, who takes away the sin of the world!" (John 1:29)

Jesus said this about himself:

The reason my Father loves me is that I lay down my life—only to take it up again. [18]No one takes it from me, but I lay it down of my own accord. I have authority to lay it down and authority to take it up again. This command I received from my Father."- John 10:17-18

During the Passover meal, Jesus used well-known ceremonies of breaking bread and drinking the cup to institute a "New Covenant" with his followers:

And he took bread, gave thanks and broke it, and gave it to them, saying, "This is my body given for you; do this in remembrance of me."
[20]In the same way, after the supper he took the cup, saying, "This cup is the new covenant in my blood, which is poured out for you." - Luke 22:19-20

The Apostle Paul actually called Christ "our Passover lamb" (1 Corinthians 5:7). So we see that it was not a coincidence that Jesus was crucified for our sins during the Passover season. The exact date of his final arrival in Jerusalem and his rejection, which led to his death on the cross, had been foretold by Daniel the prophet approximately 500 years earlier.[9]

The Feast of Unleavened Bread — Fifteenth of Nisan
Leviticus 23:6-8

This feast was to be celebrated the day after Passover (Exodus 13:3). It marked the beginning of seven days of eating unleavened bread. In Jesus' time, it appears that the Jews had combined the Passover and this first day of unleavened bread (Mark 14:12).

Separation from yeast is symbolic of purification from sin. It symbolizes the purification of Christ's disciples. This, of course is the result of his death: believers are delivered from the penalty and power of sin.

The Feast of Firstfruits — Seventeenth of Nisan
Exodus 23:19; Leviticus 23:9-14

This feast was prescribed in Leviticus 23:9-14, while Israel was still wandering in the wilderness, but it was not to be celebrated until they entered the land. When they did finally enter the Promised Land, Joshua 5 records the sequence of events.

> On the evening of the fourteenth day of the month, while camped at Gilgal on the plains of Jericho, the Israelites celebrated the Passover. [11] The day after the Passover, that very day, they ate some of the produce of the land: unleavened bread and roasted grain. [12] The manna stopped the day after they ate this food from the land; there was no longer any manna for the Israelites, but that year they ate of the produce of Canaan. - Joshua 5:10-12

On the fourteenth day of the month they celebrated the Passover. On the next day, the fifteenth, they ate "some of the produce of the land." The Hebrew word for "produce" in verse 11 meant "stored grain."

On the next day, the sixteenth day of the month, Manna was given for the last time. The next day, the 17th, would have been their first day of food from the new land. The Hebrew word translated "produce" in verse 12 is a different word meaning "income," or "fruit."

All of this speaks of their new life in the Promised Land.

Just as the Feast of Firstfruits was celebrated three days after Passover, so the resurrection of Jesus was on the third day. The concept of the "first fruits" is most appropriate since, as Paul explains,

> But Christ has indeed been raised from the dead, the firstfruits of those who have fallen asleep. [21]For since death came through a man, the resurrection of the dead comes also through a man. [22]For as in Adam all die, so in Christ all will be made alive. [23]But each in his own turn: Christ, the firstfruits; then, when he comes, those who belong to him. - 1 Corinthians 15:20-23

Pentecost — Sixth of Sivan
(50 Days after Feast of Firstfruits)
Also called the Feast of Harvest, and the Feast of Weeks
Leviticus 23:16, 21 Deuteronomy 16:9-10

It is surely no coincidence that this feast, being next in the order, was the occasion of the giving of the Holy Spirit to the Church, as explained above (Acts 2:1-4).

This leaves three of the primary seven feasts for possible symbolic meaning in regard to future prophetic events.

A Warning about Date Setting!

It is important that the reader does not think, from the remarks on the following three feasts, that we can set exact dates for future events. For a brief discussion of this topic, please see Appendix D: *Warnings and Cautions*. We do not believe in setting dates, and Jesus warned his disciples against the temptation to do that. However, it does seem likely that, in some way, future events will be tied in to the meaning of these feasts. Using the Passover, and Christ's crucifixion, as an example, it seems that he and his disciples celebrated Passover early in order that his death could take place, and his body could be removed from the cross before the beginning of the sacred day itself. Thus, even if one could have known he was going to die on Passover of that year, they still would not have been able to set the exact date. In the same way, even if we could know that the rapture would take place on Rosh Hashanah (and we can not know this), we would still not be able to predict with certainty whether it would be the exact day, or near the day, for his own purposes. Furthermore, we can not know whether it will be this year, next year, or twenty years from now. For the past several years, people have presented elaborate schemes "proving" that the rapture would be in a certain year. All such attempts have only succeeded in causing some people to doubt the whole subject of biblical prophecy.

The Feasts and Possible Future Fulfillments

Rosh Hashanah — First of Tishri - Ancient New Year's Day (Civil)
Also called The Feast of Trumpets
Leviticus 23:23-25, 27-32

This day marks Israel's ancient New Year's Day, and the beginning of the holy season of the Seventh Month (which includes the next two feasts). It began with the blowing of the shofar, or trumpet. It was to be a day of rest and sacrifice.

This day might point to the future rapture of the Church, since it is the next major feast in the Jewish calendar, and because of the prominence of the blowing of the shofar. Again, we do not believe that this theory gives grounds for any actual setting of dates for the Lord's return. *See Chapter 6 - The Rapture.*

Yom Kippur — Tenth of Tishri — The Day of Atonement
Leviticus 16; Leviticus 23:26-32

This is considered the most holy day of the Jewish year. It is a day of public fasting and humiliation as the people of Israel seek atonement for their sins.

When animal sacrifices were still being offered the high priest first sanctified himself by taking a ceremonial bath and putting on white garments. He then sacrificed a bullock to atone for himself and his fellow priests. Then two goats were chosen, one for sacrifice in behalf of the sins of the people, and one to be released into the wilderness. This "scape-goat" was symbolic of the pardon for sin brought through the sacrifice.

Since this is a day of mourning for sin, it is possibly symbolic of that future date when Christ returns to Earth in glory. At that time Israel will mourn when they see their Messiah whom they have pierced (Zechariah 12:9-10).

This future day of mourning is developed more fully in the third section of the book.

The Feast of Tabernacles (Sukkot) —Fifteenth of Tishri
Also called the Feast of Booths and the Feast of Ingathering
Leviticus 23:33-42

On the 15th day of the seventh month Israel was to commemorate their wandering in the wilderness. They constructed temporary booths in which to live during the festival to remember the 40 years of wandering when they lived in temporary shelters.

This could very well have been the time of year when Jesus was born.

The theme of the feast is appropriate since John 1:14 tells us that, "The Word became flesh and made his dwelling among us." The Greek word is *skenoo*, "to tent or encamp", as God did in the Tabernacle of old. Incidentally, if Jesus was born during this festival, his actual conception would have taken place nine months earlier, about the time of Hanukkah, the Feast of Lights, in December of the previous year. This would lend some credibility to our modern observance of Christmas in December.

As far as future symbolism is concerned, this feast is ideal for the concept of Christ ushering in the Kingdom Age. It is a picture of God dwelling, or encamping with mankind once again, this time as King of Kings and Lord of Lords!

Revelation of the Mystery of the Church through Paul
The "mystery" of the Church was revealed to the Apostle Paul, and described by him in numerous passages of Scripture. In Romans 11:25 he used the word to describe the tem-

porary "hardening" of Israel: "I do not want you to be ignorant of this mystery, brothers, so that you may not be conceited: Israel has experienced a hardening in part until the full number of the Gentiles has come in."

The word "mystery" (Greek *musterion*) meant a "secret," or something formerly hidden, but now revealed.

In Romans 16:25, Paul calls the Gospel, the proclamation of Jesus Christ, a mystery.

In Corinthians 15:51-58, he uses "mystery" to describe the resurrection and the glorified body that believers will receive.

Paul taught that it was a mystery (formerly hidden, but now revealed) that all things will eventually be brought together under the headship of Christ (Ephesians 1:9-10).

In Ephesians 3 the Apostle explained in greater detail that the mystery of the Church was part of God's purpose all along to make Gentiles heirs together with Israel.

> Surely you have heard about the administration of God's grace that was given to me for you, [3]that is, the mystery made known to me by revelation, as I have already written briefly. [4]In reading this, then, you will be able to understand my insight into the mystery of Christ, [5]which was not made known to men in other generations as it has now been revealed by the Spirit to God's holy apostles and prophets. [6]This mystery is that through the gospel the Gentiles are heirs together with Israel, members together of one body, and sharers together in the promise in Christ Jesus.
> [7]I became a servant of this gospel by the gift of God's grace given me through the working of his power. [8]Although I am less than the least of all God's people, this grace was given me: to preach to the Gentiles the unsearchable riches of Christ, [9]and to make plain to everyone the administration of this mystery, which for ages past was kept hidden in God, who created all things. [10]His intent was that now, through the Church, the manifold wisdom of God should be made known to the rulers and authorities in the heavenly realms, [11]according to his eternal purpose which he accomplished in Christ Jesus our Lord. - Ephesians 3:2-11

Again in Ephesians, Paul calls the revelation that the Church is The Bride of Christ a mystery (Ephesians 5:32). And he refers to his commission to preach the Gospel to the Gentiles as a mystery (Ephesians 6:19). This theme is also addressed in Colossians:

> I have become its servant by the commission God gave me to present to you the word of God in its fullness— [26]the mystery that has been kept hidden for ages and generations, but is now disclosed to the saints. [27]To them God has chosen to make known among the Gentiles the glorious riches of this mystery, which is Christ in you, the hope of glory. - Colossians 1:25-27

The Gospel to All Nations - "To the Jew First"

The essence, then, of the mystery of the Church is that, through this new assembly, God would include all people who would believe: both Jews and Gentiles. They would, in a sense, become one:

> You are all sons of God through faith in Christ Jesus, [27]for all of you who were baptized into Christ have clothed yourselves with Christ. [28]There is neither Jew nor Greek, slave nor free, male nor female, for you are all one in Christ Jesus. - Galatians 3:26-28 (See also Ephesians 2:14.)

This spiritual oneness does not blur the distinctions between them. Peter and Paul (and all the Disciples) became one in Christ with Gentiles like Cornelius, and Luke. Yet no one was confused about which of them was which. Likewise, oneness exists between Christian men and women, but God does not change their gender. Neither did he obliterate the difference between slaves and free men, as seen in the touching story of Philemon and Onesimus. The spiritual oneness superseded the physical differences, but did not eliminate them.

It should also be obvious that the Church did not replace Israel, because, as mentioned before, Paul was careful to always take the Gospel to Jewish believers in every new city before sharing it with the Gentiles. He said, "I am not ashamed of the gospel, because it is the power of God for the salvation of everyone who believes: first for the Jew, then for the Gentile" (Romans 1:16).

The Church: The Body and Bride of Christ

The church is distinguished from Israel in many ways. One example would be that it is called the *Body of Christ* (1 Corinthians 12:14-27; Ephesians 12:4).

The church is also called the *Bride of Christ* (Ephesians 5:22-33), whereas unfaithful Israel was sometimes called an adulterous wife (Jeremiah 16:32; Hosea 1:2). The church has not yet been married, but is a virgin bride preparing for her first wedding. However Israel was "the wife of Yahweh." Because of her spiritual adultery he has temporarily set her aside. Yet Hosea makes clear God will one day take his wife, Israel, back to himself. The common belief that Israel has been permanently set aside by God can easily be refuted from many Scriptures in both the Old and New Testaments (Hosea; Ezekiel chapters 36 through 48; Romans 11).

It is vitally important for the followers of Jesus in our age to understand the difference between Israel and the Church. Israel as a nation enjoys covenant relationships with God—other nations do not have such covenants with God. God's covenants with the Church do not include a plot of land, a temple, an earthly inheritance, etc. They are an entirely different set of promises.

Grafted in Temporarily - In Israel's Place

In Romans 11, Paul, "the Apostle to the Gentiles" explains to Gentiles that Israel has not been rejected by God, but, because of their hardness, they have suffered temporary spiritual blindness, and that Gentile believers have been grafted in, in the place of some of them. Eventually, believing Israel will be grafted back in (Romans 11:17-25).

The description of Gentile believers as wild olive branches grafted into the true olive tree suggests that Gentiles need to become more Jewish in their thinking and life styles as they grow spiritually. When we meet our Messiah and Savior face to face we shall discover that he is Jewish and was raised in Jewish culture and taught the Hebrew Scriptures. He was a devout and observant Jewish believer. Visits to Israel and cultivated friendships with Jewish people are well worth the effort in freeing us from our own ghetto mentalities and the pagan, idolatrous roots from which we have been freed as Gentiles.

Spiritual Heirs of the Covenants

In Ephesians, chapters 2 and 3, the Apostle Paul reminds his Gentile readers that before Christ, they were excluded from the covenants given to Israel, but now have been brought near through Christ's blood. The barrier between Jews and Gentiles has been abolished. Both have been reconciled by the Cross, and both have access to the Father by one Spirit. Consequently, Gentile believers in Christ have become fellow citizens with Israel.

In Romans 11, Paul shows that the Church has not replaced Israel. "I ask then: Did God reject his people? By no means! I am an Israelite myself, a descendant of Abraham, from the tribe of Benjamin" (Romans 11:1).

The institution of the Church was not meant by God to replace the earlier institution of Israel as his "chosen people." In the next verse (v.2), he stated plainly, "God did not reject his people, whom he foreknew." And he used the well-known example of Elijah, when he thought he was the only believer, and the Lord told him that he had seven thousand other true believers. Thus, Paul argues that there were many true believers in Israel. "So too, at the present time there is a remnant chosen by grace" (Romans 11:5).

After explaining that the others, who did not believe that Jesus was Messiah, had been hardened and blinded temporarily, he asks again, "Did they stumble so as to fall beyond recovery?" And then he answers emphatically, "Not at all! Rather, because of their transgression, salvation has come to the Gentiles to make Israel envious" (Romans 11:11).

One New Man

The church plus Israel is the "one new man" that God is building.

For he himself is our peace, who has made the two one and has destroyed the barrier, the dividing wall of hostility, [15]by abolishing in his flesh the law with its commandments and regulations. His purpose was to create in himself one new man out of the two, thus making peace, [16]and in this one body to reconcile both of them to God through the cross, by which he put to death their hostility. - Ephesians 2:14-16

The late Ray Stedman, former pastor of Peninsula Bible Church in Palo Alto, CA wrote,

Running all through Scripture from Genesis to Revelation, and especially in Genesis and Revelation, is the great theme that God's desire is that he may dwell amidst man. Man himself is to be the dwelling place of God. This is what our Lord and the Apostle Paul speak of when they speak of a new creation, a new man, which God is forming at this present hour. Just as there is an old man symbolized by Adam and all his descendants, so there is a new man, the true Adam, symbolized or figured in Jesus Christ and all his spiritual sons and daughters. That is the new creation.

Just as the old creation, humanity itself, is made up of body, soul and spirit, so in the new heavens and the new earth there will be a new humanity to inhabit, develop and fulfill it, body, soul and spirit. This seems to be, then, the place where we can bring together the apparent conflicting destinies of Israel as a nation and the Church as The Bride of Christ. In our human bodies we have an outward physical part of our life, i.e., the body.

That seems to be the place that Israel occupies in the new man, the new humanity. Israel's destiny is earthly. It will reign on the earth. It will govern the earth. It will be involved with the blessing and the fruitfulness of the earth as Paul so beautifully describes in the 11th chapter of Romans. But linked with the body very closely in our humanity is the soul, our inner life, our minds, our emotions, our wills, this inner functioning of which we are so aware and which links us to so much of the universe of God in terms of feeling and thinking, etc. Now, that is the Church. The special dwelling place of God is in the soul of man, and the Church is called to fulfill that, linked together with Israel as the soul in our humanity is linked with the body. And the spirit, which is the third part of man necessary to his existence is, of course, God himself. God is a spirit, and in the new humanity, God fulfills that central control place. So, you have a whole new creation in a whole new world operating on totally different principles that probably are the exact reverse of the principles on which the world functions today.

One of the great principles with which science has to deal is the so called second law of thermodynamics, the law of entropy, the idea that everything is running down, that no matter how good things are they do not eventually get better. They get worse. They fall apart. They phase out. They lose energy. That law is universal. In the new heavens and the new earth, it will be exactly the opposite. There things will start and you will not be able to stop them from developing. They get better and better, and richer and sweeter and fuller and more exciting. We are awed when we look at the vastness of the cosmos in which we now live, but everywhere we look we see the evidence of sin and decay, the futility that is present in the universe today. But according to the promises of Scripture, there is coming a new heaven and a new earth. This is why for believers the apostles and the prophets try to describe what lies beyond death, but they can only talk about what is not going to be there, no sorrow, no tears, no separations, no weakness, no fear, no war, no death, and just imply the opposite. This is the fulfillment of the dreams and hopes of mankind.[10]

Not to Antagonize Israel

Members of the Church must not feel superior to the Jewish people, since the time will come that Israel will return to the Lord. This too is part of the mystery once hidden, but now revealed:

> I do not want you to be ignorant of this mystery, brothers, so that you may not be conceited: Israel has experienced a hardening in part until the full number of the Gentiles has come in. - Romans 11:25

Now that we see how God looks at both Israel and the Church, we understand that the Church will have a definite period of existence until the End Times, when Israel will return to a right relationship with the Lord. The next chapter explains the various stages of Church history as they are revealed in the Book of Revelation.

Chapter 4
Church History

The Book of Acts tells about the history of the early church. The Epistles give instruction to the Church. But it is in the book of Revelation that a prophetic history of the Church is given. The whole book is about prophecy, so it is understandable that the messages to the seven churches of Asia were meant not only for the actual churches of that day, but for *seven periods of church history* that would describe conditions from the beginning of the Church Age to the end of it.

The book of Revelation is unique in that the opening verses tell us that what follows was given to Jesus by his Father. Jesus then passed the contents to his beloved Apostle John (now an old man in exile on the island of Patmos off the coast of Asia, or modern Turkey). John recorded for us in vivid language what he saw and heard. The information was imparted to him partly by means of a series of great visions. Information about events transpiring in heaven is juxtaposed with happenings on earth. The book contains interludes and flashbacks. Therefore, understanding the order of events in the Revelation takes thoughtful care.

Genesis, the Book of beginnings, unfolds little by little. Great themes of human history are introduced to us one by one. These themes branch out and are woven as recurring themes in the rest of the Bible. In the book of Revelation all these themes come back together in a great consummation.

The 404 verses of Revelation contain 800 Old Testament references![11] Many Jewish symbols and ideas that have not been used in the entire New Testament suddenly reappear in Revelation. Because of this, no one can hope to understand this marvelous last book of the Bible without reading the rest of the book—all that has gone before.

The Revelation gives an outline of its contents in Chapter 1, verse 19. "Write, therefore, what you have seen, what is now and what will take place later." This verse may be considered the KEY to the Book. The three parts of the Revelation are:

1- What you *have seen* - The Person of Jesus Christ - 1:1-18

2- The Things that *are now* - The Presence of Jesus Christ in This Age - 1:19-3:22

3- The things that *will take place* - The Program of Jesus Christ For The Future - 4:1-22:21

In this section we will only consider the second of these parts.

The Presence of Jesus Christ in This Age - Revelation 1:19-3:22

Following the Ascension of Jesus, Acts Chapter 1, we do not again hear directly from the Lord Jesus Christ until we come to the last book of the Bible. There Jesus is depicted for us in priestly robes walking in the midst of, and judging, his church, during the present age.

Insight about the Church: Revelation 1:19-20

These verses portray the seven churches as seven golden lampstands—they were designed to shine the Light (which is God), into the darkness of the world.

> "Write, therefore, what you have seen, what is now and what will take place later. [20]The mystery of the seven stars that you saw in my right hand and of the seven golden lampstands is this: The seven stars are the angels of the seven churches, and the seven lampstands are the seven churches." - Revelation 1:19-20

A message is to be given to each of these seven churches, and the messages to the churches follow a pattern. First, there is a description of Jesus Christ in terms that are especially important to each church. Secondly, there is affirmation of the good characteristics of the Church. Thirdly, there is a warning for each church (except Smyrna, and Philadelphia). Finally, there is a reward promised to those in the Church who are overcomers.

Instruction to the Church: Revelation 2:1-3:22
To Ephesus - Revelation 2:1-7

> "To the angel[1] of the church in Ephesus write:
> These are the words of him who holds the seven stars in his right hand and walks among the seven golden lampstands: [2]I know your deeds, your hard work and your perseverance. I know that you cannot tolerate wicked men, that you have tested those who claim to be apostles but are not, and have found them false. [3]You have persevered and have endured hardships for my name, and have not grown weary. [4]Yet I hold this against you: You have

forsaken your first love. ⁵Remember the height from which you have fallen! Repent and do the things you did at first. If you do not repent, I will come to you and remove your lampstand from its place. ⁶But you have this in your favor: You hate the practices of the Nicolaitans, which I also hate. ⁷He who has an ear, let him hear what the Spirit says to the churches. To him who overcomes, I will give the right to eat from the tree of life, which is in the paradise of God." - Revelation 2:1-7

Ephesus, the first church, portrays the Apostolic Period, from the birth of the Church, at the day of Pentecost (Acts 2), until approximately AD 100.

During the Apostolic period there were false apostles. The early church was careful to identify true apostles and reject the false. This explains the need for the Apostle Paul to defend his calling as an apostle in 2 Corinthians, chapters 11-13. In chapter 11, verse 13 he also mentions people who were masquerading as false apostles.

Believers of this period also endured great hardships without giving up their faith. Christianity was considered false by the majority of Jewish people who had been blinded because of their unbelief (Romans 11). Those who followed Christ often had to do so against the wishes of their families. Jesus warned his followers that this would happen (Matthew 10:34-39). Opposition to early Christianity became so strong that believers were scattered and many were imprisoned and even killed. Before he was converted, Paul zealously persecuted the Church (Acts 9:1-2, 21).

It is shocking that this early church had lost its "first love" for Christ. It shows that it is possible for any Christian to be distracted from his devotion to the Lord by the cares of the world. Jesus himself gave the Parable of the Sower, which teaches that some new Christians fail to develop deep roots, others are choked by the competing "weeds" that spring up around them, and others grow well and bear good fruit (Matthew 13:3-8).

The good news is that if a person, or even a whole group of people in a church, should lose their first love, they can be restored by repenting. To repent means to turn around and go the other way. Repentance requires honest self-appraisal. One must identify the sins that are separating him from the Lord, and then confess (Greek *homologeo* —" to say the same"). This means that the person agrees with God about the sin. When a person does this, God is faithful to forgive and cleanse him or her from sin (1 John 1:9).

The church of the Apostolic Period hated the deeds of the Nicolaitans. This is a Greek word, which means "conquerors of the people." This is probably a reference to the false apostles mentioned earlier, and their tendency to establish a ruling class over the rest of the people in the Church. The proper Scriptural view is that the Church is like a body, and different people in the Church have different gifts from God, but all are of equal importance to the well-being of the whole spiritual body. There is no hierarchy in the Body of Christ, and no distinction between "clergy" and "laity"—all are called to work together in the ministry as one Body headed by Christ (1 Corinthians 12, Ephesians 4).

The promise to overcomers of this period is that they will eat of the Tree of Life, which is said to now be in Paradise. Adam and Eve ate instead from the forbidden fruit of the Tree of The Knowledge of Good and Evil, thus rebelling against God and entering into sin (Genesis 3). Part of the result of this sin was to be banished from the Garden of Eden so that they would not eat of this tree and live forever in their fallen state (Genesis 3:22-24). Nevertheless, an overcomer will be delivered from this fallen state, and will be permitted to partake of this fruit, thus living forever as a redeemed person.

Who then is an overcomer? John himself explains this:

For everyone born of God overcomes the world. This is the victory that has overcome the world, even our faith. ⁵Who is it that overcomes the world? Only he who believes that Jesus is the Son of God. - I John 5:4-5

To Smyrna - Revelation 2:8-11

"To the angel of the church in Smyrna write:
These are the words of him who is the First and the Last, who died and came to life again. ⁹I know your afflictions and your poverty—yet you are rich! I know the slander of those who say they are Jews and are not, but are a synagogue of Satan. ¹⁰Do not be afraid of what you are about to suffer. I tell you, the devil will put some of you in prison to test you, and you will suffer persecution for ten days. Be faithful, even to the point of death, and I will give you the crown of life. ¹¹He who has an ear, let him hear what the Spirit says to the churches. He who overcomes will not be hurt at all by the second death." - Revelation 2:8-11

Smyrna was a city, of course, but its name is derived from "myrrh," a valuable spice used in the process of embalming. Myrrh symbolizes death and yet is a sweet fragrance. This is an appropriate word picture for the period of church history characterized by martyrdom. This period lasted from approximately AD 100 to 312 when Constantine established Christianity as the state religion of the empire. During these two centuries there were ten definable periods of persecution of Christians under ten of the emperors of Rome. To these believers, Jesus identified himself as the resurrected one!

There is no warning to this church, since it was a church constantly purified by the rigors of persecution. To put it simply, only a strong, dedicated Christian would be willing to die for Christ. A hypocrite would quit the Church long before he would risk losing his life. True believers would be faithful unto death, and they would receive a crown of life. This is one of the special believers' crowns mentioned in the Bible. Faithful believers will be able to lay these at the feet of Christ in the future to prove their love for him (Revelation 4:10).

Jesus had taught earlier,

"I tell you, my friends, do not be afraid of those who kill the body and after that can do no more. [5]But I will show you whom you should fear: Fear him who, after the killing of the body, has power to throw you into hell. Yes, I tell you, fear him." - Luke 12:4-5

The promise to overcomers of this period is that, though they might need to die physically, they would not be hurt by the "second death." This subject is revisited in Revelation 20:12-15 where it is equated with eternal punishment and being cast into the Lake of Fire. The biblical concept of death is not annihilation, but separation. When a person dies physically, the material part (body) is separated from the immaterial (soul and spirit). The person does not cease to exist. Spiritual death is seen in the Scriptures as separation from God (Genesis 3, Ephesians 2:1). Those who are spiritually dead may be brought back to life, that is, be born again. (Ephesians 2:2-10; John 3:3-18). See Appendix T - *Do You Know Christ Personally?*

To Pergamum - 2:12-17

"To the angel of the church in Pergamum write:
These are the words of him who has the sharp, double-edged sword. [13]I know where you live—where Satan has his throne. Yet you remain true to my name. You did not renounce your faith in me, even in the days of Antipas, my faithful witness, who was put to death in your city—where Satan lives. [14]Nevertheless, I have a few things against you: You have people there who hold to the teaching of Balaam, who taught Balak to entice the Israelites to sin by eating food sacrificed to idols and by committing sexual immorality. [15]Likewise you also have those who hold to the teaching of the Nicolaitans. [16]Repent therefore! Otherwise, I will soon come to you and will fight against them with the sword of my mouth. [17]He who has an ear, let him hear what the Spirit says to the churches. To him who overcomes, I will give some of the hidden manna. I will also give him a white stone with a new name written on it, known only to him who receives it." - Revelation 2:12-17

Pergamum, also known as Pergamos, had a colorful history as a major city of Asia Minor. It was steeped in pagan idolatry, serpent worship, and Caesar worship. Alexander Hislop, Archbishop of the Anglican Church in the late 19th Century, wrote a book called *The Two Babylons*, in which he showed how the satanic religious system of Babylon was transferred to the city of Pergamum.[12]

Pergamum means "thoroughly married." It represents the period of church history when the Church became married to the world. Constantine, the Emperor of the Roman Empire probably meant well when he issued a decree that all his subjects should become Christians, but it actually did much damage to the Church. The majority of people became

Christian in name only, bringing their pagan practices and lifestyles into a compromised church. This merger of the Church and state took place with Constantine's conversion to Christianity in AD 312 and the Edict of Milan in AD 313. This period lasted until about AD 476 when the Western Roman Empire fell. During this time the Bishop of Rome assumed the title, Pontifex Maximus[13].

To this church Jesus revealed himself as the one with the sharp double-edged sword proceeding from his mouth. Hebrews 4:12 calls God's Word a double-edged sword, able to divide even between soul and spirit. In the same book Jesus is considered God's ultimate Word (Hebrews 1:1-2). In John's own writings Jesus is called The Word (John 1:1, 14). If the Church would follow Jesus and his Word, they would be able to separate the truth from the pagan influences that had come in like a flood.

The warning to this church is about those who allowed the teaching of Balaam. This refers to a fascinating story from the Old Testament book of Numbers, chapters 22 through 24, where the prophet Balaam was hired by Balak, king of the Moabites, to curse Israel. He tried repeatedly, but God would not allow him to utter a curse against his people. However, he evidently advised Balak to involve the Israelites in worldliness and immorality (Numbers 31:16). Thus Israel could be corrupted from within. This, of course, is exactly what happened to the Church during this period of time. They were corrupted by worldliness.

This church was also corrupted by the teaching of the Nicolaitans. These church clerics who exercised authority over the people are the same as those seen above in the message to the Church at Ephesus. They had now entrenched their position by their doctrine.

Overcomers are promised hidden manna and a white stone with a new name written upon it. The hidden manna might be the truth of Scripture that was in the process of being hidden by the worldly church. The white stone is a symbol taken from the ancient custom of giving a black stone to one judged guilty, and a white stone to one who is acquitted.

To Thyatira - Revelation 2:18-29

"To the angel of the church in Thyatira write:

These are the words of the Son of God, whose eyes are like blazing fire and whose feet are like burnished bronze. [19]I know your deeds, your love and faith, your service and perseverance, and that you are now doing more than you did at first. [20]Nevertheless, I have this against you: You tolerate that woman Jezebel, who calls herself a prophetess. By her teaching she misleads my servants into sexual immorality and the eating of food sacrificed to idols. [21]I have given her time to repent of her immorality, but she is unwilling. [22]So I will cast her on a bed of suffering, and I will make those who commit adultery with her suffer intensely, unless they repent of her ways. [23]I will strike her children dead. Then all the churches will know that I am he who searches hearts and minds, and I will repay each of you according to your deeds. [24]Now I say to the rest of you in Thyatira, to you who do not hold to her teaching and have not learned Satan's so-called deep secrets (I will not impose any other burden on you): ²⁵Only hold on to what you have until I come. ²⁶To him who overcomes and does my will to the end, I will give authority over the nations—

²⁷'He will rule them with an iron scepter;

he will dash them to pieces like pottery'— just as I have received authority from my Father.

²⁸I will also give him the morning star. ²⁹He who has an ear, let him hear what the Spirit says to the churches." - Revelation 2:18-29

Thyatira stands for a dark period of the Church from about AD 476 (The fall of the Western Roman Empire) until the time of the Reformation, which began in 1517. During this time such unfortunate historical events, as the inquisitions and the Crusades demonstrated the deepening lack of spirituality of the Church. It was also the time when indulgences were sold, whereby people could pay money to supposedly have their sins removed. This led to the posting of Luther's 95 Theses on the door of the Wittenberg Church and the beginning of the Reformation.

The Thyatira church received at least a mild commendation for doing some things right, but it also was given a stern warning about the toleration of Jezebel whose practices included false prophecy, immorality, and eating food offered to idols. It seems unlikely that Jezebel was an actual person during this period of time. This is more likely another of the many symbols in the book. Jezebel, an Old Testament queen, was an incredibly wicked person who was known for her idolatry, immorality, and hatred of the true prophets (1 Kings Chapters 18 through 21 and 2 Kings 9). This would then symbolize the Church hierarchy with its growing spiritual unfaithfulness and idolatry that eventually caused the splitting of the Church at the Reformation. It also prefigures the specter of the Woman Riding the Beast in Revelation 17.

The promise to overcomers is to give authority over the nations. This stands in contrast to the deep secrets of Satan, which may be a reference to the unholy alliance between the Church and various governments. God was not pleased with Papal influence over the nations, but he will be pleased to allow his righteous followers to rule and reign with Christ when he returns as King of Kings (Revelation 19:11-16).

The overcomer will also receive the Morning Star. Jesus calls himself the Morning Star in Revelation 22:16.

To Sardis - Revelation 3:1-6

"To the angel of the church in Sardis write:

These are the words of him who holds the seven spirits of God and the seven stars. I know your deeds; you have a reputation of being alive, but you are dead. ²Wake up! Strengthen what remains and is about to die, for I have not found your deeds complete in the sight of my God. [3]Remember, therefore, what you have received and heard; obey it, and repent. But if you do not wake up, I will come like a thief, and you will not know at what time I will come to you. [4]Yet you have a few people in Sardis who have not soiled their clothes. They will walk with me, dressed in white, for they are worthy. [5]He who overcomes will, like them, be dressed in white. I will never blot out his name from the book of life, but will acknowledge his name before my Father and his angels. [6]He who has an ear, let him hear what the Spirit says to the churches." - Revelation 3:1-6

The Sardis church represents the Reformation period from 1517 until the mid-1700's when the great revivals and modern missions movement began. This was a time when the Church had a reputation for being alive, but, as God saw it, they were really dying. History reveals that, though the churches of the Reformation did break away from problems in the Roman Catholic Church, they still did not return to thoroughly biblical practices, and had many problems of their own, including the union of church and state and the persecution of other reformers such as the Anabaptists who practiced believer's baptism and were pacifists. The Reformation churches did not in general deal with the faulty eschatology held by the Roman Church since early times.

Jesus reveals himself to this church as the one who holds the Seven Spirits, and the seven stars, identified earlier as the *angels* of the seven churches. These images indicate his sovereignty and his right to tell them to repent and change their ways.

The overcomer will be given white garments and his name will not be blotted out of the Book of Life. It seems that each person's name is already in the Book of Life, but those who are not true believers will have their names blotted out. This book is also mentioned in Revelation 20:12 where those not found in it are cast into the Lake of Fire.

To Philadelphia - Revelation 3:7-13

"To the angel of the church in Philadelphia write:

These are the words of him who is holy and true, who holds the key of David. What he opens no one can shut, and what he shuts no one can open. [8]I know your deeds. See, I have placed before you an open door that no one can shut. I know that you have little strength, yet you have kept my word and have not denied my name. [9]I will make those who are of the synagogue of Satan, who claim to be Jews though they are not, but are liars—I will make them come and fall down at your feet and acknowledge that I have loved you. [10]Since you have kept my command to endure patiently, I will also keep you from the hour of trial that is going to come upon the whole world to test those who live on the earth. [11]I am coming soon. Hold on to what you have, so that no one will take your crown. [12]Him who overcomes I will make a pillar in the temple of my God. Never again will he leave it. I will write on him the name of my God and the name of the city of my God, the new Jerusalem, which is coming down out of heaven from my God; and I will also write on him my new name. [13]He who has an ear, let him hear what the Spirit says to the churches." - Revelation 3:7-13

Philadelphia is the missionary church. It began in the mid 1700's with the great revivals and the modern missions movement, and it gradually lost much of its power during the 1900's. Philadelphia means "brotherly love." It is this love that causes the desire to evangelize others (Romans 5:5). Jesus is seen as having the keys of David. He was of the line of David, and thus eligible for the throne of Israel. The key is for opening the door of opportunity for missions. No one can close what he has opened. No one can open what he has closed.

There is no warning to this church, but many promises including these: "I am coming soon.", and a promise to keep them from the hour of trial that is coming on the world. These are definite allusions to the rapture and to its timing: before the trials of The Tribulation. There is also a warning not to let anyone take their crown. This refers to one of the believers' crowns: possibly the crown of life that was promised to the overcomers of the Smyrna church above.

To the overcomers of this period there is a promise of a new name and permanent residence in the New Jerusalem.

To Laodicea - Revelation 3:14-22

"To the angel of the church in Laodicea write:
These are the words of the Amen, the faithful and true witness, the ruler of God's creation. [15]I know your deeds, that you are neither cold nor hot. I wish you were either one or the other! [16]So, because you are lukewarm—neither hot nor cold—I am about to spit you out of my mouth. [17]You say, 'I am rich; I have acquired wealth and do not need a thing.' But you do not realize that you are wretched, pitiful, poor, blind and naked. [18]I counsel you to buy from me gold refined in the fire, so you can become rich; and white clothes to wear, so you can cover your shameful nakedness; and salve to put on your eyes, so you can see. [19]Those whom I love I rebuke and discipline. So be earnest, and repent. [20]Here I am! I stand at the door and knock. If anyone hears my voice and opens the door, I will come in and eat with him, and he with me. [21]To him who overcomes, I will give the right to sit with me on my throne, just as I overcame and sat down with my Father on his throne. [22]He who has an ear, let him hear what the Spirit says to the churches." - Revelation 3:14-22

The Laodicean church is the last church of the seven, and stands for the last of the Church periods. The name Laodicea means "rule of the people." It is a picture of a church controlled by the people instead of being controlled by God. It is the church of the apostasy, or the great "falling away" of believers.

Jesus reveals himself as ruler of all creation, and as the faithful and true one in contrast to the unfaithfulness of the Laodiceans. He says they are neither spiritually hot nor cold, but lukewarm, and that he will spit them out of his mouth. This is shocking news to a people who have a very good feeling about themselves. They say they are rich, but they are poor and wretched and blind. If they were spiritually "hot" they would be like the flaming evangelists of the Philadelphia church. If they were "cold" perhaps they would recognize their spiritual plight. But they are active in their church work, doing what they want instead of what God wants. They are like those about whom Jesus warned—they call him Lord, but he never knew them (Matthew 7:21-23).

Jesus counsels them to buy gold, symbolic of faith (1 Peter 1:7), white garments, which are like the linen of imputed righteousness with which the Bride of Christ is dressed (Revelation 19:7-8), and eye salve, showing dependence on God's spiritual healing for their blinded eyes.

To this church Jesus says he is standing outside the door, knocking. If they will open the door, he will come in. This is a church full of so-called Christians who have never really given their hearts to Jesus. Since it comes at the end of the Church Age, it is easy to see that there will still be many who call themselves Christians left behind when the rapture takes place.

Still, there are overcomers even from this church. Those who will open the door to Christ will be overcomers. To them, Jesus will grant the right to sit with him on his throne. This is undoubtedly a reference to the future privilege of believers to reign with Christ.

Many Bible commentators note that the seven churches are representative of various congregations that can be found on the earth at any one time during the entire 2000 year history of the Church. These distinctively different congregations each have strengths and weaknesses, and each has a core of faithful believers within them—designated by the word "overcomers." Also, each of the seven churches has enjoyed its season of prominence as the dominant church during a given period of time. Most scholars who hold to this view believe we are now moving, or have already moved, out of the Philadelphian age into the Laodicean age. This is the final stage of church history before the rapture.

Having considered the progress of the Church during these past two thousand years, we should now look at the gradual preparation for a final evil world empire that will fulfill the prophecies of the Book of Daniel and its New Testament counterpart, the Book of Revelation.

Chapter 5
Satan's Final Empire: Global Governance and Religion

Ever since sin entered the human race there has been a problem with government. We often hear the saying, "Power corrupts; absolute power corrupts absolutely."[14] The Bible records that it did not take long for sinful decadence to set in. Adam and Eve sinned and were driven from the Garden of Eden (Genesis 3). In the famous story of two of their sons, Cain and Abel, Cain displeased God by the type of sacrifice he offered. He killed his brother Abel in a jealous fit after God accepted Abel's sacrifice. Then God sent him away from the rest of the family. But as time went on[15], Cain actually built the first city! He named it Enoch, after his son (Genesis 4:1-17). But was this city a great achievement, or was it something evil? Given his background, and God's will for him to be separated from others, it is clear that it was an act of rebellion. There were evidently other rebels by then also who were attracted to his project.

The same thing happened after the Flood of Noah's time. Once again, the survivors of the Flood were told by God to spread out and replenish the earth. For some time they did what God wanted them to do, but by the time of Noah's great-grandson, Nimrod, there was a new rebellion against God's will. Nimrod was a mighty warrior and builder of several cities (Genesis 10:8-11). One of these was Nineveh, which would later become the capital of the Assyrian Empire. Another of his cities was Babylon, which eventually became the capital of the Babylonian Empire.

Rise of Satan's Final Empire

Nimrod's goal was to gather people together and rule over them. He was called "a mighty hunter before the Lord" (Genesis 10:9). In the context of what he was doing, this was not just a biographical note of his ability to hunt animals, but a condemnation of his desire to hunt men and turn them from the Lord. He led them in rebellion against God's will to migrate and repopulate the earth.

Nimrod was probably still governing Babylon when the people there built a great tower (Genesis 11). It was a monument to their own achievements and evidently a place where astrology was practiced and false gods were worshipped. The Lord confused their languages so they had to stop their work and were scattered from that place.

Nebuchadnezzar's Dream and Daniel's Visions

Hundreds of years later, Nimrod's kingdom-building vision was revived by Nebuchadnezzar, king of Babylon, and ruler of the Babylonian Empire. Nebuchadnezzar had a mysterious dream and did not know what it meant. His magicians, astrologers and fortunetellers could not help him interpret it (Daniel 2:31-35). Daniel was one of the captives who had been carried off from Israel to Babylon. Nebuchadnezzar called for Daniel to see if he could explain the dream to him.

First God showed Daniel that Nebuchadnezzar had dreamed about a huge statue made of various kinds of metals. The head was gold, the chest and arms were silver, the waist and thighs were brass, the legs were iron, and the feet were iron, mixed with clay. A stone came out of heaven, landing on the feet, and causing the whole statue to topple and break into pieces. God then showed Daniel what the dream meant.

Since Nebuchadnezzar was the head of the Babylonian empire (which virtually ruled the then-known world), he was the head of gold. But the prophecy meant that another empire would arise that would overtake them. There were scores of other, minor kingdoms. Some of them were small empires that ruled over a certain number of countries for a period of time. But what Nebuchadnezzar saw in his dream were *world* empires. From the time of Nebuchadnezzar until now there would only be four of them, including his Babylon. The second empire was silver, meaning that it was inferior to the first in some ways, and it had two parts, like two arms (the Medes and the Persians). Then there was another empire, symbolized by brass waist and thighs (Greece), and a fourth Empire, described as legs of iron (Rome). The feet of the statue were made of iron and clay. This fifth and final empire has not yet come to power. (See Appendix C -*Harmony of Prophecy Chart.*)

The Babylonians gave way to the Medo-Persians, the Medo-Persians gave way to the Greeks, and the Greeks gave way to the Romans. It was the Romans who were in power at the time of Christ. There had been almost an unbroken succession of world empires from Nebuchadnezzar until the time of Christ. Nebuchadnezzar's dream indicated that one empire would be replaced by another. There is still one empire that has not yet come.

After the Roman Empire ceased to exist, how many world empires have there been? Can you think of any? Not really. There have been some serious attempts. Mohammed, Charlemagne, Napoleon, and Hitler all tried to conquer the world in their times, but none of them succeeded. The Bible says there are only four of these world empires, and then a final form of the fourth one—symbolized by the feet made partly of iron and partly of clay.

What would the iron and clay mean? It is a Revived Roman Empire—partly of the old iron of the ancient Roman Empire, and partly of clay, something weaker and brittle. It would include some of the old areas, but it would not be as strong and monolithic as the old Roman Empire. When the stone comes out of Heaven and lands on these feet they will break. The stone from Heaven represents the coming of the Lord Jesus Christ as King of Kings. When he comes he will destroy the final evil empire and set up the Millennial Kingdom.

Later, when Nebuchadnezzar was gone, and Belshazzar was king of Babylon, Daniel had a dream of his own (Daniel 7). He called it a night vision. It was about four great beasts representing the same world empires that Nebuchadnezzar had seen, but in a different form. This dream was given to confirm what Nebuchadnezzar had seen in his dream: that there would be a succession of four empires, and that they would become successively more fierce. The first one, symbolic of Babylon, was a lion with wings of an eagle. The second was a bear. It would correspond to the Medo-Persian period. A third beast was a leopard with four wings, prefiguring the Greek Empire, and its dissolution into four parts. The fourth beast was a terrifying creature with iron teeth. This one would represent powerful Rome. It had ten horns, symbolizing the still-future form of the old Roman Empire in the End Times. Daniel also saw a brief sequence of the rise of an evil world ruler and his overthrow by The Lord, the "Ancient of Days."

A couple of years later Daniel had another vision featuring different animals (Daniel 8:1-12). The activities of these animals added detail to the future existence of Medo-Persia and Greece. In this vision there was also an individual who was extremely powerful. He came on the scene at the end. This is a picture of the end-time dictator. The first specific teachings about him are from Daniel, chapters 7 to 9. Chapter 9 gives details of his treaty with Israel, which he breaks in the middle. He will then set up a statue of himself to be worshiped in the Temple (Daniel 9:20-27).

The interesting thing to notice here is that, in Nebuchadnezzar's dream, there are ten toes on the feet, and in Daniel's dream, the final form of a world government had ten horns. So the number ten is very significant in the last form of world governments that is still future.

We are looking for another empire that will come out of ten nations and then become a world power.

Satanic Control of World Empires

Again, the devil took him to a very high mountain and showed him all the kingdoms of the world and their splendor. "All this I will give you," he said, "if you will bow down and worship me."

Jesus said to him, "Away from me, Satan! For it is written: 'Worship the Lord your God, and serve him only.'"
Then the devil left him, and angels came and attended him. - Matthew 4:8-11

What business does the devil have offering Jesus, God the Son, the Creator of the World, these kingdoms? Was that nonsense? Or was it a legitimate offer? Satan is called "The god of this age" (2 Corinthians 4:4), "The prince of this world" (John 12:31), and "The prince of the power of the air" (Ephesians 2:2). Because of the fall of man and the corruption that resulted from the fall, the devil does have control of the kingdoms of the world today. That is not to say that every single nation is corrupt. There was a time in our country that we were not influenced much by Satan. Godly people came here to begin a nation under God with religious freedom. In those days, before we had a federal government, there were states, like William Penn's "Holy Experiment" in Pennsylvania, that were almost theocracies. A theocracy is a government where God rules literally. But, for the most part, nations become ungodly. The people forget their blessings from God. Leaders become corrupt, and even a good nation like ours drifts, until they no longer seek and receive God's blessing. We have reached the point where many people say America is a "post-Christian" nation. It hurts to admit this. The good news is that we can return to our devotion to the Lord. We could have a revival. Many people feel there is a great renewal of faith brewing in our nation. However, America is not the Christian nation it once was.

In terms of world empires, there have only been, since Nebuchadnezzar, four world empires, and all of them have been dominated by evil. Your history teachers have probably told you this is true even if they were not Christians. These evil empires tolerated immorality and became corrupt. They were brutal. And they collapsed internally because of their sin and corruption. The devil had a right to offer these kingdoms to Jesus. But why would Jesus want those corrupted kingdoms? Jesus is going to come back as King of Kings and Lord of Lords, to set things up as they ought to be. He doesn't need the devil's help, and he doesn't need the devil's kingdoms. He would never have accepted that offer, but the devil thought that was his "best card." Unfortunately, Satan does have control over the corrupt kingdoms of the world today.

Revelation's Beasts

The Revelation picks up the theme of the final evil world empire in chapters 12 through 18. To summarize what is given in Revelation 12, the devil is symbolically pictured as a great red dragon with seven heads. The dragon tries to destroy Israel and Israel's Messiah as soon as he is born. The seven heads are explained in Revelation 17:9-11 as seven empires that have opposed God's will. In that description, it is said that five have come and gone, one still exists, and one is yet to come. The one that existed at that time was Rome. The five that had come and gone would undoubtedly be Egypt, Assyria, Babylon, Medo-Persia, and Greece. The future evil empire will be formed in the End Times, and we could well be witnessing the creation of this monstrosity in our generation.

One striking aspect of the seven-headed dragon is the fact that his final head has 10 horns.

> "The ten horns you saw are ten kings who have not yet received a kingdom, but who for one hour will receive authority as kings along with the beast. [13]They have one purpose and will give their power and authority to the beast." -Revelation 17:12

In various prophecies, horns are symbols of power. In Nebuchadnezzar's dream, the final evil world empire was symbolized by the feet of iron and clay. The feet would have 10 toes. Details of how this prophecy will be fulfilled can only be educated guesses at this point, but there will be 10 rulers who will give their power to him. One possibility comes from the history of the formation of the European Union, which now occupies much of the old Roman Empire. The first 10 nations to join the European Economic Union (EEU), which was the precursor of the modern European Union (EU), still held exclusive membership in the Western European Union (WEU) until recently. Jack Kinsella explains that these 10 nations represent "Old Europe." They have maintained Europe's military security,[16] but those functions were scheduled to be transferred to the EU in July, 2011.[17]

In Revelation chapter 13, the Beast, who is controlled by the devil, is also depicted as a seven-headed dragon, though this one is not red. This chapter reveals details about the Beast's economic dictatorship, the erection of a statue in the Temple, which becomes the prophesied "Abomination of Desolation," and the imposition of the "Mark of the Beast."

Rise of Satan's Final Religion

This horrific story is carried forward in chapters 17 and 18 of Revelation with a vision of the final evil empire, again seen as a seven-headed dragon, energized by the devil and led by the Beast. In this chapter a prostitute is riding the Beast. The title on her forehead reads in part, "Mystery Babylon the Great, The Mother of Prostitutes." The woman is symbolic of a false world religion. Because it is false, it is considered unfaithful to God and therefore a prostitute. It is identified with Babylon, the fountainhead of all false religion.

As mentioned above in Chapter 4, Alexander Hislop wrote a fascinating history of world religions called *The Two Babylons*. In this classic work Hislop demonstrated that Nimrod's false religion in Babylon spread through succeeding ages, manifesting itself as idolatrous worship in virtually all nations. In fact, Hislop demonstrated that most false religions are just corruptions and perversions of the true faith originally held by Adam and Noah.[18]

Returning to the vision of the woman riding the beast in Revelation 17, this is a symbol that a global religion will evidently endorse and further enable the beastly empire to dominate the world.

A New World Order

We have already studied the rise and fall of various world empires under Satan's control and the emerging final form of that political structure. We have also mentioned the course of false world religions from the time of Nimrod in Babel through the period of The Tribulation. Now we will examine the secret societies that have controlled wealth and power from behind the scenes, and the sinister religious connections with these secret societies. Some people refer to this power behind the scenes as the Invisible Government.

Note: The implication in this section that there is a conspiracy to produce a universal government is accepted by many prophecy scholars, but rejected by others. There is no doubt that there will be a One-World Government, but there are differing views on the processes that lead to it. Some have called this an "open conspiracy," meaning one that is not totally hidden, but is more of a one-world agenda by the rich and powerful. This elite group publishes their ideas, but the public is never made aware of their ultimate plans. (For balance here, see Appendix D - *Warnings and Cautions.*)

A number of secretive organizations are listed now. These groups have kept the vision of a world empire, or global government alive. The first two in our list are included, not because of their governmental concepts, but because of their spiritual influence on the later organizations

Kabbalism

This was an ancient system of Jewish theosophy and mysticism. It denies the inspiration of Scripture and blends metaphysical and occult practices, trying to mesh them with the Old Testament. This secretive organization attracts many of the rich and famous of our generation.

Gnosticism

This system of belief flourished during the time of the writing of the New Testament. It is a dualistic philosophy that there are two equally powerful forces in the universe- one good and one evil. It still exists today, and was recently depicted in the book and movie, "The Da Vinci Code."

Knights Templar

This fraternity, whose name means "Knights of the Temple," arose during the period of the Crusades. Some may have meant well at the beginning, but it was so corrupted that it became a great blight on Christian history and a serious stumbling block between Christians and Jews and between Christians and Muslims.

Here are some of the highlights of this movement:[19]
- 1119 - Established in Jerusalem by 9 French knights to protect pilgrims on their journey to visit the Holy Land.
- 1129 - Officially recognized by the [Roman Catholic] Church.
- 1187 - Defeated by Saladin at the Battle of the Horns of Hattin. This was a turning point in the Crusades.
- 1291 - Moved to Cyprus (when Acre fell to Muslims). By then they had become influential bankers of Europe. They especially influenced Spain, France, and England.
- 1308 - Philip IV of France arrested many of them, charging them with conspiracy, heresy and Satan worship. Historical records are not clear whether or not they were really guilty and how many of them were put to death.
- 1314 - The Grand Master, Jacques de Molay, was burned at the stake.

Rosicrucians

In the early 1300's, the surviving Knights Templar merged with the Order of the Rose-Croix (red cross) since they were not allowed to continue their own organization.

The beliefs and practices of this group were very secret through the 1600's. They may have been the pre-cursors of the Masonic Orders. The names of the last three Masonic degrees of the York Rite are: Knight of the Red Cross (means the same thing as Rose-Croix), Knight of Malta, and Knight Templar. The 18th Degree of Scottish Rite of the Masonic Order is called the Sovereign Prince of Rose-Croix.

In 1717 the world's first Grand Lodge of the Masonic Order was established in London. According to Gary Kah, it had Rosicrucians deep within its structure. These were the Princes of Freemasonry.[20]

The Illuminati

The Illuminati were an order within an order of Freemasons. This order was founded on May 1, 1776 by Adam Weishaupt, a college professor in Ingolstadt, Bavaria, a part of modern Germany.

Gary Kah cites John Robinson, 18th Century historian and prominent Mason, writing that the express aim of the order was to abolish Christianity and overturn government.[21]

Weishaupt said the name is derived from Lucifer, and means "Holders of the Light." Lucifer is one of the names of Satan in our Bible. He was created as an angel of light (Isaiah 14:12; Ezekiel 28:14; 2 Corinthians 11:14), then he rebelled against God and fell.

At the Masonic Congress of Wilhelmsbad, in July, 1782 the Illuminati reached the zenith of their power. This conference solidified Weishaupt and his order as undisputed head of the occult one-world movement. Weishaupt also forged an alliance with the growing Rothschild banker network.

The Illuminati were banned in Bavaria in 1786 as subversive. Their work was apparently exposed by an act of God when a messenger carrying secret information to members of the Illuminati was struck by lightning. His documents were exposed, and used as the basis of action by the government of Bavaria to ban the organization. Copies of this information were sent to heads of government all over Europe, but most people did not take it seriously. These people continued to exert influence through the network of illuminated Masonic Lodges already in place, especially through the Grand Orient Lodge of France.

Kah says that The Illuminati were condemned by George Washington in 1798.[22] Our first president was a Mason, but he was a godly man. He was a surveyor, and would naturally belong to Masonic trades. But there is no evidence that he personally was involved in any of the unfortunate secret aspects of the founding of our nation and its capital, such as the city of Washington D.C. being laid out in the form of a pentagram. He wrote,

"I have heard much of the nefarious and dangerous plan and doctrines of the Illuminati. It was not my intention to doubt that the doctrine of the Illuminati and the principles of Jacobinism had not spread in the United States."[23]

This discussion is about orders within orders in Freemasonry, and about the illuminated orders in particular. However, that does not necessarily mean that all Masons believe the same thing. There is so much about secret societies that we do not know. But we do know about the terrible corruption that permeated some aspects of Freemasonry from the time of the Illuminati. We might expect a person who is a high order Mason to say, "Honestly, we don't have any of this stuff in our literature." There may be some branches of Masonic Orders that are not corrupted, but there are some, and maybe all of them that do have these beliefs. Some of our own close relatives were Masons, and we don't think they had any idea about these things. They didn't go high enough in the organization to discover the deeper truth. Like most people, they were in it for the business networking and the idea of good works. Masons have a great image as humanitarians.

Another aspect of this study is in answer to the question, "Why would the rich and powerful people want to control the world?" You would think they would be happy to retire on the French Riviera with their millions, and just enjoy the good life. But history teaches us that as people become richer, they also become greedy for power. They want to control more and more. Finally, some of these rich and powerful people reached the obvious conclusion that they would like to control the world. Some of these people have conspired together to do just that. They have planned how they or their descendants can literally control the whole world.

Taylor Caldwell's *Captains and the Kings* was an artful novel about an immigrant who made good here in the United States against terrible odds. The underlying theme of the book was that the really powerful people in the United States were not the people in congress, but the ones who "bought" congressmen. They were the ones who held something over congressmen's heads so they could manipulate them. Truthfully, this is not so hard to believe today. There are some notable exceptions. But, since it costs huge amounts of money to successfully run for congress, it is obvious that the rich can have great influence on campaigns, and therefore, on the allegiance of the politicians they have helped. Today there are laws about campaign practices, but there are ways of getting around them. No one admits that they are "owned" by anyone, but if one of a congressman's big backers calls and asks him to vote a certain way, he will have to seriously consider doing it.

Today you could not prove that any organization is the Illuminati, but the principles they established are very much alive in the various organizations that we will consider.

The Scottish Rite of the Masonic Order
The Scottish Rite of the Masonic Order was established in 1801 in Charleston, South Carolina. It later moved to Washington D.C. A Masonic publication, *Facts of Scottish Rite*, states that all regular Supreme Councils have descended from it.

The Palladian Rite
The New and Reformed Palladian Rite was established in 1870 by Albert Pike, the leader of Scottish Rite Freemasonry in the United States and Giuseppe Mazzini, an Italian revolutionary leader and worldwide director of illuminized Freemasonry from 1834 to 1872. The purpose of the Palladian Rite was to be behind the scenes and control all the other Masonic groups. Most people don't know much about this group. According to Gary Kah, Mazzini wrote to Pike that this would be the supreme rite; that it would be somewhat unknown, but through it, the hand-picked high degree Masons who became a part of it would secretly govern all Freemasonry.[24]

On July 14, 1889, Pike instructed twenty-three Supreme Councils of the world to tell people that Masons worship a God, but one who is adored without superstition. Further, they were told to explain to Masons only of the 30th through 32nd degrees that the "Masonic religion" should be kept in the "purity of the Luciferic doctrine."[25]

Kah then goes on to say that the belief in Lucifer is not revealed until a higher level. He quotes from A.C. De La Rive's, *La Femme et L'Enfant dans la Franc-Maconnerie Universelle*, who recorded Pike's instructions on that date. Pike claimed that Lucifer was the good God of Light, and Adonay (The God of the Christians) is a cruel and barbaric God of darkness and evil. He believed in the dual god theory of Zoroaster, and the Gnostics and Templars after them. According to this view these two gods are always fighting.[26]

How could more terrible words ever be penned by a person who supposedly knows the message of the Bible?

Notice that they do not equate Satan with Lucifer. This is also true of the New Age religion. Those who follow Lucifer usually think that he is actually the good god, and the whole idea of Satan is just a myth and a heresy.

Kah also shows the connection between these beliefs and communism. Mazzini and Karl Marx were closely associated. He says that the early Russian revolutionaries called themselves Spartacusts, after Adam Weishaupt's Illuminati pseudonym. They were later called Bolsheviks. Still later they became known as Communists.[27]

Recent Developments toward a New World Order
Council for a Parliament of World Religions - 1893

The Parliament for the World's Religions came into existence in 1893 to promote inter-religious harmony.

At least four sessions of the parliament have been held: Chicago in 1993; Cape Town in 1999; Barcelona in 2004; and Melbourne in 2009.[28]

The parliament includes followers of Buddhism, Christianity, Judaism, Hinduism, Islam, new age groups and other recognized religions.

There were approximately 6500 representatives from 80 nationalities and more than 220 faith traditions in attendance at the latest meeting of this parliament in Melbourne. They spent a week of dialogue about how to increase understanding and cooperation between their various religious traditions. They also discussed such topics as climate change and the west's relationship with Islam.

The Federal Reserve System - 1913

The Federal Reserve System is not a government institution, but a privately held corporation owned by stockholders. The top eight stockholders have been Rothschild Banks of London and Berlin; Lazard Brothers Banks of Paris; Israel Moses Seif Banks of Italy; Warburg Bank of Hamburg and Amsterdam; Lehman Brothers Bank of New York; Kuhn, Loeb Bank of New York; Chase Manhattan Bank of New York; and Goldman, Sachs Bank of New York.

Jacob Schiff came to America from Germany with specific directives from Rothschild, the major banking mogul of England and Germany: to gain control of the U.S. money system. He bought into a banking house he could control: Kuhn & Loeb. He married Loeb's daughter, Theresa, eventually bought out Kuhn's interest, and moved to New York as sole owner. He posed as a philanthropist and man of holiness. He won over J.P. Morgan and others by offering help from Rothschild financing. These people were having a heyday with their businesses, but they were at a point where they needed a lot of capital to expand their businesses. Through loans to these people he gained great financial power. He also had to convince congressmen to enact the Federal Reserve Act. Some say that he used racial strife to plant liberals in congress and control media.

The Federal Reserve Act was originally voted down as unconstitutional (Art. 1, Sect. 8 - the power of issuing money and regulating value belongs to Congress). It was later reintroduced in another form, when many opponents of such a system had left for Christmas holidays, and was rammed through Congress on Dec. 23, 1913.

Now this private enterprise can control how much money will be printed and what the interest rates will be. Therefore, the powerful elite can know what to do about buying and selling, etc., while the rest of us are influenced negatively by their policies. They can drive prices up and down. They have an unfair control of what they can do with our fortunes.

The League of Nations - 1920

The League of Nations was established in 1920 in Geneva, Switzerland. It was an attempt to move toward a one-world government, but it failed because the Congress of the United States disagreed with its purpose and would not allow us to join it.

This global experiment came out of the same period of time as World War I. President Woodrow Wilson, and his Secretary of State, Colonel House, who was the champion of one-world thinking of his time worked for its establishment. It probably was a result of a euphoric feeling on the part of the people, who had long believed that the time was right for going public with their ideals. We saw the exact same thing during the Gulf War when President Bush started talking about "The new world order." You may not have heard a president say those words before (some say Kennedy and Nixon did, but if so, it wasn't obvious). President Bush used the expression over 200 times. The need was obvious to them for a world police force. It was very interesting that he suddenly stopped using the expression. Apparently the secret powers said, in essence, "Don't tell the people yet. They aren't quite ready."

The Council on Foreign Relations -1921

World War I lasted from 1914 to 1918. The United States' was involved during the last two years. Woodrow Wilson's Secretary of State, Colonel Edward Mandell House, had supported the Federal Reserve Act and planned the League of Nations. He favored allowing Americans to enter this war in the hope of establishing a new world order of peace and security.

Colonel House was also a prime mover in the formation of the Council on Foreign Relations in 1919.

Virtually all the literature about a conspiracy in the last thirty years has mentioned the Council on Foreign Relations as a key element. Most people know little about the organization because they are very private. Their agenda has been supra-national (above or beyond national interests) from the beginning.

Most Presidents and nearly all Secretaries of State in our generation have belonged to the CFR. Even the strong "Christian" presidents have generally filled their cabinets with CFR members. George Bush was a good example of this.

The CFR has several branches. They are the Institute for Pacific Relations - New York; the Royal Institute of International Affairs in London, the Centre d'Etudes de Politicque Etrangere - Paris; and the Institut fur Auswartige Politick - Hamburg.

The CFR is now so old that many other organizations have been formed to carry out their objectives. The network of influences controlled by these people, including the major news networks, is unbelievable.

The admitted goal of the CFR is to abolish the Constitution and replace our once independent Republic with a World Government.[29]

Some of their purposes are hair-raising. For instance, Study Number 7, CFR position paper 11/25/1959 - stated its purpose was to advocate the "building [of] a new international order [which] must be responsive to world aspirations for peace...including states labeling themselves as 'Socialist.'"[30] Today we have become complacent about this alarming goal, but we should be all the more upset because the U.S. is making great strides toward their socialist agenda.

Pyramid on the One Dollar Bill - 1935

The pyramid was placed on the back of our dollar bills during the term of President Franklin Delano Roosevelt. This is the Masonic pyramid. It was always on our Great Seal, but most people weren't aware of it. It was only after we lost our "real money," Silver Certificates, which were based on actual reserves of Gold and Silver, and were given Federal Reserve Notes instead, which were easily inflated, that the pyramid side of the Great Seal was put on the dollar bill. It has 13 courses. The all-seeing eye goes back to Egyptian idolatry of Osiris, and ultimately to Lucifer. It is not the eye of God. In the early orders, there is frequent mention of God, but not much about Jesus. It is only later that one learns who their god is. There are constant references to mythological characters and gods of other religions. President Roosevelt was himself a thirty-third degree Mason and a close associate of the CFR.

The words *Novus Ordo Seclorum*- "New Order of the Ages" in Latin—appear on the dollar bill. Basically this has the same meaning as "The New World Order." Many feel that the big banking houses of Europe saw the United States as a new world where they purposely sent their representatives so that it could be the kingpin of their future one-world government.

The United Nations -1945

The United Nations grew out of the world conditions leading to the start of World War II. By then the Council on Foreign Relations wielded great control of the State Department and of our foreign policy.

Hitler was financed by The Warburgs, The Rothschilds, and others. This demonstrates the practice of actually fomenting war by enabling it, financing both sides of various wars to keep the people in a state of unrest, waiting for a peacemaker and a one-world government.

Ten of the original 14 founding council members of the United Nations were also members of the Council on Foreign Relations.

Alger Hiss was the Secretary General of the U.N.'s founding conference. He was later exposed as a Soviet spy.

To keep the United States involved, the land was donated by John D. Rockefeller, Jr.

In 1995, delegates from more than 170 sovereign nations attended the U.N. 4th World Conference on Women, held in Beijing, China. This was the most anti-family conference in the history of the world. China was a terrible site for any conference on human rights, and especially on the rights of women, because of that country's dismal record of discrimination against women. Their family planning policies only allow one child per family, so nearly all baby girls are aborted. One of their topics was: Gender Feminism- a new way of looking at human sexuality. The way some of them see it, we end up with 5 sexes: male, female, homosexual, lesbian, and transsexual - all equally good. You decide what you are. They also promoted safe sex, condoms, and abortion. For the most part the churches were silent.

The United Nations is the parent organization of the World Bank Group consisting of these agencies: The International Monetary Fund (IMF), established in 1944, the International Finance Corporation, begun in 1956, and the International Development Association, founded in 1960.

The United Nations also has a World Court, otherwise known as the International Court of Justice created by the charter of the United Nations in 1945. At present the decisions of the World Court are not always honored, but as the military strength of the U.N. grows, the actions of its court will also become more binding.

Once we have surrendered our power to the United Nations, we will have no power to stand for our uniquely American ideals.

The Gulf War and Bosnia air strikes are examples of U.N. police work, using the U.S. as world cops.

The United Nations appears to be ineffective in keeping peace. It may be that they are purposely using wars and rumors of wars, economic instability, and environmental crises to finally bring the world to the place where we will say, "OK, if you have the plan and the power to bring order, we will accept it because things have been so bad." Purposely allowing things to get worse now would help them achieve their objectives at the proper time. At last, hope for all these political, economic and ecological issues would be offered when it is time for a one-world government.

The United Nations does not have the will or the power to enforce the resolutions that they pass. This became painfully obvious when Saddam Hussein ignored all their warnings against Iraq's apparent plan to develop nuclear weapons in 2003. At this time (2010) the same useless exercise is going on in opposition to Iran's nuclear ambitions. Iran laughs at the United Nations' frustration

Twenty years ago those who study prophecy did not put much emphasis on the United Nations because it seemed that everything they tried was a failure, and no one took their actions seriously. However, if the United Nations ever accomplishes what it wants to do, it could be the fulfillment of the prophecy of a final world empire. Time will tell what role the United Nations will play in the End Times drama.

In any case, the push toward a future global government has already begun in earnest. It appears that the growth of the next organization, the European Union has led the way.

European Union - 1948

Today we have what you might call a United States of Europe. The first step toward the formation of a European superstate was the Benelux Agreement on June 8, 1948. This was a treaty between three very small countries, Belgium, The Netherlands, and Luxembourg. Several years later, in 1957, in the city of Rome, and with a document called "The Treaty of Rome," those three countries joined with three other countries, Italy, France, and Germany to form the EEC (European Economic Community), which was called the Common Market. In 1973 the United Kingdom or England came in along with Ireland and Denmark, making a total of nine nations. In 1981 Greece became the tenth member of the union. As shown earlier in this chapter, the original 10 nations of the European Union could be the fulfillment of the prophetic 10 horns on the last head of the seven-headed beast of Revelation.

Later Spain, Portugal, Austria, Sweden, and Finland also joined. In 1993, with the adoption of The Treaty of Maastricht, the organization became known as the European Union (EU).

In 2010 there are 27 member nations in this European superstate.[31] Since 2008 there has been another alignment of countries around the Mediterranean Sea. It is called The Union for the Mediterranean. It includes EU member states and a number of North African and Middle East countries, making a total of 44 countries in the region.[32] Libya's Muammar Gaddafi declined to join, calling it "another Roman empire."[33]

The progress of the European Union is seen by many as an example of how global government can be constructed. 2010 was an important year for the EU because its member nations finally ratified its constitution, The Lisbon Treaty, and elected its first set of permanent officers.

The EU represents 500,000,000 people, a larger population and larger total economy than the U.S. A new study about the economic crisis showed that Europe is now the richest region in the world. North America's wealth plummeted by 21.8 percent, the steepest decline in the world. European assets only dropped 5.8 percent.[34]

Prophecy students notice with interest that the EU considers itself one of ten world regions, following the concept suggested by the Club of Rome (see below).

However, In spite of all its promise for a bright future, Europe has one overwhelming problem. The Muslim population is exploding all over Europe while its traditional residents are declining in numbers.[35] Europe is weak culturally, having lost its Christian conscience. And, as Christopher Caldwell warns in his book, *Reflections on the revolution in Europe: Immigration, Islam and the West*, "European culture is about to be extinguished by Islamic culture."[36] This could very well be the "clay" that is mixed with the Roman "iron" in the feet of Nebuchadnezzar's vision.

The Bilderberg Group - 1954

The Bilderberg Group was established in 1954 in The Netherlands. This is a similar organization to the Council on Foreign Relations. Its annual meeting of about 100 power-elite members is by invitation only. It does now publish its agenda but the meetings and their plans are top-secret.

The fact that there is such a meeting of top politicians, military leaders, business moguls, bankers, and selected representatives of the media is a sure sign that global planning for our future is underway.

The World Constitution and Parliament Association -1959

The World Constitution and Parliament Association was organized in 1959 in Lakewood, Colorado. Several sessions have been held since 1982. At the third, a Provisional World Presidium and World Cabinet were appointed to serve as the equivalent of an executive branch for the emerging world government. This organization's top figures are closely allied and interlocked with leaders from many other "one-world"/interfaith groups such as the World Federalist Association, World Union, Greenpeace, and the World Council of Churches.

New Age Spirituality - 1960's

While the structure for a one-world government has been growing, there has been a parallel spiritual development that could be the vehicle for a one-world religion. It is the New Age Movement, sometimes simply called "New Age" or "New Age Spirituality."

New Age is an individual approach to the blending of various beliefs and practices from the occult, astrology, paganism, pantheism, holistic health, metaphysics, Eastern meditation and bits and pieces of all major religions.

It seemed to be a new thing in the 1960's when the concept was co-opted by the counterculture. It actually had roots in the thinking of a number of popular writers in the 1800's and early 1900's, including Helena Blavatsky, H. G. Wells, George Bernard Shaw, William Butler Yeats and Edgar Cayce. Gary Kah notes that Alice Bailey, a writer from the Theosophical Society, "was probably the most instrumental in developing the infrastructure and presenting the strategies of today's New Age movement."[37] She founded Lucis Trust and Lucifer Publishing Company in 1922.[38]

New Age thought reached the masses in the 1960's and 1970's. It was popularized by the song, "Aquarius" in the theatrical production, "Hair: The American Tribal Love-Rock Musical." The song proclaimed, *This is the dawning of the Age of Aquarius.* The mysterious message was evidently meant to convey the belief by astrologists that the existing Age of Pisces, which lasted approximately 2,150 years, was beginning to give way to the new Age of Aquarius.

Most proponents of this theory think the Age of Pisces represents the Christian era. The last two thousand years have obviously been an era of Christian expansion. In addition, Christianity is symbolized by the fish (Pisces). Persecuted Christians of the First Century used the symbol to convey their belief to fellow-Christians. The Greek word *ichthus* became a code for "*iesus christus theou uios, soter*" meaning "Jesus Christ, Son of God, Savior".

Barbara Curtis, who spent seven years as a former New Age seeker before learning the truth about Jesus Christ, described New Age this way:

> What exactly is the New Age? Impossible to narrow down, the New Age is actually a vast smorgasbord of beliefs and practices. Each New Ager fills his tray with whatever assortment fits his appetite. All is liberally seasoned with self-centeredness. It's really a Have-It-Your-Way religion – thus its modern appeal.[39]

Recently the name "New Age" has somewhat gone underground (like the political expression, "New World Order"), but the popularity of the concept has grown exponentially. One reason for this is the endorsement by Oprah Winfrey of "A Course in Miracles," which was originally channeled to the writer of the course from a spirit guide who called himself "Jesus," but denied that the cross was significant and claimed that there is no sin.[40] CNN and Time have called Oprah "arguably the most influential woman in the world,"[41] and many consider her America's spiritual leader.

The 2009 movie "Avatar" broke all previous box-office records. It was rated PG-13, but intentionally targeted the younger children through McDonald's happy meal program. It was a fascinating production with an interesting story line. However, the underlying message of the movie was about pantheism (all living things are part of God) and New Age religion. It will undoubtedly have a profound influence on the cultural drift toward mixing and unifying religions.

Many New Age teachers see a connection between their beliefs and the supposed end of the Mayan calendar in 2012. They consider that a prime time for the beginning of the "Age of Aquarius" and the coming of their messiah. See the discussion of Mayan Prophecies and 2012 in Chapter 1 - *What in the World Is Happening?*

The Club of Rome - 1968

The Club of Rome, formed in 1968 in the city of Rome seems to be another level of informal hierarchy for the planning of a one-world government. Their 1973 report entitled *Regionalized and Adaptive Model of the Global World System*, divides the world into ten political/economic regions.[42]

According to its website, the Club of Rome is driven by the participation and efforts of its membership. Its members come from the scientific, political, business, financial, academic, religious, cultural and civil society communities.[43]

One of the stated objectives of this think-tank is to lower the population of the earth by some two billion people.

Environmental Issues - 1970's

In December of 1970 The Environmental Protection Agency began operating. In 1992 alone EPA regulations cost taxpayers over $130 billion (over $1000 per family per year).

An international Earth Summit was held in Rio de Janeiro in June of 1992. This event, sponsored by the United Nations Conference on Environment and Development, was the largest event of its kind in history. One hundred sixty heads of state, including George Bush, attended this event, which some are calling the launching pad for a quantum leap into the New World Order and the New Age."

The continuing emphasis on environmental problems such as global warming, acid rain and depletion of the ozone layer is part of the long-range strategy to prepare the people of the globe to accept a universal government.

In spite of the release of controversial e-mails from some climate scientists that global warming calculations are not accurate, thousands of enthusiastic delegates from all over the globe met in Copenhagen in 2009 at the United Nations Climate Change Summit to further their plans to limit carbon emissions and provide up to $150 billion in aid to developing countries to gain their cooperation. This gathering made another strong argument for the development of a One-World Government.

The Trilateral Commission - 1973

The Trilateral Commission was founded in 1973 in New York. It deals with issues concerning North America, Western Europe, and Japan. This group was formed by David Rockefeller. Zbigniew Brzezinski was its first director, and they hand-picked the elite members of this power team who would evidently influence the choice of leaders and the adoption of policies that would lead to an eventual global government and economy.

Dissolution of the USSR -1991

The dissolution of the Soviet Union in 1991 seemed very strange. It looked "orchestrated" by one-world leaders when Mikhail Gorbachev suddenly allowed major shifts in soviet policy leading to a bloodless revolution.

Russia is still a major nuclear threat to the world, and recent events in the former Soviet Union indicate a possible return to Communism.

Russia is still the military champion and source for most of the Islamic world. Their ties with Iran's nuclear program have escalated concerns that a great war against Israel, like the one prophesied in Ezekiel 38 and 39 might be imminent.

The Gulf War -1991

In 1991 Saddam Hussein's Iraq invaded Kuwait, but was turned back by the US with some help from the United Nations. After the war, President George Bush Sr., in a nation-wide address said, "This is an historic moment. We have in the past year made great progress in ending the long era of the cold war. We have before us the opportunity to forge for ourselves and for future generations a New World Order, a world where the rule of law, not the law of the jungle, governs the conduct of the nations. When we are successful, and we will be, we have a real chance at the New World Order, an order in which a credible United Nations can use its peacekeeping role to fulfill the promise and vision of the UN founders."

We saw this speech on live television. It was unbelievable because this was the first time we had heard a high official speak of the future in those terms. Now it seems common enough, but it had really been kept under wraps until that time. It simply wasn't something we ordinarily heard. This is their agenda: to have a global economy, a global politic, global education, and a global religion. They do not know that the future dictator will take over all of that, but this is exactly what the Bible has prophesied. The Beast will take over this system once it is in place. It is a sad scenario, but it is great to be on the winning side. As the darkness gets darker, the light gets brighter. We see that in the polarizing of churches. For example, some are in favor of accepting homosexuals, others are opposed to it. Never before in our generation have we seen so many signs of a coming revival. If revival comes to the United States, it will push back this timetable. And that would be great! Most of us would be glad if Jesus came today, but we would also be glad if we could win a few million more to Christ!

United Religions Initiative - 2000

United Religions is an organization begun in 1997 with the express goal of forming a world body of religions patterned after the model of the United Nations.

The URI Charter was signed by more than two-hundred people present, and hundreds more joining over the Internet, at a ceremony in Pittsburgh, Pennsylvania, USA on June 26, 2000.[44]

The heart of this organization is the existence of "Cooperation Circles" that range in size from a minimum of seven members to tens of thousands, representing at least three faiths or traditions, including the non-religious, and subscribe to the shared vision outlined in URI's Charter. Each Cooperation Circle seeks to address one or more pressing issues facing their collective communities, including poverty, religiously motivated violence, environmental degradation and more. In 2010 they claimed to have 487 Cooperation Circles in 76 Countries.[45]

9/11 Attacks and the War on Terrorism - 2001

The world was changed instantly when Islamic terrorists attacked the World Trade Center and the Pentagon on September 11, 2001. The threat of terrorism became a worldwide issue. During the following decade the world gradually came to realize that this blight will not go away until there is peace among the factions in the Middle East. With the rebirth of radical Islamic belief and practice during the Islamic Revolution in Iran in 1979, the old conquest mentality of Islam, which had been dormant for some time, was revived. See "Chapter 7 - Historical Developments" for more information on this topic. Supposedly only about 10% of Muslims subscribe to this viewpoint, but the majority is either unable or unwilling to put a stop to it.

Because of the threat of terrorism people have become more willing to allow governmental surveillance and access to personal information, which can eventually result in technological control of the type needed to institute a global economic dictatorship and the "Mark of the Beast."

The Great Recession - 2008

In 2008 the bottom fell out of real estate, banks and financial institutions became unstable, and the stock market plummeted. Our confused government tried to fix the problem by massive spending. The economies of other nations fell too, leaving the world in serious economic trouble. This resulted in what is generally agreed to be the worst recession since the Great Depression of the '30's. In a matter of weeks, untold millions of people all over the world lost a large percentage of their savings and investments. The economy has begun to recover from the financial storm, but there are still many problems, and some things about the world have changed forever. The United States is in a much weaker condition financially, and our current government evidently plans to lead us into a socialistic way of life.

When Nikita Khrushchev was the leader of the Soviet Union in the 50's and '60's, he predicted that various countries would fall into the lap of socialism like "ripe apples." It was implied that even the United States would someday succumb to this inevitable destiny. At the time it seemed absurd to nearly every American. But one of Newsweek's cover articles in 2009 exclaimed, "We Are All Socialists Now."

It seemed that no one expected the great economic collapse. Where did that money go? At the beginning of the unexpected crisis, major unknown investors harvested huge profits from the stock market. Was it a coincidence that so many of the super-rich decided to cash out at the same time? Now they have the funds that we lost! And when the time is right, they will buy back the properties and the stocks that have plummeted in value. The very rich will be richer still, and the majority of middle class people will be reduced to lower income status. Socialism is not a true "share the wealth" program. It has an extremely wealthy "elite" at the top that controls the government and the economy.

Whether or not America will resist this "fall" remains to be seen. But political analysts have warned that democracies are in danger once the majority of the people realize that they can use their vote to provide government benefits to themselves.

Europe has, for the most part, already adopted a form of socialism. Russia and China are socialist, and the global economic crisis is the perfect opportunity for greater government intervention to institute socialism everywhere. Now it doesn't take much imagination to understand how this collapse could lead us into a one-world government state of mind.

The venerable Henry Kissinger said that the global economic crisis has weakened the United States' position of leadership, but it also provides an opportunity for building new international relationships. He also warned that the alternative to a new international order is chaos.[46]

Britain's former Prime Minister, Gordon Brown, warned the nation not to retreat from globalism in the face of the crisis. He said, "We could view the threats and challenges we face today as the difficult birth-pangs of a new global order — and our task now as nothing less than making the transition through a new internationalism to the benefits of an expanding global society."[47]

Speaking in Prague, Barack Obama said, "All nations must come together to build a stronger, global regime."[48]

Iran's President Mahmoud Ahmadinejad told an international gathering in Moscow that a new world order is needed to deal with the many challenges arising in the international political arena. He said, "Western-style capitalism is falling apart, marking the end of the age of Imperialism."[49]

A report published by The United Nations Conference on Trade and Development said that the U.S. dollar should be replaced as the world's standard reserve currency.

This world currency would be managed by an as-yet undetermined financial regulatory organization.[50]

The total debt in America (Federal, municipal, corporate, real estate & consumer debt) in 1980 was about $2 1/2 Trillion. Presently it is over $13 Trillion! We have a collapsing economy that is not capable of repaying that debt! This indebtedness exceeds the total real estate and corporate equities of the entire country! We're insolvent. We owe Chinese and European bankers. Worst of all, some financial experts warn that this situation will hasten our slide into socialism.

Other countries are in the same mess! What can we do now? Some are saying we will have hyper inflation- printing more and more money to pay old debts. This is what ruined the economy of Germany before World War II. The effect of this is that people's hard-earned savings will become practically useless. In Germany people had to take a wheel-barrow full of money to the store just to buy a few groceries.

Everything considered, it is fair to say that the world in which we live has been fully prepared for an economic messiah who could take financial control of a desperate situation. Furthermore, the philosophies and organizations are in place for both a one-world government and a one-world religious system.

But before this false Christ is revealed, the Church must be taken away by the rapture. We will now turn our attention to that great event.

Chapter 6
The Rapture of the Church:

The Next Major Biblical Event in History

[13]Brothers, we do not want you to be ignorant about those who fall asleep, or to grieve like the rest of men, who have no hope. [14]We believe that Jesus died and rose again and so we believe that God will bring with Jesus those who have fallen asleep in him. [15]According to the Lord's own word, we tell you that we who are still alive, who are left till the coming of the Lord, will certainly not precede those who have fallen asleep. [16]For the Lord himself will come down from heaven, with a loud command, with the voice of the archangel and with the trumpet call of God, and the dead in Christ will rise first. [17]After that, we who are still alive and are left will be caught up together with them in the clouds to meet the Lord in the air. And so we will be with the Lord forever. [18]Therefore encourage each other with these words. - 1Thessalonians 4:13-18

Meaning of "Rapture"

"Rapture" comes from the words "caught up" in I Thessalonians 4:17. In the Greek the word is *harpazo* - "to seize upon by force", "to snatch up." The Latin translators used the word *rapturo*. Some people claim that "rapture" is not a biblical term. This is untrue, unless they want to say that "God" and "Jesus" are not biblical terms. Almost all words in our English Bible are translations of Greek or Hebrew expressions, and are, therefore, not in the Bible in the form we know them. "God" is a proper and meaningful translation of certain words in the original languages, and "Jesus" is a good translation of his name (*Jesus*, "Joshua," "The Lord Saves," in Hebrew). In the same way, the English word "rapture," which means "to be caught up" is an excellent translation for the Greek *harpazo*.

Three Events That Happen at the Rapture

The scriptures of First Thessalonians 4 and 5 are familiar to most Christians as a description of the "rapture of the Church." The rapture can be thought of as a point in eternity that will protrude into our historical time frame at some fixed point on God's calendar. However, as we have seen, God has not given us the date.

Three specific events take place at the time Jesus calls his Church out of the world:
For the Lord himself will come down from heaven.
(a) With a loud command
(b) With the voice of the archangel
(c) And with the trumpet call of God
The "loud command" from the lips of Jesus is to awake the dead in Christ and to call them forth from their graves as God called his friend Lazarus forth (John 11:43).

Only one archangel is called by name in Scripture. He is Michael whose specific jurisdiction is over the people of Israel. At the time of the rapture, the archangel will signal to Israel that God has returned the focus of his attention at last to the final redemption of his chosen nation. This event was spoken of by Daniel:

> "At that time Michael, the great prince who protects your people, will arise. There will be a time of distress such as has not happened from the beginning of nations until then. But at that time your people—everyone whose name is found written in the book—will be delivered." - Daniel 12:1

This trumpet call is not to be confused with the last of the seven trumpets in Revelation. It is a trumpet call associated with Rosh Hashanah, the Jewish New Year.[51] It will be used to call the living saints at the time of the rapture to be caught up and transformed together with the just-raised saints of the past. This is described also in 1 Corinthians 15,

> I declare to you, brothers, that flesh and blood cannot inherit the kingdom of God, nor does the perishable inherit the imperishable. [51]Listen, I tell you a mystery: We will not all sleep, but we will all be changed— [52]in a flash, in the twinkling of an eye, at the last trumpet. For the trumpet will sound, the dead will be raised imperishable, and we will be changed. - 1 Corinthians 15:50-52

When an individual dies he or she leaves time and enters eternity. Some scholars think that all believers travel through eternity immediately, "in a moment, in the twinkling of an eye," to arrive at the rapture the next instant in his or her personal experience. If that is the case, all believers arrive in heaven at the same "time." Thus, "to be absent from the body is to be at home with the Lord" (2 Corinthians 5:8). We may have difficulty picturing this if we do not realize that eternity runs according to an entirely different time than the one-dimensional time frame in which we are constrained to live while in our mortal bodies. (For more on the issue of time, see Appendix F - *The Complexities of Time.*)

Other Important Terms

As you probably know, there are many different ways of looking at biblical prophecy. Here are a few other terms you will hear in discussions about the future.

Millennium - 1000 years of history during which Christ will reign as King of Kings (Rev. 20:2-7).

Premillennialism - The belief that Christ returns visibly and bodily at the beginning of the thousand-year reign of Christ on the earth. He will rule the nations from Jerusalem.

Postmillennialism - The belief that Christ will return at the end of the present age to take over the earth. Meantime, he is assumed to reign on earth through the Church now. Postmillennialists do not necessarily believe in a literal millennial age. Satan was defeated at the cross and is now bound; hence the final triumph of the Church in history is assured.

Amillennialism - The belief that there will be no literal 1000 year reign of Christ. Thus Revelation 20 is taken symbolically, not literally, by adherents of this view. Amillennialists generally believe that Israel has been permanently set aside for all time and that God's current plan of salvation involves only the Church.
(See also: Appendix B - *Definition of Common Terms Found in Eschatology.*)

The authors' understanding of future things is firmly premillennial. A literal interpretation of Scripture requires belief in an actual thousand year period of time during which Christ will reign as King of Kings and Lord of Lords. The book of Revelation describes these periods of time clearly: The Church Age (chapters 1-3), The Tribulation (chapters 4-19), The Millennium (chapter 20), and then the new heaven and new earth (chapters 21-22).

Most of the Bible teachers who write and speak about prophecy are also premillennial. Among them there are various viewpoints about the timing of the rapture. Here is a brief summary of these positions:

Pre-Tribulation Rapture - That Christ will rapture the Church before the Tribulation begins

Mid-Tribulation Rapture - That Christ will rapture the Church at the Mid-point of The Tribulation

Post Tribulation Rapture - That Christ will rapture the Church at the end of the Tribulation

Pre-Wrath Rapture - That Christ will rapture the Church just before the Battle of Armageddon

Partial Rapture - That Christ will rapture those who are ready and leave the rest to go through the Tribulation

Multiple Rapture - That there are more than one rapture, during which Christ receives those who are ready

"Pan-Trib" Position - No clue about future events, but think it will "all pan out in the end."

The last term is not really funny. There are too many people who just claim ignorance of this vital subject. When one pastor was asked recently what his views of prophecy were, he said, "I just don't handle it." Can you imagine? A pastor, who has the responsibility of teaching the whole counsel of God's Word, refusing to "handle" nearly one third of Scripture?

Those who are "in Christ"

Returning to the rapture passage in 1 Thessalonians 4, the last part of verse 16 and first part of verse 17 say,"... the dead in Christ will rise first. [17]After that, we who are still alive and are left will be caught up together with them in the clouds to meet the Lord in the air."

This event is only for those "in Christ." It does not, therefore, include Old Testament Saints. We will study the time of their resurrection later. The point here is that all believers of the Church Age, and only believers of this age are included; those who have died "in Christ," and those believers who are alive at the time. It should be added that the rapture does include all Jewish people during this present time who have placed their faith in Jesus as Messiah. They too are part of the Church, though they have not lost their identity as descendants of Israel.

Why the Rapture Will Take Place before the Tribulation

We believe that, by far, the strongest biblical evidence is in favor of the pre-tribulation rapture position. There are many reasons for this. Here are some of the most obvious ones.

Any-moment Expectation (Imminence)

In every age Christians have been expecting the return of Our Lord. Twice in the last chapter of the Revelation he tells us, "I am coming quickly" (Revelation 22:7, 12, 20).

Paul referred to this ever-present possibility of Christ's return as "the blessed hope" (Titus 2:13).

He also taught that his coming will be like a thief in the night (1 Thessalonians 5:1-6, which is a continuation of the primary rapture passage in 1 Thessalonians 4:13-18).

John also spoke of Christ's appearing:

Dear friends, now we are children of God, and what we will be has not yet been made known. But we know that when he appears, we shall be like him, for we shall see him as he is. Everyone who has this hope in him purifies himself, just as he is pure. -1 John 3:2

The pre-Tribulation position is the best from this point of view. If the rapture takes place before the Tribulation, we can truly expect it "any day." If it is delayed to the middle or end of the Tribulation, we could not honestly have that expectation now.

Deliverance of the Saints from Wrath

Here are some of the passages that indicate that believers of this Church Age will not be left to suffer the outpouring of God's wrath:

"Be always on the watch, and pray that you may be able to escape all that is about to happen, and that you may be able to stand before the Son of Man." - Luke 21:36

And to wait for his Son from heaven, whom he raised from the dead—Jesus, who rescues us from the coming wrath. - 1 Thessalonians 1:10

For God did not appoint us to suffer wrath but to receive salvation through our Lord Jesus Christ. - 1Thessalonians 5:9

If he condemned the cities of Sodom and Gomorrah by burning them to ashes, and made them an example of what is going to happen to the ungodly; [7]and if he rescued Lot, a righteous man, who was distressed by the filthy lives of lawless men [8](for that righteous man, living among them day after day, was tormented in his righteous soul by the lawless deeds he saw and heard)— [9]if this is so, then the Lord knows how to rescue godly men from trials and to hold the unrighteous for the day of judgment, while continuing their punishment. - 2 Peter 2:6-9

In the message to the Church of Philadelphia (Missions Period), God said:

"Since you have kept my command to endure patiently, I will also keep you from the hour of trial that is going to come upon the whole world to test those who live on the earth." - Revelation 3:10

Keep in mind that the Bible does not teach that Christians are delivered from persecution, trials and temptations. In fact, the opposite is true. In 2 Timothy 3:12 we are told, "In fact, everyone who wants to live a godly life in Christ Jesus will be persecuted." The books of James and 1 Peter were written to encourage Christians when they are called upon to go through trials. Paul himself spoke about his "thorn in the flesh" as a trial allowed by God in order that God's strength could be shown through him (2 Corinthians 12:7-10).

Belief in the pre-tribulation rapture has nothing to do with a cowardly desire to escape persecution. Scriptural examples and history itself teach us that, when called upon to suffer for the name of Christ, it is actually a privilege to die for him. In fact, we are being reminded today that more Christians have been persecuted and even put to death in our own generation than in all other periods of Church history combined. For two thousand years God has allowed his people to suffer trials and persecution and even martyrdom. Why, however, should he ask only the final generation of the Church to endure an unprecedented time of terrible destruction that is not intended for the Church, but as a judgment of unbelieving world?

The belief that the Church will be delivered from the Tribulation is based in part on the biblical pattern that when God pours out his wrath he always gives opportunity for the righteous to escape it. This was true of Noah and his family, of Sodom and Gomorrah in the days of Lot, and even of the pagan Ninevites to whom Jonah was sent.

The Church is the Bride of Christ. God intends that she join her Bridegroom for a great wedding feast and after that share with him in ruling the nations. Allowing his bride to suffer through The Tribulation is inconsistent with the specific purposes for which he has called out the Church from the world; why he has rescued her "from the coming wrath" (1 Thessalonians 1:10).

Some recent teaching about the Tribulation tries to make a distinction between Satan's wrath, which they say characterizes most of the book of Revelation, and God's wrath, which is poured out at the Battle of Armageddon. From their point of view, the Church could then be subjected to most of the Tribulation, but delivered from the last part. The problem with this position is that it ascribes to Satan the powers of nature: weather conditions, earthquakes, asteroid collisions, and other "terrors in the heavens." Satan, however, has no power to do anything that has not been appointed for him by God. This theory also fails to notice that the Church is missing from the Tribulation, as explained toward the end of this chapter. (Also See *Appendix K - Pretribulation or Prewrath?*)

The Lawless One Not Revealed until Hindering Force Removed

In 2 Thessalonians we are told that the "man of sin (or lawlessness)" will not be revealed until "he who now restrains" is taken out of the way.

> Concerning the coming of our Lord Jesus Christ and our being gathered to him, we ask you, brothers, [2]not to become easily unsettled or alarmed by some prophecy, report or letter supposed to have come from us, saying that the day of the Lord has already come. [3]Don't let anyone deceive you in any way, for (that day will not come) until the rebellion occurs and the man of lawlessness is revealed, the man doomed to destruction. [4]He will oppose and will exalt himself over everything that is called God or is worshiped, so that he sets himself up in God's temple, proclaiming himself to be God.
> [5]Don't you remember that when I was with you I used to tell you these things? [6]And now you know what is holding him back, so that he may be revealed at the proper time. [7]For the secret power of lawlessness is already at work; but the one who now holds it back will continue to do so till he is taken out of the way. [8]And then the lawless one will be revealed, whom the Lord Jesus will overthrow with the breath of his mouth and destroy by the splendor of his coming. - 2 Thessalonians 2:1-8

In John 16:7-8 we are told that it is The Holy Spirit who will "convict the world concerning sin..." God the Holy Spirit can never be removed from the earth, but, in the sense that he is effectively restraining sin through Christians in whom he dwells, the time will come, once those Christians are gone, that wickedness will abound. Today Christians are everywhere: in their occupations, in the market place, in the schools, even in government halls. But during the Tribulation, true believers will be persecuted and either killed or driven underground, so that their godly influence will not be felt in the world. When the Church is taken in the rapture, the world will be ripe for the evil one to step forth with his ungodly plans. True, multitudes of people will turn to Christ and will become true believers in the Tribulation Period. They will also be indwelt by the Holy Spirit, but they will not be permitted to take the place of the missing Christians in society. They will be outcasts, and therefore the Holy Spirit will not have the same restraining influence on the world that he now has. Most, or even all of them, will be quickly put to death by the man of sin.

The Death of the Believer: Time and Eternity

The Apostle Paul adds further to our understanding of what happens when an individual Christian dies:

> Now we know that if the earthly tent we live in is destroyed, we have a building from God, an eternal house in heaven, not built by human hands. [2]Meanwhile we groan, longing to be clothed with our heavenly dwelling, [3]because when we are clothed, we will not be found naked...

⁶Therefore we are always confident and know that as long as we are at home in the body we are away from the Lord. ⁷We live by faith, not by sight. ⁸We are confident, I say, and would prefer to be away from the body and at home with the Lord. - 2 Corinthians 5:1-3, 6-8

There is no hint here of an intermediate state between dying and going into the presence of the Lord. Indeed the Apostle tells us that our resurrection bodies are already prepared for us; they are waiting for us to "put on" exactly as one would put on a new set of clothes over the old!

Events between the Rapture and Christ's Return
There are certain future events that evidently will take place between the rapture and Christ's glorious return as King of Kings and Lord of Lords. Two of them are The Bema Seat Judgment, and The Marriage of the Lamb.

- The Bema Seat Judgment
According to 2 Corinthians 5:10, all believers of this age must appear before the judgment seat of Christ. Information about this event is also found in Romans 14:10; in 1 Corinthians 3:10-15; and in 1 Corinthians 4:2-5. This evaluation of every believer is not for the purpose of dealing with sin, which was fully dealt with on the cross by the Lord Jesus. Rather it is a reviewing stand where the quality of our Christian performance can be evaluated and rewarded. The motives of the heart will be made known, and most importantly, only the works the believer has undertaken by faith "in the Spirit" — by faith in the indwelling presence of God, will survive. The "works of the flesh" (our self-efforts to serve God) will be taken away and only what God has built into our lives since we came to know him will go with us into the next life. (See -N: *The Judgment Seat of Christ,* for further details.)

- The Marriage Supper of the Lamb - Revelation 19:7-9
During his lifetime on earth, Jesus did not marry. For a man not to marry was very rare in Israel (then as now). Following the typology in the story of Abraham's servant going to a far country to select a bride (Rebekah) for the patriarchs beloved son Isaac (Genesis 24), we could say that God the Father dispatched the Holy Spirit into the world to call out and prepare a people who would be a suitable bride. The Spirit would also give the Church a suitable wedding dowry that she might be a fitting love-gift from the Father to his beloved Son, Jesus. All sorts of people are welcome to be part of Christ's bride. The invitation is open to everyone (Luke 14:16-24).

The Church can be thought of as the "Second Eve." But whereas the original Eve was one woman, the Bride of Christ consists of millions of men, women, and children! When we are all brought together as a family following the rapture we shall join with our Lord in a great marriage feast.

Christ's Bride is in Heaven before he returns in glory to the earth!

⁷Let us rejoice and be glad
    and give him glory!
  For the wedding of the Lamb has come,
    and his bride has made herself ready.
⁸Fine linen, bright and clean,
    was given her to wear." (Fine linen stands for the righteous acts of the saints.)
⁹Then the angel said to me, "Write: 'Blessed are those who are invited to the wedding supper of the Lamb!' And he added, "These are the true words of God." - Revelation 19:7-9

Our Return with Christ
To understand the events that take place after the rapture, we need to bear in mind that there is a sequence of events taking place that occurs "in heaven" and there is a parallel sequence of events occurring "on earth." In the book of Revelation note is made of those who "dwell in heaven" and those who dwell on earth" during The Tribulation Period. The former group "dwelling in heaven" is the Church. We who comprise the Church will have been given our resurrection bodies and will walk in the company of the Lamb and his holy angels. Others who will be living during this same time period will be:

- Non-believers,
- God's 144,000 Jewish evangelists and,
- Their converts, who are the saints of the Tribulation period.

Many of these saints will become martyrs during the Tribulation period, but they will not be given their resurrection bodies until the Tribulation ends (Revelation 20:4).

Appendix L: *The Return of Jesus Christ in Power Glory and Splendor*, helps to understand that the return of Christ has two aspects.

His silent return for his Church at the rapture is described by the use of the Greek word *parousia*, which means "coming alongside and remaining with" someone. We should think of the rapture as the first phase of the second coming of Christ. He will come for his Church, and he will remain with them forever after. But he will also come to be with the 144,000 and with the Tribulation Saints as well during the final seven years of world evangelism, judgment and restoration.

After the seven years of the Tribulation has run its course Jesus will step out of hiding, and appears in the sky, bringing us with him. This event, described by the Greek word *epiphaneia*, which means "shining forth," is the open public unveiling of Jesus—the second coming in power and glory.

All this careful reading of scripture tells us that heaven is not far away. It is in fact merely another dimension of reality. Earthly, material realities occupy only a small localized region of the realm the Bible calls the heavenly places. The material world is *embedded* in the spiritual. Therefore Jesus is never far away from any of us. The old notion that when Jesus takes us to heaven we are somehow far removed to a golden land beyond the farthest star is not a biblical view of heaven at all! We need to adjust our thinking to the likelihood that Jesus will be on the earth during the entire Tribulation Period, invisible, but probably appearing and disappearing in the same mysterious manner he did during the 40 days following his resurrection and his ascension. On earth, but unseen by unbelievers, Jesus will be the Commander and Chief of the armies of the Lord. He will also direct the 144,000 and their strategic work. Jesus will apparently involve himself personally in the shepherding of his faithful remnant hidden at Petra during the last half of the Tribulation period. When Jesus returns, he will come not from "outer space," but simply step back into our space-time frame once again, bringing his Church with him.

The Bible assures us that authority has been given to Jesus (Matthew 28:18). However, he does not yet *reign* on the earth. For two thousand years the saints of God have prayed that he might soon come and reign on earth as he already does reign in heaven. In Revelation Chapter 4, a great scroll, which we may think of as the title deed to the earth, is handed to Jesus by his Father. Jesus is called to begin his long awaited reign on earth.

He will accomplish this in stages, by first coming for his Church, and then by strategically directing and orchestrating all of the events of the end time. Evidently he will establish a beachhead on the planet, a command center for those military operations that will culminate in his final appearance in public as earth's legal King of Kings and Lord of Lords. His activities during the Tribulation will not be detected by unbelievers, though there will be rumors he has returned. Many events occurring on earth, due to the clandestine operations of the 144,000, will cause earth's inhabitants to be nervous (Matthew 24:21-30).

If we consider all the parallel events the book of Revelation describes, including the throwing-down of Satan and his hosts to earth during this last three and a half years, then it makes sense that our Commander-and-Chief should establish his battle headquarters for the end time right here on earth. This is where the final conflict will be fought, including the Seed of the Woman winning a final victory over the Seed of the Serpent.

But the Church is the Body of Christ and the Head can not be separated from the Body! So we might begin to think of ourselves as present on earth with Jesus during the Tribulation period. Our resurrection bodies would make us invulnerable to sin and death. Furthermore, like our Lord, we would be invisible to the inhabitants of the earth.

When Christ returns, it is with "armies in heaven, clothed in fine linen, white and clean." [11]I saw heaven standing open and there before me was a white horse, whose rider is called Faithful and True. With justice he judges and makes war. [12]His eyes are like blazing fire, and on his head are many crowns. He has a name written on him that no one knows but he himself. [13]He is dressed in a robe dipped in blood, and his name is the Word of God. [14]The armies of heaven were following him, riding on white horses and dressed in fine linen, white and clean. - Revelation 19:11-14

This is undoubtedly a picture of his redeemed (Revelation 3:18), with glorified, immortal bodies (1 Corinthians 15:35-50), able to descend from the heavens without the aid of a spacecraft! We are told in Colossians 3:4, "When Christ, who is your life, appears, then you also will appear with him in glory."

The book of Revelation tells what we will do, once we have returned with Christ:

Blessed and holy are those who have part in the first resurrection. The second death has no power over them, but they will be priests of God and of Christ and will reign with him for a thousand years. -Revelation 20:6

The Centrality of Israel and Jewish People during the Tribulation

A great body of converted people from all the nations is mentioned several times in the book of Revelation—after the rapture of the Church. Usually they are called the "Saints." They are believers in Christ—Jews and Gentiles alike, but they are not referred to as the Church, nor are any of the usual descriptions of the Church attached to them. The apostate church of the period will be corrupt, and will give its influence to the Beast (Revelation 18), so these Tribulation Saints will not in any way be associated with this apostate church, the great harlot of Revelation 17.

The theme of Israel's place during The Tribulation Period will be expanded in the third section of the book, but here are some of the key points that illustrate the centrality of Israel and Jewish people during this period of time:

- It is synonymous with Daniel's 70th Week (Daniel 9:27; Revelation 13).
- The 144,000 are sealed from the 12 Tribes of Israel (Revelation 7:1-8).
- The Two Witnesses are probably Old Testament leaders - Moses and Elijah; or, as some think, Enoch and Elijah. (Revelation 11:1-12).
- Israel will flee from Satan's wrath (Revelation 12).
- There will be a treaty with Israel and defilement of Israel's Temple (Revelation 13).

Other views of the rapture have the Church going through at least part of the 70th week.

Population of the Millennium by Mortal Believers

The pre-tribulation rapture interpretation best explains this important feature of God's future plan. According to Jesus' teaching on the Mount of Olives, there will be a judgment of the nations (Sheep and Goats - Matthew 25:31-46) just before the Millennium, just prior to the commencement of the thousand-year reign of Christ (Revelation 20:1-6). This taking of some and leaving of others is not the rapture, but it corresponds to the Parable of The Wheat and The Tares (Matthew 13:24-30). In that parable, the tares are collected FIRST, and tied into bundles to be burned (later, at the Great White Throne judgment), then the wheat is gathered into the barn. The wheat represents true believers who have survived the Tribulation period, and are thus permitted to enter the Millennial Age.

If the rapture took place at, or near the end of the Tribulation, all believers would have glorified bodies, and there would be no righteous mortals left to enter the Millennium!

Differences between the Rapture and the Second Coming

We believe that much of the confusion about the rapture is caused by a lack of understanding that Christ comes first for believers, and then comes later in what is properly called the Second Coming, or his Glorious Return as King of Kings. Here are some of the differences between these two events.

The Rapture	The Second Coming
Christ comes for His own 1 Thessalonians 4:13-18	Christ returns with His own Revelation 19:14
Believers taken to Father's House John 14:3	Believers come to Earth Matthew 24:30
Jesus seen only by believers 1 Corinthians 15:52, 19:11-16;	Every eye will see Him Revelation 1:7 Matthew 24:30
No reference to Satan	Satan bound Revelation 20:1-3
Earth not judged	Earth judged Revelation 20:4-5
A Mystery 1 Corinthians 15:51	Foretold in Old Testament Dan. 12:1-3; Zechariah 12:10; 14:4

Absence of the Church

Finally, and probably most significant of all, is this fact:

The Church Is Missing from the Tribulation (Revelation Chapters 4-19).

In the first three chapters of Revelation, there are constant references to the Church and to the Seven Churches. However, starting at chapter 4, verse 1, where John is told to "come up here," the Church is obviously absent throughout the Tribulation period. The expression "come up here" does mean leaving the earth in Revelation 11:12 where the translation of the Two Witnesses takes place. (We are not suggesting that the rapture takes place in chapter 11, only that the same expression, used there, does mean virtually the same thing for the Two Witnesses that the rapture does to the Church.)

There are numerous references to believers in these chapters, but they are not called the Church. What might be called the church on the earth during this time is the apostate shell of nominal Christianity, which has lost its true believers, and has joined with other religions of the world to become a "United Religion," which, in turn will give its power to the Beast. This apostate church is pictured as a prostitute riding the beast in Revelation 17.

Finally, the absence of the Church will undoubtedly account for the lawlessness spoken of in 2 Thessalonians 2:3.

In the next chapter we will explore one other major movement in human history that has a bearing on End Times prophecy. That historical development is the rise of Islam and its effects on Israel and the Church.

Chapter 7
Historical Developments: Israel Scattered, The Church Age, and The Rise of Islam

This chapter serves as an annex to Section Two. It traces the major movements of Israel and the Church during the past two thousand years. It also includes highlights of the rise of Islam as it affects Israel and the Church. It is not possible to recognize the rapid fulfillment of prophecy in these days without understanding the impact of radical Islamic history.

The birth and growth of the early Church was a tumultuous season of change as God began to move in the power of his Spirit to bring men and women into the New Covenant relationship. The book of Acts tells us about the first three decades of the Works of the Spirit through the Apostles, beginning with Peter's mighty sermon on the Day of Pentecost. Within months the believing community in Jerusalem, (all Jews), who followed Jesus (Yeshua), numbered several thousand.

The Apostles instituted a division of responsibility in the Church by appointing elders to oversee teaching and deacons to be responsible for serving and meeting the immediate physical needs of people in the assembly. Among the newly appointed deacons were two great teachers: Philip the Evangelist and a young man named Stephen. Stephen's stirring speech (Acts 6-7), recounting the history of the Jews to the assembled crowds on the Temple Mount, resulted in his own death by stoning—and this was quickly followed by growing persecution of the "Way" of Jesus. The opposition came from the traditionally-oriented elements of Jewish leadership.

Jews who had given their allegiance to Jesus moved in large numbers to other countries beginning what would be later known as the great "Diaspora" of the Jewish people. Their exodus from their own land would continue for the next 1900 years. Later, as Jewish rebellion against Roman rule continued, the Romans began to forcefully expel the land of its residents, leaving Eretz Israel (the land of Israel) nearly empty of the Jewish people of all classes and belief.

It was soon obvious to the followers of Jesus (the early Church) that God in his sovereign movement in history was also adding multitudes of Gentiles to the Body of Christ. A young Pharisee named Saul was responsible for the persecution of Christians, and was present when Stephen was killed. He was suddenly converted on the road to Damascus, and within a decade became the mighty Apostle Paul. He was called specifically by the Lord to spearhead the world wide evangelism of the Gentiles.

Peter meanwhile led the Apostles who were to focus on bringing the good news of Jesus to Jewish communities beyond the borders of Israel. The other disciples scattered near and far, carrying the message of Jesus to all lands and peoples.

So it was that the focal point of Christianity moved quickly out of Jerusalem to Antioch—about 300 miles to the North—in Syria. While there remained a strong but persecuted Church in Jerusalem, the rapid growth of the Church was now in Asia Minor, in Africa, Europe and India.

Jewish resistance to Roman rule in Jerusalem increased in cycles until finally Jerusalem became off limits to Jews all together. Most of the Jews in Israel were forced to flee to foreign lands. They remained in these countries for the next 19 centuries in small communities where their culture and values could be preserved.

The history of Israel in the Diaspora is an utterly amazing chapter of world history, virtually unknown by most Christians today, yet it is a subject most worthy of study. Often ill-treated, forcefully converted, persecuted and frequently killed, these amazing people persisted. God watched over them as he had promised through Ezekiel long ago. He would bring them back to the land when the out-calling of the Church was complete (Ezekiel 11:14-21).

The definitive history of the Christian Church has not yet been written. The book of Acts was just the introduction; the whole story remains yet to be told in full. But all the evidence suggests that the end of the age of the Church is now very near.

After most of the Jews left their homeland in the second Century of this era, the land fell into disuse. Once cultivated land reverted to desert and fresh water lakes became useless silted marshes. The land was rocky and devoid of mineral resources in the first place, of little use to anyone except wandering tribes of Bedouins with their flocks, and a few caravan-route travelers. The great ancient civilizations that had ruled the ancient world—Egypt, Babylon, Persia, Greece and Rome—had long since faded away, and the Holy Land became an unimportant part of the Byzantine Empire. The Emperor Constantine had made Christianity the official state religion of the Roman Empire with headquarters in Constantinople. Foreign rule of Israel by the shifting Gentile world powers (as Jesus predicted) continued. Israel was visited by occasional tourists but the surrounding nations were also poor and backward, not at all the great world powers they once had been. Small numbers of Jews continued to live in the land. They succeeded in preserving the Jewish heritage so that it could later blossom again into life in the Return to the land in our day.

The Rise of Islam
Mohammed
Mohammed instituted a third major monotheistic religion during the 7th Century AD. He was born in Mecca, Arabia about AD 570. He was familiar with Jewish and Christian beliefs and supposedly received revelations from an angel. He was rejected by his associates and migrated to Medina in 622. This marks the beginning of the Islamic era.

Two years later Mohammed and his followers defeated the Meccans at the Battle of Badr. In 630 he conquered Mecca and made it the spiritual center of Islam. His goal was to unite the warring tribes under one chief God, whom he called Allah.[52]

The Spread of Islam
Mohammed died in 632, and was succeeded by Abu Bakr, who was the first Caliph, or successor of Mohammed.[53] Between 633 and 643 his followers conquered Syria and Iraq (ancient Babylon), the Holy Land, Egypt and Persia.

By 656 the first official version of the Qur'an was established. As time went on, Mohammed's followers experienced disputes and civil war. Shiite extremism, the belief system that gave rise to modern Islamic terrorism, began in 685.

Jerusalem was evidently not considered of great importance to the Muslim armies. They first called the city Ilya (Aelia Capitolina) rather than Beit el-Maqdas (the holy house). An early Muslim proverb says, "One prayer in Mecca is valued as ten thousand prayers; a prayer in Medina is valued at one thousand prayers; and a prayer in Jerusalem at five hundred prayers."[54]

The Dome of the Rock
The rest of this section is taken from The Temple Mount website by permission.[55]

Although Abd El-Malik had commissioned the structure, it became known as "The Mosque of Omar." The structure, however, was not (and is not today) a mosque, but rather a shrine.

Inside the Dome is an outcropping of the bedrock of Mount Moriah, the "Sacred Rock." On the rock's pock-marked surface is one indentation, which Muslims believe is the footprint left by Mohammed as he leapt into heaven. (Pilgrims over the centuries have whittled off pieces of the rock. The Crusaders especially were known to chip "holy souvenirs" from it.) Mount Moriah is a long, extended hill in Jerusalem, extending north from the City of David and beyond the present North wall of the Old City. That same hill is the traditional site of Abraham's sacrificial altar for Isaac, the threshing floor or Araunah, and the site of the First and the Second Temple.

The Foundation Stone is not solid. Beneath it is a cave and a well, known as "the well of souls."

East of the exposed bedrock in the Dome of the Rock is a tall cupboard where it is believed hairs from the beard of Mohammed are kept. Within the hollowed out chamber of under the rock are the "places of prayer" of Elijah, Abraham, David, and Solomon. The Muslims call this cave the "well of souls" where they believe the dead meet twice a week to pray.

In medieval times this spot was considered to be the "center of the world" and was marked such on maps. Since the rock under the Dome of the Rock, where the cave is, shows the effects of quarrying above the level of the cave, it is logical to hold that the rock stood higher originally and that the threshing floor surrounded the rock and the cave.

The exterior of the Dome is covered with tiles from Persia as well as marble. The "Golden Dome" is not made out of gold but rather anodized aluminum. The original dome was wooden, later covered with brass, and then lead sheathing in 1448. The excess weight of the lead-clad dome caused grave concern for the entire building because of periodic severe earthquakes in Jerusalem and finally the anodized aluminum dome was installed. Most recently, in 1993, a million dollars in gold foil was provided by the government of Saudi Arabia as a gift. As of this writing the installation of the gold leaf has now been completed and the dome is today resplendent in brilliant pure gold.

During the seventeen centuries of the Dome's existence it has undergone many repairs, but it has not been substantially changed in overall appearance since its completion in AD 691. After one of the earliest renovations in A. D 820, Caliph al-Mamun removed the name of Caliph Abd el-Malik from the dedication plate and inserted his own name instead. However he neglected to change the dates and his fraud is there for all to see.

The Dome's Beauty [56]

Writing about A. D 985, Mukadassi, the famous Muslim traveler born in Jerusalem, wrote:

> At the dawn, when the light of the sun first strikes on the cupola and the drum catches the rays, then is this edifice a marvelous site to behold and one such that in all Islam I have never seen its equal; neither have I heard tell of aught built in pagan times that could rival in grace this Dome of the Rock.

A Denial of Christianity [57]

From the Muslim point of view the Dome of the Rock was an answer to and a denial of the attractions of Christianity and its Scriptures, providing the "faithful" with arguments to be used against Christian theology.[58] The inscriptions are seven hundred and thirty-four feet long in all, amongst the lengthiest inscriptions in the world. There is a great amount of repetition and many quotations from the Qur'an.

The following extracts are relevant:

Inner Face: South Wall. "In the name of Allah the Merciful the Compassionate. There is no God but Allah alone; he has no co-partner. He is the Kingship and his the praise. He giveth life and He causeth to die, and He hath power over everything."

South-East Wall. "Verily Allah and his angels pronounce blessing upon the Prophet. O ye who have pronounced blessings upon him and give him the salutation of peace. O, People of the Book [i. e. the Jews and Christians always referred to as such by the Muslims] do not go beyond the bounds in your religion and do not say about Allah anything but the truth. The Messiah, Jesus, son of Mary, is but a messenger of Allah and his word which he cast upon Mary, and a spirit from him. So believe only in Allah and of his messenger, but do not say "Three" [Trinity] and it will be better for you. Allah is only one God. Far be it from his glory that he should have a son."

North Wall. "The Messiah will not deign to be in the service of Allah nor will the angels who stand in his presence. O Allah; pray upon Thy messenger "the servant Jesus - [N-W Wall] the son of Mary and peace be upon him the day of his birth, the day of his death and the day of his being raised alive. That is Jesus, son of Mary - a statement concerning which YOU are in doubt. It is not for Allah to take for himself any offspring, glory be to him."

West Wall. "Allah bears witness that there is no God but him, likewise the angels and the people possessed of knowledge [S-W WALL] - Upholding justice. There is no God but He, the Almighty and All wise. Verily, the religion in Allah's sight is Islam."

Outer Face: West and North-West Walls. "In the name of Allah the Merciful and Compassionate. There is no God but Allah alone. Praise be to Allah who hath not taken to himself offspring. To him there has never been any person in the sovereignty. Mohammed is the messenger of Allah, may God pray upon him and accept his intercession."

"Praise be God who has not taken unto himself a son and who has no partner in sovereignty nor has He any protector on account of weakness."

If religious Jews are offended by the presence of this Islamic shrine on their holy mountain, Christians have even more reasons to take offense at these misrepresentations of the character of their God, and the deliberate insults to biblical revelation that the interior inscriptions clearly intend.

Since it is an historical fact that Mohammed never came to Jerusalem, why is the Temple Mount considered holy to Muslims? One passage from the Qur'an does link Mohammed with Jerusalem and the Temple Mount. It is the seventeenth Sura, entitled "The Night Journey." In this Sura there is a dream or vision by Mohammed in which he is carried by night "from the sacred temple to the temple that is more remote, whose precinct we have blessed, that we might show him of our signs."

Islamic tradition identifies the first temple as Mecca and the second as Jerusalem. Mohammed's journey was with the Archangel Gabriel. Muslim belief says they rode together on a winged steed called El Burak ("lightning"). El Burak is not mentioned in the Qur'an, its first mention is two centuries after Mohammed's death in a document called Hadith, a collection of oral traditions.

After they arrived at the Temple Mount, tradition says that Mohammed and his horse ascended through the seven heavens into Allah's presence. Various spots on the Mount were later indicated as the place where El Burak was tied up before the ascent into the presence of Allah.

Al-Aqsa Mosque[59]

Al-Aqsa is a large mosque built on the Temple Mount south of the Dome of the Rock. It is mentioned in the Qur'an in a vision of Mohammed's ascension. It means the "distant place." This refers to its geographical location far from Mecca. Al-Aqsa is regularly referred to as Islam's third holiest shrine after Mecca and Medina. The present mosque is believed to stand over the area where Solomon built his magnificent palace south of the Temple.

The Al-Aqsa Mosque was built between A. D. 709-715 probably by Caliph Waleed, son of Abdel-Malik, the man who constructed the Dome of the Rock. Throughout the years the mosque has been destroyed several times by earthquakes and subsequently rebuilt. The most prominent remains of the original mosque that has survived are a few supporting columns east of the cupola.

The most important reconstruction was after an earthquake in AD 1034 when the mosque was enlarged to house 5000 worshipers. The builders used capitals and columns of destroyed Byzantine churches in their reconstruction work.

Jewish Hopes under Islam[60]

The conquering Muslims brought a different attitude with them. In contrast to the Byzantine and Roman conquerors, who let the Temple Mount remain in ruins as a proof of the destruction of Jewish nationalism, the Muslims restored worship to the Mount. Yet the worship was not of Yahweh, the God of the Bible, but of Allah.

When the Muslims became the rulers in Jerusalem some matters became easier for the Jews. They were officially allowed to live in the city and there is evidence that on certain holy days they were even permitted on the Temple Mount.

Reports say that the Jews would march in procession around the walls of the Temple Mount on feast days and pray at the gates. A document written in the tenth century indicates that one of the conditions for allowing the Jews to pray at the gates was that the

Jewish community would be responsible for keeping the Mount clean. The Jews, the document states, were responsible to sweep the Mount. Other accounts indicate that Jews were employed in the Mosque area and that Jewish craftsmen made lamps for the Mosque.

The Mishna (Berachot 9:5) reveals that the Jews of all ages are required to show reverence for the site of their former temples:

> No man shall behave frivolously when standing near the eastern gate, which looks to the Holy of Holies: he shall not enter the temple mount with his cane, his shoes, his purse, or the dust on his feet, nor shall he use it as a short cut, still less shall he spit there.

Inscriptions have been found at the gates of the Temple Mount that were probably put there by Jewish Pilgrims during the early Arab rule. One such inscription, when translated, reads: "You Lord of Hosts build this House in the lifetime of Jacob ben-Joseph, Theophylactus, and Sisinia and Anistasia. Amen and amen."

The names on the inscription indicate they were Jews from a Greek-speaking country. Though the Jews were allowed more access than in the Roman or Byzantine period, they were still far from their desired goal of retaking Jerusalem and the Temple Mount.

The Crusaders Capture Jerusalem[61]

In the last 1300 years, with only one exception, the Temple Mount has been in the hands of Muslims. On July 15, 1099 Jerusalem was taken from the Muslims by the Crusaders from Europe. The Crusaders slaughtered the inhabitants of Jerusalem in an unjustified carnage. The Dome of the Rock was converted into a Christian church called the Templum Domini - "Temple of our Lord."

The Crusaders then began to use the Al-Aqsa Mosque as headquarters for the Knights Templar who officiated over the Temple Compound. A remnant of the Crusader occupation still exists today, the tombs of the assassins of Thomas Beckett, the Archbishop of Canterbury (1118-1170). After murdering Beckett, the assassins traveled to Jerusalem and took up with the Knights Templar. Their tombs are situated near the main entrance.

The Western world rejoiced that Jerusalem was in the hands of "Christians. " The victory, however, caused Muslims to immediately launch campaigns to regain the city and the Dome from the Christian infidels. The Crusader occupation was relatively short-lived. The Muslim leader Saladin (Salah al-Din) proclaimed a jihad, or holy war, to retake the land of Palestine. After ninety years of Crusader control, Jerusalem surrendered to Saladin's army on October 2, 1187. In contrast to the brutality of the Crusaders, Saladin treated the defeated Crusaders with kindness and mercy.

The golden cross that was placed on the Dome of the Rock was torn down. Saladin rededicated the Templar's headquarters as a mosque. The Dome was covered with beautiful mosaics and a prayer niche facing Mecca was added.

Jerusalem was back in the hands of the Muslims and Europe was ready to avenge the defeat. A Third Crusade was undertaken (1189-1192) to free Jerusalem from the armies of Saladin. Richard the Lion-hearted led England and other Crusaders in a fruitless attempt to retake the city. To this day, the Temple Mount remains in Muslim control.

Jerusalem Lies Desolate[62]

In 1267 the Jewish sage Nahmanides wrote a letter to his son. It contained the following references to the land and the Temple.

> What shall I say of this land? The more holy the place, the greater the desolation. Jerusalem is the most desolate of all... There are about 2,000 inhabitants ... but there are no Jews, for after the arrival of the Tartars, the Jews fled, and some were killed by the sword. There are now only two brothers, dyers, who buy their dyes from the government. At their place a quorum of worshipers meets on the Sabbath, and we encourage them, and found a ruined house, built on pillars, with a beautiful dome, and made it into a synagogue...People regularly come to Jerusalem, men and women from Damascus and from Aleppo and from all parts of the country, to see the Temple and weep over it. And may He who deemed us worthy to see Jerusalem in her ruins, grant us to see her rebuilt and restored, and the honor of the Divine Presence returned.[63]

An account exists of Napoleon's visit to the Temple Mount on the 9th of Av, the day of the commemoration of the Temple's destruction. When asked what all the crying and wailing was about, Napoleon was told that the Jews were mourning their Temple that had been destroyed 1800 years previously. Touched by the incident the French Monarch said, "A people which weeps and mourns for the loss of its homeland 1800 years ago and does not forget - such a people will never be destroyed. Such a people can rest assured that its homeland will be returned to it."[64]

Jerusalem under Turkish Rule[65]

The Ottoman Turks, non-Arab Muslims, became the dominant power in the 15th century. In 1453 they captured the city of Constantinople and brought about the final destruction of the Eastern Roman Empire (Byzantine). They renamed the city Istanbul and made it the center of their empire.

In 1517, under Sultan Selim I, the Turks captured Jerusalem and all of Israel. The rule of the Turks over Jerusalem would last exactly four hundred years. The walls that today surround the Old City were built by Suleiman the Magnificent, son of Sultan Selim. Suleiman restored the Al-Aqsa Mosque and some of the present stained glass windows date from this period.

The Arabs found themselves under the domination of the Turks. For four hundred years of Turkish rule the Arabs did not possess even a single, independent state.

Jews Hope for Return[66]

Even during the Jewish exile extending over many centuries, the people continually expressed hope for a return to Jerusalem, for the rebuilding of the city and of the Temple. Two eighteenth century rabbis, Jacob Emden and Jonathan Eibschutz were fierce rivals. On the subject of returning to Jerusalem, however they saw eye to eye. Emden wrote:

> We do not mourn properly over Jerusalem. Were we guilty of this transgression alone, it would be sufficient reason for the extension of the period of our Exile. In my opinion this is the most likely, most apparent and the strongest reason for all of the dreadful terrifying persecutions which have been fallen us in Exile, in all the places of our dispersion. We have been hotly pursued. We have not been granted rest among the nations with our humiliation, affliction and homelessness, because this sense of mourning has left our hearts. While becoming complacent in a land not ours, we have forgotten Jerusalem; we have not taken it to heart. Therefore, "Like one who is dead we have been forgotten. From generation to generation sorrow is added to our sorrow and our pain."

Eibschutz concurred:

> One must weep ceaselessly over the rebuilding of Jerusalem and the restoration of the glory of King David, for that is the object of human perfection. If we do not have Jerusalem and the kingdom of the House of David, why should we have life? Since our many transgressions have led to the Destruction and to the desolation of our glorious Temple and the loss of the kingdom of the House of David, the degree which we suffer the absence and the lack of good is known to all. Surely have we descended from life until death. And the converse is also true: "When the Lord restores the captivity of Zion," we shall ascend from death unto life. Certainly the heart of anyone who possesses the soul of a Jew is broken when he recalls the destruction of Jerusalem.
>
> The hope of the Jews in Diaspora is that one day they would again come to their land, rebuild the Holy City, and their Temple.

Non-Muslims Barred from the Temple Mount[67]

J. T. Barclay in the mid 19th Century wrote about the barring of those from the Mount who were not of the Islamic faith:

> When the clock of the Mosque needs repairing, they are compelled, however reluctantly to employ a Frank. But in order to have a clean conscience in the commission of such an abominable piece of sacrilege as the admission upon the sacred premises, they adopt the following expedient. The mechanic selected being thoroughly purged from his uncleanness ablution a certain formula of prayer and incantation is sung over him at the gate. This being satisfactorily concluded, he is considered as exorcised, not only of Christianity (or Judaism, as the case may be), but of humanity also; and is declared to be no longer a man

but a donkey. He is then mounted upon the shoulders of the faithful, lest the ground should be polluted by his footsteps; and being carried to the spot where his labours are required, he is set down upon matting within certain prescribed limits; and the operation being performed, he is carried back to the gate, and there, by certain other ceremonies, he is duly undonkeyfied and transmuted back into a man again.

More Jewish Persecution[68]

Toward the end of the nineteenth century, Jewish persecution was on the increase. In 1882, as a result of persecution of the Jews in Russia and Romania, the first immigration of Jewish settlers to Palestine began.

In 1891 Arab leaders prepared a petition to the Ottoman government in Constantinople to demand an end to Jewish immigration into Palestine and prohibit Jewish land purchases.

In 1896 Theodor Herzl, the founder of the modern Zionism, promoted the founding of a Jewish State. He argued that the only way in which the "Jewish problem" can be resolved is by establishing a Jewish state in Palestine. Herzl's writing started the Jews on the road back to their promised homeland.

World Wars I and II

End of Ottoman Empire

Beginning in the 13th Century, Turkish tribes united under Osman I and eventually formed the Ottoman Empire. This super-state greatly extended Islamic expansion in the Mediterranean and South-Eastern part of Europe. It captured the Byzantine capital of Constantinople in 1453. However, by the beginning of the 1900's it was gradually losing ground to other competing European empires. It sided with Germany in World War I, and in the end, was forced to disband in 1918. In 1922 the nation we now know as Turkey began in a portion of the old Ottoman territory.

The Balfour Agreement and the British Mandate

Meanwhile, the plight of European Jews continued to grow. The more they were persecuted, the stronger the concept of Zionism grew. In 1917, just before the end of World War I, the government of Great Britain became gradually committed to the idea of establishing a Jewish home in Palestine. This policy was revealed in a letter by Arthur James Lord Balfour to Lord Rothschild. It was the first political recognition of Zionist aims by a major power. It said in part:

"His Majesty's Government view with favour the establishment in Palestine of a national home for the Jewish people, and will use their best endeavours to facilitate the achievement of this object, it being clearly understood that nothing shall be done which may prejudice the civil and religious rights of existing non-Jewish communities in Palestine, or the rights and political status enjoyed by Jews in any other country."[69]

In 1922 the newly formed League of Nations issued *The British Mandate for Palestine.* This document charged Great Britain with the task of administrating the area of Palestine and Transjordan (land now designated as Israel, The West Bank, The Gaza Strip, and Jordan), "until such time as they are able to stand alone."[70]

The Holocaust

One of the worst horrors of World War II was the construction of Nazi death camps and the destruction of some 6 million Jews. Because of this Holocaust, world sympathy for Jewish people was awakened. There was a sense everywhere that it would be fair to give these persecuted people a homeland. Hundreds of thousands of persecuted Jews from Europe and all over the world fled to the Holy Land.

End of the British Mandate

As Zionism grew and hostilities increased between the Jewish immigrants to Palestine and Arab Palestinians, the British found themselves increasingly unable to maintain order in the area. They announced their intention to end the British Mandate as of May 14, 1948.

Rebirth of the Nation of Israel

Some of the following information was given briefly in Chapter 1 - What in the World Is Happening? At this point a little more detail will help explain the present situation in the Middle East. From the day of Israel's rebirth, to the present day, Zechariah's prophecies about the End Times has been coming to pass:

> This is the word of the LORD concerning Israel. The LORD, who stretches out the heavens, who lays the foundation of the earth, and who forms the spirit of man within him, declares:
> [2] "I am going to make Jerusalem a cup that sends all the surrounding peoples reeling. Judah will be besieged as well as Jerusalem. [3] On that day, when all the nations of the earth are gathered against her, I will make Jerusalem an immovable rock for all the nations. All who try to move it will injure themselves...
> [9] On that day I will set out to destroy all the nations that attack Jerusalem." - Zechariah 12:1-3, 9

Independence -1948

Ezekiel, chapters 36 and 37, give a most remarkable prophecy of the rebirth of the Nation of Israel. In great detail, the future plan for Israel was described; bringing back God's dispersed Israelites from all over the world to the mountains of Israel. The prophet saw a vision of a valley where the dry bones miraculously came together, and then the muscles and the skin were re-created over the skeleton. This is a picture of the migration of people from the most remote parts of the world back to their homeland.

Independence Day for Israel was May 14, 1948. On the very first day of their independence, all of Israel's neighbors declared war against them. They had to fight them off, and amazingly, they won this first war with practically no resources. Jordan controlled the "West Bank", most of the land on the West side of the Jordan River, and other sections extending inland, including the western portion of the city of Jerusalem and the Temple Mount area.

Previous residents of the land were invited to stay in Israel if they were willing to become Israeli citizens. Thousands of Arabs remained and did indeed become citizens of the new nation. Other Arabs fled Israel and became refugees in neighboring countries and in the areas occupied by Jordan. The Arab countries would not assimilate them. Thus they continued year after year as poor, disgruntled people, and enemies of Israel.

One part of Ezekiel's prophecy has not yet been fulfilled. The last part of the vision is the breath of life entering into the re-constituted body (Ezekiel 37:14). The body has been brought back together, but is not yet spiritually alive. In Israel, most people do not follow the Lord even in the old way of Judaism. The future fulfillment of this portion of the prophecy will be during The Tribulation when Israel will once again be spiritually alive. The rapture will probably play a part in bringing about their awakening.

The Suez Canal War of 1956

This was started by Egypt and her allies, but it resulted in the loss of the whole Sinai Peninsula and the Suez Canal to Israel. These were later given back.

The PLO - 1964

The Palestine Liberation Organization (PLO) was begun in 1964 to represent Palestinians who felt that they had been unfairly deprived of their land by the establishment of the nation of Israel. They originally called for the elimination of Israel. Yasser Arafat was their Chairman from 1969 until his death in 2004. He was succeeded by Mahmoud Abbas.

Fatah, a left-wing nationalist group is the largest political component of the PLO. The Popular Front for the Liberation of Palestine is the second largest group. It is a Marxist-Leninist resistance organization. Several other groups representing Palestinian issues are also part of the PLO.

The United States and Israel considered the PLO a terrorist organization until the Madrid Conference in 1991. In 1992 the PLO negotiated an agreement in principle with the government of Israel to occupy and control, under self-rule, portions of the land, including the Gaza Strip and Jericho with a view to further negotiations in the future. By 1993 it had recognized Israel's right to exist in peace.[71]

The 6-Day War of 1967

On June 5, 1967 Israel responded to an imminent attack by her neighbors: Egypt, Syria, Jordan and Iraq. This was an amazing war! Israelis destroyed the aircraft of their hostile neighbors before they even had time to launch them. They even knew which planes of the Arab nations were decoys, and didn't bother to bomb them. They took control of the Golan Heights and the West Bank, including East Jerusalem. The Sinai Peninsula was also taken.

The Yom Kippur War of 1973

This is the one war they almost lost because even the non-religious Jews observe Yom Kippur, The Day of Atonement. The nation was unprepared, but The Lord still preserved his Chosen People.

The Islamic Revolution - Iran 1979

As noted in Chapter 1, these victories were embarrassing to the Islamic nations that surrounded the new country of Israel. Shiite clerics in Iran resented Israel's presence in the Middle East and evidently desired to rekindle Islamic aspirations to rule the world that had been stopped by World War I. They overthrew the democratic government of the land, and imposed Islamic Sharia law. They held Americans hostage there for 444 days, and began to refer to the U.S. as "The Great Satan." Since that time, Iran has exported radical Islamic beliefs and the philosophy of "jihad" (meaning "struggle") that has been responsible for a whole new kind of conquest that we now call "terrorism." They have also provided funds and training for terrorists in many parts of the world.

Wars with Lebanon and Hezbollah - 1982 and 2006

In 1982 Israel invaded southern Lebanon to weaken the forces of the Palestine Liberation Army (PLO), which had moved there from Jordan. A new Islamic political and paramilitary group called Hezbollah ("Party of God") grew out of this conflict. They were a guerrilla force at first, but now have become a large army, and a controlling power in Lebanon. They are considered terrorists by the U.S., Israel, Egypt, Saudi Arabia, Jordan and others; but supported and rearmed by Iran and Syria.

A second war between Israel and Lebanon came in 2006 as the result of numerous rocket attacks launched into Israel by Hezbollah. This war was not executed as definitively as usual by the Israelis, so when they left Lebanon, claiming victory, Hezbollah also claimed a victory over Israel.

United Nations personnel were employed to help keep the peace, and UN Security Council Resolution 1701 called for the disarmament of all militias in Lebanon and the implementation of the Lebanese cabinet decision of July 26, 2006, which stated that "there shall be no weapons or authority in Lebanon other than that of the Lebanese state." This resolution was ignored as usual, and Hezbollah has been rearmed with better rockets and other weapons by the Syrians and Iran. Hezbollah has in effect become Iran's forward military arm in its aim to destroy Israel.

Tensions are increasing between Israel and Lebanon again in 2010, with many predicting that this could lead to a third, and greater, war between them. In July of 2010 UN Secretary-General Ban Ki-moon expressed concern that Israel and the Lebanese terrorist militia Hezbollah may go to war again in the very near future. [72]

Another war in Lebanon could spread to Syria. Israeli forces quickly and effectively destroyed a nuclear reactor that was being built there in 2007. A future war could involve the destruction of Damascus, which some prophecy scholars note must one day take place (Isaiah 17, Jeremiah 49, and Zechariah 9).

Hamas (Islamic Resistance Movement) - 1987

In 1987 the Palestinians began an *intifada* (uprising) against the control of Israel. Hamas was born from this unrest, and was an outgrowth of the Palestinian branch of the Muslim Brotherhood. It is not closely aligned with the Iran-Syria-Hezbollah movement because the Muslim Brotherhood began in Egypt where the majority follows the Sunni branch of Islam. Iran, on the other hand, is the champion of the Shiite branch. Hamas was founded on the belief that Allah had given the land to them and Israel had no right to it. They are listed by the U.S. and other countries as a terrorist organization. They have used terrorism, including suicide bombings and rocket attacks to try to establish a Palestinian state.

In the book, "Son of Hamas," Mosab Hassan Yousef explains his upbringing as the son of one of the founders of Hamas. As a young man he admired his father and was involved in leadership of the youth of the movement. He was imprisoned for his activities, and witnessed the brutality of Hamas against its own people. He became disillusioned with the movement. After he was released from prison he was drawn to a Bible study in Jerusalem where he became a born-again Christian.[73] He now lives in the United States.

Rocket attacks from Hamas in Gaza led to a brief war between Israel and Gaza in 2008.

In 2010, according to Aziz Dwaik, Hamas' most senior representative in the West Bank, Hamas would now accept Israel's right to exist. This means that they would be willing to nullify the part in the Hamas charter that calls for the destruction of Israel.[74]

The Palestinian Authority - 1994

The Palestinian Authority is an elected body of representatives prescribed by the "Oslo Peace Process" in 1993. Its purpose is to control areas in the West Bank and The Gaza Strip when Israel would withdraw from them.

Hamas was not in favor of the peace talks and ultimately refused to participate in the peace process.

Suicide Bombings Introduced - 1994

Palestinians and the world were startled on February 25, 1994 when an American-born physician, Baruch Goldstein opened fire in the mosque in Hebron, killing 29 people and injuring more than one hundred others. He was beat to death by an angry and grief-stricken mob.[75] Bombing incidents had become commonplace, but to avenge this massacre, 21 year-old Amar Salah Diab Amarna detonated a bomb he was carrying on a bus to Tel Aviv. Six were killed and thirty were wounded.[76] Amarna and the scores of young suicide bombers who would follow him were considered heroes among the Palestinians, and especially among Hamas followers.

Because of the bombings and suicide missions, Israel decided to build a massive barrier between Palestinian areas, especially the Gaza Strip, and Israeli communities. The wall was begun in 1994, and more than 200 miles of it have been completed, effectively stopping the carnage until Hamas began to use rockets to attack Israeli areas.

Interference from Saddam Hussein's Iraq - 2002

In 1981 Israeli fighter jets destroyed the Osirak nuclear reactor that was being built by Iraq. Ten years later, during the Gulf War in 1991, Saddam Hussein launched numerous Scud missiles at Israeli targets, including Tel Aviv.

In 2002 and 2003 Saddam gave $10,000 charity checks to families of Palestinian martyrs, and $25,000 to families of suicide bombers, thus encouraging the ongoing terrorism against Israel.[77]

Nuclear Iran - 2010

Nuclear fuel was loaded into Iran's first nuclear reactor at Bushehr on Aug. 21, 2010. This was done against the wishes of most of the people of the world, including major Arab nations in the Middle East, against numerous resolutions by the United Nations, and in spite of embargos from the U.S. and others. The project was made possible by the Russians, who provided materials and expertise at every stage, and who actually started the reactor for them. Their installation was not attacked by Israel because of the immense complications of Iran's multi-faceted nuclear power and nuclear weapons programs.

Worst of all, Iranian President Mahmoud Ahmadinejad has consistently called for the elimination of Israel since he was first elected in 2005. He chaired a conference in Teheran in that same year called "A World Without Zionism and America." He sincerely hates the U.S., whom he calls "The Great Satan," and has vowed to destroy Israel when it is possible, presumably when Iran has nuclear weapons. Many experts believe that it will not be long before he has these weapons of mass destruction. But will he use them?

Author Mike Evans warns that Ahmadinejad is not constrained by the "MAD deterrent" (mutual assured destruction) that kept the U.S. and Russia from bombing each other during the cold war. Neither side would attack first because of the certainty that the other would respond with enough force to destroy the enemy many times over.[78] Evans calls Ahmadinejad's Iran "the suicide regime" because of his belief that he has been chosen to help bring back their Mahdi (Messiah), the Twelfth Imam, who has supposedly been in hiding since the eighth century, waiting for the right time to return. In 2006 Evans interviewed James Woolsey, former head of the Central Intelligence Agency, who said that his plan is to "get a lot of people killed as quickly as possible." This will summon the Mahdi. Woolsey added,

> And then they also believe once the Mahdi comes, the world will only exist for a brief period of time. So Ahmadinejad is effectively on a campaign to see if he can't get the world to end.[79]

Of course, many Bible students see all of this as a build-up to the War of Gog and Magog (Ezekiel chapters 38 and 39), See *Chapter 9 - The First Half of the Tribulation* for more detail about this great war near the beginning of the 7 year "Tribulation." (Daniel 9:27)

Concern for Muslims

Christians continue to affirm their love for Muslims because Christ died for all men, and to stand against any persecution of Muslims based on their religion or ethnicity. In 2010 there was a big debate about whether or not to allow the building of a 13-story mosque near New York's "ground zero" from the 9/11 attacks. It was a difficult question because Americans generally are very committed to the concept of freedom of religion. Americans have believed that through this freedom, people of all beliefs will explore the truth and some will find Christ in the process. But it was clear that the proposed mosque would be a symbol of Islamic conquest in New York. In the same way, they have built their shrines over other political or religious focal points like the Kaaba, the Temple Mount in Jerusalem, and the Christian Church of Saint Vincent in Cordoba, Spain. Furthermore, it was considered very insensitive to the feelings of the families of those who died in the attacks. Muslims have been allowed to build more than a thousand mosques in the U.S. This is as it should be, even though Christians would not be allowed to build churches in some Islamic countries of the world. But Americans wanted an answer to the question, "Why build here?"

Evangelical Christians also seek to enter into dialog with Muslims wherever possible, so that they might learn more about Jesus, whom they respect as a prophet, but do not accept as savior. At the same time, they should not give the false impression, so prevalent in our culture today, that Christianity is just one way to God. Jesus said that he is the only way to God the Father (John 14:6).

Muslim evangelism is difficult in most Islamic countries. It is actually illegal in many of them. But in these critical days, Christians are praying for them that they will accept Christ. There have been many amazing stories of Muslims who have been converted by appearances of Jesus in their dreams. Some, like Mosab Hassan Yousef, the "Son of Hamas," have been drawn to Christ through the love of Christians. According to some missionaries, large numbers of Muslims are becoming Christians now.[80]

In Sections One and Two we have considered God's dealings with Israel, his "Chosen People," the Church, the mystery age not revealed in the Old Testament, and the rise of Islam. We now turn our attention to the future—to The Tribulation period, the time just beyond the rapture, which signals the end of the Church period.

Part III - Tribulation Saints:
The Destiny of Believers during the Coming Tribulation

Chapter 8
Believers during the Tribulation

We come now to the third section of this book, and to things that are yet future. After considering the history of Israel, the Chosen People, and of the Church, we can not help wondering who the true believers of the Tribulation period will be. According to the book of Revelation, starting with Chapter Four, the next period of human history will be a time of trial for the earth. This is generally called "The Tribulation," from Christ's own words in Matthew 24:9. "Then they will deliver you to tribulation, and will kill you, and you will be hated by all nations on account of my name." The word for "tribulation" is the Greek word *thlipsis*. This word literally means "pressure" and can be translated as "affliction, anguish, persecution, or tribulation." (Usually the seven-year period after the rapture and before the Second Coming is called "The Tribulation Period," however the last 3.5 years is frequently called "the *Great Tribulation*" because of the terrible violence loosed on the earth during the last half of these seven years.)

If Israel has rejected her Messiah and has been blinded, and if true believers from the Church have been taken away, who then are these believers of the Tribulation period?

Saints and Martyrs of the Tribulation Period

Future believers will basically be the same as the believers of today. They will be Christians: people who have put their faith in Jesus Christ who have repented of their sins, asked Christ to come into their lives, and have been "born again," just like the Christians of the Church Age (Luke 24:46-47; John 1:12; Revelation 3:20; John 3:3-16).

It is true that God works different ways in every age. The Church, for instance is called the "Body of Christ" and the Bride of Christ. All Christians are said to be "members one of another" in a special organic way. The Church was not promised a plot of land, nor a temple nor an earthly king and inheritance. God's promises to her are "heavenly" blessings while those given to Israel are "earthly."

Actually, salvation has been offered by God to people of all ages on the same basis: that of grace and faith. God's grace has always preceded man's response, because, as the Bible says, "There is no one righteous, not even one; there is no one who understands, no one who seeks God" (Romans 3:10-11). We have only glimpses of God's work in other nations down through history. For instance many Ninevites evidently became believers in the one true God because of the preaching of Jonah, yet these peoples were not part of believing Israel, or of the Church.

Even in the Garden of Eden God took the initiative to restore our fallen, sinful parents to fellowship. It was God's idea to call Abraham and Moses and David. It has always been God's idea to call and enable every person to believe. Men do not seek God on their own initiative (Romans 3). God seeks out and saves everyone who ever comes to know him. The proper response to God's call is faith—trust in him, and actions based on that trust. According to Ephesians 2:8-9, even that faith is a gift from our loving God. "For it is by grace you have been saved, through faith—and this not from yourselves, it is the gift of God—not by works, so that no one can boast."

In the Old Testament, faith in God involved belief in the promise that He would provide a payment for sin. That is what the sacrificial system was all about. When an animal was being sacrificed, the one offering the sacrifice would place his hand on its head and acknowledge that the innocent animal was dying in his place.

In the New Testament Jesus was shown to be the Messiah and the Savior whose death provided a once-for-all payment for our sin. Messiah's sacrifice was retroactively effective for all those who had believed in the promises that sin would one day be not merely "passed-over" or "covered"—but removed (John 1:41; 4:25-26; Hebrews 9:26-28; 13:11-12).

Believers of the Tribulation period will undoubtedly have the Holy Spirit (Acts 2:38; Romans 8:9-11), but since they will not be accepted into the dictator's evil world system, they will not be allowed into public places of influence, as teachers business leaders, and government positions, etc. The Holy Spirit in them will not have the same restraining influence that he had during the Church Age when believers were united in one body, the Body of Christ (2 Thessalonians 2:6-8).

Believers of the Tribulation will not be affiliated with the organization of the Church that remains on earth following the rapture. That church will be a totally apostate group commonly called "the harlot church." After the rapture, some churches will be quite empty, and some may not be affected much at all, depending on what percentage of true born-again believers belonged to each church. Many of those who are left behind will actually be relieved to be rid of the fanatical ones who were taken in the rapture. They will believe whatever lie is proposed by the Evil One to explain this great disappearance. Some churches will close down, and some will merely reorganize and go on with their religious activities. These spiritually dead organizations will not attract new true believers in Christ. They may even turn them in as troublemakers to the evil government of that time. Therefore, the saints and martyrs of the Tribulation period are never called the Church (Revelation chapters 4-19). As noted there will indeed exist a "renewed" church on the earth after the rapture, but she will be a counterfeit, apostate organization and will give her power to the Beast. She is thus depicted as a prostitute riding the beast in Revelation chapter 17.

Are you among those who know Christ personally? If you are not sure, we urge you to turn to Appendix T - *Do You Know Christ Personally?*

Believers in Christ from All Nations

The covenant with Abraham and his seed was for the purpose of blessing all nations (Genesis 12:2-3; 22:17-18). It was a promise to an earthly people ("as numerous as the grains of sand by the sea shore") *and* to a heavenly people ("as numerous as the stars of the sky").

The promise to Abraham was fulfilled specifically in the person and work of Jesus the Messiah (Galatians 3:16).

In the book of Acts we gain a glimpse of this blessing extended to the Gentiles.

Simon has described to us how God at first showed his concern by taking from the Gentiles a people for himself. - Acts 15:14

Sudden Belief of Many after the Rapture

Since the rapture will have taken all true Christians, one might ask how there are believers during The Tribulation. There could well be hundreds of thousands of immediate conversions right after the rapture by those who had heard the Gospel, and, though they were not hardened against it, had not yet actually received Christ as Savior. These people will remember the earnest pleading of friends and family members who had disappeared. They could respond quickly, turning to Christ in prayer, confessing their sins and asking him to save them.

Thousands of others will not know what to do, but will be convinced in their hearts that their missing loved ones had been taken by Christ. Perhaps some of them will not believe the lie that is put forward by the ungodly media, which may be saying that the Earth has at last been cleansed of its narrow-minded trouble-making Christian extremists. Officials may even suggest that UFOs had abducted them— our planet's population has been con-ditioned for decades now to believe in the existence of UFOs. See Chapter 13 - *The Plot Thickens.*

These honest seekers will turn to the Bibles and prophecy books that have been left by their missing friends. Their minds and hearts will be open to the Gospel when they read it or hear it explained by the thousands of instant converts. Even if they do not find the truth immediately, they will respond when evangelists like the 144,000 specially sealed Israelites mentioned below, boldly proclaim the Gospel during this period.

Messianic (Jewish) Leadership

It is apparent that the spiritual leaders of this period will be "completed" or "fulfilled" Jews, those who have accepted Yeshua (Jesus) as their Messiah. They will receive God's mercy when they return to him (Romans 11:25-32).

The Central Role of Israel

There are many indications that Israel is once again on center stage of history during the Tribulation period. Even now, before that time begins, our newspapers and television programs are preoccupied with the events of the Middle East, and especially of the tiny nation of Israel. The miraculous rebirth of the nation in 1948 was the fulfillment of the prophecies of Ezekiel chapters 36 and 37!

The importance of Israel in current events was prophesied in Zechariah:

> "I am going to make Jerusalem a cup that sends all the surrounding peoples reeling. Judah will be besieged as well as Jerusalem. [3] On that day, when all the nations of the earth are gathered against her, I will make Jerusalem an immovable rock for all the nations. All who try to move it will injure themselves. " - Zechariah 12:2-3

Israel is also portrayed in the Old Testament as the central nation of major future events. Especially in the Book of Daniel we are told of a "seventieth week," a seven year period that still belongs to Israel's future.

> "Seventy 'sevens' are decreed for your people and your holy city to finish transgression, to put an end to sin, to atone for wickedness, to bring in everlasting righteousness, to seal up vision and prophecy and to anoint the most holy.
> [25] "Know and understand this: From the issuing of the decree to restore and rebuild Jerusalem until the Anointed One, the ruler, comes, there will be seven 'sevens,' and sixty-two 'sevens.' It will be rebuilt with streets and a trench, but in times of trouble. [26] After the sixty-two 'sevens,' the Anointed One will be cut off and will have nothing. The people of the ruler who will come will destroy the city and the sanctuary. The end will come like a flood: War will continue until the end, and desolations have been decreed. [27] He will confirm a covenant with many for one 'seven.' In the middle of the 'seven' he will put an end to sacrifice and offering. And on a wing *of the temple* he will set up an abomination that causes desolation, until the end that is decreed is poured out on him." - Daniel 9:24-27

In his classic book *The Coming Prince*, Sir Robert Anderson, who was a high official in Scotland Yard, calculated the exact duration of the first sixty nine of these "weeks" of years. Sixty-nine times seven is four hundred eighty-three. These years were lunar years of exactly 360 days, as in all the biblical references. Anderson showed that from the decree by Artaxerxes Longimanus to rebuild Jerusalem until the day that Jesus offered himself as Messiah and was rejected by the officials of Jerusalem (the day of his "Triumphal Entry"), was exactly four hundred eighty-three years, that is 173,880 days (360 x 483).[81]

This leaves one seven year period of Israel's history to be fulfilled before the time of "everlasting righteousness." At the beginning of this last seven year period, the Beast (the "prince" or "ruler" who will come), will make a seven year covenant with Israel, but will break it in the middle by setting up an "abomination" in the newly rebuilt Temple in Jerusalem (Revelation 13). This time table agrees exactly with the timing of the Book of Revelation. This will be shown later. The Beast will have a statue of himself set up in the Temple (Daniel's "abomination that causes desolation"). This period will last exactly three and one half years, and will fulfill the second half of Daniel's seventieth "week."

This period of upheaval is also characterized in Jeremiah 30:7 as the "Time of Jacob's Trouble."

Perhaps the best way to set the scene for this section is to study the wonderful overview of Israel's history in Revelation chapter 12.

A Symbolic Overview of All of Israel's History

The book of Revelation, Chapter 12:1-17, presents a great vision of the nation of Israel portrayed as a woman. The vantage point is that of eternity.

In his sermon series on Revelation, Ray Stedman offers the following commentary on this passage.[82]

> There is no mystery to the dragon's identity, for John will disclose that to us in verse 9: "that ancient serpent called the devil, or Satan, who leads the whole world astray." In the opening verse of chapter 12, the devil is symbolized as a great red dragon with seven heads and ten horns and seven crowns upon his heads. But he is also "that ancient serpent" the very one who appeared in the Garden of Eden to the first woman, Eve, deceiving her and introducing sin into the human race. Dragons, of course, symbolize satanic worship in many cultures around the world. As John says in verse 9, the career of the devil has been devoted to deceiving the entire human race and leading human beings astray.
>
> The male child who is born to the woman is the next easiest to identify because verse 5 says that he is the one "who will rule all the nations with an iron scepter." This is one of four references in Revelation to Psalm 2. In verse 9 of that prophetic, messianic psalm we read, "You will rule them with an iron scepter."
>
> Though the book of Revelation is truly rooted in the entire Old Testament, it would be a valid analogy to compare Revelation to an oak tree that grows and expands out of the

acorn of Psalm 2. In this Psalm we read that the One enthroned in heaven says, "I have installed my King on Zion, my holy hill," and that this King will rule the nations with an iron scepter. Clearly this is a reference to the thousand-year reign of Jesus Christ during the Millennium, as is pictured for us in the book of Revelation. The reference to an iron scepter (in Psalm 2 and Revelation 12:5) always indicates a millennial scene. The iron scepter speaks of strict justice. The Millennium will be a time of worldwide blessing and prosperity when the curse of sin will be at least partly removed from the natural world. But sin will still manifest itself to some degree—hence the iron scepter of Christ. As we shall see in Revelation 20, righteousness will reign on earth during the Millennium, but it will have to be enforced.

After the Millennium the new heaven and the new earth will appear. At that time Christ will no longer reign with a scepter of iron. Nothing evil can enter into the new heaven and the new earth. When sin is finally extinguished forever, the defining characteristic of Christ will no longer be his iron reign but tender, shepherd-like love as he ministers personally and kindly to his redeemed people.

That brings us to the mystery of the woman. Why is she clothed with the sun? Why is the moon under her feet? Why are twelve stars arranged in a crown over her head? There are several theories as to whom or what this symbolic woman represents. Roman Catholic scholars have concluded that she is Mary, the mother of Jesus. Having understood that the child who will rule the nation with an iron scepter is Jesus, it certainly makes sense that the mother of that child would be Mary. The problem with this theory, however, is that there is no way you can fit Mary into verse 6 where we read that she "fled into the desert to a place prepared for her by God, where she will be taken care of for 1,260 days." That never happened to Mary, and never will. The woman in Revelation 12 does not represent a single individual but rather a community of people.

Some Bible scholars say she symbolizes the Church. Certainly there is some substantiation for this view, in that the Church is pictured at the close of Revelation as a woman, The Bride of Christ. But as with the previous theory this view has an insurmountable problem: It is impossible for the woman to represent the Church because she is depicted as giving birth to Jesus. The church did not produce Jesus; Jesus produced the Church! The church was "born" out of the wounded side of Jesus.

What, then, is the true identity of this woman of mystery'? Let us examine the clues one by one and see where they lead. The clues are significant: The woman is clothed with the sun, the moon is under her feet, and a crown of twelve stars is on her head. There is only one other place in Scripture where you find all these symbols clustered together in one place: Genesis 37, the story of Joseph the boy-dreamer. He dreamed one night that the sun, the moon, and eleven stars bowed down before him. The sun, moon, and stars represented his father, mother, and eleven brothers, respectively. Eventually this dream would come true—but not until after those eleven brothers sold Joseph into slavery, not until after Joseph overcame trials of false accusation and unjust imprisonment, not until after Joseph became second in command over all of Egypt.

The symbols of the sun, moon, and stars make it clear: The woman represents the people of Israel, all of whom are descendants of Joseph's father Jacob. Joseph himself would be the twelfth star. In Romans 9:5 Paul said of the people of Israel, "from them is traced the human ancestry of Christ." That is why Jesus told the Samaritan woman at the well, "Salvation is from the Jews." Even the salvation of the Gentiles comes by way of the Jews, because it is the Jewish race that produced Jesus Christ. So here again, in the symbolism of the woman clothed in the sun with the stars at her head and the moon at her feet, we have a picture of Israel coming again into prominence in the end times.

To understand the vivid images and symbols of Revelation 12 we should remember that we are viewing earthly scenes from heaven's point of view. In Revelation 4 we saw that John was caught up into heaven and shown all the things that follow in Revelation 4 through 19. When you look at earthly events from heaven's standpoint, time is never a factor. This vision does not present a sequence or an ordered chronology. It presents occurrences arranged according to their meaning and importance from a heavenly, eternal perspective. Events that may be widely separated in time may be clustered together in eternity's view. From heaven's perspective we are shown what happens, not when it happens. If we approach this chapter—and indeed all of Revelation—with this point of view, symbols that once seemed murky and obscure will pop into focus.

What we have in Revelation 12 is a kind of tableau, like a scene in a wax museum, of three-dimensional figures frozen in place at the climactic moment of a dramatic event. Satan, the great dragon, is crouched with its fangs bared and its eyes smoldering, watching Israel as she prepares to give birth to her long-promised Son. Israel is pregnant and crying out in her labor pains. The dragon's intention is clear: it seeks to devour Jesus as soon as He emerges from the womb of Israel and makes his appearance upon the earth. What is the historical reality represented by this grim and symbol-laden tableau?

This scene takes us back to the historical birth of Jesus, to the time of the Roman Empire and its subjugation of Israel. It takes us back to time of King Herod the Great and the demonic malice and enmity filled his heart when he learned of the birth of Jesus. It is easy to see events of that time in the symbolic tableau of Revelation 12:1-4. The dragon of world power in Jesus' day was the Roman Empire, which, in the Jewish land of Judea, was represented by the person of Rome's puppet king Herod the Great. Though in his early career Herod had been a comparatively progressive and benevolent despot, his notorious cruel streak and murderous paranoia were already in full evidence by the time Christ was born. In a fit of jealous rage Herod murdered his favorite among his eight wives, as well as several of her family members. He later murdered his own firstborn son Antipas. So his attempt to kill the newborn Son of God by slaughtering the infants of Bethlehem was true to form for this brutal and unfeeling man. Like a dragon, he lay in wait for the child to be born—then pounced, beast-like, spilling blood as if it were water. But God intervened, sparing the infant Jesus from the maw of the dragon. Warned by the appearance of an angel in a dream, Joseph and Mary took Jesus on a secret journey to Egypt beyond the reach of Herod.

This brings us to verse 5. It is at this point in the symbolic allegory of the dragon, the woman, and the child that we come upon a startling statement. John writes, "She gave birth to a son, a male child, who will rule all the nations with an iron scepter. And her child was snatched up to God and to his throne." Completely ignoring any chronology or .sequence of historical events, this symbolic scene takes a sudden jump from the birth of Jesus to his ascension some 30 years later, skipping over his life, ministry, death, and resurrection in a single breath. In this image, John is shown only the birth and ascension into heaven of Jesus. This symbol encompasses both the beginning and the ending of his earthly ministry.

But a problem of interpretation arises at this point. The problem is this: The clear implication of Revelation 12:5 is that Jesus was "snatched up to God" in order to deliver him from harm, from the reach of the dragon. Yet we know from reading the gospels and the book of Acts that Jesus' ascension was by no means an escape from harm. Rather it was a triumphal exit following his victory over death. The resurrected Lord was completely beyond the reach of his enemies, and there was no harm anyone could do to him. Why, then, does this tableau in Revelation 12 depict Jesus as having been "snatched up to God" as a child is snatched out of the path of an onrushing car?

Here is where the interpretation of Revelation becomes sensitive, because of the non-linear, non-chronological nature of the vision. The interpretation is this: There is an aspect of our Lord Jesus Christ that does find deliverance from danger, from the rage of the red dragon, by being snatched away into heaven. By this I mean the Body of Christ that is on the earth today—that is, the Church. Throughout the New Testament, the Lord and his church are regarded as one. When Saul (later the apostle Paul) was confronted by an appearance of Christ on the Damascus Road, Jesus said to him, "Saul, Saul, why are you persecuting me?" Saul had never even met Jesus—but he was persecuting the Church. When Jesus spoke to Saul of his church he identified completely with that church. If Saul was persecuting the Lord's church, Saul was persecuting him, because they were one. Paul later wrote to the Corinthians, "Now you are the body of Christ, and each one of you is a part of it." The church, he said, is a body, and "the body is a unit, though it is made up of many parts; and though all its parts are many, they form one body. So it is with Christ." The church and the Lord together are the body of Christ. So when we come to Revelation 12 and see that the child, representing Christ, was "snatched up to God and to his throne," it becomes clear that this is a reference to the removal of the Church from the world and from the threatening presence of the dragon."

It should be remembered that Christ himself ascended into the heavens (Acts 1:9-11). This passage might only have that ascension in view. However if, as Stedman suggests, this is a reference to the rapture of the Church, it is still an event that will take place before the Tribulation, when Israel will be driven into the wilderness. Thus, even if the Church is in view, it is not a violation of the concept that the Church is never mentioned during the Tribulation period.

Ray Stedman continues: [83]

Verse 6 carries us on into the Tribulation period. In leaping immediately from the birth of Christ to the removal of the Church and the beginning of the Tribulation, these verses in Revelation 12 completely eclipse all the centuries of the Church Age in which we now live. In verse 6, the woman (representing the people of Israel) flees into the desert to a place prepared for her by God. There she is taken care of for a period of 1,260 days—a significant time period, as can be seen in the previous chapter. In Revelation 11, the two witnesses will prophesy for a period of 1,260 days—the last 3 1/2 years of the seven-year Tribulation period. So it would be reasonable and consistent to conclude that the desert exile of the believing Jewish people (represented by the woman) would also take place during the same 3 1/2-year period in which the two witnesses prophesy against the Beast.

Notice, too, that a subtle shift has taken place in the symbolism represented by the woman. In verses 1 through 4 the woman represented the Jewish nation that was to bring forth Jesus, the Son of God. In verse 5 the child is born and is snatched up to God's throne. In verse 6 the woman flees into the desert to escape the persecution of the dictator and the horrors of the Tribulation. The fleeing woman, then, represents not the Jewish people as a whole—for many Jews will be deceived by the Beast. The believing remnant of the Jews will refuse to submit to the rule of the Beast.

This woman, you recall, represents not all Jews of the last days but only the believing remnant. Those Jews who have not believed are suffering under the judgments that are foretold in the Old Testament prophecies. This is "the time of Jacob's trouble," when apostate Jews are cruelly eliminated by the dragon and the faithful remnant is pursued and persecuted. The remnant escapes to the desert, and the swiftness of their flight from danger is symbolized by the eagle's wings.

Many Bible scholars believe the faithful Jews of the last days will flee to the city of Petra, south of the Dead Sea—a strangely beautiful city hewn out of the rock of the earth that is presently an attraction for tourists and archaeologists in the Holy Land. Perhaps this is true, but no one can say with certainty.

What is important in these verses is that God will care for this believing remnant in a supernatural way. They will be borne out of danger on the metaphorical wings of an eagle. It is no coincidence that this is the very same metaphor God used when the nation of Israel was led out of Egypt by Moses. "You yourselves have seen what I did to Egypt," God said to Israel through his servant Moses, "and how I carried you on eagles' wings and brought you to myself" (Exodus 19:4). This is a picture of God's loving protection and care for the people who are his faithful remnant in that day.

The symbolism of the river of water that the serpent spews in an effort to overtake the woman is likely an image of a vast host of soldiers sent by the Beast to overtake and destroy the faithful of Israel in the last days. But God will protect his faithful remnant, probably by means of a natural cataclysm—perhaps an earthquake—that causes the destruction of the Beast's armies and the frustration of his plans.

The dictator will be diverted from attacking the faithful Jews of Israel (symbolized by the woman), and will instead turn his attention to "the rest of her offspring" and make war against them. Who is John describing in this phrase? Most likely "the rest of her offspring" refers to "Christ's commandos," the 144,000 Jews we first met in Revelation 7 and will meet again in Revelation 14. They are the special band of believing Jews who move out into the four corners of the world, preaching the gospel of the kingdom to all the nations. The devil gives his final attention to destroying this group because of their powerful and effective witness to the world. The rage of the devil is increasing as he grows more and more desperate, knowing that his time is short. Like any wild and dangerous beast, the devil becomes more deadly and ferocious as he is backed into a corner.

In this chapter we have seen that there will be many true believers in Jesus Christ during the Tribulation Period, some being former unbelievers from a Christian background who suddenly realize that the rapture has really happened and they have been left behind; and some from the Jewish heritage who likewise understand that the Old Testament prophecies were true, and that Yeshua (Jesus) is the Messiah.

All of these new believers will face persecution, and most will probably be martyrs. In the next chapter we continue our study of prophecy by considering the events of the first half of the Tribulation.

Chapter 9
The First Half of the Tribulation

The fourth Chapter of the Book of Revelation begins with two often-quoted Greek words:

Meta tauta

These words mean "after these things." The authors join company with a good number of conservative Bible scholars who see these words as marking a major division in the last book of the Bible. John was told to "Write, therefore, what you have seen, what is now and what will take place later." (Revelation 1:19).

Chapters 1 through 3 of Revelation cover the first two subjects. "What you have seen," referred to the visions of chapter one. "What is now" points to the contents of Chapters 2 and 3, which trace the progress of the Church in its different forms and stages of history. Beginning with Chapter 4, verse one, the scene shifts to Heaven and to events that are yet to come. These things are in the future for John in the First Century and for us as well in our day.

John sees in a vision a great worship scene of elders and angels around the throne of God the Father. They are engaged in worship and adoration of the Father and they sing a hymn of praise to the One who has created and who sustains the universe. The One seated on the throne holds a mysterious scroll, written on both sides—not one side as would be usual—and sealed with seven wax seals, instead of the usual one.

The seven-sealed scroll is a document of great importance and a search is made for a person worthy to receive this scroll from the Father's hand—for evidently the contents of the scroll contain delegated authority for the unfolding of the final chapters of this age. Some have called the scroll, "the title deed to the earth."

The only one found worthy to open the scroll is Christ Jesus, who is described here in symbols that combine the Old Testament figure of the Lion out of the Tribe of Judah (Genesis 49:8) and the New Testament figure of the submissive lamb who has been slain voluntarily for the sins of the world. (John 1:29). The Messiah, son of God, takes the scroll from his Father's hand.

Immediately the worship shifts to a new song of praise centered on Jesus. He is the one who has ransomed men "from every tribe and tongue and nation," and the only one worthy to receive such important delegated authority.

The unfolding of the fate of the earth is now totally in the hands of Jesus who proceeds to open the seven-sealed scroll, one seal at a time. The message of the scroll pertains to judgment about to fall upon an evil, unbelieving world, from which the true church has already been removed.

The First Four Seals

There are seven seals in all, describing major aspects and events of the Tribulation period. The first four are depicted as riders on four horses of different colors. Horses in the Bible often depict angelic activity (this image occurs in Zechariah for instance). Swift angelic messengers in the invisible spiritual realm rapidly carry out and bring into effect a series of world-wide changes in society on earth. The "Four Horsemen of the Apocalypse" have been universal portents of coming evil in art and literature down through all of history.

The First Seal - The Man of Sin revealed

> I watched as the Lamb opened the first of the seven seals. Then I heard one of the four living creatures say in a voice like thunder, "Come!" ²I looked, and there before me was a white horse! Its rider held a bow, and he was given a crown, and he rode out as a conqueror bent on conquest. - Revelation 6:1-2

The first significant event of the future Tribulation will be the emergence of a false man of peace, symbolized here as the rider on a white horse. In the Bible, there is another rider on a white horse at the opposite end of the Tribulation. In the second case, Revelation 19:11-21, Jesus Christ is clearly the conquering hero on the white horse. But in this first instance, a human who is energized by Satan begins his campaign of world conquest. He does not appear as a horrible or evil monster, but as a benevolent dictator. He is seen as a messiah, who has come to solve the world's great problems.

It is possible that his authority to control the world will come into effect silently without open war. Ray Stedman writes,

> He is given a bow, but no mention is made of arrows. This appears to be a bloodless conquest he launches. When you ask, "What is this describing?" I think it is clear that it suggests some kind of overpowering of the minds and wills of men, without physical

destruction. How is that done? The answer is: by some form of deceit, by lying that misleads and deceives men and thus overcomes them without the shedding of blood. It is noteworthy that in Matthew 24, the first word Jesus speaks to his disciples is, "Watch out that no one deceives you." You will find references to the possibility of deception throughout that chapter.

We are bemused by delusions today. We are hardly aware of how much we are being deceived all the time. Turn on the television and fraudulent ideas, along with a mixture of truth, are immediately poured into your brain. Pick up a magazine or read a newspaper and you will find they make false claims that certain acquisitions will produce great blessing and liberty for you. But trying them will soon tell you that it is a lie. They do not work. We are constantly offered much of promise but which are totally unable to deliver....What this rider on the white horse tells us, however, is that the worst is yet to come. We are living amidst great deceit, it is true, but it is not as bad as it is going to be. There is coming an even greater lie.[84]

Many people speculate about the identity of the Beast. However, we can not know who he is at this time. 2 Thessalonians 2:1-10 tells us that "the man of lawlessness" will not be revealed until the one who holds evil back is "taken out of the way." This is an unmistakable reference to the Holy Spirit. One of the main purposes of the indwelling work of the Holy Spirit is to convict the world of sin and guilt (John 16:5-11). He does that by His power in the lives of Christians who are committed to Christ and "filled with the Spirit" (Ephesians 5:18). At this time Spirit-filled Christians occupy key positions as teachers, government employees, and influential people in the workplace and the marketplace. When the rapture has taken place and Christians are suddenly removed, the Holy Spirit will still be in the world, but as new converts accept Christ during the Tribulation period they will be persecuted, driven underground, or even killed for their faith. Thus they will not have public testimonies and the ability to restrain evil around them.

The Second Seal - War

> When the Lamb opened the second seal, I heard the second living creature say, "Come!" [4]Then another horse came out, a fiery red one. Its rider was given power to take peace from the earth and to make men slay each other. To him was given a large sword. - Revelation 6:3-4

The second symbolic rider comes on a red horse. This speaks of the ravages of a great world-wide war. It is not likely that this war is started by the rider on the white horse, since, as the previous verses indicate, he is seen as a messianic hero.

Before we consider what this particular war might be, let us recall that Jesus told us that the period leading up to the Tribulation would be characterized by "wars and rumors of wars" (Matthew 24:6; Mark 13:7).

People of all ages have been subjected to the horrors of war, but in our generation we have had an almost constant pre-occupation with war. There are usually several wars going on at various places in the world at the same time. There have been as many as forty at one time in our lifetime.

World War I was called "The War to end all war." It did not end war. It only taught us more about how to fight in a more deadly way, using the air to deliver death from the sky.

World War II brought the world to the brink of nuclear destruction, introducing the first use of the atomic bomb. The Korean War and The Vietnam War were very disheartening because of the great loss of life without gaining a definite victory. The Vietnam War was especially frustrating to Americans causing great internal strife at home as well as the loss of lives abroad.

The Persian Gulf War brought us the ability to "be there" as an audience in the thick of the battle by way of television—even as bombs were dropped. This war also introduced us to "smart weapons" that could find their way to the exact buildings great distances away for which they were programmed.

The terrorist attacks of September 11, 2001 against New York's Twin Towers and Washington D.C.'s, Pentagon gave cause for wars against Al-Qaeda in Afghanistan and Saddam Hussein's reckless dictatorship in Iraq.

It is interesting that Jesus not only foretold the abundance of wars, but also that there would be "rumors" of war. Some of our generations' variations on war could qualify as "rumors." The intense "Cold War" lasted from the end of World War II until the demise of the Soviet Union on December 25, 1991. It was a serious battle of words and philosophies, mainly between the United States and Russia over our mutual capabilities to destroy the world with nuclear weapons. By the 1960's the U.S. and Russia both had developed Hydrogen bombs with 1000 times the destructive power of the ones used to end World War II.[85] At the height of nuclear stockpiling, in 1986, there were more than 65,000 nuclear weapons, which was enough to destroy the world many times over.[86] Before the dissolution of the Soviet Union our defense policy was called MAD (Mutual Assured Destruction), meaning that we did not have anything that could actually destroy incoming missiles with atomic warheads, but were counting on the fact that no one would attack us since they would be destroyed in retaliation.

Another "rumor" aspect to war is the endless tension of the "War on Terrorism." It is fed by the previously unimagined power of the Internet to spread fear and misinformation. The Middle East is constantly upset by frequent acts of terrorism, but nearly every nation is affected by its reach as well.

Cyberwar could also be called a rumor of war. It is the threat that professional hackers could break into vital control systems of an enemy's superstructure to disrupt their communications, their transportation, their electrical or water supplies, their financial systems or other necessary functions. Computer "viruses," "worms," and other threats have grown along with the advance of computing power. In 2010 a shocking break-through in this technology came to light. The so-called "Stuxnet malware" infiltrated industrial computer systems worldwide. It was a search-and-destroy weapon meant to hit a single target, presumed to be Iran's nuclear facilities. It has the unprecedented ability to cause the control computers in these targets to allow malfunctions of equipment that could cause it to self-destruct.

War has been more common down through history than we might at first suppose. Bruce Menzies in his online book, "Studies in Eschatology," says,

> "The Norwegian Academy of Sciences has determined
> that since 3600 BC there have been 14,531 wars
> and only 292 years of peace.
> This is approximately 2.6 wars per year,
> and one year of 'peace' out of every two decades,
> or a little over 36 hours of peace per month,
> or about a minute of peace every four hours."[87]

When the seals are opened God will release, step by step, the last restraints holding back the evil that already exists in men's hearts. Even now in our violent age bad men, as well as good, enjoy "common grace" from God—and a great deal of protection every day of our lives, all from God's benevolent hand. We ought to be thankful every day for this restraining hand of God that allows us to live in comfort most of the time. But the end time is a season in which evil is allowed to run its full course, unchecked and unimpeded—except for God's final intervention. One possibility for this war was given by Ray Stedman in his message called "Four Terrible Horsemen:"

This rider is easy to recognize. It is war, of course, but not war between great armies—at least not at first. The word for "slay" is really the word "slaughter." It is a reference to civil war or civil anarchy where mobs of people group together to attack and destroy other peoples whom they do not like... We have had further examples of it in El Salvador, in Nicaragua, and in the gang wars raging in the streets of Los Angeles, Miami, New York City, and other places. It is a murderous slaying of others by people unrestrained by any control.[88]

Another possibility is that this is the war of Ezekiel 38 and 39 that results in fiery destruction of the aggressors from the north when they try to conquer Israel. This could very possibly escalate to nuclear warfare, which involves more than one of the present-day nuclear powers. The emerging world dictator could take credit for the destruction of Israel's invaders, or at least take advantage of the situation, to bring about the seven-year peace treaty between himself and Israel that was prophesied by Daniel. If this is the case, this war would take place at the very beginning of the seven years of the Tribulation.

- The Aggressors of the War of Gog and Magog - Ezekiel 38:1-4

According to Ezekiel, an alliance of enemies will attack Israel in the End Times. The leader will be Gog of the land of Magog, who is the chief prince of Meshech and Tubal. He is assisted by Persia, Cush, Put, Gomer, Beth Togarmah, and other nations. Most of these names are listed in the genealogies of Genesis 10. Gog is not listed in Genesis 10, but he is evidently the head of the land of Magog, who is mentioned as a son of Japheth, one of Noah's sons. It is known that Japheth traveled north from Mt. Ararat after the flood.

Hesoid, a Greek writer of the 7th century BC, and contemporary of Ezekiel, identified Magog with the Scythians and southern Russia. Flavius Josephus, a 1st century Jewish historian said that Magogians were called "Scythians" by the Greeks. Philo, a 1st century Greek identified Magog with southern Russia.[89]

Commentators from the turn of this century and before have generally identified Gog and Magog with Russia even though, at the time, they could not explain why Russia would turn against God's people. They conjectured that perhaps the time would come when there would be animosity between Russia and Israel.

Rosh ("head", "chief") sounds like Russia. Meshech sounds like Moscow or Mushkovi, the old name for Russia. Tubal sounds like Tobolsk.

- The Target: Israel - Ezekiel 38:2-12

This is the only time in history that this could be said of Israel, that they were brought back from many nations. It is true that they were brought back from Babylon and Persia in the Old Testament, but it is only since the Zionist movement, which began in the late 1800's, that Jewish people have returned from nations all over the world. They had been scattered abroad even in New Testament times. On the Day of Pentecost, for example, the various languages spoken by the Apostles, when the Holy Spirit came upon them, represented the many lands where they had settled. But they had not returned to stay. This really never happened until the amazing events that led to the rebirth of Israel in 1948. What thoughts would come into Russia's mind to make them want to attack Israel? A consideration of Russia's instability and the plans of some of their leaders for expansion throughout the Mediterranean area is given below. Israel has always been a key land bridge between

Russia's allies and is presently an enemy of some of those allies. Any number of scenarios in the always-volatile Middle East politics could lead to a Russian attack in the future.

- Russia's Allies - Ezekiel 38:5-6

Persia is now known as Iran, and there is an amazingly close relationship now between Russia and Iran. Cush is Ethiopia, Put is Libya, Gomer and Beth Togarmah may well be Turkey and/or other Islamic nations like those once part of the Soviet Union.

It is interesting that Mizraim, the forefather of Egypt is apparently missing from this lineup. This, of course, fits the current world scene, with Egypt being the first Arab nation to make peace with Israel.

- Israel's Allies - Ezekiel 38:13

Israel's allies appear to be few and feeble. Some of Saudi Arabia was populated by Sheba and Dedan. The merchants of Tarshish could be England and English colonies. In that case, The United States could even be included since we were once an English colony. These allies ask why Russia and its allies are coming, but do not appear to deter them.

- The Outcome - Ezekiel 38:22

The quick end of this future war will be with God's judgment. It could be God's personal power, raining literal fire and brimstone, as in the days of Sodom, or it could be God using nation against nation, as he often did in the Old Testament, to precipitate a nuclear exchange.

> And with pestilence and with blood I shall enter into judgment with him; and I shall rain on him, and on his troops, and on the many peoples who are with him, a torrential rain, with hailstones, fire, and brimstone. - Ezekiel 38:22

The next chapter of Ezekiel continues to give details of this great conflict. Again, it is a scene of utter destruction.

> "And I shall strike your bow from your left hand, and dash down your arrows from your right hand. 4 "You shall fall on the mountains of Israel, you and all your troops, and the peoples who are with you; I shall give you as food to every kind of predatory bird and beast of the field. 5 "You will fall on the open field; for it is I who have spoken," declares the Lord GOD. 6 "And I shall send fire upon Magog and those who inhabit the coastlands in safety; and they will know that I am the LORD." - Ezekiel 39:3-6

The Third Seal - Famine

When the Lamb opened the third seal, I heard the third living creature say, "Come!" I looked, and there before me was a black horse! Its rider was holding a pair of scales in his hand. ⁶Then I heard what sounded like a voice among the four living creatures, saying, "A quart of wheat for a day's wages, and three quarts of barley for a day's wages, and do not damage the oil and the wine!"- Revelation 6:5-6

This third seal and third rider appears on a black horse that symbolizes terrible famine, probably as a result of the previous world-wide warfare. Famine results from war directly when crops are destroyed by the warfare, and indirectly when the process of farming and distribution of food is disrupted by blockades, and when there is a diversion of manpower and resources for the war effort.

The result is an extensive and ruinous famine. The price of food will be prohibitive. The economic impact of this famine will undoubtedly prepare the people of the world to be willing to have a benevolent dictator.

Matthew 24:7, Mark 13:8 and Luke 21:11 all mention famines and plagues (pestilence) as factors that would characterize the End Times.

Famine is usually the result of changes in weather patterns or of war. Both of these are characteristic of our times. For most of our generation there have been great numbers of deaths, especially of the young because of famine. At times this problem reaches staggering proportions: 40,000 babies starve to death every day.

Ray Stedman suggests another type of shortage: the shortage of all necessities that comes as a result of runaway inflation.

Most scholars take this to be a reference to widespread famine on the earth. They say that the scales symbolize food being weighed out carefully. It is in such short supply that it must be rationed. Even then no one can get very much because it takes a day's wages to earn a single quart of wheat or, because it is cheaper, three quarts of barley. This would only be enough food for one person for a day. You would work all day long and all you would be able to earn at best would be enough for your own physical needs. There would be nothing for your family or for anyone else. But the luxuries, the oil and the wine, are left untouched.

But perhaps this is not referring to famine because in the next seal, as we will see, famine is specifically mentioned as part of that judgment. What else causes terrible shortages and creates high prices so that people cannot buy adequate amounts of food? It is inflation: economics out of control. That is what runaway inflation does. It makes money worthless. That in turn becomes an excuse for the rigid controls over buying and selling which we find in chapter 13 when, under the reign of the Beast, the whole world is subjected to enormously restrictive controls so that "no one can buy or sell without the mark of the beast."[90]

The Fourth Seal - Plagues and Death

When the Lamb opened the fourth seal, I heard the voice of the fourth living creature say, "Come!" [8]I looked, and there before me was a pale horse! Its rider was named Death, and Hades was following close behind him. They were given power over a fourth of the earth to kill by sword, famine and plague, and by the wild beasts of the earth. - Revelation 6:7-8

The color of the fourth horse is translated many ways. Some Bible versions translate it as "pale," others as "ashen," or "pale green." The Greek word is *chloros*, "greenish." It is the root of the well known "chlorophyll", the tiny green chemical converters in the leaves of most plants. Chlorine gas was deadly in warfare during the First World War.

Chloros also suggests deadly chlorine gas, which is pale green in color and quickly fatal to all who breathe it. The intended picture here is a sickly pale green that symbolizes death as a result of the former terrors of war and famine and the added threats of plague and wild beasts. All of this is the result of a world becoming progressively damaged, corrupted and neglected.

Once again we consider Stedman's commentary on this section:

This rider is named "Death"; and floating along behind, was a figure that is identified as "Hades," or Hell. Death takes the body and Hades takes the soul. As someone has put it, "Death rides the horse, but Hades follows with the hearse." There are four forms of death that are related to this attack. First, the sword, which here is not war but murder; individual assault upon one another. It is people taking the law into their own hands and murdering other people without regard to justice or law.[91]

Many people are fearful about the senseless violent crime of our days. Gang warfare, riots, carjacking, follow-home robberies, ATM muggings, and drive-by shootings have become commonplace. Just imagine the wanton looting and killing that could be ahead in a world already decimated by the events of the first three seals!

There have always been plagues, but they do seem to be increasing in our times. Cancer is an ever-growing threat. AIDS is a new disease of the most sobering proportions. So far there is no cure for this plague. Alzheimer's is a new, incurable ailment of the elderly. We are constantly hearing of serious outbreaks of such diseases as the Ebola Virus that can destroy whole towns. There have been recent outbreaks of a rare flesh-eating Strep disease that disfigures or even kills its victims in a matter of hours. Resistant strains of "conquered diseases," such as tuberculosis are now reappearing. Some people are even wondering if some of these problems are the result of genetic engineering. Recent information about the rampant production of chemical and biological weapons of mass destruction also helps us picture the disastrous effects of these plagues.

One other possibility for the meaning of the green horse has been suggested by some Bible teachers in the light of the growing threat by Islamic radical terrorists. They wonder if the green could come from the well-known fact that Islamic countries all use green in their flags and seem to prefer that color. Time will tell if there is any connection here.

A Seven Year Treaty with Israel

The seven year period following the *parousia* (the rapture) and preceding the *epiphaneia* (the Second Coming in power and glory), is normally divided into two halves. The first three and a half years are characterized by some degree of apparent world peace as the false Messiah (Revelation 13:11-18, 2 Thessalonians 2:1-10, Matthew 24:15) in Israel negotiates a favorable Middle Eastern peace treaty. That peace treaty, described by Isaiah as Israel's "covenant with death," will fail, and terrible war will break out in Israel. The second half of the Tribulation Period is usually called "The Great Tribulation" (Matthew 24:21) or "the Day of the Lord." Jeremiah calls it "the time of Jacob's trouble" (Jeremiah 30-31, Daniel 12:1).

Trust in a Counterfeit Messiah

The Book of Daniel, chapter 9, tells of a future seven year period when "the ruler who will come" will confirm a covenant, presumably with Israel.

> After the sixty-two 'sevens,' the Anointed One will be cut off and will have nothing. The people of the ruler who will come will destroy the city and the sanctuary. The end will come like a flood: War will continue until the end, and desolations have been decreed. [27] He will confirm a covenant with many for one 'seven.' In the middle of the 'seven' he will put an end to sacrifice and offering. And on a wing of the temple he will set up an abomination that causes desolation, until the end that is decreed is poured out on him. - Daniel 9:26-27

This "ruler who will come" is the Man of Sin. As mentioned above, he will probably use the wars of the Second Seal as the occasion for instituting this treaty.

Jesus may have been alluding to this future event when He said, "I have come in my Father's name, and you do not accept me; but if someone else comes in his own name, you will accept him" (John 5:43).

The 144,000 Called

Revelation Chapter Seven describes the calling out of 144,000 select Jewish evangelists from the nation Israel at the beginning of the Tribulation period, probably soon after the rapture of the Church. As you can see from Revelation 7:3-8, the 144,000 are specifically God's chosen people, 12,000 from each of the twelve tribes *of Israel*.

Sealed - for what?

Immediately after the verses about the calling of the 144,000, this information is added. It depicts the result of the sealing of these people: the evangelization of multitudes of people.

> After this I looked and there before me was a great multitude that no one could count, from every nation, tribe, people and language, standing before the throne and in front of the Lamb. They were wearing white robes and were holding palm branches in their hands. [10]And they cried out in a loud voice:
> "Salvation belongs to our God,
> who sits on the throne,
> and to the Lamb." - Revelation 7:9-10

The 144,000 will vigorously evangelize Israel, completing the task begun by the disciples of Jesus, within Israel but also extending their field to all the nations. The result of their bold and fearless evangelism program will be hundreds of thousands of converts to Jesus Christ.

The following chapters describe various aspects of the second half of the seven year Tribulation. This second half is known as The Great Tribulation (Matthew 24:21). The seven-year treaty will be broken by the Beast when he has an image of himself set up in the newly rebuilt Temple in Jerusalem (Daniel 9:27; Matthew 24:15; Revelation 13:11-18). Since the Temple does not exist in Israel yet, we will now consider the possibility that it could be built quickly, perhaps during the first 3 ½ years of the seven-year covenant.

Chapter 10
The Rebuilt Temple

The major biblical prophecies relevant to the Tribulation indicate that there will be a Temple in Jerusalem, at least by the middle of the seven year covenant or treaty between the false peace-maker and Israel. In this chapter we will discuss the history of the Temple and consider what would be necessary to rebuild the structure in the near future.

Background: Jerusalem

When the sons of Noah spread out, Shem, the father of all the Semitic people, may well have gone to the area we now call Jerusalem. The earliest mention of the area was when Abraham was returning from a battle with Sodom (Genesis chapter 14). He met Melchizedek, King of Salem. Salem is the oldest name for the city. The root word means "peace." Melchizedek means "king of righteousness." So this is probably a title rather than a proper name. Melchizedek is important also because the dual offices of King and Priest of El Elyon ("God Most High") were resident in this one man.

The priesthood that Jesus Christ would later grant to his Church is modeled after Melchizedek as the book of Hebrews tells us. During Israel's history the office of king and priest were always separate. But Zechariah the prophet looked forward to a future day when these offices will be combined in Messiah (Zechariah 6).

It may be demonstrated from the life-spans and genealogies in Genesis that Shem should still have been living at that time. Some scholars believe that Melchizedek was actually Shem. All of Noah's sons and their wives were believers in the one true God (or they would not have been saved on the Ark). In one or two generations most of their offspring had already "forgotten" about God and gone their own way, following a rebellion led by Nimrod against the rule of God (Genesis 10:8-12).

Remaining a godly, wise follower of Yahweh, Shem lived to the age of 600 years and surely would have been the most revered of the ancient fathers at that time.

Jewish legends claim that God stood on the Foundation Stone of what later would be the Holy of Holies of Jerusalem's Temple. Eden, these rabbis remind us, was to the East, so Adam was probably formed of the clay of the ground in what is now the land of Israel. In any case, Jerusalem was already a center for the worship of the Lord under the leadership of Melchizedek.

Jerusalem seems to have been chosen by God long before the Jewish people came into existence. It is mentioned by name nearly 800 times in the Bible! The city is also called "Zion" ("fortification") or Mt. Zion, one of the hills of the city. In the Psalms God is said to dwell (present tense) in that city. A number of Psalms highlight the central importance of the "City of Peace" in God's eternal plans for mankind.

> Those who trust in the LORD are like Mount Zion,
>   which cannot be shaken but endures forever.
> As the mountains surround Jerusalem,
>   so the LORD surrounds his people
>   both now and forevermore. - Psalm 125:1-2

The city, also called Jebus (Judges 19:10; 1Chronicles 11:4), had become a pagan city by the time of the occupation of the land by the Hebrews when they returned from Egypt.

There is reason to suspect that source documents existed from before the Flood of Noah—perhaps "Adam's Diary" and the records of his sons in the line of Seth down to Noah. It is possible that these records were preserved on the Ark by Noah and handed down to Noah's son Shem for safekeeping. Perhaps Shem left these ancient documents in the care of Melchizedek? We simply do not know, but the speculation is interesting, because when we first meet Abram in Genesis he is 70 years old and living in Ur of the Chaldees. His father and his family had evidently lapsed into the idolatry of the region and God had to call him back so that he was restored into the godly line of Shem, the promised line of descent, which would lead to Messiah.

Did Melchizedek transmit to Abraham ancient written documents or carefully preserved oral legends that eventually were handed by Abraham's descendants on down to Moses? Did Moses write the Pentateuch with the help of some source documents of which we are now unaware? No one knows. We will have to ask Moses when we meet him!

The Tabernacle

The Tabernacle was the precursor of the Temple. Detailed information about the Tabernacle is found in Exodus chapters 25 through 27.

Instruction for the Tabernacle was given to Moses at the same time as the giving of the Ten Commandments. It was a portable place of worship that would serve as the point where God met with his people. It was small but very lavish, with gold and silver work, and elaborate hangings and curtains, some of which were woven with beautiful patterns. It was completely portable, so that it could be broken down on short notice and moved with the nation as they followed the Lord.

All of the articles of the Tabernacle are types or pre-figures of Christ.

The Outer Court

The Brazen Altar is a picture of Christ's sacrifice as the Lamb of God who takes away the sins of the world.

The Laver is symbolic of confession and regular spiritual cleansing.

The Holy Place

The Golden Lampstand pictures Jesus as the Light of the World.

The Table of Showbread is symbolic of Jesus as the Bread of Life.

The Altar of Incense (drawing attention to the importance of prayer), reminds us that Jesus is our intercessor and Great High Priest.

The Holy of Holies

The Ark of the Covenant is a type of Jesus as the presence of God with us.

Solomon's Temple

This first temple was built in the 10th century BC, right after Solomon became king. David had wanted to build it, but was not allowed by God because of the bloodshed in his past. Nevertheless, he collected all the materials for the Temple, so that, as soon as his son Solomon became king, he could construct it. It was erected on the property bought by David from Araunah (2 Samuel 24). The site had been a threshing floor, a place where grain was winnowed by tossing it up into the air. The wind would carry the chaff away while the heavier grain would fall back down. Eventually there would be a pile of grain in the center and a large section of chaff further away. The chaff could be raked up and burned, and the grain could be put into baskets. This threshing floor was probably on a higher part of Mount Moriah where the winds were strongest. Here, a thousand years earlier, Abraham had demonstrated his faith by being willing to offer Isaac, though he was not required to carry it out (Genesis 22). This is a beautiful preview of the willingness of our Heavenly Father to sacrifice his own son, Jesus, for the sins of the world. An especially remarkable fact is the connection between Mount Moriah (the Temple Mount) with the hill of Calvary where Jesus was crucified. When Solomon built the Temple, stones were quarried from the northern and western slope of the same mountain, and from underneath the mountain. Stones quarried to build the temple cut a large gorge, leaving the westernmost portion of the mountain standing alone. In Jesus' day this portion was called Golgotha, "the place of the skull"! Even today if you visit Jerusalem, the visitor can see the high steep cliff where the bedrock of the mountain was cut away. There is a man-made valley between that cliff and Golgotha, about two blocks away. Damascus Street, the old Damascus Road, passes through this cut just outside the Western Wall of the Old City.

Solomon's Temple was destroyed by the Babylonians in 586 BC.

The Second Temple

This modest structure was built by Zerubbabel with encouragement of the prophets Haggai and Zechariah in the 6th century BC. The books of Ezra and Nehemiah recount the drama of the return of a Jewish remnant from Persia and the rebuilding of the Temple as well as the city of Jerusalem. These are great stories of courage and dedication, but the Temple was smaller and much less beautiful than the original. It is said that some who remembered the original temple wept when they saw it (Ezra 3:12). This Second Temple was desecrated by Antiochus IV (Epiphanes), the Seleucid ruler who had a pig slaughtered on the altar, and set up an image of a pagan god in the Holy of Holies. This is the event that triggered the rise of the Hasmonean family of the Maccabees. They eventually took Jerusalem and the Temple back and ruled there independently for a few years. The Jewish celebration of Hanukkah comes from this time of restoration and renewal in their national history.

"Herod's Temple"

The reconstruction of the Second Temple was begun by Herod the Great about 20 BC. It was an enhancement of Zerubbabel's Temple. Herod was an ungodly foreigner, an Edomite (Idumean), who had been given the kingship by the Romans. He was the greatest builder in the world during that period of time. Herod built seven palaces and forts, and the work on the Temple was truly magnificent. The stones (ashlars) used were huge, and every one had a border (embossing) carved around it. The work on the temple and courts continued long after his death until it was finished in AD 63. It was about twice the size of the Second Temple. Some call it the Third Temple, but Jews do not think of it as other than their Second Temple. It had already been 46 years in the rebuilding process when Jesus ministered there (John 2:19). Neither Herod nor most of the Jewish leaders were at all godly during this period. The Temple was built for show and for political reasons, but a faithful remnant of priests and Jews worshiped Yahweh there nevertheless, in accordance with the teachings of the Torah.

The Gospels tell us of a few godly priests and citizens at the Temple during the child-hood of Jesus and give us brief glimpses of temple life in that day. The account of Jesus' circumcision is one of these stories (Luke 2:21-38).

Every year Jesus' parents went to Jerusalem for the Feast of the Passover. When he was twelve years old, they went up to the Feast, according to the custom. After the Feast was over, while his parents were returning home, the boy Jesus stayed behind in Jerusalem, but they were unaware of it. Thinking he was in their company, they traveled on for a day.

Then they began looking for him among their relatives and friends. When they did not find him, they went back to Jerusalem to look for him. They found him talking with the teachers in the Temple (Luke 2:43-51).

Herod's Temple evidently did not have God's blessing. Expressing his grave displeasure at the desecrating of the Temple, Jesus cast out the money changers on two occasions—at the beginning of his ministry and again at the start of his final week in the city before his death. On that second occasion Mark tells us he would not allow anything to be carried in or out of the Temple. Thus he also stopped the continual temple sacrifices, in effect declaring them null and void. Within a few days, at Passover, the true Lamb of God would die—one death for all, offering himself as the foreordained perfect sacrifice for the sins of the world. All the temple sacrifices were but shadows. Indeed, when Jesus died, the veil of the Temple was torn from the top to the bottom (Matthew 27:51), thus signifying that Jesus had made a way for all men to come into the holiest place of intimate presence with God because of his perfect sacrifice (Hebrews 9).

Destruction of the Temple

The destruction of the Temple was prophesied by Jesus.

Some of his disciples were remarking about how the temple was adorned with beautiful stones and with gifts dedicated to God. But Jesus said, 6"As for what you see here, the time will come when not one stone will be left on another; every one of them will be thrown down." - Luke 21:5-6

Herod's Temple was destroyed in AD 70. It was torn down by four Roman legions under the command of Titus. The Jewish people have not been able to practice animal sacrifices since that time, although the Muslims do so every year in Mecca! The Temple was burned, so the gold melted and ran into the cracks in the stones. That is why the destruction was so great. The conquerors literally removed every possible stone in order to find all the gold.

From that time until the present, the Temple Mount and all of Jerusalem has been under the control of various people. The Romans built a temple to a pagan god there. Later a Christian church was built. When the Muslims took control they built a mosque and a shrine.

The Temple Mount Today

The 35 acre site is under the control of The Supreme Muslim Council—the Waqf (religious endowment). Even though Israel took all of Jerusalem in 1967, this concession was made by then Israeli Minister of Defense Moshe Dyan to keep peace.

Jews are not allowed on the Temple Mount by the laws of their own Rabbinical Council because of concern that visitors might tread on the Ark of the Covenant if it is buried somewhere on the grounds. The Muslim authorities do not allow Jews or Christians to pray, worship, or even read the Bible there.

Two Muslim Holy Places

- The Dome of the Rock

This ornate building is sometimes called The Mosque of Omar. It isn't really a mosque, but a shrine, built over the rock venerated by the Muslims. The rock under the dome is where Mohammed is said to have ascended to heaven on his "Night Journey". Actually Mohammed was never there, but in the Qur'an, in the seventeenth Sura a dream or vision is recorded in which he was carried from the temple in Mecca to the one in Jerusalem.

This rock is thought by many to be either the place of the Holy of Holies or of the Altar of Sacrifice. As shown below, there are other theories about the location of this most sacred portion of the Temple, which held the Ark of the Covenant.

More detail about the Dome of the Rock is given in *Chapter 7 - Historical Developments.*

- Al-Aqsa Mosque

The name means "the distant place." It is Islam's third most holy place, after Mecca and Medina. This is the building where the Muslims actually gather to worship.

The Western Wall

The Western Wall, also called "The Wailing Wall," is the one part of the old Temple area that is still standing, and that is only because it is a retaining wall. This wall was not part of the Temple itself, so it is not a violation of the prophecy that these stones still stand. This is considered the holiest place on the earth to Jewish People today. They are allowed to worship there, but are prohibited by their own rabbinical rulings and by the Muslims to go onto the Temple Mount itself.

The Rabbinical Tunnel opened recently to tourism allows one to walk under the city Northward from the Western Wall prayer area (Ha Kotel). In this tunnel, at the walled-off entrance to Cistern 30, devout Jews who believe the Temple occupied the spot where the Dome of the Rock now stands, can get somewhat closer to their favorite Temple site. Therefore a small synagogue area has been placed there.

The Dome of the Tablets / Dome of the Spirit

This neglected portion of the Temple Mount is covered by a simple cupola, without a sign or anything that would indicate its importance, but, as can be seen by the discussion below about the future location of the Temple, it may well be the location of the Holy of Holies! The Arabic name does suggest both the Tablets of Moses, which were placed within the Ark, or the Shekinah, or Spirit of God.

Necessity for a Temple

There are at least two reasons why we expect the Temple to be built again: because the Jewish people want it rebuilt, and because Bible prophecy says it will be constructed again, perhaps twice.

Because of Israel's Desires

Jewish law requires the Temple be rebuilt where it once was. One third of the Torah's 613 commandments involve rituals that require the Temple be rebuilt. A poll of Israelis during preparation for observance of Tisha B'Av, the national day of mourning over the loss of their ancient temples, revealed that 49 percent of the population said they do. Only 23 percent said they do not want a Third Temple. Many of them fear the hostile reaction of Muslims that would be caused by trying to build the Temple now.[92]

Because of Bible Prophecy

The following section shows that prophecies in the Bible point to the existence of a rebuilt Temple during the Tribulation and another one during the millennial reign of Christ.

A Third Temple during the Tribulation

Jesus' mentioned the future desecration of a temple in Jerusalem at the mid-point of the Tribulation (Matthew 24:15-22). He said it would be the "abomination of desolation" that was predicted by Daniel (Daniel 9:24-27). This is part of Daniel's vision about a period of time described as "seventy sevens" (or weeks), which amounts to 490 years. The first 483 years (69 times 7) were fulfilled exactly on the day that Jesus entered the City of Jerusalem riding on a donkey, and offering himself as king. According to Daniel's vision, there is yet to come a seventieth week, the last seven years, which is separated from the others. The Man of Sin, who is called the "ruler who will come" in Daniel 9:26, will make a treaty with Israel to protect her for seven years, but will break the covenant in the middle of the treaty. See *Chapter 8 - Believers during the Coming Tribulation.*

The Apostle Paul speaks of this same event (2 Thessalonians 2:1-4) and calls the desecrator "the man of sin."

Thirdly, seeing ahead into the distant future, the aged Apostle John wrote about this same Temple, which has never yet been built (Revelation 11:1-2; 13:14-15).

This subject is explored more fully in *Chapter 11 - The Great Tribulation.*

Location of the Future Temple

Since the Bible teaches that the Temple will be rebuilt, and it is obvious that it must be in the general area of the Temple Mount, there is much speculation about exactly where the Temple might be situated. There are several possibilities for the place where the Temple will be rebuilt. Here are the main theories, summarized briefly. Detailed information on all these theories is found on the Temple Mount web site.[93]

- **Where the Dome of the Rock stands**

That the First and Second Temples stood where the Dome of the Rock now stands is the traditional, conventional view. Former Jerusalem District Archaeologist Dan Bahat represents this point of view with considerable authority and knowledge. Everyone used to assume that the Dome of The Rock had to be torn down before the Temple could be built, because the rock was thought to be either the place of the Holy of Holies or of the Altar of Sacrifice. However, it is unthinkable to Muslims to have anyone harm or destroy this shrine without bringing the greatest of all jihads, or "holy wars," by all of Israel's Muslim neighbors.

- **North of the Dome of the Rock**

This theory, proposed by Physicist Asher Kauffman, suggests that the new Temple could be built north of the Dome of The Rock without tearing it down. Asher Kaufman is a faculty member in physics at Hebrew University and a devout observant Jew who was born in Scotland. He has explored the Temple Mount more than 100 times since 1974.

This view is based on the known location of the Eastern Gate ("The Golden Gate"), the location of the Dome of the Tablets, and various alignments of ancient stones on the Mount. Due East of the Dome of the Tablets is the Eastern Gate, which may have been the very gate Jesus entered when he offered himself as Messiah and was ultimately rejected by the religious authorities of Jerusalem. It is thought to be the gate of the future coming of Messiah into Jerusalem, so the Turkish Muslims walled it up completely in the hopes of keeping this prophecy from being fulfilled. Verification of the ancient position of the Eastern Gate was made recently with the discovery of an arch from an older gate directly below the existing one. The older gate may even date back to the time of Solomon. The Dome of The Tablets is a cupola, also called *Dome of the Spirits* in Arabic.

Whether or not there are other ancient gates in the East wall is not known because of the depth of the rubble in the area, and a Muslim cemetery conveniently located along the Eastern wall, both to stop excavation there and to deter a holy priest such as Messiah from entering the area from that direction. Muslim, Christian and Jewish cemeteries are found all along the Kidron Valley and up the adjacent Mount of Olives. All three religions have traditions about the resurrection of the dead and the last judgment being located there. That dreadful day is described in Joel's prophecy ({Joel 3:1-21). The newly discovered Western

Gate, underneath the present city is also interesting since it is on the same basic line that could be drawn through the temple area.

This theory would place the Dome of The Rock in the outer court, the Court of The Gentiles. Perhaps this is why Revelation 11:1-2 says:

> I was given a reed like a measuring rod and was told, "Go and measure the temple of God and the altar, and count the worshipers there. ²But exclude the outer court; do not measure it, because it has been given to the Gentiles. They will trample on the holy city for 42 months.

This could be the key to peace between Israel and the Palestinians. Both want Jerusalem for their capitals. Both want control of the Temple area. If an agreement could be made to allow the Palestinians to have a part of Jerusalem, including the portion of the Temple Mount where their holy places stand, and Israel would have the rest of Jerusalem, including the place where they can build the Temple, the peace process might be completed.

- South of the Dome of the Rock

This view is advocated by Tuvia Sagiv in his paper "The Hidden Secrets of The Temple Mount,"[94] 1992. Chuck Missler also considers this theory credible.[95] Factors discussed by these scholars include:

- Ancient accounts that the Temple was visible from certain places, not from others, suggest that it was further south at a slightly lower altitude.
- Aerial infrared pictures of the Dome of The Rock show a pentagonal structure below the shrine, raising the possibility that this was part of the Antonia Fortress, which was north of the Temple. Pentagonal structures were uncommon in Israel, and when found have occultic significance, so the site of the Dome of the Rock may have been a Canaanite High Place and a shrine to Ashtoreth.
- There is reason to believe the caves under the Dome may have been an ancient burial site in which case a holy temple could never have been built there.

One big problem with this view is that it would place the Temple between the Dome of The Rock and the Mosque of Al-Aqsa, which would be more awkward than if it were built on the north. Sagiv's historical research suggests that Hadrian rebuilt Jerusalem rather thoroughly after excluding the Jews so that the buildings on the Temple Mount may reflect more of Hadrian's work than that of Herod the Great.

The Ark of the Covenant

There are also several interesting theories about the present location of the Ark of the Covenant. These include:

- Under the Temple Mount

Jewish scholars believe that it is quite possible for it to be under the Court of Wood of Solomon's Temple, near the Western Wall ("The Wailing Wall").

- In Ethiopia

In an underground Temple beneath the ancient church of Zion in Aksum, northern Ethiopia, it is said that there are seven concentric rings of interior circular walls. The Ark of the Covenant is supposedly in the innermost ring, "The Holy of Holies."

The Ethiopian monarchy began with the Queen of Sheba and her son, Menelik I. Menelik I was the offspring of her marriage to King Solomon of Israel. This royal dynasty has lasted for three thousand years. The late Emperor Haile Selassie was part of this dynasty.

Emperor Haile Selassie, in our generation, called himself "The Conquering Lion of Judah."

Ethiopian tradition explains that the Ark of the Covenant was brought to Ethiopia by Prince Menelik, who was raised until he was 16 years old in Jerusalem. Solomon had a copy of the Ark made for Menelik, but he supposedly took the original because of Solomon's apostasy.

The history of both the Ethiopian Jewish community (the Falashas) and the history of the ancient Christian Coptic community in that country are fascinating and certainly go back two or three thousand years.

- On Mount Nebo

The apocryphal book of II Maccabees says that Jeremiah the prophet hid the Ark in a cave on Mt. Nebo (Jordan) at the time of Nebuchadnezzar's destruction of the City when the prophet was kidnapped by his own countrymen and taken to Egypt.

In 1982, a team that included Tom Crotser, Jim Bollinger, and the astronaut Jim Irwin, claimed to have found and photographed the Ark in a cave on the mountain.[96]

- Other Possibilities

The late explorer, Ron Wyatt, gave a report of discovering the Ark of the Covenant in a cave at Golgotha. He took pictures, but they were too foggy to validate his claims. He also claimed that the Ark was under an earthquake fissure so that the blood of Christ that poured out when he was pierced by a sword dripped onto the Mercy Seat.[97]

In the "Ark of the Covenant" section of Prophecy Central we have listed several other theories that have been promoted by various individuals. These stories have proposed that the Ark might someday be found in Zimbabwe, The Dead Sea area, an Egyptian temple in a Hamas camp in the West Bank, in Rennes-le-Chateau in southern France (by the Knights Templar), and in Heaven.[98]

Of course it is very possible that it simply does not exist any longer because it would be defiled in the coming Third Temple, and would no longer be necessary in the Forth Temple because God himself will be with us in person by that time. Jeremiah 3:16 says that when Messiah returns the Ark will be remembered no more.

Preparations for the Temple

Many people in Israel are convinced that the Temple will be rebuilt soon, and are preparing to help make it a reality. Here are some of the signs of this preparation:

- Training

The Seminary of Ateret Cohanim (Glory of the Priests) in the Old City of Jerusalem is training priests and Levites in priestly rituals and animal sacrifice.[99]

In their book, *Are We Living in the End Times*, Tim LaHaye and Jerry B. Jenkins write, "Many yeshivas [religious schools] have arisen throughout Jerusalem to prepare for the eventuality of a rebuilt, fully functioning temple service."[100]

Gershon Salomon, Chairman of the Temple Mount and Eretz Israel Faithful Movement, periodically attempts to place the cornerstone for the new temple on the Temple Mount. Their organization's goal is "the building of the Third Temple on the Temple Mount in Jerusalem in our lifetime in accordance with the Word of G-d and all the Hebrew prophets and the liberation of the Temple Mount from Arab (Islamic) occupation so that it may be consecrated to the Name of G-d." They have produced architectural plans for the Third Temple.[101]

- Materials

An organization known as The Temple Institute has already spent approximately 27 million dollars on preparations for the rebuilding of the Temple. Their Museum in Jerusalem's Old City contains solid gold service vessels, trumpets made of silver, garments to be worn by future priests made from golden thread, copper urns and many, many other items that have been painstakingly designed to biblical specifications for use in the future Temple.[102] They have even started the building of the massive sacrificial altar. It obviously can not be built where it belongs, but it is being erected off site, and will be transported to the new Temple when it is ready. The rocks for the sacrificial altar were gathered from the area around the Dead Sea and they were individually wrapped in order to ensure that they are not touched by metal as the Torah requires.

- Ashes of a Red Heifer

According to Numbers 19:1-9, it is necessary to use the sacrificial ashes of a young red cow, which has not yet reproduced for ritual cleansing of the Temple.

Until recently, this was considered a serious hurdle to the establishment of a new Temple. There had been some hopes of finding ancient ashes among the Dead Sea Scrolls, but when that no longer seemed likely, representatives of the Temple Institute started looking throughout Europe for pure red cattle. They found that they do exist. There is a breed called the Red Angus, but they were not sure whether or not the existing specimens would be pure enough to qualify.

An American rancher was known to have a herd of these red cattle, which he hoped could be used.

In May of 1997 a shocking announcement was made that a red heifer had been born unexpectedly in Israel! Examination of the animal revealed that, though it was born to parents that were not red its features would qualify it to be used in this way when it is of age. In early 1998 a few white hairs developed on its tail, making it no longer acceptable, but there is optimism that a suitable heifer will become available in the near future.

Another interesting twist in this matter is the successful cloning of sheep recently, opening the way for possible genetic engineering of a red heifer if it is necessary.

- Timing

Using older methods, it would take many years to build the new temple like it did in King Herod's days. But with modern equipment, it could be erected quickly if the plans and materials were ready to begin the process. Some Temple advocates have even said the project could be done in less than a year. It is believed that cedar from Lebanon was obtained in the war in 1982 and hidden for future use in building of the Temple.

A controversial mega-church in Sao Paulo Brazil has been given permission to build a $200 million dollar full-scale replica of Solomon's Temple. The massive structure will be twice the height of the famous Christ the Redeemer statue in Rio de Janeiro. It will be constructed from stone imported from Israel, and should be completed in four years.[103] This project has no direct bearing on the prophesied temple in Jerusalem, but it demonstrates that the structure could be built during the first half of the Tribulation (3 ½ years).

A Fourth Temple during the Millennium

There will be a Fourth Temple built in Israel during the thousand-year reign of Christ as King of Kings. The prophet Zechariah says that Messiah, whom he calls the "Branch" will yet build a temple in Israel (Zechariah 6:12-15).

This temple may well be that seen by Ezekiel (Ezekiel 40-45), in a vision. A temple that matches his description has never yet been built.

According to many Bible scholars, the fourth or "millennial temple" will be a memorial. It will be a teaching center to instruct men about the holiness of God and proper worship. As sinful men and women continue to be born into the world in the Millennium the temple is supposed to remind everyone of the substitutionary death of Jesus on the cross, as the "Lamb of God," some two thousand years earlier.

For more information and latest developments regarding the Temple Mount visit the Temple Mount Web Site and The Temple section at Prophecy Central.[104]

We now turn our attention to the dreadful events that transpire at the midpoint of the seven-year treaty with Israel, plunging the world into The Great Tribulation.

Chapter 11
The Great Tribulation

"So when you see standing in the holy place 'the abomination that causes desolation,' spoken of through the prophet Daniel—let the reader understand— ¹⁶then let those who are in Judea flee to the mountains. ¹⁷Let no one on the roof of his house go down to take anything out of the house. ¹⁸Let no one in the field go back to get his cloak. ¹⁹How dreadful it will be in those days for pregnant women and nursing mothers! ²⁰Pray that your flight will not take place in winter or on the Sabbath. ²¹For then there will be great distress, unequaled from the beginning of the world until now—and never to be equaled again. ²²If those days had not been cut short, no one would survive, but for the sake of the elect those days will be shortened." - Matthew 24:15-22

This abomination was mentioned by Jesus as the first major event of the "Great Tribulation" ("great distress" in the NIV). The blasphemous announcement by this false messiah in the Temple Holy of Holies will also mark the one clear "sign of the end of the Age" given to us by the Lord himself (Matthew 24).

The term "Antichrist" is widely used today. In his epistles, the Apostle John used this word to refer to a succession of evil world rulers, one of whom would be the final world dictator. "Anti" can mean "against" or "opposed to" in Greek, but it also can mean "instead of." Thus this man is a clever counterfeit of God's Messiah (*christos* means messiah or "anointed one"). See: "About the Name 'Antichrist'" at the end of Chapter 1.

The event that will precipitate a last desperate flight of the believing remnant of the Jewish people from Jerusalem and Judea will be "The Abomination of Desolation," which was predicted in Daniel 9:27 at the mid-point of the seven year peace treaty.

He will confirm a covenant with many for one 'seven.' In the middle of the 'seven' he will put an end to sacrifice and offering. And on a wing *of the temple* he will set up an abomination that causes desolation, until the end that is decreed is poured out on him. - Daniel 9:27

This same event is mentioned by the Apostle Paul in 2 Thessalonians 2:1-4.

Actually, two great world leaders, prominent on the world stage for the final three and one-half years of the world-wide Tribulation period, are described for us in Revelation Chapter 13. The imagery used is that of two wild beasts (Revelation 13:1-2, 11). The man who desecrates the temple is evidently the second of these two men also called "the false prophet." Jesus warned the Jews that such a man would come among them at the end of the age. He said, "I have come in my Father's name, and you do not receive me; if another comes in his own name, him you will receive" (John 5:43).

This man was also predicted by Zechariah (Zechariah 11:15-17).

Thus it is clear that this second three and one half years of the Tribulation are the worst years of human history. This also corresponds to the Old Testament prophecy of the "Time of Jacob's Trouble" (Jeremiah 30:1-7). Secular Jews, who constitute the majority of the people of Israel today, will not heed the ancient warning of Jesus in the Olivet Discourse, nor heed his 144,000 end-of-the-age witnesses who will surely warn the world afresh. Indeed most of the world will probably herald—with approval—the public announcement that a great and powerful world leader has found a formula for world peace. This same man will claim that he is also God incarnate, and his claims will be accepted. It will be a time of unprecedented world-wide deception as Jesus has already warned. Paul reasserts this in his description of this event in 2 Thessalonians 2:1-12.

The Abomination of Desolation in the Temple

What is this "Abomination of Desolation"? In addition to the Scriptures given above, there is this description of this detestable event in 2 Thessalonians 2.

Concerning the coming of our Lord Jesus Christ and our being gathered to him, we ask you, brothers, [2]not to become easily unsettled or alarmed by some prophecy, report or letter supposed to have come from us, saying that the day of the Lord has already come. [3]Don't let anyone deceive you in any way, for (that day will not come) until the rebellion [*apostasia*] occurs and the man of lawlessness is revealed, the man doomed to destruction. [4]He will oppose and will exalt himself over everything that is called God or is worshiped, so that he sets himself up in God's temple, proclaiming himself to be God. - 2 Thessalonians 2:1-4

According to Revelation 13, the Beast, who will be energized by the devil, will be considered so wonderful that many of the people of the earth will voluntarily offer to worship him. They will see him as a benevolent dictator. Not content with this, at the height of his power, he will make it mandatory for everyone to give him homage. In order to enforce this, he will have his religious leader, The False Prophet, set up an image of the Beast in the newly rebuilt temple. The image (an *idol*) must also be worshiped. The two Leaders will also institute a system of economic dictatorship that allows only those who agree to worship him to receive a mark (666). Without the mark, no one will be able to buy or sell anything. Those who believe in Jesus Christ will not be willing to accept the mark. No one who does receive the mark will ever be able or willing to repent and become a true Christian (Revelation 14:6-11; 20:4). Those who refuse the mark will be forced underground, living with other true believers in out of the way places. If they are caught they will be put to death for treason against the dictator's world government (Revelation 13:10; 20:4).

The final form of world government in this Tribulation period will have two aspects: Military, political and economic power will revolve around the first Beast. Subservient to him will be the harlot church. In Israel a powerful religious coalition will be led by the Second Beast. Both of these Leaders are Satan's masterpieces for deceiving the world. Both are energized by Satan, who until now has never found a complete way of expressing himself in human form ruling the earth.

The Mark of the Beast

There is another earth-shaking event that will take place at the same time. A one-world economic dictatorship will be established, and only those who follow the Beast's leadership and worship him will be permitted to buy or sell.

> He also forced everyone, small and great, rich and poor, free and slave, to receive a mark on his right hand or on his forehead, ¹⁷so that no one could buy or sell unless he had the mark, which is the name of the beast or the number of his name. - Revelation 13:16-17

The false Messiah (Paul's "man of sin" in 2 Thessalonians 2:1-12) will enter the Third Temple in Jerusalem and declare himself to be God. That event Jesus had said, in the Olivet Discourse, would bring great peril to the residents of Jerusalem. The peril for believers in Jesus at that time period will include the immediate danger of military invasion of Jerusalem by foreign armies (Luke 21:20). The believing remnant of Jews, who are in Jerusalem at the time the false messiah makes this move, will also be in grave danger of their lives because of his vigorous persecution of believers—that is, those few Jews who believe in the God of Abraham, Isaac, Jacob and Jesus.

Earth's last Caesar will rise to the position of virtual dictator of the earth. With the help of the "False Prophet," he will require people to receive a "mark" on their right hand or forehead in order to be able to buy or sell (Revelation 13:7-18). An angel will warn everyone that all who receive the mark will be doomed to eternal punishment (Revelation 14:9-11; compare Revelation 20:4).

There are at least three powers at work in the world even now that make this economic dictatorship possible.

Political Power - Revelation 13:5-7 - One-World Government

The beast was given a mouth to utter proud words and blasphemies and to exercise his authority for forty-two months. [6]He opened his mouth to blaspheme God, and to slander his name and his dwelling place and those who live in heaven. [7]He was given power to make war against the saints and to conquer them. And he was given authority over every tribe, people, language and nation. - Revelation 13:5-7

The first beast will lead the development of the emerging one-world government, or New World Order, which has been planned for centuries by the super rich behind the scenes. See *Chapter 5 - Satan's Final Empire.*

These power brokers are used to controlling who will be chosen for political positions, based on their ability to manipulate their pawns in high places. They will present the Beast as a benevolent dictator. They will undoubtedly think that they can control him for their own advantage. But he will be very powerful, drawing his energy from the devil. He will do as he pleases, though it is likely that much of what he does will also please the powerful elite group who has given him support.

Religious Power - Revelation 13:8, 11-15 - False Prophet

All inhabitants of the earth will worship the beast—all whose names have not been written in the book of life belonging to the Lamb that was slain from the creation of the world...
[11]Then I saw another beast, coming out of the earth. He had two horns like a lamb, but he spoke like a dragon. [12]He exercised all the authority of the first beast on his behalf, and made the earth and its inhabitants worship the first beast, whose fatal wound had been healed. [13]And he performed great and miraculous signs, even causing fire to come down from heaven to earth in full view of men. [14]Because of the signs he was given power to do on behalf of the first beast, he deceived the inhabitants of the earth. He ordered them to set up an image in honor of the beast who was wounded by the sword and yet lived. [15]He was given power to give breath to the image of the first beast, so that it could speak and cause all who refused to worship the image to be killed. - Revelation 13:8, 11-15

As can be seen even in our own American politics, support from religious groups can be very helpful to a politician. Revelation 13:11-15 tells about a False Prophet who is most likely the head of a one-world religion. This religious unity will finally be possible because after The rapture, born-again Christians will be absent from public life. Even in the Churches, those who are left are those who have never had a personal relationship with Christ. These people, for the most part, will not take the Bible literally. They will be willing to give up their doctrines for the sake of unity. The New Age Religion may be the uniting force behind this since it already draws heavily from various religions. The head of this union could be the leader of the United Religions, the World Council of Churches or an apostate denomination.

Technological power - Revelation 13:16-17 - Electronic Commerce

> He also forced everyone, small and great, rich and poor, free and slave, to receive a mark on his right hand or on his forehead, [17]so that no one could buy or sell unless he had the mark, which is the name of the beast or the number of his name
> [18]This calls for wisdom. If anyone has insight, let him calculate the number of the beast, for it is man's number. His number is 666. - Revelation 13:16-18

According to Revelation 13, the Beast, energized by the devil, (who is called the "god of this age" in 2 Corinthians 4:4) will be considered so wonderful that many of the people of the earth will voluntarily offer to worship him. They will see him as a benevolent dictator. Not content with this, at the height of his power, he will make it mandatory for everyone to give him homage. In order to enforce this, his religious leader, the False Prophet, will set up an image of him to be adored. (Revelation 13:11-15).

This "living image" will probably be a technological deception; perhaps some marvelous new holographic image, a genetically-engineered clone, or some other bio-tech "invention." In any case, it is clear that it represents the Beast, and it must be worshiped.

Modern technology has made it possible, not only to produce this deception, but to also do what the Bible predicts about literally controlling the right of individuals to buy and sell.

Here are some of the technological wonders of our age.

Computers

Before computers were such a vital part of our lives it was hard to imagine how this prophecy could be enforced. It is really humorous how limited human predictions have been about future developments. Here are a few examples from an article in the Wall Street Journal in 2009:

> "Inventions have long since reached their limit, and I see no hope for further developments." - Roman engineer Julius Sextus Frontinus in AD 10.

> "Everything that can be invented has already been invented." - Charles Duell, commissioner for the U.S. Patent Office, 1899.

> "I think there is a world market for maybe five computers," - Thomas Watson, chairman of IBM, 1943.

'No one will need more than 637 kb of memory for a personal computer." - Bill Gates, 1981.[105]

Amazingly, in our generation we have seen the development of all aspects of the electronic network necessary for one person to wield total economic control.

We are living in "The Information Age." In this generation science and knowledge have increased at a rate never imagined by our forefathers. Yet, this knowledge explosion was predicted by Daniel more than 2500 years ago! Daniel 12:4 says, "But you, Daniel, close up and seal the words of the scroll until the time of the end. Many will go here and there to increase knowledge."

Our generation has been a time of unprecedented invention, space exploration, and, above all, development and use of the computer. The advent of small, inexpensive, and powerful microcomputers has caused nearly every field of science and technology to take quantum leaps forward. Here are just a few of the emerging tools and methods that are making more information available.

The Personal Computer

In 1976 the Apple I computer was introduced at the retail of $666.66. Since then computers have become a necessary business and household appliance. The ever-present, ever-improving personal computer has become the primary tool of creativity. Practically everything that was once done by pencil and paper, drafting tools, and artistry is now being done faster, easier, and better with the help of the computer. A person of average income may now own a computer that is more powerful than the million dollar main-frames of just a few years ago. Beautiful color, digital stereophonic sound, DVD libraries of knowledge, modem connectivity to the entire world via the Internet, and an exploding source of helpful, inexpensive software applications all make this device a necessity for many people today. Smaller, more powerful laptop, notebook, and even hand-held computers make it possible for people to take this essential productivity tool with them wherever they go.

In a little more than 30 years we have witnessed the speed of personal computer processing units (CPU) rise from 1 million cycles per second to 3.33 Gigahertz (3 billion, 33 million cycles per second)![106] Intel's Core i7-980X Extreme processor is a single chip with six cores and more than 1 billion transistors.[107] You see, Andy Groves, Intel's CEO, predicted that the power of a computer chip would double every 18 months, and so far, Intel has lived up to that "law."

In 2009 Uruguay and a few other nations began offering a laptop computer to every child attending state primary school. The XO model laptops cost the state $260 per child, including maintenance costs, equipment repairs, training for the teachers and internet connection.[108]

Artificial Intelligence

Artificial Intelligence is also a field that is improving steadily. It gained new respect and interest in February, 1996 when Garry Kasparov, reigning chess champion of the world, lost the first of five games against IBM's "Deep Blue" computer. AI programming allows the computers at credit card companies to analyze customers' spending habits and project safe credit limits. It also helps them spot unusual activity with the cards so that fraudulent use can be minimized.

Supercomputers

Behind the scenes, giant companies and government agencies have highly advanced supercomputers. If the average person now has the power of yesteryear's main frame computers in his lap-top, imagine the increased capabilities that exist in the largest state of the art computers!

IBM is working on its new Sequoia computer, to be delivered in 2011 to the Department of Energy's Lawrence Livermore National Laboratory. It will have the computing power of 2 million laptops! It will operate at 20 petaflops (20 quadrillion floating point operations per second!).[109] At that speed, one computer could theoretically devote nearly 3 million calculations to each person's credit rating, bank account balance, physical location, and other matters. In fact, it could do all that for each of the nearly 7 billion people of the world in one second before starting the whole process all over again! Of course, the Beast's system will not depend on just one computer, but will use thousands of them working in parallel, just as Google does already with smaller computers. Such a system could permit or forbid buying and selling just as prophesied in Revelation 13.

Fiber Optics / Quantum Computers

Fiber optic "wires" now service our businesses and many homes. These cables, which use light instead of electricity, are able to carry thousands of conversations, video images, and data transfers all at the same time. One small Fiber Optic cable can replace 10,000 ordinary telephone lines!

Computer scientists are working on optical microprocessing, using light and fiber optics —instead of electricity and wires—to increase the speed by another factor of 1000 or more.

A new kind of computer, known as a "quantum computer," is being developed. It will use light waves to solve very difficult problems. Until now it has required laboratory-sized optical computers to do this work. Now researchers have designed a silicon chip that can do these calculations.[110]

Experimental work is being done on the concept of biochips, living, self-repairing, and incredibly compact memory devices.[111]

Credit Cards, Debit Cards, Smart Cards

The first credit cards were issued in 1950, and have become the preferred method of paying for most things. The card introduced electronic accounting of purchases, but the owner of the card still needed to settle the account once a month by paying for the purchases, usually with a check. Using a credit card allowed people convenience without having to carry large amounts of cash, and provided a record of how and where their money was spent.

The next step was the actual transfer of money electronically. For decades now the banking industry has been pressing for the use of electronic funds transfer. A growing number of people now have their paychecks deposited electronically into their accounts, pay their bills automatically by electronic checks, or use their personal computer to make these payments.

ATM machines were introduced to allow people to make deposits and withdrawals at any hour of the day. Debit cards were introduced to enable users to buy most of what they need electronically, with virtually immediate transfer of funds from the buyer's bank account to the seller's bank account.

"Pay Point" devices allow the use of either credit cards or debit cards to buy your gas without the help of an attendant. At your supermarket or fast-food restaurant one may pay for purchases the same way. In fact, if the buyer needs a little cash, he can get it out of his bank account at the same time. The checker will gladly give you the cash because that lowers the amount of cash on hand, discouraging robbers.

Smart cards are another development in the cashless trend. Smart cards are different from the cards most of us have in our wallets. They look the same, except a little thicker. Some of them have small contacts in the middle of the card. Inside the card there is actually a little computer, with a tiny battery, and up to 1 megabyte of memory. This already makes them more powerful than the earlier personal computers.

Some smart cards can be loaded with specialized applications. This will allow users do all kinds of things they couldn't do with a magnetic stripe card like the ones we have now. Some smart cards can literally transfer "money" from your bank account into the card. The electronic money is placed in one or more "wallets" in the card. This stored money can be used to operate vending machines, pay tolls, and whatever else people need.

These cards could eventually manage all of the users' PINs and passwords, so they won't have to worry about forgetting them. Smart Cards could also manage loyalty programs, from frequent flier miles to product discounts at the local grocery store.

Smart Cards are already very popular in Europe, but have had limited success in the United States. One of the reasons for this is the lack of standards by card manufacturers. Another reason is the fact that the new smart phones, which are described below, are becoming extremely popular, and can theoretically do the same things better.

All of the cards mentioned above may be equipped with a radio frequency identification chip (RFID) so that they may be used without actual contact with a card reader. These cards, or in some cases, just a wand on a key ring, or a sticker on the car's dashboard, will communicate to a RFID receiver to complete the transaction, These devices speed the process of purchasing and eliminate the need for handling money.

The Internet / Grid

Parallel to the development of computers has been the emergence of a method of connecting computers. This indispensable network is the Internet. It has been around for several decades, but has recently mushroomed in size and popularity. It is a high speed data transmission system, now often called the information "super highway." It was originally used by major corporations and universities to connect their main-frame computers together. Today it is considered an essential aspect of education, business, government, and homes. This global network (thus called the "world-wide web,' and the "net") connects people and devices in a way that enhances our education and productivity, our purchasing power, our social networking and communication, and our entertainment. As mentioned above, Daniel 12:4 predicts that in the End Times, "Many will go here and there to increase knowledge." What could be a better description of the Internet from more than 2500 years ago?

In 2008 China became the nation with the largest number of users. At that time more than 253 million Chinese were using the Internet, compared to the United States' 223 million users.[112]

Scientists have begun to use a new generation of the Internet. It is called Internet 2, or "The Grid." It is described as vBNS (very high speed Backbone Network Service). At full speed (2.5 billion bits per second) it will be about 10,000 times faster than a typical broadband connection.[113] At that speed it will be able to transmit the contents of two public libraries per second.[114]

"The Cloud"

Users of computers and other devices connected to the Internet may purchase data space and services from a variety of suppliers. Data and computing activity performed by these remote hosts is sometimes called "cloud computing." The name cloud computing was inspired by the cloud symbol that is often used to represent the Internet in flowcharts and diagrams. One seldom knows or cares where his data and services are located. It really doesn't matter since any place on Earth is instantly accessible via the Internet.

Satellites

Even people in remote areas of the Earth may obtain Internet service, thanks to the satellite networks of HughesNet and other providers. This means that control of world-wide commerce is possible when the coming world dictator makes his move to control all buying and selling (Revelation 13).

Smart Phones/ GPS

Now the incredible and fast-growing power of cell phones and GPS devices bring us a bewildering choice of "smart phones." This new phenomenon started with the advent of cell phones with additional features in the 1990's. In 2002 the first BlackBerry was released with the ability to handle Email. The Apple iPhone, introduced in 2007, and the open source Android, backed by Google in 2008, gave phones the same computing power and memory as a personal computer but with enhanced capabilities for mobile usage. Advanced touch screen, built in high resolution cameras, Global Positioning System (GPS) information, and high-speed Internet connectivity became standard equipment for the new generation of smart phones. All of this cost the user only a fraction of the price they could have ever imagined such devices would cost. With the computing power and memory of a personal computer and with tens of thousands of applications available, people can even run their businesses from their hand-held phones.

The next step for smart phones is to replace credit and debit cards with the phone's own functionality. In 2010 AT&T and Verizon Wireless announced plans for this game-changing move.[115] The cell phone will communicate with the vendor the way a contact-less card does, but unlike a card, it will be able to keep track of charges and payments through one of the phone's apps. There will undoubtedly be docking stations for future smart phones so users can use a large screen and keyboard at home or at work. They should also be able to keep all our passwords and download electronic cash the way a smart card could, and then spend those funds for every-day purchases.

However, there is one big problem. Once the smart phone has all our personal data and becomes our universal commerce device, and maybe even has a large amount of money stored electronically, what will happen if we lose it? Would someone else be able to take over our finances and have access to all our secret information? Losing one's phone would be worse than losing one's wallet (we may not even have one once it is all in the phone) or one's car. The solution will be to make the phone useless to anyone but its rightful owner. This can be done with biometrics, as shown below, or with an RFID device implanted in the owner. Thus the smart phone would not work unless it was near its owner. Meanwhile, the phone could be located by its built-in GPS device. And what criminal would want to take the phone if he couldn't use it, and it leads the police to his door?

With the right combination of features, the smart phone could become a powerful personal security system, automatically notifying authorities when something is amiss, and, of course letting them know exactly where the user is. This, of course, can also be a very negative feature for those who do not want to be located.

Biometrics

Fingerprints, palm prints, face and eye prints (retinal imaging) are some of the high tech methods now used to verify a person's identity. These, of course, cannot be stolen or lost. How far away from public acceptance of these devices are we? We may be closer than we think!

Other technologies are also leading in the same direction. A face recognition program or a fingerprint or iris scanner could be used by your smart phone through its camera. Once the phone knows it is "seeing" its owner, it could let the user proceed.

Implanted Transponders

Implanting a tiny identification chip under the skin of the phone's owner would be an even better solution to the problem of losing the smart phone and its valuable contents. Such a rice-sized chip has already been inserted under the skin of countless livestock and pets so that they can be identified if lost. A version of this device approved for use in humans is the VeriChip. It doesn't need batteries. It has a little coil, and a pre-programmed number, all encapsulated in glass, and is easily inserted by a nearly painless hypodermic needle. It has been available for some time now, but truthfully, not many people have been eager to experiment with it yet.

The Beast's Dictatorial Control

Nothing more is necessary for the future dictator to take over. Science, technology, and business have already prepared the way for him. Now the whole world can participate in the Beast's economic experiment. Revelation 13:16-17 reminds us that the day will come when he will be able to cut off the privilege of buying and selling for anyone who will not worship him and receive the "mark of the beast."

Control of Commerce

Most people have had the embarrassing experience of hearing a vendor say, "Your card is not accepted, sir." It could be a mistake by the card company, or a miscalculation on the user's part, but it can usually be corrected the next day or so. Once the economic dictator's team is in charge, anyone who refuses to accept the mark will be flagged by the system to automatically deny the privilege of electronic commerce anywhere on the globe. And that prohibition will be permanent!

Control of Travel

Toll booths register and deduct payment from vehicles passing through their scanners. Smart highway projects are in the planning stages to literally guide vehicles from one point to another on safer highways. Obviously, those in the future who have not paid, or who are not allowed to buy and sell can be kept off these highways!

Most people are aware of the growing number of people who are on the airlines' "no-fly list." This same electronic commerce system will undoubtedly keep the Beast's enemies from buying a ticket in the first place, but it will also put his name on the "no-fly list" and flag his interactive passport so he can't even drive across the border to another country.

Control of the Media

Another very significant development in the world of modern technology is the recent merger of huge communications and media corporations. In August, 1995 Disney and ABC agreed to the largest merger in history, and the next day a merger of Westinghouse with CBS was announced.. These things lead us closer to a one-world economy. Smaller operations will continue to be swallowed up by larger ones so they have more control.

It is normal in any dictatorship for the political powers to literally control what can be said and done on radio, television, and the printed media. Current reminders of this fact can be seen in Russia's return to media control after a brief period of free speech after the collapse of the Soviet Union, and China's censoring of Internet traffic.

Programmable Tattoos

Since the "mark of the beast" will be placed on the right hand or forehead of those who choose to follow the Beast, it has often been suggested that the name or number will be some kind of tattoo.

There now exists a "Programmable Tattoo" that can be implanted under your skin. It is actually an LCD display panel that can serve as a watch to tell the time, or give reports on your vital functions like blood pressure or insulin count: anything you need to know about yourself. The people who have the patents on this are from a company called Interval Research Corporation. You may not have heard of them. They say they don't even know what they want to do with this invention yet. Interval was co-founded by Paul Allen, who was also co-founder of Microsoft. Most of the things they are doing right now, they are keeping secret. There is an "interval," you see.[116] They are thinking that five, ten, or twenty years in the future, all the things they are developing will be put into service.

Maybe they will be put into service when the Mark of The Beast is ready.

The Actual Mark
The Beast's name or number (666)

Again, we read the prediction about the "mark of the beast":

> He also forced everyone, small and great, rich and poor, free and slave, to receive a mark on his right hand or on his forehead, [17]so that no one could buy or sell unless he had the mark, which is the name of the beast or the number of his name.

[18]This calls for wisdom. If anyone has insight, let him calculate the number of the beast, for it is man's number. His number is 666. - Revelation 13:16-18

At this future point in time these two powerful leaders—one religious, the other political and military—will have arranged world-wide control over buying and selling. The fate of the world will apparently rest solely with them.

Computers do all kind of wonderful things, but, because of the way they work, everything they do must be converted to numbers. Every letter on this screen, every colored pixel, every tone produced by the computer (including your favorite music CD) is saved and processed as a number.

Our number(s)

Now that modern technology has reached the stage where it is truly feasible for a world ruler to exert economic dictatorship it is increasingly important for everyone to have a distinctive number. Most of us have several numbers already: our Social Security number, drivers' license number, phones, FAX and pager numbers, credit card numbers, and so on.

It was recently revealed that America's Social Security numbers are badly compromised. Millions of Americans have more than one Social Security number, and millions of Social Security numbers are shared by more than one person. Identity theft accounts for some of the duplications. Other causes include bad memories, careless record-keeping and data input errors. More than 40 million numbers are associated with more than one person.[117] As the issue of illegal immigration became a heated issue in 2010, a proposed immigration bill would require all U.S. workers to use a biometric Social Security card in order to work within the United States. John W. Whitehead, founder and president of the Rutherford Institute warns that this would become a national ID card under a different name.[118] Other countries are also moving in this direction. The same year Germany unveiled a new generation of identity cards with RFID chips.[119] At a certain point in time, after such worldwide economic turmoil and identity theft, people will welcome a fresh personal identification number.

The number of the Beast

What does the Beast's personal number, 666 mean? Please notice that the Scripture says plainly that it is "the number of his name." This is significant because the issue in this future story is that of worship. People will have to vow their devotion to this worst of all the false christs by allowing either his name, or else the number of his name, to be placed on them in a prominent place as a symbol of their allegiance.

We have been warned that we can not know who this evil dictator is until he is revealed, and that will not happen until the Restrainer (The Holy Spirit) is no longer holding back sin (2 Thessalonians 2:1-11). But those who are alive during that time might recognize him partly by this number. It will be wise and proper for those living during that time to "calculate" his number (Revelation 13:18).

There are many possible ways of converting a name to a number. Here are some of them:

- Assignment

This is how you received your Social Security number, or credit card numbers. When it was time to be "numbered" the next number in a sequence was assigned. Some systems pick numbers randomly instead of sequentially, and check to make sure no one else has that number before issuing it.

- Choice

This is the process if you, or someone else, should choose a number to represent you. This is sometimes done for jerseys of famous athletes. Other examples of this are when you order a personalized license plate for your car or pick your own phone number.

- Conversion

Returning to the fact that our lives are run, or at least monitored, by computers, there is another way of deriving a number from a name. There are several different numbering systems used by computers to convert any given letter to a number. One of these is the ASCII code (A=65, B=66, etc.) Using this system, and adding up the total of the values of the letters, it is interesting that some names do add up to 666. Some famous names produce this result.

Another type of conversion is based on the alphabet (A=1, B=2, etc.) Such a system would not produce a number as big as 666, so some have suggested converting this way and then multiplying by the "number of man", which some believe is 6 - one short of the number of perfection. Again, some notable people's names produce 666 in this way.

There are also various techniques for coding this number. These include:

- Printing

Checks, Invoices, and many other documents that need to be recognized and handled by people simply print the number. Data processing clerks or scanning devices convert these numbers back into the numbers needed by the computers.

- Magnetic stripe

Credit cards and debit cards (and a host of other identifying devices) use these little strips of magnetic tape to store your number and other information.

- Transponders

As explained earlier, a tiny electronic chip that may be injected into an animal or a human will respond to the stimulus of a certain kind of scanner by transmitting your numerical data.

These radio-frequency identification (RFID) chips can now even be printed on paper or cardboard to allow better electronic inventory control.

- Bar Code

Laser scanners use the bar codes on products to print your sales receipt. The number on the package is converted to a name, a price, and at the same time it is subtracted from inventory and placed on the store's next re-order form.

It has been noticed by some that the UPC bar codes are generally divided into two parts by three bars, one at the beginning, one at the end, and one in the middle. These marks may be longer than the numbers, but they may look the same as one of the codes for the number six. Thus, some bar-codes do have the number 666 built into it. This may or may not have any significance in future understanding of prophecy.

In 2009 the Media Lab at Massachusetts Institute of Technology introduced a new kind of optical data storage tag. It has the capacity to store more than a million times more data than a bar code in only 3mm of space, and it can be "read" by a smart phone with the proper application installed.[120]

Receiving the Mark

At the same time that the Beast's followers receive his mark (tattoo?), they will probably also have a RFID chip with their own ID Number inserted under their skin.

It should also be noted that, even though it is logical for us to have our own numbers, and that, for security reasons, these numbers might even be tattooed on or implanted in us, the number that will be displayed on the hand or forehead will not be our number, but the Beast's. Those who are more bold in their devotion to him will not have his number, but his actual name!

Implanted chips will be considered acceptable because they will provide improved security measures in an age of terrorism. They will have the added benefit of making one's medical history and records quickly accessible in case of an emergency. As mentioned above, these chips may provide the necessary link to one's own smart phone.

What we are assured of by the Bible is that these sophisticated tools will be usurped and used against God-fearing people during the Tribulation period, because the world government of that time period will be entirely under Satanic control and the restraining influence of the Church will no longer restrain evil at all levels of society.

In the next chapter we will study the biblical teaching about a protected place for the Chosen People during the Great Tribulation. When the Abomination of Desolation is set up in the Temple, and believing Jews are outraged by the desecration, they will be driven out of Israel.

Chapter 12
Petra

The Flight of the Remnant from Jerusalem at Mid-Tribulation

Earlier it was pointed out that Revelation 12 is a symbolic overview of all of Israel's history. In Revelation 12:6 we read, "The woman fled into the desert to a place prepared for her by God, where she might be taken care of for 1,260 days." The woman is symbolic of Israel. 1260 days is exactly three and one half years—the standard lunar (prophetic) years of the Bible, with 360 days each.

Later in the same chapter, this event is described this way:

> he woman was given the two wings of a great eagle, so that she might fly to the place prepared for her in the desert, where she would be taken care of for a time, times and half a time, out of the serpent's reach. [15]Then from his mouth the serpent spewed water like a river, to overtake the woman and sweep her away with the torrent. [16]But the earth helped the woman by opening its mouth and swallowing the river that the dragon had spewed out of his mouth. - Revelation 12:14-16

This also corresponds to Jesus' warning in his sweeping outline of the future, known as the "Olivet Discourse" because it was delivered on the Mt. of Olives. He warned that when "the abomination that causes desolation" takes place, the inhabitants of Judea should flee immediately, because that would be the beginning of a great time of distress, "unequaled from the beginning of the world" (Matthew 24:15-22).

Jerusalem Surrounded by Armies

The parallel passage in Luke 21 adds what Matthew does not tell us, that Jerusalem will be surrounded by hostile armies at the time of the end.

When you see Jerusalem being surrounded by armies, you will know that its desolation is near. [21]Then let those who are in Judea flee to the mountains, let those in the city get out, and let those in the country not enter the city. [22]For this is the time of punishment in fulfillment of all that has been written. [23]How dreadful it will be in those days for pregnant women and nursing mothers! There will be great distress in the land and wrath against this people. [24]They will fall by the sword and will be taken as prisoners to all the nations. Jerusalem will be trampled on by the Gentiles until the times of the Gentiles are fulfilled.
- Luke 21:20-24

Jerusalem, "trodden down by the Gentiles" again and again since the time of the Babylonian captivity is yet to suffer one last final, terrible invasion by the Gentiles.

Flight of Jews from Judea

The size of this believing remnant at the mid-tribulation point is open to discussion, but for the sake of argument it would seem to be some thousands or perhaps tens of thousands of believing Jews who are warned to flee from Jerusalem.

The words and teachings of Jesus to his people Israel were not heeded when he was with them during his First Advent. We can not expect the entire nation to take this warning to leave Jerusalem seriously even though it will no doubt be heralded again by a new generation of prophets in the end time. Those Jews in Israel who have come to know Yeshua (Jesus) personally during the first half of The Tribulation *will* be responsive and it is to this believing remnant that Jesus makes his appeal.

Ray Stedman remarks on this event,

Who are they who must flee so urgently when the last days begin? Who dare not hesitate long enough even to go back into the house to pick up a wrap, but must immediately head for the hills? There is no need to wonder, for the Lord says plainly, "those who are in Judea" Now Judea is a geographical part of the land of Israel, ancient Palestine. It comprises the hill country surrounding the city of Jerusalem and includes the city as well. It is to the residents of Jerusalem and Judea that this warning is addressed.

Furthermore, the Lord's mention of the Sabbath establishes the fact that these residents of Judea are Jews. He urges them to pray that their flight will not be in the winter, with its distress of cold, or on the Sabbath, with its travel limitations, for Jews are allowed to travel only a short distance on a Sabbath day. Later in this passage these Jews are called "the elect" ("for the sake of the elect those days will be shortened"), and this makes clear they are believing Jews, that is, men and women of faith who know and love Jesus Christ as Lord and are prepared to live or die for him.

They are not Christians in the usual sense of that term, referring to those who are members of the Church, for we are told that in the Church there is neither Jew nor Gentile, bond nor free. Jews are not to be distinguished from Gentiles within the Church. These distinctions, we are precisely told by the apostle Paul, have been invalidated in the Church.

The "middle wall of partition" has been eliminated; there are no distinctions of background, race or religious training that are recognized within the Church of Jesus Christ.

Furthermore, Christians, we are told, are free from the law and no longer observe special days, special feasts, new moons and Sabbaths. In his letter to the Colossians the apostle Paul clearly speaks of the fact that the Sabbaths were included in those shadows which were done away in Christ. But here the Sabbath distinctly will be a restricting factor in the flight of these people. Here then will be a class of people who cannot be identified with the present day church. They will be Jewish believers in Christ who will be converted after the removal of the Church and before the time of the Great Tribulation.[121]

Jesus does not tell the residents of Tel Aviv or Haifa to flee. The greatest danger is in Jerusalem and the peril is so great that the true believers in Yahweh must leave town immediately. They are called to flee to the mountains, and since Jerusalem is already in the mountains of Judea, the flight will evidently be down to Jericho, then across into Jordan.

Petra - The Prepared Place
Historical Background of Petra

Most Bible scholars believe this godly remnant who flees from Jerusalem will find refuge in the ancient rock-hewn cliff city of Petra, and in the surrounding region in the land of that once belonged to the descendants of Esau, that is Edom (Southern Jordan). Petra is not mentioned by name in the Scriptures, but Bozrah, the ancient capital of Edom (Gen 36:31-33; Amos 1:12), is said to be the place where God will care for them as his sheep (Hebrew *botsrah* = "sheepfold" - Micah 2:12-13), and it is the place where Messiah will tread the winepress of his vengeance against the nations of the Earth (Isaiah 63). Bozrah was on the North-South caravan route known as "The King's Highway" (Numbers 20:17), south of the Dead Sea. Petra is about 7 miles from the ancient location of Bozrah.[122] Petra may not be large enough to hold all the people who will flee from the terrors in Jerusalem. However, since Bozrah is near Petra, it is likely that the whole area will be God's prepared place for the refugees. The remnant will survive there, protected by God, for three and a half years. Meantime terrible destruction will come upon the land of Israel—which will be the focal point of war. The entire world will suffer terrible destructive judgments, all from the Lord on that Day—but the believing refugees who constitute what the Bible calls "true Israel" will be safe in the sheepfold around Bozrah and Petra. See also, Appendix H - *The History of Edom.*

Edom, as the territory allotted to Jacob's brother Esau, is documented in Genesis 36. A man named Bozrah was a descendant of Seir the Horite, who inhabited the land "before there were any kings in Israel" (Genesis 36:31-33).

Edom's long-standing enmity against Israel ultimately brought God's judgment on them. Obadiah the prophet devotes his short but potent message to the judgment of Edom, telling us of her pride and arrogance and the reasons for God's final judgment on these people. Amos, the shepherd of Tekoa, wrote of impending judgment on Edom (Amos 1:11-12).

Various writers have given fine descriptions of Petra and the history of that region of ancient Edom. The Nabataeans displaced the descendants of Esau probably in the 6th Century BC. They controlled the entire region as far North as Damascus until the First Century. The Greeks and Romans built extensively in Jordan and the area around Bozrah and Petra was well populated as late as Roman times. Today the area is desolate and sparsely populated because of the very low rainfall and scarcity of natural resources there.

Petra was the capital city of the Nabataeans. Tourists to this vast mountain-enclosed ancient city in the Wadi Musa generally enter from the east on foot or on horseback through El Siq, a 6000 feet long narrow cleft (width: 12-30 feet) with 100-500 foot high cliff walls. Tombs and houses carved into the bedrock over a vast area at Petra would be suitable for temporarily housing many thousands of people. Mt. Hor is nearby, where Aaron died after Moses passed the high priestly garments of Aaron on to Eleazer in the sight of the congregation (Numbers 20:23-29).

Not to Be Conquered by the Beast

The future world dictator's military will pursue and seek to annihilate the Jewish believing remnant as they flee from Jerusalem. But their route of escape will have been made ready by the Lord.

> He [the last king of the North] will also invade the Beautiful Land. Many countries will fall, but Edom, Moab and the leaders of Ammon will be delivered from his hand. - Daniel 11:41

A Hiding Place

Evidently this part of Jordan will be given special protection during the last great invasion of Israel. Isaiah the Prophet instructs the believing remnant of Israel to find a safe hiding place during the time of Jacob's trouble when God's judgment will fall on the whole earth (Isaiah 26:20-21).

During the second half of The Tribulation Period there will be no safe place to hide anywhere on the earth—except in the refuge God will provide, probably at Petra. We gain glimpses of how terrible life will become for non-believers in those days from many passages in the Book of Revelation. For example at the opening of the Sixth Seal of judgment John notes:

> I watched as he opened the sixth seal. There was a great earthquake. The sun turned black like sackcloth made of goat hair, the whole moon turned blood red, ¹³and the stars in the

sky fell to earth, as late figs drop from a fig tree when shaken by a strong wind. [14]The sky receded like a scroll, rolling up, and every mountain and island was removed from its place.

[15]Then the kings of the earth, the princes, the generals, the rich, the mighty, and every slave and every free man hid in caves and among the rocks of the mountains. [16]They called to the mountains and the rocks, "Fall on us and hide us from the face of him who sits on the throne and from the wrath of the Lamb! [17]For the great day of their wrath has come, and who can stand?" -Revelation 6:12-17

Believers' Underground

These fleeing refugees from Jerusalem will become a part of a believer's underground in those days. True believers in Jesus as they are converted by the vigorous world-wide evangelistic campaign of the 144,000 will not be allowed the privileges of citizenship and commerce in the Beast's world government, as we have noted. They will refuse to participate in worship of the beast, and consequently will not be allowed to buy or sell anything. Therefore, they will be forced to hide in secret places, or die, as the early Christians did when the Church was young.

Christians went underground during the persecutions in Rome. They literally lived in the vast network of catacombs beneath the city of Rome. Visitors to Rome today can visit the places where they lived, including large cavernous rooms where they met for worship and prayer, and hundreds of tombs carved into the sides of the tunnels for those who died during this time.

Groups of "underground" believers during the Tribulation Period will no doubt form their own alliances for survival, including sharing of resources, bartering, and standing guard for one another. They may well have the use of the Internet, satellite communication, and other high tech methods in their struggle.

According to Revelation 12, which records the cosmic drama of Israel and the Dragon, the devil will be thwarted in his attempt to capture the fleeing remnant of Israel and will be enraged at "the rest of her offspring" who are described as true believers in Jesus (Revelation 12:14-17). Evidently this latter group will be converts from all the Gentile nations.

It is possible that the underground followers of Jesus during The Tribulation period will receive special divine guidance and help from this place to which Israel will flee, because it will be protected by God. Petra is certainly one of the best natural places on earth for protection, because it can only be entered by one narrow valley ("El Siq"), which would be easy to guard. However, given the modern capabilities to fly over the city and bomb even mountain sanctuaries, it seems clear that God himself will provide the necessary supernatural protection for Israel.

The Fifth Seal - Martyrdom

The Greek word "martyr" actually means "witness" or "one who gives a testimony." Early Christians were very bold witnesses for Christ in fulfillment of his command to be his witnesses in all the earth (Acts 1:8). In those days every Roman subject was expected to acknowledge Caesar as god. They were required to say "Caesar is Lord." Christians, of course could not say this. Instead, they acknowledged "Jesus is Lord" (1 Corinthians 12:3). For this reason many early Christians were put to death by a variety of cruel methods, such as crucifixion, burning at the stake, beheading, and being fed to lions. Historical accounts of these people refer to them as martyrs.

There have been a great many Christian martyrs down through the centuries. In fact, our own generation has seen the persecution and death of more Christians than any other age. This is especially true in fundamentalist Muslim countries, and in the totalitarian communistic regimes of the former Soviet Union and China.

During the Tribulation there will be many martyrs—perhaps *the majority* of those converted to faith in Jesus around the world will be put to death as a threat to the New World Order established by the Beast. The fifth seal (Revelation 6:9-11) is about these martyrs, who ask the Lord, "How long...until you judge the inhabitants of the earth and avenge our blood?" (Revelation 6:10)

It is also clear that those who trust in Christ and refuse to receive the mark of the beast will be put to death for treason against the one-world government (Revelation 13:10; 20:4). Surely the Lord will give them the strength to stand for Christ even if it means suffering in this extreme way. Believers are not promised deliverance from persecution. 2 Timothy 3:12 says, "In fact, everyone who wants to live a godly life in Christ Jesus will be persecuted."

The Concept of the Remnant

From the Old Testament it is clear that the majority of the Jewish people within the nation were not necessarily believers. Elijah lamented that he was the "only one" left who knew God after his successful defeat of the priests of Baal at Mt. Carmel. But God responded telling him that he had, at that time, "more than seven thousand who had not bowed the knee to Baal" Numbers 19:9-18).

From 1 Corinthians 10:1-5 we get the clear picture regarding Israel that "with most of them God was not well pleased, for their bodies fell in the wilderness"—referring to the generation that left Egypt under Moses.

Thus at any point in time "true Israel" means the believing community within the nation. Sometimes it was substantial, at other times few in number.

Likewise within the professing church of Jesus Christ around the world, not all are true believers by any means,

"Not everyone who says to me, 'Lord, Lord,' will enter the kingdom of heaven, but only he who does the will of my Father who is in heaven. [22]Many will say to me on that day, 'Lord, Lord, did we not prophesy in your name, and in your name drive out demons and perform many miracles?' [23]Then I will tell them plainly, 'I never knew you. Away from me, you evildoers!'" - Matthew 7:21-23

God gets his work done by a "remnant" in every generation it would seem.

Christ's Presence

Ray Stedman has proposed the interesting possibility that Jesus Christ, following the rapture of the Church, will be present on the Earth during this time, appearing and disappearing at will as he did for a few weeks following the Resurrection.

In contrast to the false propaganda of the last days, in Matthew 24:27-28, Jesus unveils the true method for locating him in the day of his presence. To do so he uses a parable from nature and a proverb from life: "For as the lightning comes from the east and shines as far as the west, so will be the coming of the Son of man. Wherever the body is, there the eagles will be gathered together."

The word the Lord uses for "coming" here is the now familiar "parousia." It is quite a different word than he uses a few verses farther on when he speaks of "the Son of man coming on the clouds of heaven with power and great glory." It is easy to confuse these two comings because of his reference to lightning in verse 27. Since lightning is a form of power and glory, many feel the Lord is using it as symbol of his coming in glory. But note carefully what he says.

Lightning flashes in the east, but the effect of it is seen all over the sky. Yet the flash itself does not involve the whole inverted dome of the heavens from east to west. When he uses the symbol of lightning, therefore, he is not describing a universally visible manifestation of his glory, but the universal effect of his presence behind the scenes. Like lightning flashes he will be seen by his own in different places, at all different times, but the effect of those appearances will be felt throughout the earth.

Furthermore, lightning is sovereign, unpredictable, uncontrollable. So will be the presence, the parousia, of the Son of man. He will appear and disappear at will. Whenever there is need for him he will be there, just as he was during the post-resurrection period. There will be no need to search for him for he cannot be found that way. There will be no need to look for him in the wilderness nor in the inner rooms, for he will come whenever and wherever he finds a heart ready to know him. In the passage parallel to this in Luke 17, Jesus says, "For as the lightning flashes and lights up the sky from one side to the other, so will the Son of man be in his day." A "day" used in that sense always refers to a period of time, not a sudden, climactic event.[123]

We won't be dogmatic about this, but if Ray Stedman's interpretation is correct, it would certainly help explain the supernatural protection that the refugees from Israel will enjoy during this time.

An interesting corollary to this idea is that the raptured Church might be involved in this activity of protecting the Saints during the Tribulation. This could be true because we know that we, the Church, are destined to rule and reign with him when he appears later as King of Kings. In any case, we are assured in 1 Thessalonians 4:17 that once we have met The Lord in the air, we will always be with him! The church is called the "Body of Christ" in the New Testament, so wherever the Lord of the Church is at work, there also is his Body, the Church.

If the above scenario is correct, it is important to remember that the members of the Church as well as their Lord will all have their new resurrection bodies. It should not surprise us that our ministry during this time period might well be like that of our Lord Jesus during the 40 days after his resurrection and prior to his ascension when he came and went at will, appearing and disappearing in the midst of followers to continue to teach them and guide them. The Church may well have a similar role of encouragement in the lives of the 144,000 who will still be mortal and not immune from suffering and martyrdom in their heroic acts of evangelism.

Next we turn our attention to the plight of those who do not have God's special protection during the awful three and a half years of the Great Tribulation. The events prescribed for this period of time are almost beyond belief.

Chapter 13
The Plot Thickens

Not All the Jews Flee to Edom

> A day of the LORD is coming when your plunder will be divided among you.
> ²I will gather all the nations to Jerusalem to fight against it; the city will be captured, the houses ransacked, and the women raped. Half of the city will go into exile, but the rest of the people will not be taken from the city.
> ³Then the LORD will go out and fight against those nations, as he fights in the day of battle.
> - Zechariah 14:1-3

These verses lead us up to the Battle of Armageddon, which will be discussed in the next chapter. Jerusalem appears to have been occupied by "foreign armies" from the mid-point of the Tribulation when "The Abomination of Desolation" is set up—until the great battle at the end of the Tribulation. According to the above text half of the city will go into exile and the other half will remain.

The Jews who will remain in Jerusalem, and elsewhere in Israel during the second half of The Tribulation, will be ignoring the warning of Jesus given some 2000 years earlier. These Jews in fact will stay—and will maintain their secular, apostate, stance opposing the God of their forefathers, and continuing to stumble over their own cornerstone, Jesus (Romans 9:32). God will continue to warn them through a new generation of prophets. Their message will be like that of Jeremiah at the time of the Babylonian captivity. At that time, when Nebuchadnezzar pillaged Israel, remnants led by Daniel and Ezekiel had escaped to Babylon where they enjoyed God's protection and blessing. God clearly spoke to the Jewish people urging them to go to Babylon. Jeremiah's warnings went unheeded in Jerusalem, yet God did not leave himself without a witness in the capital. Most of those who remained in Jerusalem died in the terrible destruction of 586 BC. The glorious Temple of Solomon was pillaged, burned and destroyed on the 9th of Av. Jeremiah was taken by rebellious countrymen to Egypt where he was soon martyred, according to tradition.

Two Fearless Witnesses on the Temple Mount

At the mid-point of the Tribulation period Jesus will call his faithful remnant to flee Jerusalem and hide in the desert place, and he will place two powerful witnesses on public display in Jerusalem. For a full three and a half years they will speak to the nation and to the world of impending judgment. In spite of the enormously hostile environment of Jerusalem in that Day, these bold spokesmen for the Lord will be kept safe until their mission is accomplished.

Revelation, Chapter 11, gives us details concerning two special servants God sets before his nation during the final turbulent months just prior to the return of Messiah in power and glory:

[1]I was given a reed like a measuring rod and was told, "Go and measure the temple of God and the altar, and count the worshipers there. [2]But exclude the outer court; do not measure it, because it has been given to the Gentiles. They will trample on the holy city for 42 months. [3]And I will give power to my two witnesses, and they will prophesy for 1,260 days, clothed in sackcloth." [4]These are the two olive trees and the two lampstands that stand before the Lord of the earth. [5]If anyone tries to harm them, fire comes from their mouths and devours their enemies. This is how anyone who wants to harm them must die. [6]These men have power to shut up the sky so that it will not rain during the time they are prophesying; and they have power to turn the waters into blood and to strike the earth with every kind of plague as often as they want.
[7]Now when they have finished their testimony, the beast that comes up from the Abyss will attack them, and overpower and kill them. [8]Their bodies will lie in the street of the great city, which is figuratively called Sodom and Egypt, where also their Lord was crucified. [9]For three and a half days men from every people, tribe, language and nation will gaze on their bodies and refuse them burial. [10]The inhabitants of the earth will gloat over them and will celebrate by sending each other gifts, because these two prophets had tormented those who live on the earth.
[11]But after the three and a half days a breath of life from God entered them, and they stood on their feet, and terror struck those who saw them. [12]Then they heard a loud voice from heaven saying to them, "Come up here." And they went up to heaven in a cloud, while their enemies looked on.
[13]At that very hour there was a severe earthquake and a tenth of the city collapsed. Seven thousand people were killed in the earthquake, and the survivors were terrified and gave glory to the God of heaven.
[14]The second woe has passed; the third woe is coming soon. - Revelation 11:1-14

This parenthetical section describes Two Witnesses who are given supernatural power to prophesy, to perform miracles and to speak the truth boldly without fear of being captured or killed for a period of 1260 days, which is the same length of time as the 42 months of verse 2 in this same chapter. The 42 months, in turn, is the same as 3 1/2 years, the exact duration of the second half of the Tribulation. This also corresponds to the period of the evil dictator's reign in chapter 13, verse 5.

The identity of these two is not certain, but they could be Enoch and Elijah since these are the two people who were taken to heaven without dying (See Genesis 5:24 and 2 Kings 2:11). Since it is "appointed for men to die once" (Hebrews 9:27), God may be planning to send these two back to conclude their life's work in this striking manner, and to die. Elijah was, of course, a prophet and it is said of Enoch that he prophesied also (Jude 14).

It is also possible that they will be Moses and Elijah since these were the two who appeared with Jesus in his transfiguration (Matthew 17:3). If this is the case, they would represent the two Old Testament periods of The Law and The Prophets. Moses did die, but he was with God alone when he it happened, and was personally buried by God (Deuteronomy 34:1-8). He was considered the greatest of prophets (Deuteronomy 34:10).

These Two Witnesses are identified as "two olive trees." This is reminiscent of the imagery in Zechariah's prophecy of two olive trees that automatically supplied oil continuously to the Golden lampstand in the Temple (Zechariah 4:1-14). The meaning given in the passage is that the work of rebuilding the Temple in Zerubbabel's days was "'Not by might nor by power, but by My Spirit,' says the LORD of hosts" (Zechariah 4:6). Likewise, though enemies are arrayed against God in the last days, his purposes will prevail by the power of his Holy Spirit.

The miraculous powers that these two demonstrate will be very much like the miracles performed by Moses and Elijah (Exodus chapters 4 through 12; 1 Kings 17:1,7; 18:1,19-45; 2 Kings 1:10-14). This is another indication that the Two Witnesses could be Moses and Elijah.

When their work is finished, God will allow them to be put to death. The place of their death will be Jerusalem, probably on the Temple Mount. The City greatly loved by God is known for killing the prophets (Matthew 23:37). On his way to be crucified, Jesus remarked that God's prophets were always killed in Jerusalem!

Conservative Bible commentators on the book of Revelation are divided about the time period of the work of the Two Witnesses (followed of course by their death, resurrection and ascension). Does this work take place in the first half or the second half of The Tribulation Period? If their ministry is during the first half of The Tribulation they will presumably have a bigger audience on site. The completion of their ministry is marked by an earthquake. Then, presumably, the False Prophet of Revelation 13, Paul's man of sin, will step into the newly completed Third Temple and defile it. Followers of Christ who are in Jerusalem at that time have been told ahead of time by Jesus himself to flee Jerusalem at once when that desecration happens (Matthew 24:15-22).

If, on the other hand, the Two Witnesses engage in their bold preaching during the *Great* Tribulation, (i.e., the second 3.5 year portion of the Tribulation period, the "time of Jacob's trouble") they will need God's maximum protection—the man of sin will surely do all he can to wipe them out. Horrific violence will occur all over the earth, Israel and Jerusalem will be invaded and nearly destroyed completely. The earthquake that marks the end of the ministry of the Two Witnesses from the Temple Mount could then be the same earthquake marking the second coming of Jesus Christ to the Mount of Olives as described in Zechariah 14.

Spiritually speaking, Jerusalem can be compared to Sodom and Egypt, immoral places that were condemned by the Lord. Ungodly people rejoice at their death because they had stood against all their evil deeds.

After three and a half days, the Two Witnesses will be raised from the dead and caught up to heaven when they heard the words from heaven, "Come up here." The rapture of the Church happens at the beginning of The Tribulation, but this event toward the end of these seven years is similar, and may even be representative of what happens to the believing martyrs of this period of time.

Disasters of the Great Tribulation

There will be great earthquakes, famines and pestilences in various places, and fearful events and great signs from heaven. - Luke 21:11

A great amount of attention is focused on the skies in our times. There are several reasons for this. Scientific advances in observation technologies have allowed us to learn much more about our space neighbors. We now know much more about the existence and orbits of small objects that could come near, or even strike the Earth.

Our own ventures into space are a second major reason for this interest. In 2009 an Iridium communications satellite collided with a Russian Cosmos 2251 satellite directly above the International Space Station. Space junk is a growing problem. At that time scientists were trying to keep track of 13,000 pieces of space debris that are tennis ball-sized or bigger.

Asteroids

There is an "Asteroid Belt" between the orbits of Mars and Jupiter. The NASA site reports that Scientists estimate that there are more than 750,000 asteroids with diameters larger than 3/5 mile (1 kilometer), and there are millions of smaller asteroids[124].Many of them are known to intersect the Earth's orbit. (At the writing of the first edition of this book, it was thought that there might be 30,000 asteroids in our Solar System. Only about 5,000 had been identified at that time.)

Most known asteroids are not a direct threat to Earth. NASA list less than 100 that could impact Earth. These are known as Near-Earth Asteroids (NEAs). NASA says the odds that they will strike Earth in our lifetime are virtually zero. However, the various craters on Earth remind us that it has happened in the past.

In 1937 the asteroid Hermes came very close to earth. It passed within 500,000 miles, only twice the distance between the Earth the Moon. This is a "near miss." Our gravitational pull can affect something that passes this close.

In 1989 an asteroid that was 5 miles in diameter came dangerously close. It will pass again some time after the turn of the century.

Russell Chandler, former religion editor for the Los Angeles Times, reports in his book called *Doomsday*, that

On March 23, 1989, a half-mile-wide asteroid flew through Earth's path at forty-six thousand miles an hour. Nobody saw it coming. A scientific team convened by Congress a year later noted that "the Earth had been at that point only six hours earlier." Had it struck the Earth, it would have caused a disaster unprecedented in human history.[125]

Some asteroids we know about are:
Ceres - largest known - 580 miles diameter[126]
Pallas - 379 miles diameter
Vesta - 336 miles diameter
Junu - 120 miles diameter
Icarus - 1 mile diameter: a "small flying mountain."

In the book of Revelation one often reads about a "falling star." The Greek word for star is *aster*. This word is the basis for "Esther" and "asteroid."

Scientists have often suggested that an earlier collision with an asteroid may have caused mass extinction and the onset of an ice age. However, a literal interpretation of the Book of Genesis would suggest these events were caused by the great flood of Noah's days.

Meteors and Meteorites

These are "boulder-sized" asteroids. The largest one discovered was about 70 tons. They are often called "shooting stars," since they leave bright streaks in the atmosphere as they burn up. Those that do not completely burn up before hitting the earth are called meteorites.

One hit Arizona in prehistoric times causing a crater 4,100 feet across and 600 feet deep! About 500 of them strike the earth each year. About 120 impact sites are known.

Comets

We hear of comets occasionally, such as Haley's Comet, The Swift Tuttle Comet, and the Hale-Bopp Comet.

In 1994, Shoemaker-Levy 9, a comet with 21 fragments collided with Jupiter from July 16 through 22. The speed of this "comet train" was 37 miles per second (133,200 mph). This is 60 times the speed of an average bullet! (The energy carried by a moving object is proportional to the velocity squared!) At comet speed, one could go from New York to Los Angeles in 1 minute and 22 seconds. The first chunk of this comet hit Jupiter with a force of perhaps 6 million hydrogen bombs.[127] It was photographed by powerful telescopes on earth that showed that it caused a mushroom cloud of gas nearly 1000 miles into space, and left a dark splotch, half the size of Earth.

The combined size of the 21 pieces was between 1/2 mile and 2 1/2 miles in diameter. The combined energy could be 20 million megatons (compare the largest bomb ever made: the Soviet's 58 megaton behemoth)! This total impact of Shoemaker-Levy 9 was greater than the combined force of all nuclear devices ever made.

One writer said that such a comet train hitting the Earth could incinerate whole countries and produce a dust cloud that would bring on nuclear winter. It would kill millions, or perhaps billions, of people.

In 1908 a comet in Siberia flattened the surrounding forests for 40 miles, and could be felt more than 100 miles away. Pressure waves from this event were recorded in London.

Coronal Mass Eruptions / Solar Storms

On Aug. 1, 2010 a few hours of heavy activity on the Sun produced a large Coronal Mass Eruption (CME) that NASA said produced large clouds of charged particles that could carry up to ten billion tons of plasma. "They expand away from the sun at speeds as high as a million miles an hour."[128] This phenomenon caused an aurora all around the Earth similar to the Northern Lights, but it did not cause damage. In the past, CMEs have knocked out satellites and shut down electrical power grids. Scientists say the event marks the awakening of the Sun to its regular 11 year cycle of activity, which is expected to peak in 2012 or 2013. According to NASA, if we were to have the same kind of "perfect storm" as the so-called Carrington event of 1859, we could expect "disruption of the transportation, communication, banking and finance systems, and government services; the breakdown of the distribution of potable water owing to pump failure, and the loss of perishable foods and medications because of a lack of refrigeration."[129]

Ecological Issues

Many of the ecological problems of our age are related to the skies. Some of these are:

Depletion of the Ozone layer and the resultant increase in Ultra Violet Rays reaching the Earth.

Nuclear Radiation from bombs, power plants and satellites,

Space Junk falling every few days from old satellites and their rocket boosters,

Acid Rain, which is a result of dangerous chemicals in the air, and

Solar storms, mentioned above.

UFOs

Periodic reports about UFOs may be setting us up for great deception. After decades of inquiry there is still serious interest in the Roswell, New Mexico stories, and accounts of the findings of the Air Force's Project Blue Book, which supposedly give some credence to the existence of these objects.

Some prophecy scholars think that the belief in UFOs might cause authorities of the Tribulation Period to use them as an explanation of the disappearance of Christians during the rapture.

> And then the lawless one will be revealed whom the Lord Jesus will overthrow with the breath of his mouth and destroy by the splendor of his coming. [9]The coming of the lawless one will be in accordance with the work of Satan displayed in all kinds of counterfeit miracles, signs and wonders, [10]and in every sort of evil that deceives those who are perishing. They perish because they refused to love the truth and so be saved. [11]For this reason God sends them a powerful delusion so that they will believe the lie. - 2 Thessalonians 2:8-11

Some New Age practitioners are already suggesting that extraterrestrials might someday "cleanse" the Earth of troublemakers. Interest in such UFOs goes in cycles. There is a current rise in interest, and several recent movies about UFOs.

During one week in September of 2010 two sensational stories, reported by major news sources, brought UFOs and extraterrestrial life back into the public eye. The first was about a press conference in Washington D.C. UFO researcher Robert Hastings announced that some 100 former and retired members of the US Air Force claim sightings of UFOs and say that aliens interfered with nuclear weapons.

The second big story was that the United Nations was seriously considering appointing an "Ambassador to Extraterrestrials." The most likely person to be appointed to such a position was named as Mazlan Othman, a Malaysian astrophysicist. News sources were asked to recast the story to include that Othman denied the appointment. However, she does already hold the position of director of the United Nations Office for Outer Space Affairs.

Many Christians suspect that UFO appearances are often demonic manifestations. In any event, the end of the age will be a time of unprecedented deception. Satan's power to imitate and counterfeit the miracles of God will increase and in those days, separating the real from the counterfeit will become increasingly more difficult.

The Seven Trumpets
The First Trumpet - Scorching of the Earth

> The first angel sounded his trumpet, and there came hail and fire mixed with blood, and it was hurled down upon the earth. A third of the earth was burned up, a third of the trees were burned up, and all the green grass was burned up. - Revelation 8:7

The events of the previous section, the Seven Seals, were events caused by human activity and natural, earthly disasters. This next series brings what might be called supernatural judgments. The first three appear to be the result of asteroids, meteors or comets. These are also natural, but in the sense that they are divinely directed judgments on the earth, they have a supernatural element. There seems to be a progression of disasters from space: first hail and fire mixed with blood, then what seemed like a large mountain, and later, a "star."

It should be noted that these trumpet judgments could be caused by a nuclear war just as well. Hal Lindsey thinks it is more likely that the events of this chapter are the result of nuclear activity than supernatural activity; that they are the result of man's evil actions once the restraining hand of God is removed.[130] As mentioned before, some scholars expect the war of Ezekiel 38 and 39 at the beginning of the Tribulation, and some expect it to occur at the end. In any case, the language of these two chapters clearly describes God raining "fire" down from heaven on Israel's invaders from the North and also upon the "coastlands," or the "remote continents."

The first catastrophe in this series could also be caused by a comet or by very severe weather conditions. Comets are made of ice, which would provide the water for hail. It would first vaporize, and then perhaps, depending on other weather conditions descend to earth as hail. This sudden intrusion of a comet could cause extreme world-wide storms. The blood might be caused by animals being sucked up by waterspouts and tornadoes. And the fire could be extraordinary displays of lightning, which, in turn, could start forest fires in many places. All of these events have happened before, but never to the extent of this plague, burning up one third of the earth's vegetation!

The Second Trumpet - Slaughter in the Sea

> The second angel sounded his trumpet, and something like a huge mountain, all ablaze, was thrown into the sea. A third of the sea turned into blood, ⁹a third of the living creatures in the sea died, and a third of the ships were destroyed. - Revelation 8:8-9

This judgment could be caused by an asteroid plunging into the sea. Icarus, one of the smaller asteroids known to us is about one mile in diameter and is sometimes described as a small flying mountain. Other asteroids may be as large as Ceres, which is about 580 miles in diameter. Even a small asteroid crashing into one of our oceans would cause utter devastation. The fiery impact would burn and crush all life in a large portion of the ocean, and the resulting tidal waves would be beyond comprehension. These waves could capsize ships in every direction for hundreds of miles.

The Third Trumpet - Souring of the Water

> The third angel sounded his trumpet, and a great star, blazing like a torch, fell from the sky on a third of the rivers and on the springs of water— ¹¹the name of the star is Wormwood. A third of the waters turned bitter, and many people died from the waters that had become bitter. - Revelation 8:10-11

As we now know, a star is a large body of burning gases. Our own Sun is a comparatively small star, though it is 860,000 miles in diameter, compared to the Earth's diameter of 7,900 miles.

The largest known star was recently identified as R136a1 with 365 times the mass of our own Sun and is said to be ten million times brighter than our Sun![131]

This means, of course, that a star can not "fall" to the Earth, though the Earth could presumably "fall" into the Sun. However, the Greek word for star is *aster*, from which we get our word asteroid and the name "Esther." Thus, it is not a star as we know it, but a large asteroid that is in view here. As in the previous plague, the asteroid strikes earth, but, in this case, on land, causing widespread destruction and poisoning of the waters in a large area.

A "Falling Star" can also describe one of the angels, as in Revelation 9:1. In this judgment it seems more reasonable to expect an asteroid than an angel.

The Fourth Trumpet - Smiting of the Planets

> The fourth angel sounded his trumpet, and a third of the sun was struck, a third of the moon, and a third of the stars, so that a third of them turned dark. A third of the day was without light, and also a third of the night.

[13]As I watched, I heard an eagle that was flying in midair call out in a loud voice: "Woe! Woe! Woe to the inhabitants of the earth, because of the trumpet blasts about to be sounded by the other three angels!" - Revelation 8:12-13

This judgment affects the entrance of light from space. The amount of light from the sun, moon and stars is diminished by one third. This could be a description of what, in our generation, has been called "nuclear winter." One of the most serious side-effects of a nuclear war (or an asteroid strike) would be the wide-spread burning of cities and forests and the resulting soot and smoke reaching the stratosphere. This diminishing of the Sun's radiation could cause the average temperature of the Earth to cool between 18 and 36 degrees, resulting in crop failures and great ecological damage.

Alternatively, we cannot rule out that the actual light and heat output from the sun might be diminished by God during this judgment of mankind.

The eagle flying through the heavens with a message of woe is most likely a symbolic image of an angelic being. The three-fold repetition of "woe" is a biblical way of intensifying the terrible nature of the impending doom soon to follow.

In Revelation 4:7 one of the faces of the Four Living Creatures was the face of an eagle. The message is a warning of the dreadful nature of the next three trumpet judgments.

The Fifth Trumpet - Striking by Locusts

- The Diabolical Pit

The fifth angel sounded his trumpet, and I saw a star that had fallen from the sky to the earth. The star was given the key to the shaft of the Abyss. [2]When he opened the Abyss, smoke rose from it like the smoke from a gigantic furnace. The sun and sky were darkened by the smoke from the Abyss. - Revelation 9:1-2

In this case the falling star is actually an angelic being. Satan fits this description best since he was created as the Anointed Cherub, a position of prominence among the angels. Ezekiel 28:14 Isaiah 14:4-17 and Ezekiel 28:12-19 are addressed to earthly rulers, but obviously refer to Satan's own history and work since he controlled the human rulers. Isaiah 14:12 says "How you have fallen from heaven, O star of the morning, son of the dawn! You have been cut down to the earth, you who have weakened the nations!"

The Dragon of Revelation 12 is the devil, another name for Satan (v.9). He is seen there sweeping away a third of the stars (angels) of heaven, and waging war against God, then being cast out of heaven (vv. 7-9, 12-13).

Satan is given the key, presumably from Jesus Christ, who, according to Revelation 1:18 holds the keys of death and Hades. This key to the Abyss might well be one of these keys.

-The Demonic Plague
- *Their Actions*

> And out of the smoke locusts came down upon the earth and were given power like that of scorpions of the earth. ⁴They were told not to harm the grass of the earth or any plant or tree, but only those people who did not have the seal of God on their foreheads. ⁵They were not given power to kill them, but only to torture them for five months. And the agony they suffered was like that of the sting of a scorpion when it strikes a man. ⁶During those days men will seek death, but will not find it; they will long to die, but death will elude them.
> - Revelation 9:3-6

Once the Abyss or Bottomless Pit is opened, its demonic inhabitants are set loose for the purpose of torturing people. Like locusts, they are numerous and destructive. Like scorpions, they inflict pain. But they are not allowed to kill. Here, as in the whole book of Revelation, God's sovereignty is seen. He sets the limits of what is permitted (Job 2:6; 1 Corinthians 10:13).

Those who have the seal of God on their foreheads can not be harmed by these demonic mutations. Some take this to mean all believers, since we are sealed by the Holy Spirit (2 Corinthians 1:22; Ephesians 1:13; 4:30). However, it probably refers to the 144,000 servants of God from Revelation 7:3 who are marked or sealed on their foreheads before any further plagues were permitted.

The pain inflicted by this judgment is so severe that people who suffer it would rather die than endure the continuous torment (five months), but they are not allowed to take the easy course of death. This length of time may be allowed by God to give men the opportunity to repent, though it appears from the last verses of this chapter that none of them do (Revelation 9:19-20). Those who have hardened their heart against God would probably not even repent in hell itself.

- *Their Appearance*

> The locusts looked like horses prepared for battle. On their heads they wore something like crowns of gold, and their faces resembled human faces. ⁸Their hair was like women's hair, and their teeth were like lions' teeth. ⁹They had breastplates like breastplates of iron, and the sound of their wings was like the thundering of many horses and chariots rushing

into battle. [10]They had tails and stings like scorpions, and in their tails they had power to torment people for five months. - Revelation 9:7-10

Further information is given about these malignant creatures. Each description is symbolic of some aspect of their power and activity.

They are like horses prepared for battle: descriptive of strength. They seem to have crowns of gold, standing for power and authority, yet they are limited by God that they may not kill their victims. Human faces imply intelligence. Hair like a woman's hair would be totally unnatural for insect-like monsters and would add to the confusion about their nature. The lion's teeth picture ferocity, breastplates of iron show that they are invincible. Like normal locusts, they have wings. Wings symbolize mobility and speed. Because of their extraordinary powers, their sound in flight is loud and terrifying, like horses and chariots in battle.

- The Destructive Potentate

They had as king over them the angel of the Abyss, whose name in Hebrew is Abaddon, and in Greek, Apollyon. The first woe is past; two other woes are yet to come. Revelation 9:11-12

Perhaps the most terrifying aspect of this fifth trumpet judgment is that these monstrosities are actually the demons that have been imprisoned in the Abyss (Luke 8:31; Jude 6).They have a leader of their fallen ranks, named Abaddon, or "Destroyer." This is a Hebrew word that is used in connection with hell, and normally refers to it as the place of destruction (Job 26:6; Proverbs 15:11; 27:20). It occurs only here as the name of a person. Apollyon is the exact Greek equivalent of the same name. This name is also found only here.

The Sixth Trumpet - Slaying of One-third of the Population

The sixth angel sounded his trumpet, and I heard a voice coming from the horn of the golden altar that is before God. - Revelation 9:13

The Sixth Trumpet is also called the Second Woe. It is a judgment of terrible magnitude. It begins with the release of four evil angels (demons) from the area of the Euphrates River, the approximate location of the early evil empires of Babylon, Medo-Persia, and Assyria. They are allowed to kill a third of the people on the Earth. They accomplish this by mobilizing a force of 200 million soldiers. It is only in recent times that it would be conceivable to raise an army of that size. Today China has that many people who could serve as soldiers.

Each of these 200 million troops has equipment resembling modern weaponry, with fire, smoke and sulfur coming out of their mouths. They employ horses, symbolic of modern tanks, with "tails" able to inflict injury.

Even after all the agony and death inflicted by these judgments, the survivors are not willing to repent or to stop worshiping demons and idols. There is a process of hardening one's heart. It is illustrated in the case of Pharaoh during the days of Moses. He hardened his heart repeatedly. As a result, God actually hardened it more (Exodus 8:19, 32; 9:12, 34; 10:1).

This hardening is explained in Romans 1:21-32. It starts with a conscious decision not to honor God, but to honor themselves instead. This results in idolatry. Idolatry in our age can take many forms. The word means "to worship what can be seen." Some practice idolatry in the ancient way of venerating a man-made image of something that represents their false god. In New Age religious practice there is worship of the creation itself, such as "Mother Earth," or use of sacred objects, such as crystals. Other people, who do not consider themselves religious at all, often venerate material possessions: in essence, worshiping materialism and wealth.

Idols are not devoid of power to influence men; the Apostle Paul tells us that demonic, destructive powers come into play when we give ourselves to any master except Jesus.

> Do I mean then that a sacrifice offered to an idol is anything, or that an idol is anything? [20]No, but the sacrifices of pagans are offered to demons, not to God, and I do not want you to be participants with demons.. - 1 Corinthians 10:19-20

God is not willing that any should perish (2 Peter 3:9), but when man's rebellion has reached a certain point, he "gives them over" to their lusts and degrading passions.

Since the Trumpet judgments appear to take place during the Great Tribulation, the second half of the seven years of the Tribulation, these people will have received the Mark of The Beast, which is the unforgivable act of worshipping the imposter (Revelation 14:9-11; 20:4). This also helps to explain why none of them are willing to repent.

The Seventh Trumpet - Sovereignty of God

> The seventh angel sounded his trumpet, and there were loud voices in heaven, which said:
>> "The kingdom of the world has become the kingdom of our Lord and of his Christ, and he will reign for ever and ever." [16]And the twenty-four elders, who were seated on their thrones before God, fell on their faces and worshiped God, [17]saying:

> "We give thanks to you, Lord God Almighty,
>> the One who is and who was,
>> because you have taken your great power
>> and have begun to reign.
> [18]The nations were angry; and your wrath has come.
>> The time has come for judging the dead,
>>> and for rewarding your servants the prophets
>> and your saints and those who reverence your name,
>>> both small and great—
>> and for destroying those who destroy the earth."
> [19]Then God's temple in heaven was opened, and within his temple was seen the ark of his covenant. And there came flashes of lightning, rumblings, peals of thunder, an earthquake and a great hailstorm. - Revelation 11:15-19

The Seventh Trumpet, like the Seventh Seal, does not introduce an activity on earth, but looks to Heaven in anticipation of the next series of events. In this case, the next step is God taking his great power and beginning to reign on earth. This last trumpet introduces the events leading up to the Battle of Armageddon.

The great earthquake mentioned in this passage is probably the same earthquake that marks the Sixth Seal (Revelation 6:12-17), the last of the Seven Trumpets (Rev. 11:19), and the last of the Seven Bowls of wrath (Revelation. 16:18-21) —which all run in parallel. (See also Ezekiel 38:19-20 and Zechariah 14:4-5.) Many Bible scholars hold that all these scriptures are homing in on one or possibly a connected series of great cataclysmic earthquakes that punctuate the end of the age, the open return of Messiah and the dawning of the millennial age. Not only does the city of Jerusalem suffer great damage from this earthquake, but "the cities of the nations fall," "And every island fled away, and no mountains were to be found." according to Revelation 16:19, 20.

The next few chapters of the book of Revelation explain important aspects of the total story, but they cannot be taken strictly in chronological order. They focus on particular topics, some of which we have already considered: Israel (chapter 12); The Beast, the False Prophet and the Mark of the Beast (chapter 13); the 144,000 sealed ones (chapter 14); preparations for judgment (chapters 14-15); and then the Seven Vials (chapter 16), which are poured out in rapid succession; culminating in Judgment of Babylon (chapters 17 and 18); the Battle of Armageddon, and the glorious return of Christ as King of Kings and Lord of Lords (chapter 19). As the time approaches for Christ to return, it is also nearing the time for judging the dead and rewarding the faithful (chapters 20 to 22).

As we continue our study of future things, the next topic is one of special interest to most people: The Battle of Armageddon.

Chapter 14
Armageddon

The awful culmination of the Great Tribulation will be the Battle of Armageddon. This conflict gets its name from Revelation 16:14-16. Actually it might be better to speak of the "campaign" of Armageddon, since it is not one single battle but a series of events in which all the nations of the world are drawn in as participants. The word "Armageddon" is formed from the Hebrew Words "Har" or mountain, and "Megiddo," a city on a hill—actually an archaeological site. It is in the northern part of the Holy Land, inland from Mount Carmel. It is near the modern seaport of Haifa. It is at the "crossroads of the crossroads" where the ancient Via Maris ("Way of the Sea") crosses the central transverse highway of Israel. This commands a view of the Valley of Jezreel, known as the "breadbasket of Israel." It was a strategic command post for control of the entire area for many centuries. The transverse highway led to the other major caravan route of the day, "The King's Highway." Travelers from Egypt to Syria, Babylon, Persia, and Asia Minor would normally pass this way, and could be taxed by whoever controlled the city. For this reason, the city was often conquered by the various powers that occupied the Holy Land.

Two important issues need to be considered. As may be seen from the following section, Jerusalem is actually the focus of the battle, but Megiddo, is 55 miles away from Jerusalem. This may be understood when the huge numbers of soldiers involved in this battle are considered. This area, Megiddo, and the Valley of Jezreel, (also known as the Plain of Esdraelon) will be the staging area where the multi-national troops will assemble prior to their advance on Jerusalem. Haifa, at the West end of the Valley, is the logical seaport for major troop landings.

The other issue is the question of who is fighting whom in this battle. It is apparent that at the end of his career, the Beast is fighting against various alliances, and his empire appears to be crumbling. On the other hand, according to Revelation 19, all the forces gathered for that battle will be arrayed together against Jesus Christ. Verse 19 states "Then I saw the beast and the kings of the earth and their armies gathered together to make war against the rider on the horse and his army." The probable scenario is that the Beast, realizing that his power is waning, manages to unite all the forces of earth together against their common enemy—The King of Kings and Lord of Lords. Like all non-believers do, they think they can prevail against him!

This dreadful battle is the subject of many Old and New Testament passages. It is actually a series of inter-related disasters. In this section we will first look at some of the Old Testament predictions about this terrible day. These passages remind us that God's chosen people, Israel, and her capital, Jerusalem, are the focus of the campaign. They also show God's compassion for Israel. We will then examine the steps that lead to the battle, and to the glorious return of The Lord Jesus Christ.

Old Testament Previews of the Battle of Armageddon
Zechariah

The post-exilic prophet Zechariah gave insight about the close of the age in which we live. God himself will fight against those who will gather against Jerusalem (Zechariah 12).

> "I am going to make Jerusalem a cup that sends all the surrounding peoples reeling. Judah will be besieged as well as Jerusalem. " - Zechariah 12:2

The expression, *on that day,* used frequently by prophets, is a clue that the passage is referring to the Great Tribulation.

> On that day, when all the nations of the earth are gathered against her, I will make Jerusalem an immovable rock for all the nations. All who try to move it will injure themselves. 4 On that day I will strike every horse with panic and its rider with madness," declares the LORD. "I will keep a watchful eye over the house of Judah, but I will blind all the horses of the nations...
> 9 On that day I will set out to destroy all the nations that attack Jerusalem." - Zechariah 12:3-9

Near the end of the coming Tribulation Period, Jerusalem is to come under military siege and be overrun by foreign armies one more time. Zechariah announces that this will happen just prior to Messiah's final return to the city,

> A day of the LORD is coming when your plunder will be divided among you.
> 2 I will gather all the nations to Jerusalem to fight against it; the city will be captured, the houses ransacked, and the women raped. Half of the city will go into exile, but the rest of the people will not be taken from the city.

³ Then the LORD will go out and fight against those nations, as he fights in the day of battle. ⁴ On that day his feet will stand on the Mount of Olives, east of Jerusalem, and the Mount of Olives will be split in two from east to west, forming a great valley, with half of the mountain moving north and half moving south. ⁵ You will flee by my mountain valley, for it will extend to Azel. You will flee as you fled from the earthquake in the days of Uzziah king of Judah. Then the LORD my God will come and all the holy ones with him. - Zechariah 14:1-5

Daniel

The Book of Daniel is known as "The Apocalypse of The Old Testament." The visions of this book establish the framework of the entire history of evil world empires, from the time of Nebuchadnezzar (and even before), until the final despotic rule of end-times ruler. In the ninth chapter there is a brief allusion to the Battle of Armageddon where he will be defeated. This one verse speaks of three and one half years: from the "middle" of the "seven," until the end of that time.

> He will confirm a covenant with many for one 'seven.' In the middle of the 'seven' he will put an end to sacrifice and offering. And on a wing *of the temple* he will set up an abomination that causes desolation, until the end that is decreed is poured out on him. - Daniel 9:27

The eleventh chapter of Daniel foretells some of the activity of the last evil king's military campaigns, leading up to his bold establishment of himself as ruler, and the "abomination of desolation" at the mid-point of the Tribulation. The first twenty verses of this chapter describe the rise of Alexander's Greece (verse 3) at the end of the Medo-Persian era, then the emergence of the Roman Empire as a "King of the North." At verse 21 the scene shifts from the ancient Roman Empire to the future appearance of a contemptible person who will seize the kingdom by intrigue (conspiracy).

At the height of his power he will decide to break his covenant with Israel. At that time he will abolish the daily sacrifice (in the newly rebuilt Temple in Jerusalem), and the False Prophet will set up the "abomination of desolation," which Revelation 13:14-15 reveals will be an image of the First Beast that is to be worshiped.

Most conservative commentators find the events of Daniel 11 were partially fulfilled by Antiochus Epiphanes as a type of the final world ruler.

> "At the appointed time he will invade the South again, but this time the outcome will be different from what it was before. ³⁰ Ships of the western coastlands will oppose him, and he will lose heart. Then he will turn back and vent his fury against the holy covenant. He will return and show favor to those who forsake the holy covenant.

[31] "His armed forces will rise up to desecrate the temple fortress and will abolish the daily sacrifice. Then they will set up the abomination that causes desolation." - Daniel 11:28-31

A great gap or "parenthesis" is found in Daniel Chapter 11. The first part of this chapter is a long history of ancient rulers, the Selucids and the Ptolemies, who struggled back and forth for many years between one another—with Israel in the middle. At verse 28 there is a sudden break in the text, and Scripture leaps over centuries of intervening history down to "the time of the end." Then the final war will begin by an Egyptian king invading Israel from the South and being met by the opposing forces of the last king of the North.

"At the time of the end the king of the South will engage him in battle, and the king of the North will storm out against him with chariots and cavalry and a great fleet of ships. He will invade many countries and sweep through them like a flood. [41] He will also invade the Beautiful Land. Many countries will fall, but Edom, Moab and the leaders of Ammon will be delivered from his hand. [42] He will extend his power over many countries; Egypt will not escape. [43] He will gain control of the treasures of gold and silver and all the riches of Egypt, with the Libyans and Nubians in submission. [44] But reports from the east and the north will alarm him, and he will set out in a great rage to destroy and annihilate many. [45] He will pitch his royal tents between the seas at the beautiful holy mountain. Yet he will come to his end, and no one will help him." - Daniel 11:40-45

Joel

The prophet Joel also describes this final invasion,

Blow the trumpet in Zion;
sound the alarm on my holy hill.
Let all who live in the land tremble,
for the day of the LORD is coming.
It is close at hand-
[2] a day of darkness and gloom,
a day of clouds and blackness.
Like dawn spreading across the mountains
a large and mighty army comes,
such as never was of old
nor ever will be in ages to come.
[3] Before them fire devours,
behind them a flame blazes.
Before them the land is like the garden of Eden,
behind them, a desert waste—
nothing escapes them. - Joel 2:1-3

Joel wrote of the approaching invasion of Israel by Nebuchadnezzar in his own day, and also about the final invasion of foreign armies that would come just prior to Messiah's appearance in power and glory. The clue to the end-time application is the phrase "the Day of the LORD," which occurs again at the end of the following section (Joel 2:4-11).

God in mercy has previously saved the godly remnant in Israel at the mid-tribulation point and taken them safely to refuge in Petra for the last half of The Tribulation Period. Still, Yahweh calls to the remaining Jews in Israel to turn to him, even at the late hour in which they are now living.

Joel's words apply well to both the approaching captivity in Babylon—which was on the near horizon in Joel's day- - but are even more relevant to the situation during the closing days of this age. God pleads with his people to come back to him, even at the midnight hour (Joel 2:12-17).

> "Even now," declares the LORD,
>> "return to me with all your heart,
>> with fasting and weeping and mourning."
> [13] Rend your heart
>> and not your garments.
>> Return to the LORD your God,
>> for he is gracious and compassionate,
>> slow to anger and abounding in love,
>> and he relents from sending calamity. - Joel 2:12-13

Joel also foresees the final conversion of Israel at the very last minute—just preceding the final return of Messiah. In mercy and grace God will at that time turn one third of the nation back to himself. In fact the prayers of this remnant are necessary for Messiah's return to his own land for the final time. This eleventh-hour conversion of great numbers of Jews to Messiah could well amount to more than one million new believers coming into the kingdom just as the Messiah is returning to the land for the final time(Joel 2:18-32).

> "And afterward,
>> I will pour out my Spirit on all people.
>> Your sons and daughters will prophesy,
>> your old men will dream dreams,
>> your young men will see visions.
> [29] Even on my servants, both men and women,
>> I will pour out my Spirit in those days.
> [30] I will show wonders in the heavens
>> and on the earth,
>> blood and fire and billows of smoke.
> [31] The sun will be turned to darkness

and the moon to blood
before the coming of the great and dreadful day of the LORD.
[32] And everyone who calls
on the name of the LORD will be saved;
for on Mount Zion and in Jerusalem
there will be deliverance,
as the LORD has said,
among the survivors
whom the LORD calls." - Joel 2:28-32

Joel's apocalyptic warning is but one of many in the Old Testament that has a double fulfillment. Joel warned against the devastating invasions of Nebuchadnezzar that lay just ahead in his own day. But the Spirit of God also had in mind a greater and more complete fulfillment of this passage at the end of the age in which we now live.

The Seven Vials of God's Wrath

These vial judgments seem to come in rapid succession, leading up to the Battle of Armageddon. Little detail is given, but they are supernatural judgments that seem to affect the whole earth.

The First Vial - Damaging Sores

Then I heard a loud voice from the temple saying to the seven angels, "Go, pour out the seven bowls of God's wrath on the earth." [2]The first angel went and poured out his bowl on the land, and ugly and painful sores broke out on the people who had the mark of the beast and worshiped his image." - Revelation 16:1-2

The first vial will cause ugly and painful sores. If mankind has the ability to develop biological warfare, just imagine what the Creator could do in this area. The result is painful, but evidently not deadly. Actually, all of these plagues cause torment rather than death.

The Second Vial - Deadly Seas

The second angel poured out his bowl on the sea, and it turned into blood like that of a dead man, and every living thing in the sea died. - Revelation 16:3

This is reminiscent of the plague of Exodus 7 in Moses' times, when the Nile River, and all the water in Egypt, was turned to blood. In this case, it will affect "the sea," meaning at least the Mediterranean, and perhaps all of the oceans of the earth.

The third angel poured out his bowl on the rivers and springs of water, and they became blood. [5]Then I heard the angel in charge of the waters say:

"You are just in these judgments,
you who are and who were, the Holy One,
because you have so judged;
[6]for they have shed the blood of your saints and prophets,
and you have given them blood to drink as they deserve."
[7]And I heard the altar respond:
"Yes, Lord God Almighty,
true and just are your judgments." - Revelation 16:4-7

This judgment is a continuation of the last one, spreading the horror of bloody water from the seas to all sources of water. As repugnant as this plague is, it is just because rebellious mankind has shed the blood of the saints and the prophets.

The Fourth Vial - Dangerous Sunlight

The fourth angel poured out his bowl on the sun, and the sun was given power to scorch people with fire. [9]They were seared by the intense heat and they cursed the name of God, who had control over these plagues, but they refused to repent and glorify him. - Revelation 16:8-9

Many natural causes could account for this scorching by the Sun. Violent eruptions of the Sun itself, a slight change of orbit, or even depletion of the ozone layer around the earth, could cause this. See the discussion of Coronal Mass Eruptions in the previous chapter.

It is very significant that, even with these stern reminders of the power and anger of God, rebellious people still refuse to repent.

The Fifth Vial - Dark Seizure

The fifth angel poured out his bowl on the throne of the beast, and his kingdom was plunged into darkness. Men gnawed their tongues in agony [11]and cursed the God of heaven because of their pains and their sores, but they refused to repent of what they had done. - Revelation 16:10-11

Coming on the heels of terrible burns from the Sun, there will be complete darkness and the cold that comes from this lack of light. Chills are common among those who have suffered burns, and this will make their situation worse yet. However, instead of repenting, mankind will curse God.

The Sixth Vial - Drying of the Strait

> The sixth angel poured out his bowl on the great river Euphrates, and its water was dried up to prepare the way for the kings from the East. - Revelation 16:12

These events will lead up to the great confrontation with Christ: The Battle of Armageddon. The drying of the Euphrates River by angelic agencies will make it easier for far eastern troops to enter the Middle East to prepare for the battle.

There are many dams on the Euphrates. Turkey completed construction of the Ataturk Dam on the Euphrates in 1990. It is one of the world's largest earth-and-rock fill dams. Whether the angel will make use of these dams or do something completely supernatural, the purpose will be to allow troop movement toward Israel.

Demonic Spirits

> Then I saw three evil spirits that looked like frogs; they came out of the mouth of the dragon, out of the mouth of the beast and out of the mouth of the false prophet. [14]They are spirits of demons performing miraculous signs, and they go out to the kings of the whole world, to gather them for the battle on the great day of God Almighty.
> [15]"Behold, I come like a thief! Blessed is he who stays awake and keeps his clothes with him, so that he may not go naked and be shamefully exposed."
> [16]Then they gathered the kings together to the place that in Hebrew is called Armageddon.
> - Revelation 16:13-16

The invitation to this battle is not by conventional political alliances, but by a demonic seduction.

The Seventh Vial - Destructive Scourge

> The seventh angel poured out his bowl into the air, and out of the temple came a loud voice from the throne, saying, "It is done!" [18]Then there came flashes of lightning, rumblings, peals of thunder and a severe earthquake. No earthquake like it has ever occurred since man has been on earth, so tremendous was the quake. [19]The great city split into three parts, and the cities of the nations collapsed. God remembered Babylon the Great and gave her the cup filled with the wine of the fury of his wrath. [20]Every Island fled away and the mountains could not be found. [21]From the sky huge hailstones of about a hundred pounds each fell upon men. And they cursed God on account of the plague of hail, because the plague was so terrible. - Revelation 16:17-21

This judgment is identical to the Great Earthquake, which will be described below.

The "Campaign" of Armageddon

As we have said, it is obvious that the final conflict of the Tribulation is not one simple battle, but a complex series of military movements and engagements. Biblical scholars have proposed a variety of possible steps in this process. It is not wise to be dogmatic about the exact sequence. Like the prophecies of the first coming of Messiah, the various aspects were known, but there were many ways it could be envisioned. No one could have written the specific order and details of the Gospel before Christ came to fulfill the predictions about his earthly life and ministry.

Here are key elements of Christ's second coming, and a proposed sequence. Some of these features have already been discussed, and some of them will be explained more fully in the next chapter.

1 - The Beast (the European military world dictator) will invade Israel, then take his troops to the South (North Africa, including Egypt and Libya - Daniel 11:40-43). His economic dictatorship will be challenged, involving military activity during the second half of the Tribulation. Toward the end, the "King of the South" (probably Egypt, with Libya and others) will rebel. He will bring his troops through Israel, and quell the disturbances.

2 - The Beast will be disturbed by news from the East and the North, so he will return to establish a staging area in the Valley of Armageddon ("between the seas and the beautiful holy mountain" - Mt. Zion - Daniel 11:44-45). He will return to Israel and set up his command post in the bread basket of Israel. The Valley of Armageddon is just 20 miles inland from the port city of Haifa, through which sea-borne armies of the world can enter.

3 - Kings and armies of all nations will be summoned to the battlefield. The Euphrates River will be dried up to enable the huge armies from the East to come (Revelation 9:14-16; 16:12-16). In a last futile effort to unify the armies of the Earth, and to divert attention from the fact that his strangle-hold on world powers is weakening, The Beast and The False Prophet will declare war against Jesus Christ, the common enemy of all the debased people of the Tribulation. The object of their wrath will be the chosen people in Jerusalem.

4 - Jerusalem will be devastated by the overpowering might of The Beast's forces (Zechariah 12:1-3; 14:1-2).

Many fine Bible teachers, including the late Ray C. Stedman, see the fulfillment at this point of the war of Ezekiel 38 and 39. In this view, the war, one of the campaigns of the Last War, will be against Israel, and will be provoked by Russia and her allies.[132]

Other respected prophecy scholars believe that, after the destruction of Jerusalem, the end-times ruler will mount a futile attempt to attack the protected remnant who have fled, probably to the Petra/Bozrah area (Micah 2:12; Jeremiah 49:13-14). Thomas Ice and Timothy Demy[133], following the lead by Arnold Fruchtenbaum, believe this will be part of the campaign of Armageddon.[134]

5 - Ominous signs will turn men's attention to the skies (Luke 21:25-27). Jesus will appear in the heavens, coming as King of Kings and Lord of Lords, utterly destroying the

gathered enemies with the sword from his mouth (Revelation 19:11-16). As suggested before, he would likely have been present on the Earth since the time of his *parousia* ("coming") at the rapture, appearing and disappearing as needed for the benefit of persecuted believers, like he did before his ascension. But at this momentous event he will make his presence known in such a way that "every eye will see him" (Revelation 1:7).

The annihilation of Christ's enemies will include the harvest judgments (of wheat and of grapes) described in the next chapter.

6 - Jesus will appear, blood-stained from the battle, to the sheltered remnant at Bozrah, near Petra, presumably to lead them from exile, back to the Holy City (Isaiah 63:1-6; Micah 2:12-13).

7 - When Christ's feet actually touch ground it will be at the Mount of Olives, and this event will trigger the great Earth-changing earthquake, which is discussed below (Zechariah 14:4-5; Acts 1:9-12; Revelation 16:17-19).

8 - Babylon will be destroyed (Revelation chapters 17 and 18). Revelation 16:19 implies that the destruction of Babylon takes place at the time of the great earthquake. There is considerable debate about whether or not the Babylonian system of world commerce and spiritual prostitution will have anything to do with a literal, rebuilt city of Babylon in Iraq. Saddam Hussein had managed to restore the city somewhat, and had planned to do more before his death. Only time will tell how this facet of the prophecy will unfold. Zechariah 5:5-11 also indicates that there will be future "wickedness" in a restored city of Babylon. But later still, Isaiah 13:1-20 indicates that the literal city of Babylon still has a devastating destruction coming, after which, it will never be inhabited again.

More likely *both* the destruction of the literal city of Babylon (and perhaps the nation of Iraq) as well as the destruction of "Mystery Babylon" are implied. The latter aspects of Babylon (Revelation 17 and 18) include the apostate church in league with the western confederacy of nations, and also the world-wide institutions of trade and commerce, which are part of the present world order. False religion sprang from the ancient city of Babylon after the Flood, and now has polluted the entire world, spiritually speaking. But commerce, trade and economic systems in the world, including capitalism, have likewise become corrupted and must be replaced by righteous means of economics under Messiah's reign.

Harmony of Passages in Revelation about Armageddon

The Book of Revelation can not be taken in strict chronological order. The various sequences of events, such as the Messages to the Seven Churches, the Seven Seals, Seven Trumpets, etc. are chronological, but each section stands alone to describe some aspect of the future. (See the charts in the Appendices to see how these segments fit together.)

The Battle of Armageddon certainly comes at the end of the seven years of the Tribulation, but references to it may be found in six places in the Book of Revelation. It serves as the end point of several of the separate sequences found in the book. A study of these six references helps us understand the total picture of the future.

You will notice that most of the Scripture references in this section are also explained in another place. We list them here for the sake of clarity.

1- The Sixth Seal - Revelation 6:12-17

This first description comes very early in the Book of Revelation, but it is near the end of the Seven Seals. The Seventh Seal - Silence in Heaven - is not an event in itself, but is the introduction to the next segment of the book, the Seven Trumpets. "When he opened the seventh seal, there was silence in heaven for about half an hour" (Revelation 8:1).

Signs in the heavens and a great, geography-changing earthquake are part of the description of the Sixth Seal, indicating that it actually does take place at the end of the seven years. Some commentators take this to be an earlier occurrence of these things, but if that were the case, the Battle of Armageddon with its accompanying signs would be anticlimactic.

From this it may be concluded that the Seven Seals cover the whole period of the Tribulation. This is perfectly fitting since it is given at the beginning of the events of this period, and serves as an overview of the entire seven years.

2- The Sixth Trumpet - Revelation 9:13-21; 11:13

Everything about this battle is too grand to be a minor campaign of the Tribulation Period. It can not be the final carnage of the Battle of Armageddon, since all the destruction of that climactic event will be accomplished by Jesus Christ himself! (See Revelation 19:11-21 below.)

It could, however, very well be a major aspect of the military events that frustrate the Beast and cause him to refocus the attention of all the world's forces on their common enemy in Israel: The Lord Jesus Christ. (See notes on Daniel 11:36-45 above.)

It is also very significant that this battle is called the Second Woe. The Seventh Trumpet, which is The Third Woe, in chapter 11, verses 14-19, is Christ taking control of the kingdoms of the world and the coming judgments. This, of course, will take place immediately after the Battle of Armageddon.

3- The Winepress of God's Wrath - Revelation 14:14-20

This is the next place in the Book of Revelation, which evidently refers to the Battle of Armageddon. It is called "the great wine press of the wrath of God" (v.19). The battlefield is some 200 miles long! There will be blood up to the horses' bridles (v.20). We have a picture given to us of utter destruction!

4- Sixth and Seventh Vials of God's Wrath - Revelation 16:12-21

Again, the similarities between this passage and the earlier ones in Revelation can only be explained by the fact that this pivotal event is given in relation to several separate sequences so that the reader will know how to put them all together. The Battle of Armageddon is the common anchor of all of these segments.

5 - War against the Lamb - Revelation 17:14

This verse is part of the description of the ten kings who will form an evil governmental alliance.

6- The Coming of Christ as King of Kings - Revelation 19:11-21

In the next chapter we will discuss the Glorious Return of Jesus Christ to the Earth. As this passage shows, his coming in glory will take place at the very end of the Battle of Armageddon. The end-times ruler and kings of earth will be assembled to make war against him. the Beast and the False Prophet will be thrown in to the Lake of Fire, and rest of the rebels will be killed with the sword from Christ's mouth, which is symbolic of his Word.

Signs in the Sun, Moon and Stars

The additional events described below either happen at the same time, or in rapid succession.

> "Immediately after the distress of those days
>   " 'the sun will be darkened,
>   and the moon will not give its light;
>   the stars will fall from the sky,
>   and the heavenly bodies will be shaken.'
> [30]"At that time the sign of the Son of Man will appear in the sky and all the nations of the earth will mourn. They will see the Son of Man coming on the clouds of the sky, with power and great glory. [31]And he will send his angels with a loud trumpet call, and they will gather his elect from the four winds, from one end of the heavens to the other." - Matthew 24:29-31

> "There will be signs in the sun, moon and stars. On the earth, nations will be in anguish and perplexity at the roaring and tossing of the sea. [26]Men will faint from terror, apprehensive of what is coming on the world, for the heavenly bodies will be shaken. [27]At that time they will see the Son of Man coming in a cloud with power and great glory." - Luke 21:25-27

Jesus himself gave this sign that will signal his return. Notice that there is a gathering of the elect associated with this event also. This cannot be the rapture of the Church. As shown before, the Church, as such, is never mentioned during The Tribulation Period. This event, immediately after his return to Earth, will be the gathering of the believers who are left on the disaster-torn planet.

> Jesus told them another parable: "The kingdom of heaven is like a man who sowed good seed in his field. [25]But while everyone was sleeping, his enemy came and sowed weeds among the wheat, and went away. [26]When the wheat sprouted and formed heads, then the weeds also appeared.
> [27]"The owner's servants came to him and said, 'Sir, didn't you sow good seed in your field? Where then did the weeds come from?'
> [28]" 'An enemy did this,' he replied.
> "The servants asked him, 'Do you want us to go and pull them up?'
> [29]" 'No,' he answered, 'because while you are pulling the weeds, you may root up the wheat with them. [30]Let both grow together until the harvest. At that time I will tell the harvesters: First collect the weeds and tie them in bundles to be burned; then gather the wheat and bring it into my barn.' " - Matthew 13:24-30

Believers will be "gathered into the barn" so they can populate the Millennial Kingdom, which will begin immediately after this. Non-believers will also be gathered together for destruction at this time so that the Millennium may begin with only believers. More will be said about this judgment in the next chapter.

The Great Earthquake

When we listed the various portions of the book of Revelation that refer to the Battle of Armageddon, it was obvious that one of the major aspects of this great judgment would be an earthquake of such magnitude that there has never been such a great one before! It will literally sink every island and shake down the mountains, and will transform the geography of the Earth completely (Revelation 6:5; Revelation 9:19; Revelation 11:13, Revelation 16:18-21).

The Promised Land, in the providence of God, lies immediately adjacent to the African Rift Zone, the deepest known break in the earth's crust. The destruction of Sodom and Gomorrah at the Southeastern shores of the Dead Sea in the time of Abraham (c. 2100-1900 BC) is vividly described in Genesis 19. Archaeological research suggests that a great earthquake opened the rift zone releasing "brimstone" (sulfur) and volatile petroleum gases, which caused a terrible firestorm.

In Zechariah 14:4-5 we are told:

On that day his feet will stand on the Mount of Olives, east of Jerusalem, and the Mount of Olives will be split in two from east to west, forming a great valley, with half of the mountain moving north and half moving south. [5] You will flee by my mountain valley, for it will extend to Azel. You will flee as you fled from the earthquake in the days of Uzziah king of Judah. Then the LORD my God will come and all the holy ones with him.

Consider this amazing Old Testament prophecy in the light of what the angel promised the Disciples on the day that Jesus ascended from the Mount of Olives,

"Men of Galilee," they said, "why do you stand here looking into the sky? This same Jesus, who has been taken from you into heaven, will come back in the same way you have seen him go into heaven." - Acts 1:11

This ultimate earthquake will evidently be preceded by others, leading up to "the big one." Jesus gave earthquakes as one of the signs of the "beginning of birth pains," the period before the beginning of the Tribulation, between his First and Second Advents (Matthew 24:7-8).

The great earthquake of Ezekiel 38:19-20 could be a foreshock, coinciding with the war at the Second Seal of Revelation 6, or it could yet be another reference to the Battle of Armageddon, depending on where this battle occurs. There are good Bible scholars on both sides of this issue.

While some people seek to demonstrate that current earthquake activity is increasing dramatically, there is need for caution on this point, earthquakes are not yet increasing. For balance on this issue, see Appendix J - *Earthquakes, Signs and Wonders*.

As terrible as the Great Tribulation will be, especially at the end, with the Battle of Armageddon, the biblical story does not end in despair. These awful events bring Jesus back to earth as King of Kings and Lord of Lords. We will study that next.

Chapter 15
Coming of the King of Kings

We come at last to the climax of the Tribulation Period, and the end of the Battle of Armageddon. Jesus Christ will literally, physically, and visibly, return to the Earth as the King of Kings and the Lord of Lords. The last two segments of the previous chapter were devoted to the signs in the sun, moon and stars, and the Great Earthquake. These events happen virtually at the same time dramatically punctuating Christ's glorious appearing. Now, when we gaze at the Lord himself, all the wondrous events in the heavens and on the Earth are suddenly not important!

The Glorious Return of Christ

> I saw heaven standing open and there before me was a white horse, whose rider is called Faithful and True. With justice he judges and makes war. ¹²His eyes are like blazing fire, and on his head are many crowns. He has a name written on him that no one knows but he himself. ¹³He is dressed in a robe dipped in blood, and his name is the Word of God. - Revelation 19:11-13

Jesus himself spoke of this magnificent event. As stated earlier, Jesus did not mention the rapture in his Olivet Discourse, but he spoke plainly of his return in glory.

> At that time the sign of the Son of Man will appear in the sky, and all the nations of the earth will mourn. They will see the Son of Man coming on the clouds of the sky, with power and great glory. ³¹And he will send his angels with a loud trumpet call, and they will gather his elect from the four winds, from one end of the heavens to the other. - Matthew 24:30-31 (See also Luke 21:27.)

Jesus also said that angels would come with him in Matthew 16:27; and Matthew 25. In the context of those passages, especially Matthew 25, the angels will be employed to gather the nations for the Judgment of Sheep and Goats, which will be discussed later.

The Church Returns with Christ

The armies of heaven were following him, riding on white horses and dressed in fine linen, white and clean. - Revelation 19:14

In the Bible, angels are sometimes dressed in white. But these riders are mentioned as a separate group from the angels. Like the Lord Jesus, they are sitting on white horses. Earlier in Revelation there are strong clues about who these people might be:

Yet you have a few people in Sardis who have not soiled their clothes. They will walk with me, dressed in white, for they are worthy. [5]He who overcomes will, like them, be dressed in white. I will never blot out his name from the book of life, but will acknowledge his name before my Father and his angels. - Revelation 3:4-5

In this passage, the message to the Church at Sardis, those dressed in white are true believers in the Lord Jesus Christ. They are those whose names will not be blotted out of the Book of Life!

White clothing is also in view from another perspective in the message to the Laodicean Church.

I counsel you to buy from me gold refined in the fire, so you can become rich; and white clothes to wear, so you can cover your shameful nakedness; and salve to put on your eyes, so you can see. - Revelation 3:18

These are self-righteous members of the apostate church. They do not realize that spiritually they are "wretched, pitiful, poor, blind and naked." What they need is salvation, which is expressed as gold, as white clothes, and as salve for their eyes. This is the Church to which Jesus needed to say:

Here I am! I stand at the door and knock. If anyone hears my voice and opens the door, I will come in and eat with him, and he with me. - Revelation 3:20

The white linen is symbolic of righteousness. It is not self-righteousness, because Isaiah 64:6 says,

All of us have become like one who is unclean,
and all our righteous acts are like filthy rags;
we all shrivel up like a leaf,
and like the wind our sins sweep us away.

The Apostle Paul spoke of a righteousness, not of our own, "but that which is through faith in Christ—the righteousness that comes from God and is by faith" (Philippians 3:9).

Righteousness is a gift of God for those who have put their faith in Christ. It is seen as part of the "Armor of God" in Ephesians: "Stand firm then, with the belt of truth buckled around your waist, with the breastplate of righteousness in place" (Ephesians 6:14).

The white clothing of this heavenly army is not the only evidence that believers of the Church Age will return with Christ. In Colossians 3:4, the Apostle Paul confidently asserted that, "When Christ, who is your life, appears, then you also will appear with him in glory."

A similar thought was expressed by Paul to the believers at Thessalonica.

May he strengthen your hearts so that you will be blameless and holy in the presence of our God and Father when our Lord Jesus comes with all his holy ones. - 1 Thessalonians 3:13

The expression "holy ones" is the Greek word *hagios* or "saints," which is Paul's normal description of believers in Christ (Romans 1:7; 1 Corinthians 1:2; 2 Corinthians 1:1, etc.). Notice that it cannot refer to the martyred Saints of the Tribulation, because their resurrection is specifically stated to be at Christ's coming, at the beginning of the Millennium, or thousand year reign of Christ (Revelation 20:5).

It should also be noted that there is a specific purpose in our coming with Christ at his Glorious Return. Revelation 20:6 explains it this way: "Blessed and holy are those who have part in the first resurrection. The second death has no power over them, but they will be priests of God and of Christ and will reign with him for a thousand years."

The "holy ones" who return with Christ from Heaven and the resurrected martyrs from the Tribulation period will assist Christ the King of Kings.

The Objects of his Wrath

Out of his mouth comes a sharp sword with which to strike down the nations. "He will rule them with an iron scepter." He treads the winepress of the fury of the wrath of God Almighty. - Revelation 19:15

This passage should be correlated with Revelation 14:14-20. In those verses two metaphors portray Christ's conquering activities. Both of these are compared to the harvesting of crops. The first metaphor is that of harvesting wheat ("a sharp sword"). The second is that of harvesting grapes ("He treads the winepress").

These harvests are final, concluding judgments since a very large fraction of the total population of the earth has already been destroyed by cascades of civil war, famine, plagues and cosmic disasters that hit earth like trip-hammer blows in the second half of The Tribulation Period.

It has been proposed by some Bible scholars that two different groups are in view in these two harvest events. It is not a matter about which we can be dogmatic, but it is likely that the first harvest (of wheat) is that of the nations of the world, while the second harvest (of grapes) relates to Israel.

Harvest of Wheat

Returning to the descriptions of Revelation 14, we read first about the harvest of wheat.

> I looked, and there before me was a white cloud, and seated on the cloud was one "like a son of man" with a crown of gold on his head and a sharp sickle in his hand. [15]Then another angel came out of the temple and called in a loud voice to him who was sitting on the cloud, "Take your sickle and reap, because the time to reap has come, for the harvest of the earth is ripe." - Revelation 14:14-16

Destruction of Gentile Unbelievers

The first sickle and the references to the reaping of the harvest of the earth indicate the reaping of the wheat and the tares from the nations. Jesus foretold this in Matthew 13.

> Jesus told them another parable: "The kingdom of heaven is like a man who sowed good seed in his field. [25]But while everyone was sleeping, his enemy came and sowed weeds among the wheat, and went away. [26]When the wheat sprouted and formed heads, then the weeds also appeared.
> [27]"The owner's servants came to him and said, 'Sir, didn't you sow good seed in your field? Where then did the weeds come from?'
> [28]"'An enemy did this,' he replied.
> "The servants asked him, 'Do you want us to go and pull them up?'
> [29]"'No,' he answered, 'because while you are pulling the weeds, you may root up the wheat with them. [30]Let both grow together until the harvest. At that time I will tell the harvesters: First collect the weeds and tie them in bundles to be burned; then gather the wheat and bring it into my barn.'" - Matthew 13:24-30

This is a final separation of unbelievers from believers before the beginning of the Millennium.

The tares or weeds are "harvested" first, and tied in bundles to be burned. When Christ comes in his glory, he will first annihilate his enemies who are gathered against him at the Battle of Armageddon. Then he will gather and eliminate the rest of these non-believers to prevent them from entering into the Millennial Kingdom, which he will immediately establish.

Physically, all unbelievers of that time will then be dead. But what of their spirits? They are gathered "to be burned." This implies a still-future event of "burning." This will be fulfilled at the time of The Great White Throne Judgment, which is discussed later (Revelation 20:11-15).

The wheat is then gathered into a barn. This is descriptive of collecting the scattered remnant of believers from their hiding places. Perhaps they will be brought to Jerusalem and other key locations to fulfill their role of occupying and replenishing the Millennial Kingdom.

Some commentators have tried to equate this gathering into a barn with the rapture. But, in addition to the many problems associated with placing the rapture at the end of the Tribulation, the imagery and timing of this gathering just do not fit the rapture. The image of gathering believers into a barn is meaningful for living survivors of the Tribulation who are being prepared to inhabit the Millennium, but it is not an adequate picture of the glorious eternal place promised by Jesus to his believers.

> In my Father's house are many rooms; if it were not so, I would have told you. I am going there to prepare a place for you. ³And if I go and prepare a place for you, I will come back and take you to be with me that you also may be where I am. - John 14:2-3

The timing of this parable is another strong argument that this gathering is not a reference to the rapture. The unbelievers (the weeds or tares) are gathered first! Then the believers (wheat) are gathered.

This series of events is also foretold by the prophet Joel. First Joel discusses the judgment of the nations on the basis of their treatment of God's people the Jews.

> In those days and at that time,
>   when I restore the fortunes of Judah and Jerusalem,
> ² I will gather all nations
>   and bring them down to the Valley of Jehoshaphat.
>   There I will enter into judgment against them
>   concerning my inheritance, my people Israel,
>   for they scattered my people among the nations
>   and divided up my land. - Joel 3:1-2

This is the same judgment we know as the "Judgment of the Sheep and the Goats" from Matthew 25. This will be a final evaluation by Jesus of the survivors of the last great terrible war, and they fall into two classes. He will separate the sheep (believers) from the goats (unbelievers). The sheep will be those who demonstrated their love for the Lord by their treatment of others. To the sheep he will say,

> Then the King will say to those on his right, 'Come, you who are blessed by my Father; take your inheritance, the kingdom prepared for you since the creation of the world. [35]For I was hungry and you gave me something to eat, I was thirsty and you gave me something to drink, I was a stranger and you invited me in, [36]I needed clothes and you clothed me, I was sick and you looked after me, I was in prison and you came to visit me.'
> [37]"Then the righteous will answer him, 'Lord, when did we see you hungry and feed you, or thirsty and give you something to drink? [38]When did we see you a stranger and invite you in, or needing clothes and clothe you? [39]When did we see you sick or in prison and go to visit you?' "- Matthew 25:34-39

Then, to the goats, the King will say that they failed to show their love for him when they neglected the opportunity to help others, so they will be consigned to eternal punishment (Matthew 25:40-46).

Joel relates the assembly of the nations to the Battle of Armageddon. It is God who draws these armies into his land.

> Proclaim this among the nations:
>   Prepare for war!
>   Rouse the warriors!
>   Let all the fighting men draw near and attack.
> [10] Beat your plowshares into swords
>   and your pruning hooks into spears.
>   Let the weakling say,
>   "I am strong!"
> [11] Come quickly, all you nations from every side,
>   and assemble there.
>   Bring down your warriors, O LORD!
> [12] "Let the nations be roused;
>   let them advance into the Valley of Jehoshaphat,
>   for there I will sit
>   to judge all the nations on every side." - Joel 3:9-12

The Valley of Jehoshaphat is most probably the Kidron Valley between the Temple Mount and the Mount of Olives. This, of course, is not the place where the battle is fought, but the place where this judgment takes place *after* the battle.

In Revelation this great event is called "the great supper of God" when it is announced ahead of time by an angel. It is so-called because of the hordes of vultures and other carrion eaters who come to devour the corpses littering the land.

> And I saw an angel standing in the sun, who cried in a loud voice to all the birds flying in midair, "Come, gather together for the great supper of God, [18]so that you may eat the flesh of kings, generals, and mighty men, of horses and their riders, and the flesh of all people, free and slave, small and great." - Revelation 19:17-18

The Harvest of Grapes

Likewise, Israel is to be judged:

> Another angel came out of the temple in heaven, and he too had a sharp sickle. [18]Still another angel, who had charge of the fire, came from the altar and called in a loud voice to him who had the sharp sickle, "Take your sharp sickle and gather the clusters of grapes from the earth's vine, because its grapes are ripe." [19]The angel swung his sickle on the earth, gathered its grapes and threw them into the great winepress of God's wrath. [20]They were trampled in the winepress outside the city, and blood flowed out of the press, rising as high as the horses' bridles for a distance of 1,600 stadia. - Revelation 14:17-20

Destruction of Jewish Unbelievers

> "Swing the sickle,
>   for the harvest is ripe.
>   Come, trample the grapes,
>   for the winepress is full
>   and the vats overflow—
>   so great is their wickedness!"
> [14] Multitudes, multitudes
>   in the valley of decision!
>   For the day of the LORD is near
>   in the valley of decision. - Joel 3:13-14

The judgment of Jewish people alive at the time of this future battle was also foretold by Zechariah. Of that time, he said that one-third of Israel would believe, but two thirds would still be unbelievers. He used a different metaphor to describe the same judgment.

"Two Thirds" and "One Third" of All Israel

"In the whole land," declares the LORD,
    "two-thirds will be struck down and perish;
    yet one-third will be left in it.
[9] This third I will bring into the fire;
    I will refine them like silver
    and test them like gold.
    They will call on my name
    and I will answer them;
    I will say, 'They are my people,'
    and they will say, 'The LORD is our God.' " - Zechariah 13:8-9

The conversion of one-third of the Jews in Israel (if it happened today) would mean well over a million and a half converts to the true and living God. Zechariah says the new converts will be called on to undergo a terrible trial of their faith during the final days of the great military campaign of Armageddon involving as many as 200 million soldiers from the armies of the nations. While the believing remnant in Edom "passes under the rod" of God's merciful, evaluating judgment, the eleventh-hour converts in Israel must "pass through the fire."

Though our own nation, the United States, contains a professing Christian population that appears to number many tens of millions of believers, it is more realistic to say that the "believing remnant" in America today is perhaps only 5 to 10% of those professing faith in Jesus Christ.

Thus the future large-scale conversion of Jews to belief in Jesus at the close of the age will represent a very great and marvelous work of grace by the God of Israel. The end result of Jesus' work in Israel at the end of the age will be a completely righteous nation of believers chosen to be the head of all the nations.

The Return of the Remnant from Edom

What happens to the believing remnant that had fled to Petra earlier? One vivid Old Testament picture is that of Messiah coming from Bozrah (near Petra) with the remnant. Isaiah foretells this event (Isaiah 63). The imagery is that of Jesus as the greater Moses nurturing the flock of Israel at Petra and bringing them back into the land for the last time (Micah 2:12-13).

God's Dialogs with the Messiah

The latter chapters of Isaiah contain a remarkable series of dialogs between God the Father and his servant the Messiah, or between the prophet and Messiah. In Chapter 42,

Messiah is God's humble servant who will not only save Israel but aid the Gentiles and bring world-wide justice:

> "Here is my servant, whom I uphold,
>   my chosen one in whom I delight;
>   I will put my Spirit on him
>   and he will bring justice to the nations.
> ² He will not shout or cry out,
>   or raise his voice in the streets.
> ³ A bruised reed he will not break,
>   and a smoldering wick he will not snuff out.
>   In faithfulness he will bring forth justice;
> ⁴ he will not falter or be discouraged
>   till he establishes justice on earth.
>   In his law the islands will put their hope." - Isaiah 42:1-4

In Isaiah 43-44, Messiah is seen as restoring Israel by forgiving them of all their sins and delivering Jacob from all his enemies. In Chapter 44, Cyrus the Mede is designated and called by name (!) many decades before he was born. God chose him to aid in the restoration of the Jews from their captivity in Babylon. Messiah gives a personal description of his commission from the Father and contains an intimate discussion between God and his Messiah that reveals much about the content of the prayers of Jesus with his Father during his time on earth, which would come 700 years later.

In Isaiah 50, Messiah is the true Israel who fulfills all that the nation had failed to attain because of persistent rebellion and disobedience.

In Isaiah 52:13 through 53, Messiah is the suffering servant of the Lord whose death and resurrection are vividly foretold.

In Chapter 59, Messiah is Israel's *goel*, or kinsman-redeemer (Isaiah 59:15-21)

In Isaiah Chapter 63, the dialog takes the following form. Isaiah as the observer appears to be standing on the Mt. of Olives in Jerusalem in the midst of the final battles there:

ISAIAH:
Who is this coming from Edom,
    from Bozrah, with his garments stained crimson?
    Who is this, robed in splendor,
    striding forward in the greatness of his strength? - Isaiah 63:1

MESSIAH, THE WARRIOR KING AND KINSMAN-REDEEMER:
"It is I, speaking in righteousness,
    mighty to save."- Isaiah 63:1 (cont.)

ISAIAH:
Why are your garments red, like those of one treading the winepress? - Isaiah 63:2

MESSIAH:
"I have trodden the winepress alone;
>from the nations no one was with me.
>I trampled them in my anger
>and trod them down in my wrath;
>their blood spattered my garments,
>and I stained all my clothing.
[4] For the day of vengeance was in my heart,
>and the year of my redemption has come." -Isaiah 63:3-4

The blood spattering his garments is not the blood of his crucifixion, for that work on the cross was completely finished and ended 2000 years earlier. The blood is that of his enemies, slain in battle, and especially the blood of apostate Jews who have joined the armies of the Beast to oppose him.

Micah foretold the same thing.

"I will surely gather all of you, O Jacob;
>I will surely bring together the remnant of Israel.
>I will bring them together like sheep in a pen,
>like a flock in its pasture;
>the place will throng with people.
[13] One who breaks open the way will go up before them;
>they will break through the gate and go out.
>Their king will pass through before them,
>the LORD at their head."

The Final Conversion of Israel

Israel's national prayer for their Messiah to come and to forgive them is found in Hosea Chapters 5 and 6. Reputable scholars believe this prayer must be prayed *by the nation* as a precondition for their national salvation in the coming of Jesus the Messiah to save them:

"Then I will go back to my place
>until they admit their guilt.
>And they will seek my face;
>in their misery they will earnestly seek me."
[1] "Come, let us return to the LORD.
>He has torn us to pieces

> but he will heal us;
> he has injured us
> but he will bind up our wounds.
> [2] After two days he will revive us;
> on the third day he will restore us,
> that we may live in his presence.
> [3] Let us acknowledge the LORD;
> let us press on to acknowledge him.
> As surely as the sun rises,
> he will appear;
> he will come to us like the winter rains,
> like the spring rains that water the earth." - Hosea 5:15-6:3

Earlier we traced the escape of a remnant of some thousands—perhaps tens of thousands—of believing Jews from Jerusalem to Petra. This will take at the time of the desecration of the Third Temple at the mid-point of The Tribulation Period.

Yet as the age comes to a full close many passages of Scripture speak of the national conversion of Israel. However many Jewish people will still not believe when the battle of Armageddon begins. As we just saw from Isaiah 63:3-4, vengeance against the apostate Jews is symbolized as the Lord trampling out grapes in the vineyard.

The terrible judgments from God depicted in the book of Revelation will devastate the entire earth. Most of mankind will perish and the great infrastructures of the past thousand of years of civilization will be destroyed. The earth will be devastated and wasted.

Jeremiah's words at the time of the destruction of Jerusalem by the Babylonians have a double fulfillment at the time of the end.

> The word came to Jeremiah from the LORD after Nebuzaradan commander of the imperial guard had released him at Ramah. He had found Jeremiah bound in chains among all the captives from Jerusalem and Judah who were being carried into exile to Babylon. [2] When the commander of the guard found Jeremiah, he said to him, "The LORD your God decreed this disaster for this place." - Jeremiah 40:1-2

Yet Paul argues in Romans 11 that in spite of all this, "all Israel will be saved."

> I do not want you to be ignorant of this mystery, brothers, so that you may not be conceited: Israel has experienced a hardening in part until the full number of the Gentiles has come in.
> [26]And so all Israel will be saved, as it is written:
> "The deliverer will come from Zion;
> he will turn godlessness away from Jacob.

222

[27]And this is my covenant with them
   when I take away their sins." - Romans 11:25-27

Israel's National Mourning for Jesus

Paul is careful to make clear that he is not speaking of each and every Jew being converted, but true Israel is limited to those who ultimately believe in Jesus within the nation. Just how many Jews will be saved at the very end of the age? Zechariah seems to give the clue:

"And I will pour out on the house of David and the inhabitants of Jerusalem a spirit of grace and supplication. They will look on me, the one they have pierced, and they will mourn for him as one mourns for an only child, and grieve bitterly for him as one grieves for a firstborn son. [11] On that day the weeping in Jerusalem will be great, like the weeping of Hadad Rimmon in the plain of Megiddo. [12] The land will mourn, each clan by itself, with their wives by themselves: the clan of the house of David and their wives, the clan of the house of Nathan and their wives, [13] the clan of the house of Levi and their wives, the clan of Shimei and their wives, [14] and all the rest of the clans and their wives." - Zechariah 12:10-14

The Final Outcome of Christ's Glorious Return

Returning to the key passage about the return of Christ in glory, we see that He will come back for the purpose of literally reigning on the Earth. As seen above, in the Harvest Judgments, He will first annihilate all the ungodly so that he may begin his reign with people who trust in him.

His Authority to Reign

On his robe and on his thigh he has this name written: KING OF KINGS AND LORD OF LORDS. - Revelation 19:16

In his first coming to earth as Suffering Savior, his right to the Throne of David was thoroughly established, even though, to the disappointment of some like Judas, he did not come to reign, but to die. When he comes the second time in power and great glory, he will not be entitled merely to the Davidic kingship over Israel, but to the sovereign control of all of the kings and lords (other rulers) of the entire planet that he created, and for which he died. We will briefly discuss this golden period in the next section of the book.

The Death of His Enemies

> And I saw an angel standing in the sun, who cried in a loud voice to all the birds flying in midair, "Come, gather together for the great supper of God, [18]so that you may eat the flesh of kings, generals, and mighty men, of horses and their riders, and the flesh of all people, free and slave, small and great."
> [19]Then I saw the beast and the kings of the earth and their armies gathered together to make war against the rider on the horse and his army.
> [21]The rest of them were killed with the sword that came out of the mouth of the rider on the horse, and all the birds gorged themselves on their flesh. - Revelation 19:17-19, 21

This has already been discussed at length, but we should notice once again that all of the carnage of this dreadful battle will be done by Christ himself, using the incomprehensible power of his word (the sword that came out of his mouth). His words, which were sufficient to instantly bring the worlds into being, will be more than adequate to make an instant end of this ugly war.

According to Hebrews 9:27, "it is appointed unto men once to die, but after this the judgment:" (KJV) The death of these rebels is not the end of their story. They will still face the Great White Throne Judgment that will be discussed in the next section.

By contrast, two humans, though they are totally controlled by evil spirits, are judged immediately. They are "the first beast" and his False Prophet, (Revelation 13).

The Fate of the Unholy Trinity

> But the beast was captured, and with him the false prophet who had performed the miraculous signs on his behalf. With these signs he had deluded those who had received the mark of the beast and worshiped his image. The two of them were thrown alive into the fiery lake of burning sulfur. -Revelation 19:20

The two Beasts of Revelation 13 - The world dictator and the False Prophet will be immediately dispatched to the Lake of Fire. This is the same place where the ungodly will be sent for eternal punishment at the White Throne judgment that takes place later (Revelation 20:11-15 - see the next chapter).

The Apostle Paul foretold the lawless ruler's doom in 2 Thessalonians 2:8 where it is said that the Lord Jesus will overthrow him "with the breath of his mouth and destroy by the splendor of his coming"

> And I saw an angel coming down out of heaven, having the key to the Abyss and holding in his hand a great chain. [2]He seized the dragon, that ancient serpent, who is the devil, or

Satan, and bound him for a thousand years. [3]He threw him into the Abyss, and locked and sealed it over him, to keep him from deceiving the nations anymore until the thousand years were ended. After that, he must be set free for a short time. - Revelation 20:1-3

Satan's fate is different than that of his pawns, the Beast and the False Prophet. He will be cast into the Abyss (the "Bottomless Pit") for a thousand years. He has one last episode of rebellion left to play out at the end of The Millennium. He will instigate one last war. It will be discussed in the next section.

What an incredible scene is presented to the student of prophecy at the end of the Battle of Armageddon. It is a scene of mind-numbing destruction after man's battles against man, supernatural plagues on the Earth, the greatest earthquake of all time, and the sudden death of all of Christ's enemies! But it is also a scene of breathtaking glory: the glory of God the Son, standing in all his holiness and righteousness, demonstrating his everlasting love to the faithful who have survived these seven dreadful years. He is poised— ready to rebuild a new perfect environment for those who have remained true to him. He is surrounded by the holy angels, and all the saints of the Church Age who will help him.

This is not the "End of the World," but the beginning of new and better things! There is much more to come, and for those who trust in Christ, it is all good!

Part IV - After The Tribulation

Chapter 16
The Millennium and Beyond

This last section is a brief summary of those prophetic events that come after The Tribulation. This is an epilogue to the main issue of the book: the distinctions between Israel, The Church and The Saints of the Tribulation

"The Millennium" means the thousand-year reign of Jesus Christ on the earth. It will begin when he returns from Heaven as "King of Kings" and "Lord of Lords." It will be a glorious time when all of nature will be restored to an environment that is so wonderful that it reminds us of the conditions that prevailed in the Garden of Eden.

Overview of the Millennium

This is such a big subject that whole books have been written on this topic alone. Here we will simply outline some of the main teachings of God's Word about this glorious age.

The Kingdom was PROMISED to the patriarchs

Abraham was given a promise by God that he would make Abraham's descendants a great nation and give to them the land of Canaan. He was also told that through his off-spring all nations of the earth would be blessed (Genesis 12:1-3; 13:14-18; 22:15-18).

The Abrahamic Covenant was reconfirmed to Isaac and Jacob (Genesis 26:3-4, 23-24; 28:13-14).

David was told by God that his offspring would be given an eternal throne (2 Samuel 7:8-17, 24, 29; 1 Chronicles 17:7-15).

The Kingdom was ESTABLISHED by Jesus

John the Baptist announced that the Kingdom of God was near (Mark 1:15).

The Kingdom exists now and is in abeyance at the present. The Kingdom does exist, but it has not yet "come to earth" as Jesus taught us to pray (Matthew 6:10). That will not happen until He returns in power and great glory as King of Kings, and Lord of Lords. (Revelation 19:11-16).

Jesus taught much about the Kingdom of Heaven. It was the theme of his preaching (Matthew 4:17). The Sermon on the Mount explained the principles of the Kingdom (Matthew chapters 5-7). His parables were given to explain various aspects of the Kingdom (Matthew chapter 13). He related his teaching about future things (The Olivet Discourse) to the Kingdom (Matthew chapters 24-25). And he stated during his trial that his Kingdom was "not of this world" (John 18:36-38; 19:19).

The Kingdom will be DEMONSTRATED during the Millennium
The Millennium will usher in the beginning of the physical reign of Christ (Revelation 19:11-20:6).

The Kingdom will be fully DEVELOPED in the New Heaven/New Earth
The eternal Kingdom will be established when God creates a New Heaven and a New Earth (Revelation chapters 21-22).

Previews of the Millennium from the Old Testament
In contrast to the brief description of Revelation 20, the Old Testament has many lengthy passages, which describe details of the Millennium, and of the time beyond, when there will be a new heaven and a new earth. We will now turn our attention to some of these Old Testament sections.

Messiah will reign from Jerusalem

Then the survivors from all the nations that have attacked Jerusalem will go up year after year to worship the King, the LORD Almighty, and to celebrate the Feast of Tabernacles. [17] If any of the peoples of the earth do not go up to Jerusalem to worship the King, the LORD Almighty, they will have no rain. [18] If the Egyptian people do not go up and take part, they will have no rain. The LORD [will bring on them the plague he inflicts on the nations that do not go up to celebrate the Feast of Tabernacles. [19] This will be the punishment of Egypt and the punishment of all the nations that do not go up to celebrate the Feast of Tabernacles.
[20] On that day HOLY TO THE LORD will be inscribed on the bells of the horses, and the cooking pots in the LORD's house will be like the sacred bowls in front of the altar. [21] Every pot in Jerusalem and Judah will be holy to the LORD Almighty, and all who come to sacrifice will take some of the pots and cook in them. And on that day there will no longer be a Canaanite in the house of the LORD Almighty. - Zechariah 14:16-21

The survivors from all the nations that had attacked Jerusalem are the same as the sheep of Matthew 25:31-46 and the Wheat of Matthew 13:24-30, 36-43.

An enigmatic prophecy about Enoch (who was translated into heaven prior to the flood of Noah) is recorded in the book of Jude. It has a double fulfillment: First, at the time of the Flood of Noah to judge the antediluvian world, destroying probably many billions of earth's inhabitants. Then, at the end of this present age Jesus will again appear "with his ten thousands of holy ones" (Jude 14-15).

A mystery-filled prophecy in Ezekiel clearly relates in part to the end time and God's judgment of his people Israel:

> As surely as I live, declares the Sovereign LORD, I will rule over you with a mighty hand and an outstretched arm and with outpoured wrath. [34] I will bring you from the nations and gather you from the countries where you have been scattered—with a mighty hand and an outstretched arm and with outpoured wrath. [35] I will bring you into the desert of the nations and there, face to face, I will execute judgment upon you. [36] As I judged your fathers in the desert of the land of Egypt, so I will judge you, declares the Sovereign LORD. [37] I will take note of you as you pass under my rod, and I will bring you into the bond of the covenant.
> - Ezekiel 20:33-37

The promise to gather Israel from the nations was largely fulfilled during the past 100 years by the Zionist movement and the formation of the nation of Israel.

The term "wilderness of the peoples" may refer to Edom, (Southern Jordan, i.e., Petra) according to some Bible scholars.

The term "pass under the rod" appears in Leviticus 27 and symbolizes a separation of the consecrated and the unconsecrated animals of the flock.

Isaiah 11 also contains a mystery concerning the end time. In this chapter Messiah is called a "Branch" from the root of Jesse, the father of King David. As such he will have the right to rule. Because he will be filled with the Spirit of the LORD, his reign will be just. One portion of this chapter promises,

> In that day the Root of Jesse will stand as a banner for the peoples; the nations will rally to him, and his place of rest will be glorious. [11] In that day the Lord will reach out his hand a second time to reclaim the remnant that is left of his people from Assyria, from Lower Egypt, from Upper Egypt, from Cush, from Elam, from Babylonia, from Hamath and from the islands of the sea.
> [12] He will raise a banner for the nations
> and gather the exiles of Israel;
> he will assemble the scattered people of Judah
> from the four quarters of the earth. - Isaiah 11:10-12

National Repentance

As mentioned in the previous chapter, this age will begin with a great outpouring of national repentance (Zechariah 12:10-14).

> "And I will pour out on the house of David and the inhabitants of Jerusalem a spirit of grace and supplication. They will look on me, the one they have pierced, and they will mourn for him as one mourns for an only child, and grieve bitterly for him as one grieves for a firstborn son." - Zechariah 12:10

Restoration and Prosperity

Ezekiel chapters 36 and 37 describe the miraculous regathering of the Chosen People from all over the earth. The early portion of this narrative foretold the amazing rebirth of the nation of Israel that we have witnessed in our own generation. The later portion of both of these chapters goes beyond this present time to the remarkable restoration and prosperity of the Millennium.

> "This is what the Sovereign LORD says: 'On the day I cleanse you from all your sins, I will resettle your towns, and the ruins will be rebuilt. [34] The desolate land will be cultivated instead of lying desolate in the sight of all who pass through it. [35] They will say, "This land that was laid waste has become like the garden of Eden; the cities that were lying in ruins, desolate and destroyed, are now fortified and inhabited." [36] Then the nations around you that remain will know that I the LORD have rebuilt what was destroyed and have replanted what was desolate. I the LORD have spoken and I will do it.'
> [37] "This is what the Sovereign LORD says: 'Once again I will yield to the plea of the house of Israel and do this for them: I will make their people as numerous as sheep, [38] as numerous as the flocks for offerings at Jerusalem during her appointed feasts. So will the ruined cities be filled with flocks of people? Then they will know that I am the LORD.' "
> - Ezekiel 36:33-38

John's Brief Description of the Millennium

The 20th chapter of the Book of Revelation describes the Millennium. It immediately follows the Glorious Return of Christ in Revelation 19, which was discussed above. This short chapter may be considered in three parts: Preparation for the Period (verses 1-3); Progress during the period (verses 4-6); and Postscript to the period (verses 7-15).

Preparation for the Period

> And I saw an angel coming down out of heaven, having the key to the Abyss and holding in his hand a great chain. [2]He seized the dragon, that ancient serpent, who is the devil, or

Satan, and bound him for a thousand years. ³He threw him into the Abyss, and locked and sealed it over him, to keep him from deceiving the nations anymore until the thousand years were ended. After that, he must be set free for a short time. - Revelation 20:1-3

At the outset of the Millennium the devil will be cast into the Abyss. The Greek word *abussos* means "without depth." In this passage the word is used alone, but in Revelation 9:1 it is used as an adjective for another Greek word, *phrear*, which means "cistern," or "prison." Together, these words are often translated "bottomless pit."

In this pit Satan will be confined for the entire one thousand years of Christ's righteous reign on Earth. What happens when he is released is discussed below, when we look at the "Postscript to the period."

Progress during the Period

I saw thrones on which were seated those who had been given authority to judge. And I saw the souls of those who had been beheaded because of their testimony for Jesus and because of the word of God. They had not worshiped the beast or his image and had not received his mark on their foreheads or their hands. They came to life and reigned with Christ a thousand years. ⁵(The rest of the dead did not come to life until the thousand years were ended.) This is the first resurrection. ⁶Blessed and holy are those who have part in the first resurrection. The second death has no power over them, but they will be priests of God and of Christ and will reign with him for a thousand years.
⁷When the thousand years are over, Satan will be released from his prison ⁸and will go out to deceive the nations in the four corners of the earth—Gog and Magog—to gather them for battle. In number they are like the sand on the seashore. - Revelation 20:4-6

-The First Resurrection: Raised to Eternal Life

Those believers and followers of Jesus who were converted during The Tribulation Period, and had been put to death—the martyrs of The Tribulation Period—will be raised from the dead (Revelation 20:4). They are the brave ones who would not receive the Mark of the Beast, and will have been put to death for their faith in Christ. They are raised again as part of the "first resurrection." Jesus himself was the "first-fruits" of this first resurrection (1 Corinthians 15:23). At the rapture believers of the Church Age are raised as part of this first resurrection (1 Thessalonians 4:13-18). Now we see these believers also joining the ranks of this first type of resurrection.

In Daniel we read that Old Testament Saints are also resurrected to eternal life.

"At that time Michael, the great prince who protects your people, will arise. There will be a time of distress such as has not happened from the beginning of nations until then. But at that time your people—everyone whose name is found written in the book—will be delivered. [2] Multitudes who sleep in the dust of the earth will awake: some to everlasting life, others to shame and everlasting contempt. - Daniel 12:1-2

In John Chapter 5, Jesus also spoke of the coming day when the dead would rise in two separate resurrections, at his command:

I tell you the truth, a time is coming and has now come when the dead will hear the voice of the Son of God and those who hear will live. [26]For as the Father has life in himself, so he has granted the Son to have life in himself. [27]And he has given him authority to judge because he is the Son of Man.
[28]"Do not be amazed at this, for a time is coming when all who are in their graves will hear his voice [29]and come out—those who have done good will rise to live, and those who have done evil will rise to be condemned. - John 5:25-29

This resurrection of the saints of Israel who lived and died before Christ's first advent will probably take place at the same time as the resurrection of the Tribulation martyrs since they are a continuation of believing Israel during the last "week" of Daniel's "Seventy Weeks."

- Judgment of Believers

Believers of the Church Age will have already appeared at the Bema Seat Judgment where whatever was sincerely done for Christ will be the basis of rewards. Those who receive these rewards will, in turn, give them to Christ to prove their love to him (1 Corinthians 3:10-15; Revelation 4:10-11).

The exact nature of the judgment of other believers—the Old Testament believers and Saints of The Tribulation—is not described. It is possible that it will be similar to the Bema Seat.

The other type of resurrection is explained below where the ungodly are raised to stand at their judgment.

Postscript to the Period

The last part of Revelation 20 is about Rebellion (verses 7-9) and Retribution (verses 10-15). Since these events take place after the Millennium is past, they will be considered later under the heading "The Last War."

Aspects of the Millennium
Geography

The second coming of Christ—when the Lord stands upon the Mount of Olives—will be accompanied by a great world wide earthquake so that, "Every island fled away and the mountains could not be found" (Revelation 16:20). The topography of the land of Israel and the rest of the Earth will be drastically altered. The literal meaning of Isaiah 40:4 will come to pass.

> Every valley shall be raised up,
> every mountain and hill made low;
> the rough ground shall become level,
> the rugged places a plain.

The prophet Zechariah also foretold this phenomenal event:

On that day his feet will stand on the Mount of Olives, east of Jerusalem, and the Mount of Olives will be split in two from east to west, forming a great valley, with half of the mountain moving north and half moving south. - Zechariah 14:4

Jerusalem will then rise to become the capital of the Earth (Zechariah 14:9-11).

Ecology

Starting with the Millennium, there will be a removal of the Curse upon the earth that began with Adam's fall and continues down to the present unabated (Romans 8:18-23).

The Earth, and especially Eretz Israel (the Land of Israel) will become "like the Garden of Eden" (Ezekiel 36:35).

The Desert will rejoice and blossom as the rose (Isaiah 35:1), and the parched ground will become a pool (Isaiah 35:7).

The Trees...shall clap their hands, and instead of thorns there will be trees (Isaiah 55:12-13).

The earth will be fruitful, and there will be no famine (Ezekiel 34:27-29).

Animals will once again be friendly to one another and to humans.

> [6] The wolf will live with the lamb,
>> the leopard will lie down with the goat,
>> the calf and the lion and the yearling together;
>> and a little child will lead them.
> [7] The cow will feed with the bear,
>> their young will lie down together,
>> and the lion will eat straw like the ox.
> [8] The infant will play near the hole of the cobra,
>> and the young child put his hand into the viper's nest. - Isaiah 11:6-8

Health

People who live during the Millennium will not die young. A person one hundred years old will be considered a child, since, presumably, a person could live throughout the 1000 years in the restored environment (Isaiah 65:20-23).

Sickness will not be a problem because "The sun of righteousness shall arise with healing in its wings" (Malachi 4:2).

Later yet, after the New Earth is established, the Tree of Life will be accessible to mankind. Its leaves are "for the healing of the nations" (Revelation 22:2).

Politics

Jesus Christ will be King of Kings and Lord of Lords, and of the increase of his government there will be no end (Revelation 19:16; Isaiah 9:6-7),

Jerusalem will be the capital of the World, and all nations will come to Jerusalem. It will be considered the center of the nations (Isaiah 2:2-4; Ezekiel 5:5).

David will reign as king over Israel, and presumably, each nation will also have its godly king who will answer to Jesus Christ, the King of Kings (Ezekiel 34:23-24; 37:24-25).

The church will share with her Lord the rule over the Gentile nations (Revelation 4:4, 10-11; 20:4, 6).

No sin or rebellion will be allowed, because the Lord will withhold rain and send plagues on any who would rebel (Zechariah 14:16-19).

Jesus Christ will rule the nations with a rod of iron (Revelation 12:5; 19:15 - Greek: "shepherdize"). This means a strong central rule to bring prompt justice and quick control over unruly nations and individuals who revolt against God.

Sinners will be born on the earth during the Millennium. Satan will be chained and therefore not free to seduce, to tempt, and to deceive, but the flesh will still manifest itself showing how complete was the original fall of Adam and Eve. During this 1000 years men can not claim that the devil is responsible for their sinful failures.

There will be peace everywhere. People will "beat their swords into plowshares" and there will be war no more (Isaiah 2:2-4).

Worship and Belief

Messiah will build a new (fourth) temple, probably the great temple described in the final Chapters of Ezekiel. This Temple will be used for Memorial Sacrifices (Ezekiel 40:39-43).

Salvation during the Millennium will still be by grace through faith in Jesus Christ because there is "No other name given...whereby we must be saved" (Acts 4:10; Philippians 2:9-10; Revelation 22:4).

The Lord will put a new Spirit within believers whose home is on earth (Ezekiel 11:19).

Israel as a nation will be brought into the New Covenant, which Jesus put into effect at the Last Supper. This covenant, promised to Israel by the prophets, has been graciously shared with the Church during the interim period of Israel's Diaspora and unbelief.

Everything will be considered sanctified or "holy." Even the bells and pots will be holy to the Lord (Zechariah 14:20-21).

Unfortunately, some, even with this perfect environment and the opportunity to see Christ in person reigning over the Earth, will still fail to believe in him and will rebel at the end. They will follow Satan when he is released for a little while at the end of the Millennium. They will all be destroyed (Revelation 20:7-10).

After the Millennium
The Last War

> When the thousand years are over, Satan will be released from his prison [8]and will go out to deceive the nations in the four corners of the earth—Gog and Magog—to gather them for battle. In number they are like the sand on the seashore. [9]They marched across the breadth of the earth and surrounded the camp of God's people, the city he loves. But fire came down from heaven and devoured them. [10]And the devil, who deceived them, was thrown into the lake of burning sulfur, where the beast and the false prophet had been thrown. They will be tormented day and night for ever and ever. - Revelation 20:7-10

After the Millennium, Satan is allowed out of the Abyss to rally together all who do not trust in Christ. These people would have rebelled against Christ during the time of his righteous reign, but they would not dare. It is most amazing that some people, who have had the privilege of living in a perfect environment, and who have experienced a world ruled in righteousness, will still not accept God's plan for their lives. It gives us insight to the fairness of their future judgment, because they simply do not want to be with their Creator and Savior. Nothing could ever convince them how wonderful he is. They would be unhappy in his presence for ever, even in Heaven.

"Gog and Magog" is representative of rebellious nations. This imagery is taken from Ezekiel 38 and 39, an earlier war that takes place before or during the Tribulation. Once again, rebellious nations and troops who are personally rebellious against Christ will seek to overthrow his control.

This time they will be led by Satan himself.

The scene of this battle is Jerusalem, the city God loves. The outcome of this war is that those who follow Satan are destroyed by fire from above, and Satan is thrown into a Lake of Fire (compare Revelation 20:14 and 15), where the Beast and the False Prophet already had been thrown at the end of the Battle of Armageddon.

The Other Resurrection

Earlier we read about the "First Resurrection." The other type of resurrection is now seen in Revelation 20:10-15, where the ungodly are raised to stand at their judgment.

Judgment of Non-believers: The Great White Throne

> Then I saw a great white throne and him who was seated on it. Earth and sky fled from his presence, and there was no place for them. ¹²And I saw the dead, great and small, standing before the throne, and books were opened. Another book was opened, which is the book of life. The dead were judged according to what they had done as recorded in the books. ¹³The sea gave up the dead that were in it, and death and Hades gave up the dead that were in them, and each person was judged according to what he had done. ¹⁴Then death and Hades were thrown into the lake of fire. The lake of fire is the second death. ¹⁵If anyone's name was not found written in the book of life, he was thrown into the lake of fire. - Revelation 20:11-15

This is the judgment of all who do not believe in Christ. They will be judged according to their works. But, according to Romans 3:20, no one can be saved by the law and good works. Those who depend on works will have their name blotted out of the Book of Life. Even in the days of Moses, God spoke of his book and of the fact that those who sin against him will be blotted out of it. (Exodus 32:32-33). The imagery here is that people's names were at one time listed in this book, but they were blotted out because of the sin of rejecting Christ. Those who trust in Christ have had their sins forgiven, so their names still remain in the book.

In addition to the Book of Life other books are opened. This suggests that the deeds of every person are disclosed in full detail at the Great White Throne, and this in turn suggests that there may well be degrees of punishment in hell. This is hard to imagine, since hell at any level is a total, complete and final separation from God. Yet degrees of punishment would reflect the perfect justice of God, which is always thorough and overlooks nothing.

Paul wrote that "the saints will judge the world" (1 Corinthians 6:2), so it is possible that God's people will take part in this great cosmic tribunal that is more commonly called "The Last Judgment."

Those whose names are not found in this Book of Life are consigned to the Lake of Fire. This is the most vivid of the biblical pictures of Hell as a fiery eternity without Christ. John the Baptist spoke of an unquenchable fire (Matthew 3:12), and Jesus told of a fiery furnace (Matthew 13:40-42), the fire of Hell (Matthew 18:9). It is an eternal fire (Matthew 18:11), which was prepared for the devil and his angels (Matthew 25:41). The New Testament word for Hell is *Gehenna*, which means the Valley of Hinnom. This is the name of the valley on the south side of the city of Jerusalem that served as the city dump. It was a fitting picture of a place where there are worms and the fire never dies (Mark 9:45-48).

A New Heaven and Earth

> By the same word the present heavens and earth are reserved for fire, being kept for the day of judgment and destruction of ungodly men.
> [8]But do not forget this one thing, dear friends: With the Lord a day is like a thousand years, and a thousand years are like a day. [9]The Lord is not slow in keeping his promise, as some understand slowness. He is patient with you, not wanting anyone to perish, but everyone to come to repentance.
> [10]But the day of the Lord will come like a thief. The heavens will disappear with a roar; the elements will be destroyed by fire, and the earth and everything in it will be laid bare.
> [11]Since everything will be destroyed in this way, what kind of people ought you to be? You ought to live holy and godly lives [12]as you look forward to the day of God and speed its coming. That day will bring about the destruction of the heavens by fire, and the elements will melt in the heat. [13]But in keeping with his promise we are looking forward to a new heaven and a new earth, the home of righteousness. - 2 Peter 3:7-13

The Lord promised never to destroy the Earth by a flood again (Genesis 9:11), but it is destined for a fiery judgment that will cleanse it from all corruption and will result in a new, even better planet.

The heavens also are in need of cleansing and renewing since they also have been defiled by the activity of Satan and his hosts prior to their being cast down to earth during The Tribulation.

Peter's prophecies are echoed in The Revelation where the creation of a New Heaven (Revelation 21:1) and a New Earth (Revelation 21:1,3-5) are foretold.

As far as we know, this is the final realm of the believer, the place where there will be no more death, sorrow, or pain (Revelation 21:4).

Old Testament previews of this New Heaven and New Earth are also instructive.

> "Behold, I will create
>   new heavens and a new earth.
>   The former things will not be remembered,
>   nor will they come to mind.
> [18] But be glad and rejoice forever
>   in what I will create,
>   for I will create Jerusalem to be a delight
>   and its people a joy.
> [19] I will rejoice over Jerusalem
>   and take delight in my people;
>   the sound of weeping and of crying
>   will be heard in it no more.
> [20] "Never again will there be in it

an infant who lives but a few days,
or an old man who does not live out his years;
he who dies at a hundred
will be thought a mere youth;
he who fails to reach a hundred
will be considered accursed.
[21] They will build houses and dwell in them;
they will plant vineyards and eat their fruit.
[22] No longer will they build houses and others live in them,
or plant and others eat.
For as the days of a tree,
so will be the days of my people;
my chosen ones will long enjoy
the works of their hands.
[23] They will not toil in vain
or bear children doomed to misfortune;
for they will be a people blessed by the LORD,
they and their descendants with them.
[24] Before they call I will answer;
while they are still speaking I will hear.
[25] The wolf and the lamb will feed together,
and the lion will eat straw like the ox,
but dust will be the serpent's food.
They will neither harm nor destroy
on all my holy mountain,"
says the LORD. - Isaiah 65:17-25

The Heavenly Jerusalem

In the last two chapters of the Revelation, an incredible city, the Heavenly Jerusalem descends from Heaven to the New Earth. This magnificent place may be what Jesus referred to in John 14:1-3 where he told his disciples that he was going away to prepare a place for them, and that he would come again for them. He called this place "My Father's house," and said that in it are "many mansions."

This will apparently be the capital of the new Earth and the headquarters of Christ's operations. The things that are revealed about it correspond to the expectations of Christians in Heaven. Our Heaven will not be a cold ethereal place in outer space. This matchless city will be on a fantastic new Earth, which itself is a part of the new heavens. We will have glorified bodies like Christ's (1 Corinthians 15:40-44, 51-54), which was able to ascend into space (Acts 1:9). Perhaps we will be able to visit other heavenly locations without the aid of a space ship if it is God's will and purpose for us.

The imagery and symbolism of the New Jerusalem reflects both Israel and the Church, so this heavenly city is evidently not exclusively the new home for the Church.

Here are some of the unique features of this city, as revealed in Revelation 21 and 22:

- It will be the home of the Bride, the Wife of the Lamb - Revelation 21:2, 9.
- It will have twelve gates, named for the twelve tribes of Israel - Revelation 21:12-13.
- It will have twelve foundation stones, with the names of the Twelve Apostles - Revelation 21:14.
- It will be approximately fifteen hundred miles long, wide and high. - Revelation 21:16. Such a huge city would stretch from Los Angeles past Denver, and would be just as wide as it was long, and, most incredibly, it would be just as high! Actually, our present Earth is too small to accommodate such a huge city, but, at that time, there will be a new Earth.
- It will have golden walls and streets, pearl gates, and jewel foundations - Revelation 21:17-21.
- There will be no Temple in that city because God, the Almighty, and the Lamb will be there - Revelation 21:22 cf. 21:3ff.
- It will not need the sun or moon because The Glory of God, the Lamb is the light! - Revelation 21:23.
- The River of Water of Life will flow from the Throne of God and the Lamb - Revelation 22:1.
- The Tree of Life, from which Adam and Eve were barred after their sin (Genesis 3:22-24), will be a part of the city. - Revelation 22:2.
- There will be no curse there - Revelation 22:3-4; cf. 21:4.

If we take literally the dimensions given for the heavenly city, it will evidently be a cubical structure (or perhaps spherical or pyramidal) 1500 miles on a side. If the city has one billion inhabitants, each resident could have 3.37 cubic miles of space.

Incidentally, Jews in Israel today who are working towards the rebuilding of Israel's Third Temple speak about zones of holiness in the temple and its courts. But they also believe the Temple is intended to be a "time portal" of sorts. Perhaps in some wonderful way the New Jerusalem above, and the rebuilt Millennial City of Jerusalem in Israel, or Israel's Fourth (Ezekiel's) Temple, will be connected. But the portal will not permit any defilement to reach the New Jerusalem as Revelation 22:14-15 tells us.

"Blessed are those who wash their robes, that they may have the right to the tree of life and may go through the gates into the city. [15]Outside are the dogs, those who practice magic arts, the sexually immoral, the murderers, the idolaters and everyone who loves and practices falsehood."

It is a wonderful thing that the Bible ends on such a victorious note. What a glorious future the children of God have! In the end, believing Israel, The church, and the Saints from the Tribulation period will share together in a barely-imaginable place, in the presence of our Lord and Savior, Jesus Christ!

We may all join in agreement with the final statement of the Revelation,

He who testifies to these things says, "Yes, I am coming soon."
    Amen. Come, Lord Jesus.
[21]The grace of the Lord Jesus be with God's people. Amen. - Revelation 22:20-21

Appendices

Appendix A
Chart of the End Times

A Pre-Tribulational, Pre-Millennial View of Eschatology

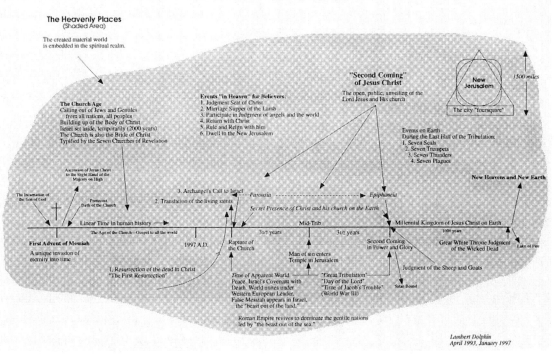

A modified version of this chart in color is available online at
http://ldolphin.org/kingdom/echart.gif

Appendix B
Definition of Common Terms
Found In Eschatology

"Last Days" refers to the entire period between the first and second advents of our Lord Jesus Christ. Since Jesus ascended into heaven from the Mount of Olives, 40 days after his resurrection, we have been living in the "last days."

Eschatology is the body of knowledge concerning the "last things," or the end of the age and the future.

Millennium. means one thousand years. (Latin, *mille* = thousand; Greek: *chilloi* = thousand, hence Chiliasm.) this is the belief, based on Revelation 20, that Christ will literally, physically reign on earth following the present age, for one thousand actual calendar years.

Amillennial. (Prefix *a* = "no"). This is the belief that there will be no literal 1000 year reign of Christ. Thus Revelation 20 is taken symbolically, not literally, by adherents of this view. Amillennialists generally believe that Israel has been permanently set aside for all time and that God's current plan of salvation involves only the Church.

Premillennial. This is the belief that Christ returns visibly and bodily at the beginning of the thousand-year reign of Christ on the earth. He will rule the nations from Jerusalem. God will resume salvation work for Israel as a nation immediately after the departure or "rapture" of the true Church.

Postmillennial. This is the belief that Christ will return at the end of the present age to take over the earth. Meantime, he is assumed to reign on earth through the Church now.

Postmillennialists do not necessarily believe in a literal millennial age. Satan was defeated at the cross and is now bound; hence the final triumph of the Church in history is assured.

Rapture. (In the Latin Bible *rapere* meaning "to catch up," is the translation of the Greek *harpazo*, 1 Thessalonians. 4:17). It refers to the coming of Jesus to take his church out of the world, "like a thief in the night", i.e., suddenly, unexpectedly. Dates for this event can not be predicted from the Bible.

Tribulation Period. This refers to the end-time period of judgment of the earth with great out-pouring of wrath on mankind from God.

The 70th Week of Daniel. From Daniel we know this period to be just 7 years in length. The last half of this "week" (3-1/2 years) is "the Great Tribulation," or "the time of Jacob's trouble" when most of the terrible judgments in the book of Revelation occur. The first half of the Tribulation period is marked by apparent world peace, especially in the Middle East as Israel's false prophet and the political/military leader of the Western confederation of nations contrive a "successful" peace plan. (Isaiah calls this treaty Israel's "covenant with death.") The onset of the Great Tribulation is marked by failure of this peace treaty and the desecration of the Third Temple in Jerusalem by the "man of sin." During the Tribulation period Israel is once again the focus for events in the Bible. Jerusalem will again be the center of reference for what God is doing in the world.

Pretribulation. This is the teaching that Jesus comes for his bride, the true Church, at the beginning of the Tribulation period.

Midtribulation. According to this belief, Jesus raptures the Church half-way through the seven-year Tribulation period.

Postribulation. This is the belief that Jesus will come for his people at the end of the Tribulation period, but prior to the Millennium.

Parousia. (Greek word meaning "coming alongside and remaining with" someone.) This describes the Second Coming of Jesus. It is used in Matthew 24:3,27,37,39; 1 Thessalonians. 4:15, 5:23, 2 Thessalonians 2:1, James 5:7, 8; 2 Peter 1:16, 3:4; and 1 Corinthians. 15:23.

Epiphaneia. (Greek word meaning "A shining-forth;" refers to the visible appearance of Jesus at the close of the age.) The word is used in 1 Timothy 6:14, 2 Timothy 4:1,8; Matthew 24:27, 2 Thessalonians. 2:8; and Titus 2:13. The words *parousia* and *epiphaneia* are combined in 2 Thessalonians. 2:8, translated "his appearing and his coming."

Apokalupsis. (Greek word for "revelation," or "unveiling," or "uncovering.") It refers to the visible appearing of Jesus to the world in full power and splendor. It also refers to the appearance of "the lawless one" on the stage of history following the rapture (2 Thessalonians. 2).

"Dominion Theology" is the teaching that the Church is responsible for taking over the world in the name and power of Christ. It is associated with "reconstructionism," and is also known and "theonomy."

"Replacement Theology" is the teaching in some circles today that the Church has replaced Israel permanently in the plan of God. It is usually associated with an Amillennial view of eschatology.

"Dispensationalism" Teaches that history is divided into various time periods during which God moves in the world in certain distinctive ways. Hence there is a "dispensation of innocence," a "dispensation of government," a "dispensation of law," a "dispensation of grace," etc. The Greek word means "economy" or "administration." Several different schools of dispensational teaching exist.

"Day of the LORD." This expression refers to the extended period of time during which God openly intervenes in human affairs both in regard to judgment and blessing. In the present age justice is deferred or applied only slowly; judgment is largely withheld or restrained; and God's people await the fulfillment of his promises and plans for them. Although Jesus the Lord rules over the universe he has not yet reigned on earth. This makes the famous prayer Jesus taught the disciples the most-often prayed and as yet unanswered prayer in the Bible, "Thy kingdom come, thy will be done, on earth as it is in heaven..."

Appendix C
Harmony of Prophecy Chart

	1580 BC	883 BC	722 BC	586 BC	336 BC	146 BC		100 AD	312 AD	476 AD	1517 AD	1900 AD	TODAY

		Old Testament			Church			Tribulation			Kingdom	

The Revelation

1:19 — Rev of THE PERSON OF JESUS CHRIST "things you have seen" [1] | THE PRESENCE OF JESUS CHRIST IN THIS AGE "the things which are" (2-3) | THE PROGRAM OF JESUS CHRIST FOR THE FUTURE "the things which shall take place" [4-22]

1-22

Eph	Smy	Per	Thy	Sar	Phi	Lao
Ephesus	Smyrna	Pergamum	Thyatira	Sardis	Philadelphia	Laodicea
Apostolic	Martyrdom	Catholic Church	Dark Ages	Reformation	Missionary	Apostate

SEVEN SEALS (6-8)
SEVEN TRUMPETS (6-8)
SEVEN VIALS (6-8) →

1000 YEARS (MORTALITY) | NEW HEAVEN AND EARTH (IMMORTALITY)

Jesus- Mt. Olives

Matthew 24-25
- "Beginning of Birth Pains" [vv. 4-8]
- "Tribulation" (vv. 9-14)
- "Great Tribulation" (vv. 15-28)
- "After the Tribulation" [vv. 29-31]

Luke 21
- "Times of the Gentiles" (v. 24)

Daniel

2:31-35
[EGYPT]	[ASSYRIA]	BABYLON	MEDO-PERSIA	GREECE	ROME
		GOLD HEAD	SILVER CHEST	BRASS THIGHS	IRON LEGS

RE-CONSTITUTED ROMAN EMPIRE IRON & CLAY FEET | GOD'S KINGDOM THE STONE

7:1-26 8:1-27
LION	BEAR	FLYING LEOPARD	DREADFUL BEAST
EAGLE	RAM	GOAT	

"LITTLE HORN" | COMING OF THE ANCIENT OF DAYS

9:24-27
- 69 "WEEKS"
- Artaxerxes' Decree 445 BC
- Triumphal Entry 1 BC
- 70TH "Abomination of Desolation" WEEK

Jeremiah

30:1-11
- RESTORED ISRAEL [vv. 1-3]
- TIME OF JACOB'S TROUBLE (vv. 4-7)
- DAVID THEIR KING [vv. 8-11]

Ezekiel

36-48
- RE-GATHERING OF ISRAEL (36-37)
- WAR (38-39)
- THE TEMPLE (40-42)
- GOD IN THE TEMPLE (43-48)

Ron Graff
Solid Ground Brethren In Christ Church

245

Appendix D
Warnings and Cautions

In these tumultuous times there is a great deal of interest in prophecy. Unfortunately, there are some dangerous temptations in the study of prophecy. Some teachers and writers go far beyond the boundaries of sound scriptural interpretation. There have already been many wild and irresponsible claims made by prophecy teachers, and there certainly will be many more errors taught during this time. The effect of this will be to mislead many and to discourage many others from study of this important aspect of the Scriptures.

Several cautions are in order for those who wish to know the truth but do not want to not be misled by false teachers. Here are some of these warnings and cautions:

1 - We cannot know the date of Christ's return. Jesus said, "No one knows about that day or hour, not even the angels in heaven, nor the Son, but only the Father." - Matthew 24:36

He also said:

Therefore keep watch, because you do not know on what day your Lord will come. But understand this: If the owner of the house had known at what time of night the thief was coming, he would have kept watch and would not have let his house be broken into. So you also must be ready, because the Son of Man will come at an hour when you do not expect him. - Matthew 24:42-44

It should be noted that the previous passages relate to Christ's Glorious Return, not to the rapture. But if it is true for that later event, how much more would it be true for the rapture, for which no specific signs are given.

In answer to their question about when he would establish his Kingdom, Jesus answered, "It is not for you to know the times or dates the Father has set by his own authority." - Acts 1:7

In another place, where Jesus' disciples wrongly thought that the Kingdom was going to appear at once, he gave them a parable about ten stewards, each of whom received money to invest. They were told to "Occupy until I come." (Luke 19:13 KJV) We do not know when he will return, but we should be busy about his business until that glorious day.

2 - We cannot know who the evil ruler will be. According to 2 Thessalonians 2:1-8, he will not be revealed until the Holy Spirit, the Restrainer, has been taken away, presumably by the rapture.

3- We must base our views on Scripture and proper methods of interpretation, and use supplemental information only for illustration.

4- We dare not be dogmatic about how future events will unfold. Like those who were looking for Christ's first coming, we should have carefully developed ideas of how his second coming, and all the related events of prophecy, might occur, but we should be open to other possibilities.

5- We must maintain respect and fellowship with other Bible-believing people who do not understand prophecy the way we do.

6- We must not ignore the importance of prophecy in the Bible. It is wrong to lose interest in this part of God's Word just because it is difficult or confusing, or even because others have made serious errors before.

7- Many times during the past two thousand years of history, events in the Middle East have escalated suddenly and rapidly, seemingly out of control, so that even careful news commentators spoke of dire, apocalyptic times. Again and again the Lord has rolled history back from the edge of the precipice to decades of relative calm. Ray Stedman once said, "What determines the future is what God has done in the past and what He has promised to do in the future. So don't look horizontally at current events."[74]

Appendix E
Notes on Covenants in the Bible
By Lambert Dolphin

The Hebrew word *berith*, covenant, occurs over 280 times in the Old Testament. (The English word covenant means "a coming together.") Covenants can include treaties, alliances, agreements, compacts, pledges, mutual agreements, promises, and undertakings on behalf of another. The translators of the OT into the Greek Septuagint chose the Greek word *diatheke* in place of the Hebrew *berith*. In the NT *diatheke* occurs 33 times.

The term "testament" (as in "Last Will and Testament") is used in some translations of the NT 13 times to translate the word *diatheke*. This adds a new depth of meaning to the idea of covenants. The New Covenant rests upon the death of the one who made it, namely Jesus. Greek has another word, *syntheke*, which means a mutual agreement, however this word is not used in the NT presumably because covenants with God do not involve joint obligations between two equals.

Covenants often exist between two unequal parties, for example between God and man, or between a conqueror and his defeated enemy. Covenants in the Bible can be agreements between two individuals, between a king or leader and his people; or between God and individuals, or God and groups of individuals.

Covenants can be conditional or unconditional. Conditional covenants are forfeited if one party violates or defaults on his part of the agreement. Unconditional covenants are arrangements in which the default of one party does not negate the ultimate fulfillment and blessing of the covenant.

In our society we all make use of various types of covenants. Credit cards, automobile loans, and mortgage agreements are types of covenants. The lending party makes money or goods available to the borrower. The borrower agrees to pay back the loan, usually with interest. Covenants of this kind are clearly conditional. A marriage agreement is not only a covenant between man and wife, but the name and blessing of God are often invoked as well. The state enters into marriage covenants because it licenses marriage, and the families involved usually pledge to work together to strengthen the marriage bond between man and wife. Marriage is the oldest institution in the world, honored in the OT and the NT and approved by God for all mankind, believers and unbelievers alike, (though believers are not to enter into marriage with unbelievers). (See especially Malachi, Chapter 2). The marriage covenant gets to the heart of what God desires in his relationship with Israel (Hosea, Ezekiel 16), with the Church as Bride of Christ (Ephesians), and with the individual believer (Song of Solomon).

Usually an individual passes along property and benefits to his surviving spouse, children or other heirs by means of a Last Will and Testament. The kind of covenant does not go into effect until the death of the Testator. Such covenants usually do not obligate the designated heirs, but this is not always the case.

All of the covenants between God and Man in the Bible are really based on our Creator's unmerited favor and loving-kindness towards his fallen and sinful creatures. Although man's expected response to God's grace may be stated differently in one covenant as compared to another, God always meets man on the basis of grace. Man's proper response is always to come from the heart-resulting in repentance, cleansing, and a renewed spirit and worship as stated beautifully in Psalm 51.

Examples of Covenants between Men

1. Abraham's Covenant with Abimelech
See Genesis 21:25-33.

2. Joshua's Covenant with the People at Shechem
See Joshua 24:19-27.

3. David and Jonathan's Covenant of Friendship
The relationship between David and Jonathan included a personal covenant between these two friends, which is described in 1 Samuel 23:15-18.

4. The Covenant between Jacob and Laban
Jacob and his uncle Laban agreed to work together under the terms of an agreement, or covenant described in Genesis 31-44-54.

5. Between Solomon and Shimei
Solomon issued a conditional covenant with Shimei, which the latter violated at the cost of his life. See 1 Kings 2:36-46.

6. Between Asa and Benhadad

Asa, King of Judah and Benhadad of Syria entered into a compact against Baasha, which is described in 1 Kings 15:17-22.

Examples of Covenants between God and Individuals

1. With Aaron

Aaron, the first of the Levitical order of priests enjoyed a personal covenant with Yahweh affecting both him and his descendants described in Numbers 18:19-23.

2. With Isaac

Isaac was personally promised by God that he was the chosen heir to the promises made to his father Abraham. This is made clear in Genesis 26:1-6.

3. God's Covenants with Jesus

Central to all the covenants is what is called "the eternal covenant" that exists between God the Father and God the Son. The following Scriptures describe that covenant: Isaiah 42:1-6, Isaiah 49:1-11.

4. King Josiah's Covenant with the Lord

When King Josiah discovered the Torah, or Book of the Law he instituted national reforms in Judah and made a covenant with God and the people described in 2 Kings 23:1-25.

5. The Beast's False Covenant (Of Death) With Israel

A future and ill-advised covenant between Israel and the end-times ruler is described in Daniel.

> He will confirm a covenant with many for one 'seven' [seven years]. In the middle of the 'seven' he will put an end to sacrifice and offering. And on a wing *of the temple* he will set up an abomination that causes desolation, until the end that is decreed is poured out on him. - Daniel 9:27

Isaiah's judgment of this covenant issued earlier than Daniel's time—in advance—annuls this covenant, because it denies the place of Jesus as rightful king and heir to the throne. See Isaiah 28:15-18.

Consequences for Despising the Sinai Covenant

Leviticus 26:3-45 spells out to Israel the consequences they would suffer if the covenant of Moses was abandoned or forsaken.

The Blessings and Curses under the Old Covenant

Under the terms of the Covenant of the Land, Moses told the people just prior to the entry of the next generation into the Promised Land that a series of blessings would follow obedience and adherence to the covenant; and on the other hand curses and terrible consequences would follow disobedience to this covenant. These are delineated in Deuteronomy 28.

Jeremiah's Solemn Warning

Jeremiah reinforced the conditional nature of the Covenant of the Land just prior to the siege of Jerusalem and the Babylonian captivity. See Jeremiah 11:1-8.

Warnings to Respond To The New Covenant

The New Covenant, superior in every way to the Old Covenant, according to the writer of the Epistle to the Hebrews. A strong admonition is included, however, about ignoring the grace of God and the wonderfully adequate and full promises of this covenant. See Hebrews 10:23-39 and Hebrews 12:12-29.

The New Covenant with Israel—A Covenant of Peace

Although Israel as a nation has not yet been brought under the terms of the New Covenant, their wonderful future when this does happen is foretold by the prophets. See Isaiah 54:1-17, Ezekiel 34:22-31.

King David, His Perpetual Throne, a Temple In Israel

God made a special covenant with King David, never repealed, never annulled, which holds to this day. See 2 Samuel 7, Ezekiel 37:21-28, Jeremiah 31.

The New Covenant with Israel—Instituted by Jesus with Israel through the Disciples

The Table of the Lord, or Holy Communion is so familiar to most Christians today that many have overlooked the momentous importance of the original Last Supper when Jesus placed this covenant into effect:

While they were eating, Jesus took bread, gave thanks and broke it, and gave it to his disciples, saying, "Take and eat; this is my body."

[27]Then he took the cup, gave thanks and offered it to them, saying, "Drink from it, all of you. [28]This is my blood of the covenant, which is poured out for many for the forgiveness of sins. [29]I tell you, I will not drink of this fruit of the vine from now on until that day when I drink it anew with you in my Father's kingdom."

[30]When they had sung a hymn, they went out to the Mount of Olives. - Matthew 26:26-30.

Gentiles Invited Into the New Covenant Jesus Made with Israel

Romans 9:22-23 indicates that God intended from the beginning to bring many Gentiles into the family of Abraham through the terms of the New Covenant instituted by Jesus. This is developed in Romans 11:13-35 and Hebrews 8:6-13.

The New Covenant as a Renewal of the Old Covenant

Note: The term "everlasting covenant" occurs 14 times in the OT. "Everlasting" is applied

(1) to the covenant with Noah (Gen. 9:16),
(2) to the covenant with Abraham (Gen. 17:7,13,19),
(3) to the covenant God made with David (2 Samuel 23:5), and
(4) to the New Covenant (Isaiah 55:3, 61:8, Jeremiah 32:40, 50:5, Ezekiel 16:60, 37:26).

The book of Hosea is especially clear about God divorcing his unfaithful wife Israel under the terms of the Old Covenant, but taking her back to himself again under the terms of the New Covenant (Hosea 2:14-23; See also Ezekiel 16:58-63).

Old Covenant and New Covenant—Compared and Contrasted

The New Testament presents strong and vivid comparisons and contrasts between the Old and the New Covenants. See especially Hebrews 9 and 2 Corinthians 3.

God's Faithfulness to His Covenants:

To better understand God's faithfulness to all his covenants the following Psalms are especially instructive: 25, 50, 89, and 132.

The Main Covenants of Yahweh Regarding Israel

As we have seen, "A covenant" is a sovereign pronouncement of God by which he establishes a relationship of responsibility

(1) between himself and an individual,
(2) between himself and mankind in general,

(3) between himself and a nation, or

(4) between himself and a specific human family.

C.I. Scofield wrote:

"A covenant in one category may overlap others...The covenants are normally unconditional in the sense that God obligates himself in grace, by the unrestricted declaration, 'I will' to accomplish certain announced purposes, despite any failure on the part of the person or people with whom he covenants. The human response to the divinely announced purpose is always important, leading as it does to blessing for obedience and discipline for disobedience. But human failure is never permitted to abrogate the covenant or block its ultimate fulfillment."[135]

Mainline Covenants

One special set of these covenants might well be called "mainline" covenants because they are connected one after another in a line, all the way from the first promise God made to Eve (that one of her sons would be the Messiah, the Savior of mankind), down through Abraham, Isaac, and Jacob, (rather than Ishmael or Esau for example), through King David and ending in Jesus Christ. Both Joseph and Mary are descended from David though through different family lines as the NT genealogies in Matthew and Luke detail.

I. The Edenic Covenant

Man is charged with responsibility for propagating the race, subduing the earth, exercising dominion over the animals, caring for the garden in Eden, and refraining from eating of the tree of the knowledge of good and evil. See Genesis 1:28-30 and Genesis 2:16, 17.

II. The Adamic Covenant

See Genesis 3. The consequences of man's fall necessitated a changed relationship between man and God including the following elements: (1) A curse on the serpent: Genesis 3:14, Romans 16:20, 2 Corinthians 11:3,14, Rev. 12:9. (2) The first promise of a redeemer (the proto-evangelium). Messiah would come in the line of Seth, Noah, Shem, Abraham, Isaac, Jacob, Judah and David. (3) A changed state of woman including bondage and subservience to man's headship, and suffering and pain in motherhood. (4) Loss of the garden in Eden as a dwelling place and light occupation changed to heavy burden of work because of a cursed earth. (5) Inevitable sorrow and disappointment in life. (6) Shortened life span and tragedy of death.

III. The Noahic Covenant

This unconditional covenant with Noah (which affects all mankind) establishes principles for all government, and includes the following: (1) Sanctity of all human life established. Man responsible to protect life, even to capital punishment. (2) A Promise that another universal flood will not occur and the ground will not be cursed further. (3) Man's relationship to the animals and to nature is confirmed (Genesis 8:22, 9:2). (4) Man, presumably a vegetarian before the flood, is now allowed to eat meat. (5) Special characteristics are assigned to the three sons of Noah, Shem, Ham, and Japheth. See Genesis 8:21-9:17.

IV. The Abrahamic Covenant

This is an unconditional covenant. (1) God gave Abraham the promise of a great nation—primarily meaning Israel, but also includes great peoples in the line of Ishmael and Abraham's others sons. In all Abraham, had eight sons, six through his second wife Keturah after Sarah died (Genesis 25:3). Two peoples descended from Abraham are named specially. They are an earthly group (Israel) "as numerous as the grains of sand on the seashore," and a heavenly group (the true church) "as numerous as the stars in the heavens." These two "family trees" form the subject of the mainstream of redemptive history in the Bible. (2) Abraham was chosen to be the father of numerous descendants, to be blessed personally, to be personally honored, to be a channel of blessing to others. (3) Those who bless Abraham are to be blessed and those who curse him will be cursed. Blessings on the nations are to come through Abraham. (4) Reaffirmation of the promise of a Messiah was made by God to Abraham. There are four major passages in Genesis specific to this covenant: Genesis 12:1-7; 13:14-17; 15:1-21; and 22:15-18.

The Covenant with Abraham Is Restated and Confirmed To Isaac by The Lord
See Genesis 26:1-5.

The Covenant with Abraham Is Restated and Confirmed To Jacob by The Lord
See Genesis 28:10-15.

V. The Mosaic Covenant

This was a conditional covenant that was connected with the giving of the Law at Sinai, and the Levitical priesthood.

The Law condemns all men. See Exodus 19 and following.

The New Testament Comments on the Mosaic (Old) Covenant
See especially 2 Corinthians 3:7-9, Romans 3:19-20, and Hebrews 10:1-10.

VI. The Covenant of the Land

This partly conditional covenant has several parts: (1) dispersion of the Jews was to be a consequence of disobedience. (2) Future repentance will be accomplished by God. (3) God will re-gather his scattered people and restore them to the land. (4) The people of Israel will be brought to the Lord as a nation. (5) The enemies and oppressors of Israel will be punished. (6) Future national prosperity and preeminence is guaranteed. See Deuteronomy 28-30. 28, 29 and Amos 9:9-15. Because of this covenant, the right of the Jews to live in the land is conditional upon their behavior.

The New Testament Promises God Will Resume His Fulfillment of Various Covenants with Israel

See Acts 15:14-18 and Romans 11:26, 27. The Old Testament Concurs on this: Isaiah 11:11,12, Jeremiah 23:3-8, Ezekiel 37:21-25, Hosea 2:14-16, Hosea 3, Joel 3:1-8 and Amos 9:11-15.

VII. The Davidic Covenant

This covenant features (1) a temple in Israel, (2) a kingdom in perpetuity, (3) a throne, i.e., royal authority in the line of David, and (4) chastisement on sons for their disobedience. The promise of Messiah in the line of David is confirmed. See 2 Samuel 7:8-16, Isaiah 1:24-28 and Psalm 89.

VIII. The New Covenant

This is an everlasting, unconditional covenant imparting a renewed mind and heart to the recipients; restored favor and blessing for Israel; complete and final forgiveness and removal of sins; indwelling of the Holy Spirit; a rebuilt temple in Israel (Ezekiel 37:26,27a); cessation of war; and institution of world peace. The Greek word *diatheke* is used interchangeably 15 times in the New Testament for "covenant" and "testament." See Matthew 26:26-28, Jeremiah 31, Hebrews 8:8-13.

Some Provisions of the New Covenant

The New Covenant promised to Israel went into effect at the Last Supper during Easter Week.

Jesus instituted this covenant with his eleven disciples who were representatives of true, believing Israel. Jesus then asked these disciples to become representatives of a new body of believers known as the Church. They were called as Apostles to invite Jews and Gentiles alike around the world to enter into this New Covenant. After the completion of this calling out of the true church, Scripture promises that God will return and bring the nation of Israel (as a nation) into the New Covenant. This will take place at the end of the age when Jesus returns to Jerusalem to sit as King on the throne of his father David. Under the new covenant all those who belong to Christ and are part of the Church benefit in the following ways: They are called children of God—Romans 8:16; called the household of God—Ephesians 2:19; called children of Abraham—Galatians 3:7; called children of promise—Romans 9:8; called a "people of his own"—Titus 2:14; called heirs of God according to promise—Galatians 3:29; called the temple of God—1 Corinthians 3:16; called "the circumcision"—Philippians 3:3; called "the Israel of God"—Galatians 6:16; called "a chosen generation, royal priesthood, peculiar people, a holy nation"—1 Peter 2:9; called heirs of the kingdom—James 2:5; called "sons of God"—John 1:12; called kings and priests of God—Revelation 1:6; called "Mount Zion", "The City of the Living God"—Hebrews 12:22; called The Bride of Christ—2 Corinthians 11:2; and called the Body of Christ—1 Corinthians 12.

The Relationship between Jesus, the Son Of God, and the Covenants With regard to the Edenic Covenant

Jesus Christ is the "Last Adam" (1 Corinthians 15:45-47) who takes the place of the First Adam and recovers all that the First Adam lost, (Colossians 2:10, Hebrews 2:7-9). Concerning the Adamic Covenant, Jesus is the promised "Seed of the Woman" (Genesis 3:15, John 12:31, Galatians 4.4, 1 John 3:8) who fulfills all the demands on man for labor and toil (Mark 6:3) as well as obedience (Philippians 2:8, Hebrews 5:8). As the son of Shem, Jesus fulfilled the promise to Noah and to Shem. Jesus Christ is the promised seed (singular) of Abraham to whom all the promises to Abraham apply (Genesis 22:18, Galatians 3:16, Philippians 2:8). Jesus is the only man who fulfilled all the requirements of the Law of Moses, and he bore the curse of the law on our behalf (Galatians 3:10-13), under the conditions of the Mosaic Covenant. Under the Palestinian Covenant he will yet perform the gracious promises, (Deuteronomy 28:1-30:9). Jesus is the Seed and Heir and King under the terms of the Covenant with David (Matthew 1:1, Luke 1:31-33). It was the sacrifice of Jesus that founded the New Covenant (Matthew 26:28, 1 Corinthians 11:25). (Adapted from the C.I. Scofield Bible notes).[136]

Appendix F
The Complexities of Time

Introduction to Time

This essay touches briefly on various aspects and dimensions of time. To a scientist, time is a relatively simple matter, but when one gets into the Bible time has qualitative and subjective aspects. There is much more to consider. The Bible contrasts time and eternity as well. God is outside of time. He is, "...the high and lofty one, who inhabits eternity" (Isaiah 57:15).

Time as we know it was created by God—it is part of the creation. However the created universe consists of a physical, material world and a spiritual realm. The latter is called in the New Testament "the heavenly places." In the heavenlies time has quite different properties than we usually think about in regard to the physical, material world. Man was created to live in both worlds (the material and the spiritual) at the same "time" and a study of time and eternity (a much neglected subject) carries a number of surprises. The physical universe has been drastically affected by the fall of Lucifer and his angels, and by the fall of man. This means we now live in a damaged, deteriorating "old creation." Time itself has been altered by the fall.

Is The Age of the Universe Indeterminate?

Virtually all modern geology and astronomy textbooks today take it for granted that the solar system is at least four or five billion years old, and it is now assumed such great ages are gospel truth. Anthropologists take it for granted that man is at least several millions of years old. But only in the past 200 years or so has Western science come to believe in a very old universe as opposed to a recent creation. The assumption of a very old universe has become such an ingrained paradigm that jokes are routinely made in classrooms and textbooks about Archbishop Usher's alleged assignment of the date, day, and hour of creation in 4004 BC.

The Bible actually opens with the statement "In the beginning God..." without making any reference to date and time. In both Hebrew and Greek, the idea of "the beginning" means the "indefinite distant past." This is not to suggest that man's early history fades into obscure mists of mythology as we go backwards in time, but that God has not revealed all that we would like to know about the exact "time" of the creation of all things.

Like Genesis, the Gospel of John opens with the words, "In the beginning was the Word, and the Word was with God, and the Word was God." It is declared in Scripture that God always was, always will be, and is unchanging—"Jesus Christ is the same yesterday, today and forever" (Hebrews 12:8). The "beginning" referred to in John's gospel is actually an earlier point in time than the "beginning" of Genesis One. John says "the Word was with God" prior to the creation of the universe, and in fact all things were brought into being through the Word.

As far as archaeology and recorded history are concerned human civilizations appear to be only of the order of thousands, not millions, of years old. The Bible is an exceptionally accurate document, and there is no ancient document for which we have better manuscript authority (or evidence), or into which more man-years of intense scholarship have been invested in recovering the original text. The Old Testament genealogies have very few gaps in them (if any at all!) and are actually quite complete so that one can estimate the time of Adam, the first man, as occurring only a few thousand years before Christ.

The internal structure of the Bible makes it difficult to place the creation of Adam more than a few thousands of years in the past. Sadly, for many secular scientists this fact is considered sufficient reason for them to ignore the Bible altogether as a relevant source of reliable information on any subject. However, a biblical world-view must in the long run be consistent with scientific data—properly interpreted. The God of the Bible is the God of truth and in the end truth from all possible sources must harmonize.

It may be, however, that the actual age of the universe is indeterminate. I believe this to be the case because God has apparently hidden from us the key evidence we need to unravel the past back to the time of creation. Twice the Bible makes important statements (consistent with each other) that suggest the fundamental nature of time, and many aspects of the actual course of history, presently escape our understanding to a large degree. Solomon says,

> I have seen the burden God has laid on men. [11] He has made everything beautiful in its time. He has also set eternity in the hearts of men; yet they cannot fathom what God has done from beginning to end. [12] I know that there is nothing better for men than to be happy and do good while they live. - Ecclesiastes 3:10-11

Just as we cannot figure out God's ways and understand precisely how he works, (Romans 11:33), so also we may not notice events that are actually crucial to his plans and programs. And we may mislabel other events in history as important when actually they turn out to be unimportant in the long run. Most of Israel totally missed the many prophetic fulfillments that took place during the First Advent of their Messiah, Yeshua (Jesus), for instance. Only afterwards did his followers figure out what actually had been happening in God's plan as revealed in the Old Testament.

Our knowledge of what actually happened in the past is inadequate; the details of what was important and what was not are obscured in the mists of time. It is most difficult for historians to reconstruct what actually happened in the past. (History books are always being rewritten). Likewise, we cannot predict what events will unfold tomorrow with any real certainty, nor set a date for the return of Christ. Yet we are restlessly preoccupied with time and frustrated when we cannot unravel its secrets with all the precision a modern atomic clock can give us.

When Jesus left his disciples forty days after his resurrection, ascending into the cloud, (that is, through the space-time gateway of the Shekinah glory cloud into the heavenly places) from the Mount of Olives in Jerusalem, his disciples were anxious for word of his return. Jesus told them,

> He said to them: "It is not for you to know the times or dates the Father has set by his own
> authority. (Acts 1:7 - compare with Matthew 24:36).

This scripture clearly implies that all attempts to set dates for the next World War and the second coming of Jesus are wasted effort. The ages past are also difficult for us to unravel and must remain full of mystery. The tapestry of the past has many folds, and we easily lose track of most of them in our feeble attempts to trace history backwards.

Modern secular science is built on the assumption that the laws of physics have never changed. Therefore we can make measurements say for 50 or 100 years and derive theories, which can then be extrapolated backwards in time to the beginning of all things. This approach to science is known as "uniformitarianism" about which we are specifically warned in the New Testament in the Apostle Peter's remark about the world-wide flood in the days of Noah (2 Peter 3:3-12).

> But do not forget this one thing, dear friends: With the Lord a day is like a thousand years,
> and a thousand years are like a day. - 2 Peter 3:8

Whether we like it that way or not, arguments about the age of the universe may be irreconcilable. There is evidence both for a recent creation, and there is also evidence for an ancient universe. It is our stereotypical thinking about the nature of time that causes us the problem. We view time as an absolute, and as a single dimension measured by a fixed master clock. In reality time is multidimensional and we are trapped in one-dimensional linear time (because of the fall). We are unable to see the broader perspective of eternity. Our vision is too narrow and needs some stretching.

The Old Testament View of Time

The Hebrew concept of time found in the Old Testament is concerned more with the quality of time as it relates to hail, rain, summer, and harvest or to "evil days" or "prosperous times." Clock or calendar time certainly is tracked in the Old Testament. Believing Jews as well as Christians believe the Old Testament is an accurate account of actual historical events and real people.

The Old Testament teaches by means of stories, by personal examples from the lives of individuals, and by case histories of God's dealings with men and angels. Scripture uses poetic images, dreams, visions and providential arrangements of circumstances to indicate God's invisible workings in human affairs from behind the scenes of history. The Hebrew year cycles around seed time and harvest and commemorative feasts and festivals. These call to mind the redemptive deeds of God and his blessings upon his chosen people Israel.

The feasts of Israel have great symbolic import both for the nation of Israel and for the Church. Many details concerning dates and length of these feasts are given in the Torah (Leviticus 23).

The Old Testament gives us a record of patriarchs and races, nations and kings. It is a selective record narrowing down to focus on the bloodline leading to the Messiah. Israel is at stage center, all directions are measured from Jerusalem, and the relationship between the Israelites and their God determines their prosperity or adversity in the land (*eretz yisrael*). The historical record of the Old Testament reveals national deterioration and repeated failures by men, but persistent, gracious intervention by God who sovereignly works out his grand strategy down through the ages. Israel typifies God's dealings with the nations. From Israel the Messiah has already come once, and through Israel will come the ultimate salvation of the nations when Messiah returns.

The Old Testament does not often speak at all about the affairs of other nations unless they impinge on events concerning Israel. Little is said about earthquakes, natural disasters, wars, the rise and fall of empires and nations, storms, or cosmic events—unless such happenings relate directly to Israel. In addition, the purpose of the biblical record is mostly moral and ethical. Because he is a personal God who makes covenants, Yahweh is evidently much more interested in helping men to know him and to understand themselves than he is in teaching us details of science or all the fine points of history.

Concerning the Old Testament, Paul plainly says in First Corinthians, 10:11, that "These things happened to them (to the Old Testament fathers) as types, but they were written down for our instruction, upon whom the end of the ages has come." In his letter to Romans, (Romans 15:4), Paul also wrote, "Whatever things were written in former times were written for our instruction, that through patience and the encouragement of the scriptures we might have hope."

Interruptions in Time Recorded in the Bible

The Hebrew language has no verb tenses in the usual sense familiar to us who speak English. In the Jewish way of thinking, the quality of an event or happening becomes more important than the minutes or hours (the measure) the event occupies in our familiar four dimensions of length, width, height and time.

For example, in the Old Testament there is Joshua's "long day," (which occurred about 1420 BC). On that day, the sun conveniently stood still for about a whole day, so Joshua could finish an important battle against the Amorites. (The battle is described in Joshua Chapter 10.) The LORD also conveniently arranged an exceptionally heavy hailstorm at the same time, suggesting that something radical happened to the earth's normal weather patterns at that time. What actually took place in nature would be, to us, of enormous scientific importance to learn more about. However, the Bible makes the stopping of the earth's rotation on its axis and the fall of enormous, deadly hailstones incidental to the main purpose of the narrative, which was recorded to show how God can use supernatural means to deliver his people. Conceiving in the mind the possibility that God actually stopped the earth's rotation and coordinated simultaneously all the forces and effects that would have been accompanied such a happening staggers the imagination—we simply don't know what actually happened except that the record says the length of one particular day was stretched by divine intervention.

Some day perhaps we will discover some supporting evidence for an unusual historic event such as a large meteor striking the earth, or a great volcanic explosion, or a close-passage of the planet Mars, which would correlate conclusively with Joshua's Long Day. The idea that God should interrupt the normal flow of time for a moral reason may strike us as "unreasonable," and, of course, explaining how he does it, (the laws of physics being what they are), is not an easy task. Critics have felt the earth would fly apart instantly if its rotation were ever stopped or even slowed. But this assumes that God lacks sufficient power to coordinate and control all related forces such as tides and stresses in the crust.

About 714 BC King Hezekiah faced the crisis of early death and asked God for help (2 Kings 20). He granted the king fifteen more years of life. As a sign, God caused the sun dial in the palace to move backwards "ten steps." Perhaps the reversed motion of the sun dial was caused by some sort of wobble in the earth's rotation? Who knows? God doesn't bother to tell us; apparently it isn't important for us to know how it happened.

The Hebrew idea of continuous present tense is found in the covenant name of God (one of many names for God in the OT). This is the God who revealed himself to Moses at the burning bush in Sinai saying, "I am Who I am. Tell Pharaoh, 'I AM' has sent you." This could be translated equally well as "I Will be Who I Will Be." The name YHWH

(Yahweh, or Jehovah) is simply derived from the verb "to be." God is the great "I AM" in the sense that each of us is a little "i am." In reading the Gospel of John it is helpful to note that Jesus used the term "I am" a number of times in the sense of the meaning of Yahweh. For instance he said, "...before Abraham was, I am" (John 8:58). Jesus was much more aware of the eternal dimension than we are. He dwelt in eternity in some sense the whole time he was present on earth as the Man Christ Jesus. Thus, some of the accomplishments by Jesus at points in time while he was on earth sent ripples into eternity, which changed both the past and the future! As God is eternal and outside of time, so our human spirits are also eternal. However, our bodies are fallen, subject to death, and not yet redeemed. It is the fact that our spirits live in bodies that places us in contact with the physical world and limits our experience of time.

To illustrate how the verb tenses in English can be either past or prophetic-future in the Hebrew in some cases, consider the prayer of Habakkuk in Habakkuk Chapter 3. This passage can be read either as a record of God's great and mighty deeds in the past, which the prophet recalls—or the passage can be read as predictive of God's mighty acts in the future. Either past or future meanings are correct. God has delivered his people Israel by great acts in history on their behalf. And, God will deliver Israel in the future by even greater deeds and mighty works. In any case, there is reason for God's people to hope for their salvation in those times when things get worse before they get better. Habakkuk lived in one of those times when there is little on the immediate horizon to give one hope.

Subjective Time

Various dimensions of time (which we usually don't stop and think about) are known to us in our daily experience. First, there is subjective time, which is the appearance of time to our sense of consciousness. Subjective time cannot be measured by a stop watch, but this type of time varies over wide limits. Sometimes we perceive a sequence of events around us as happening in a flash. Sometimes time seems to drag on "forever"—while the clock on the wall may tick off only minutes. Many of us remember how time appeared to move very slowly during childhood. A single summer day seemed to last forever, and the interval between Christmases and school vacations was an "eternity." Later in life, some of us look back and see that decades have passed almost as if they were but months. Carl Jung noted that in the second half of life it seemed as if all the events in the past are equidistant from the present. An event that took place 40 years ago may flash back into our consciousness as if it had happened yesterday. In sudden accidents some have reported that their whole lives flashed before their eyes in great detail, in what was really only a few seconds or less on the clock. When we dream at night what seems to be many hours of time is shown by REM (Rapid Eye Movement) sleep patterns to be only minutes of elapsed time. When we are bored not only does time drag on with seemingly endless monotony, the "quality" of our conscious experience is low. On the other hand when life is exciting and fulfilling, the forward movement of time is more obvious and the "quality" of the moment is greatly magnified. I have come to believe that subjective time has been greatly affected (negatively) by the fall of man. Therefore for God's people heaven will not only be life that lasts forever, it will also be life of immensely restored quality and enjoyment.

God's final judgment of all of us will no doubt reveal that what we considered important and precious was often rubbish in the eyes of God. Conversely, small forgotten moments we thought nothing of may be elevated and rewarded when God's records showed we uttered a helpful word of comfort to someone in need, or gave aid from a right motive.

Biological time has to do with wildlife migratory patterns, animal hibernation, biorhythms, jet lag, circadian (24-hour) patterns and menstrual cycles—numerous phenomena in nature that are loosely coupled to dynamical time (that is, to months and seasons). Although such biological time clocks are mysterious and still not well understood, they are probably closer to the way God keeps time, if we remember that the Jewish calendar is based on the lunar month, the cycle of harvest, and the motion of the earth, moon, planets, and stars. Seen in this light, the scientist's way of keeping time—with precision quartz clocks and atomic resonators is actually somewhat arbitrary and less "absolute" than God's heavenly clocks and calendars.

Linear Time and Cyclical Time

The Hebrew view of time also includes the concept that time moves from event to event in a line—not a straight line, to be sure, but towards a goal. The goal is always the future, yet the goal intended by God is always to be fulfilled in history. Bible prophecies frequently have both an immediate and a long-term fulfillment, for example. In the Bible, sins are seen to have consequences that follow inevitably, moral choices lead to measurable results for good or for ill, and history proceeds towards the definite outworking purposes of God.

> But small is the gate and narrow the road that leads to life, and only a few find it. [15]"Watch out for false prophets. They come to you in sheep's clothing, but inwardly they are ferocious wolves." - Matthew 7:14-15

A consummation of the ages lies ahead, for which all else has been but a shadowy preparation. In both ancient Greek culture, (among the Pythagoreans, Stoics and Neoplatonists), and in Hindu culture (especially during the Vedic period, 1500-600 BC), one runs onto the concept of circular, or cyclical time. This is sometimes symbolized by the Ouroboros, the snake chasing his own tail. In this view of time, the beginning leads back around to the end, and the cycle starts all over again. The Babylonians, ancient Chinese, Aztecs, Mayans, and the Norse had cyclical calendars.

In pantheistic religious systems of thought the universe is often depicted as going through great long epochs of rebirth, growth, decay, and destruction. The Hindu cycles, for example, range from 360 human years, to 300 trillion years (which is the lifetime of the gods before their rebirth). Reincarnation, which has no basis in the Bible at all (see Hebrews 9:27), springs from such an Eastern pantheistic point of view. Augustine was among the first to insist on linear time as opposed to cyclical, since he observed that many important events in the Bible clearly happened one time only. Since clocks were not well-developed until the 14th Century, it was perhaps easier for the ancients to imagine events in history as recurring since the four seasons and patterns of the stars in the heavens were cyclical.

The Bible depicts the human race as having a definite clear beginning, a history that has been accurately recorded by God, and an approaching day of judgment when all men will be evaluated justly by their Creator. The fact that "books are to be opened" on judgment day means God keeps track of detail (by means of his "recording angels")—even if we do not ourselves keep good record books. God even pays attention to the numbering of the hairs on our heads. He will see to it that truth and justice ultimately prevail no matter how grim things seem to us at the moment (1 Corinthians. 4:5). A good example of the work of a recording angel is to be found in Ezekiel 9:2ff.

Dynamical Time and Atomic Time

The "clock" for measuring time given us in the Bible can be called "dynamical time" because this clock is based on the motion of the earth on its axis (defining the day), the period of the moon as it revolves around the earth establishing the lunar month (used in the Jewish calendar), and the time it takes for the earth to make one trip around the sun, which defines the year. Planetary alignments, constellations, comets, meteors, special stars, and other events in the heavens are ordained by God for marking out unusual events. This time-keeping mechanism, which relies, essentially, on Newton's law of gravity, is described in Genesis One as something God put into place on the Fourth Day of creation:

> And God said, "Let there be lights in the expanse of the sky to separate the day from the night, and let them serve as signs to mark seasons and days and years, [15] and let them be lights in the expanse of the sky to give light on the earth." And it was so. [16] God made two great lights—the greater light to govern the day and the lesser light to govern the night. He also made the stars. [17] God set them in the expanse of the sky to give light on the earth, [18] to govern the day and the night, and to separate light from darkness. And God saw that it was good. [19] And there was evening, and there was morning—the fourth day. - Genesis 1:14-19

Most common clocks keep dynamical time. But also in common use today are "atomic clocks." In fact our present precision time standards are set to atomic time rather than a dynamical time standard. Atomic time would be locked in step with dynamical time if the velocity of light were an absolute, fixed constant. A careful statistical analysis of all the measured values of the velocity of light, c, shows that c has decreased during the past 300 years, and thus atomic clocks have slowed down with respect to dynamical clocks. When the velocity of light first began to be measured it appears that the annual decrease in velocity was very rapid. In fact it has been suggested that the initial value of c when the universe was new may have been as much as one to ten million times higher than its present value.

It is not possible for c to be a variable without forcing a select group of other constants to also vary. Otherwise the universe would be unstable and serious inconsistencies would occur in many equations of physics. The evidence available at the present time suggests that c, Planck's constant h, the rest mass of the electron in the atomic frame of reference, and radio-active decay rates are not fixed. The gravitational constant G is fixed, as is macroscopic mass and most other physical properties affecting life on earth, however. It seems probable that the reason c has decreased is because of an increasing permeability of free space (one of the "metric" properties of space). This would result, for example, from shrinkage of the original universe after it was "stretched out" by God to its maximum diameter on the Second Day of creation.

The observed decrease in the velocity of light originally studied in detail by Australian scientists Barry Setterfield and Trevor Norman follows a steeply decaying curve leveling off to nearly zero change in recent years.

Since it is quite possible that the velocity of light has decreased by a factor of perhaps 10 million or more, the long geological ages now in vogue, which follow the atomic clock, would actually be compressed by this amount according the dynamical time scale of ordinary history.

Time's Arrow in Physics

Many physical phenomena can be described very satisfactorily by mathematical equations. Usually these (differential) equations involve mass or similar measurable properties of the physical world, and the dimensions of length, width, height and time. From a strictly mathematical point of view it does not matter if time is positive or negative—most equations of physics are time reversible.

However it is not so in real life, because of something called "Time's Arrow." The real world we live in is governed by an important principle known as the Second Law of Thermodynamics. The Second Law can be stated in several forms, but basically it refers to the tendency of things to rot, rust, decay and fall apart with the passage of time. As we use energy, the total amount of available energy available to do additional work decreases inexorably. Orderly systems proceed to break-down in the direction of chaos, and the "information content" of things decreases with the passage of time. Both outside energy and outside organizing intelligence are required to bring order out of chaos.

In the case of living organisms, it is the genetic code that instructs cells to build themselves into orderly organisms, but this is accomplished at the expense of an overall decrease in the total available energy of the universe.

In physics this principle is often stated as "Entropy always increases." Entropy is a measure of the unavailable energy in a system or the state of disorder. Technically speaking this law of entropy applies to what is known as "closed systems." However if a sufficiently large circle is drawn around most any system one can think of the law applies without exception. The earth and its atmosphere do not comprise a thermodynamically closed system because of energy input from the sun, for example. However by drawing a circle around the solar system, one has a closed system.

Incidentally it can be shown that energy from the sun alone is not sufficient to decrease the overall entropy of earth or to drive biological organisms in the direction of increasing complexity.[137] This point is widely misunderstood among secular scientists today. It is wrongly taught that energy inputs alone are sufficient for living systems to self-organize out of simple molecules, given enough time. The above authors and other scientists as well, have shown by careful calculation that programming information from a source outside a system is required, in addition to energy, for the molecules of life and living cells to be assembled.

In conclusion, physical processes known to science require that time move from the past through the present and into the future irreversibly. "Linear," "one-dimensional" time is the time frame of the physics of the macroscopic world. This view of time is consistent with the progression of the ages in the Bible.

Time in the New Testament

The New Testament appeals to reason, to the conscience, and to the rational mind to communicate the same truths that are found in the Old Testament in story form. Someone has suggested that the Old Testament appeals to the right side of the brain and the New, to the left side. Bible teacher and former corporate executive and scientist Chuck Missler often says,

> "The New Testament is in the Old Concealed,
> and The Old Testament is in the New Revealed."

The basic message of God's love and actions in history is really the same, but it is presented in two differing formats in the two halves of Scripture. The New Testament message is addressed not only to the Jews but to the pagans, the Goyim, the entire non-Jewish world. When the New Testament was written down in the First Century AD, Greek and Roman culture and government dominated much of the ancient world. The original language now changed between the two Testaments without warning from Hebrew to Koine Greek.

The Greek language of the New Testament refers to time as measured in *chronos* and *kairos*—times and seasons. The meanings of the Greek New Testament words for times and seasons add more to an understanding of the complex nature of time in our universe. *Chronos* (Strong's Concordance Number 5550) means quantity of time, space of time, duration, succession of moments, length of time, or a bounded period of time. To understand this word, it is helpful to read the passages of the New Testament where *chronos* is used. These include Matthew 2:7, Luke 4:5; 8:27; 20:9, Acts 20:18, Romans 16:25, and Mark 2:19. *Kairos* refers to the quality of time or season, the epoch characterized by certain events, the decisive quality of happening, an opportune time, or a fortuitous moment.

The renowned Bible scholar Archbishop Trench wrote,

"The 'seasons' are the critical epoch-making periods foreordained of God, when all that has been slowly, and often without observation, ripening through long ages is mature and comes to birth in grand decisive events, which constitute at once the close of one period and the commencement of another. Such, for example, was the passing away of the old Jewish dispensation; such, again, the recognition of Christianity as the religion of the Roman Empire; such the conversion of those outside; such the great revival which went along with the first institution of the Mendicant Orders; such, by still better right, the Reformation; such, above all others, the second coming of the Lord in glory."

Kairos (Strong's Concordance Number 2540) is used in such passages as Romans 5:6, Galatians 6:10, Matthew 13:34, 26:18, Revelation 12:12, I Peter 1:11, and Luke 4:13. In the New Testament we have expressions like "times of refreshing" (Acts 3:19), "times of ignorance" (Acts 17:30), and "the times of the Gentiles" (Luke 21:24).

Greek also uses the word *aion* for age, usually referring to an indefinite period of time marked by certain moral or spiritual characteristics. The plural *aionios*, denotes the eternal or everlasting in the New Testament. For example "life eternal" (*aionios zoe*) in John 17:3 refers to an ever-increasing knowledge of God. This word and its derivatives and compounds are very common in the New Testament and can be searched by looking up Strong's Concordance Numbers 165 and 166.

Times of Stress

To illustrate the importance the Bible places on the content and quality of an interval of time within history, the expression "times of stress" occurs in one of the most interesting passages in the New Testament, Paul's second letter to Timothy 3:1-5. Our understanding of the message is enriched by looking up the individual Greek words in this passage in a lexicon. The passage in question reads as follows:

[1]But mark this: There will be terrible times in the last days. [2]People will be lovers of themselves, lovers of money, boastful, proud, abusive, disobedient to their parents, ungrateful, unholy, [3]without love, unforgiving, slanderous, without self-control, brutal, not lovers of the good, [4]treacherous, rash, conceited, lovers of pleasure rather than lovers of God— [5]having a form of godliness but denying its power. Have nothing to do with them. - 2 Timothy 3:1-5

The "Last Days"

The New Testament uses the term "last days" to refer to the entire 2000 year interval between the first and second advents of Christ. Christ was born "late" in history as God measures time—see Galatians 4:4. He will return after recurring cycles of stress have plagued mankind. These cycles will come with repeated frequency and intensity as the age draws to a close-cycles compared in Scripture to the birth pangs of a women about to give birth to a child. They will also be less and less local and more and more global. For example, only in our century have we had "World" Wars. The present world economy is another example. A recession in one nation these days affects the world economy creating a crisis not easily corrected by any individual sovereign nation.

It is not possible for us to anticipate where and when the next "time of stress" will befall us, nor can we tell what form it will take. Thus, we cannot plan ahead very well, so we must take one day at a time as Jesus advised us in the Sermon on the Mount, "...Sufficient unto the day is the evil thereof" (Matthew 6:34 KJV). During these times of stress, the real character of human beings surfaces, raw, ugly sores open in society, and the situation becomes dangerous and violent. Astrologers explain that such times are at least partially caused by "unfortunate" aspects and alignments of the planets.

For a detailed discussion of the use of the term "last days" in the New Testament see *Are These the Last Days?* by Ray C. Stedman.[138] The term "the Day of the Lord" appears frequently in the Bible. The Day of the Lord is an extended period of time, not just a 24-hour day, and is to be contrasted with the times in which we now live, which we might call "the Day of man," or "man's day." *See Appendix G - The Day of the Lord.*

For a chart of Bible prophecy and the end of the age see *Appendix A - Chart of the End of the Age.*

The Mysterious Flow of Time

Although time is measured in history in terms of clocks and calendars, it is also articulated into seasons. These periods of time bend, stretch, and unfold as God periodically moves the course of history in a different direction. Often, at the last minute, God postpones the final consummation of events, withdraws impending judgments, or even blesses us unexpectedly just when it seems to us that we are at a point of no return in our personal lives or when we think the sky is about to fall on our heads bringing an end to the world as we know it.

God is outside of time. He is an eternally self-existing, self-defining, living Being. Since he created time as we know it, we can think past, present, and future are eternally present before his eyes.

God's actions in eternity can affect past, present, and future (as experienced by mankind), simultaneously. A certain action of God completed in the past can have on-going and lasting results. Other activities of God, such as his expressions and grace and mercy towards us all, continue day after day. Certain events, such as the "appointed" hour we die or the Day of Judgment, are fixed in the future, predetermined by God. Since God is more concerned with the quality of time than the quantity or measure of time, we can all expect to experience time differently in eternity depending on the quality of our lives during our present training on earth.

Since God is outside of time, past, present and future are always present before him. Consider the case of a sudden airplane disaster where all the passengers and crew have but moments to cry out to God in a hundred or more sudden, separate, desperate prayers. God has all of eternity to hear even the shortest of these prayers, to review all the lives and facts and his own timetables for history. He knows every heart, every motive, all the facts and he has all the time in the world to take a myriad of data into consideration before answering or denying each one of those prayers! He can take his time, all the time he needs, and yet not fail to answer every one of these simultaneous prayers, each with justice, compassion, and certitude. He does not need to make split-second decisions as we do, he is never caught off guard, and when he does act he can accomplish the impossible in a flash. An example of this sudden and complete action by God will be in the coming resurrection of the dead as described in First Corinthians,

> Listen, I tell you a mystery: We will not all sleep, but we will all be changed— [52]in a flash, in the twinkling of an eye, at the last trumpet. For the trumpet will sound, the dead will be raised imperishable, and we will be changed. - 1 Corinthians 15:51-52

Some have attempted to estimate the time duration of a "twinkling of the eye." It is surely no more than milliseconds in our time frame.

There are many references in the Bible to "appointments" on God's calendar indicating that there is a divine plan for the ages in effect at all times. The age prior to the one in which we now live carries the title "times of ignorance." Speaking in Athens the Apostle Paul declared to the crowd,

> "Truly, these times of ignorance God overlooked, but now commands all men everywhere to repent, [31] because He has appointed a day on which He will judge the world in righteousness by the Man whom He has ordained. He has given assurance of this to all by raising Him from the dead." - Acts 17:30-31 NKJV)

Time Disrupted by the Fall

The universe was created for man. In science this is called the "anthropic principle." It is also evident from the opening chapters of the Bible. An empty universe inhabited only by God and the angels makes little sense to most of us. God does not "need" a universe, nor does he need man to add to his Being. He is fully sufficient and complete in all his attributes so our creation adds nothing to his essential nature. The universe was made as a home for man, and man was made for fellowship with God (see Isaiah 45:18). Man was placed in charge of the creation as Hebrews Chapter 2 recalls. God pronounced nature "good" and valuable to him before he placed man on earth. Intuitively it is unattractive to imagine that the universe sat empty for aeons before man arrived on the scene—as evolutionary thought teaches was the case. According to Genesis, God proceeded to create the universe step by step in an orderly way, and when he had the ecosystem prepared, he made man (last of all) and placed him squarely in the center of things to understand and to rule over what had been created. (Man has since lost his dominion over the creation—but that is another story. God has a restoration plan underway).

The notion of an originally upright, unflawed universe also suggests that the moon and planets may have once been more beautiful, more pristine, and more "inhabitable" than they are now. I myself happen to believe that some sort of cosmic disaster has already occurred throughout the solar system and that there is ample evidence now of destructive forces at work in the physical universe that were not put there by God. The biblical view also contradicts the notion that man is improving and society is advancing morally and socially. Rather, it is the grace of God, which makes life bearable and prevents mankind from self-destruction.

The original creation was "good" (unmarred, flawless) at the end of creation week. Then the angels fell and later man fell. The fall of man resulted in a "curse" on the physical world, a curse that has not yet been lifted. [Actually there are at least five significant curses named in Genesis that effect the world we live in today]. The fall of man and the fall of Satan seem to have made fundamental changes in certain laws of physics and biology as well. The nature of subjective time, i.e., the "quality" of time as we experience it has changed since creation. Also, man in his present condition is constrained to a rather limited "one-dimensional" time frame whereas before the fall, our first parents enjoyed a multidimensional quality of time much richer than we can even begin to imagine.

Before the fall, our first parents in their innocence and purity were in a very real sense enjoying a quality of life moment by moment that is unknown to us at the present time.

Incidentally the role of the angels in the government of the physical universe as well as in the affairs of men is confirmed in Hebrews 2:1-5. The implication of this passage is that the age in which we now live is governed by the angels, but the age that is to come will not be governed by angels, but by the redeemed of mankind who are in Christ the Lord.

A Glimpse into Eternity

The biblical view of time found in the New Testament is that time in the heavenly places, that is in the spiritual world, is multidimensional. For example, in the book of Revelation we see scenes taking place on earth in human history and scenes in the heavenly places going on at the same time. Time in heaven apparently moves in the forward direction as it does on earth. For example Revelation 8:1 describes a period of silence in heaven lasting "about half an hour." But time in heaven has a quality and a pace different from time on earth.

A good example of an event occurring in "eternity" is found in the Gospels: one day Jesus stepped up to the top of Mount Mizar, a minor peak on the slopes of Mount Hermon, above Banias (ancient Caesarea Philippi) in northern Israel, and was transfigured before his frightened disciples—Peter, James, and John. Appearing with him (about AD 30) were Moses (from about 1400 BC) and Elijah, (who was translated into heaven without seeing death about 850 BC). All were alive and well, as if they were contemporaries, oblivious to the years that had separated them by our way of reckoning time.

This incident (recorded in Luke 9:23-36; Matthew 17:1-8; and Mark 9:2-8) shows that all the usual rules and constraints of time (as we commonly think of them) were momentarily lifted. Thus, it was not only possible for men from ancient times to appear alive in the presence of the disciples of Jesus, but also for Jesus to assume his glorified body all at the same "time."

Another example of the multiple dimensions of time and eternity will be helpful to the reader. Consider the various time frames that are involved in the writing, printing, and reading of a book, for example, a mystery novel. Perhaps the author took a year to write the manuscript, but drew from many years of personal experience and from his own reading of history. Suppose six months elapse before the book is on the market and reaches the reader. The reader then begins the book, and after a period time of intermittent reading, finishes it. (The reader can even skip ahead to the end, if he wishes, to see how it all turns out). Internal to the book is the time frame of the story, which may include flashbacks in the lives of some of the characters. After reading the book, it goes on the library shelf, but the reader retains a summary version, condensed in his memory. He is free to recall the book, or read it again. In this example one can count half a dozen, or more, different time frames all co-existing!

Time As Experienced in a Resurrection Body

After his resurrection, Jesus further demonstrated the capacities of his resurrection body by appearing and disappearing at will among his disciples, in the days between the resurrection and the ascension. From such records in the Gospels, we can conclude that resurrection bodies are equipped for multidimensional space and time travel. Jesus ate food and could be touched and felt, in his resurrection body. He did not return in a ghost-like, shadowy form. In his two letters to the Corinthians, the Apostle Paul clarifies the nature of the resurrection. Physical death is the point a believer steps out of the time frame of human history. When a person leaves time and enters eternity. Once in eternity one bypasses intermediate (future) times to arrive at the resurrection at the exact same instant all other believers do, in fact "in a moment, in the twinkling of an eye."

First note carefully the wording the Apostle uses in describing the resurrection body as already in existence in eternity:

> [1]Now we know that if the earthly tent [Greek *skenos* = "tent"] we live in is destroyed, we have [now] a building [Greek: *oikos* = building] from God, an eternal house in heaven, not built by human hands. [2]Meanwhile we groan, longing to be clothed with our heavenly dwelling, [3]because when we are clothed, we will not be found naked. [4]For while we are in this tent, we groan and are burdened, because we do not wish to be unclothed but to be clothed with our heavenly dwelling, so that what is mortal may be swallowed up by life. [5]Now it is God who has made us for this very purpose and has given us the Spirit as a deposit, guaranteeing what is to come. - 2 Corinthians 5:1-5

The resurrection of Christians who have died during the past two thousand years immediately precedes the catching up of living believers at a yet-future event called the "rapture of the Church. See Chapter 6 - *The Rapture of the Church*. This appearing (*parousia*) of the Lord Jesus for his church is an event in eternity that intrudes into our time frame at some particular date on God's appointment calendar (1 Thessalonians 4:13-5:11).

In this passage three distinct events occur: (1) a great shout from the Lord Jesus that summons the dead back to life, (2) the Archangel's (Michael's) call to Israel, and the sound of a trumpet to summon those believers alive at that moment of history. That same trumpet and the immediate transformation of living Christians at the rapture is described in 1 Corinthians 15: 51-58.

In the experience of the Christian, one's personal death corresponds exactly with the Second Coming of Christ, though this event will also happen on earth at the definite date and time in recorded human history. This is what Paul meant when he said to be absent from the body was to be at home with the Lord, not as a spirit, but in a resurrection body along with everyone else who knows God. This can be seen at the Martyrdom of Stephen in the book of Acts.

> "Look," he said, "I see heaven open and the Son of Man standing at the right hand of God."
> [57]At this they covered their ears and, yelling at the top of their voices, they all rushed at him, [58]dragged him out of the city and began to stone him. Meanwhile, the witnesses laid their clothes at the feet of a young man named Saul.

[59]While they were stoning him, Stephen prayed, "Lord Jesus, receive my spirit." [60]Then he fell on his knees and cried out, "Lord, do not hold this sin against them." When he had said this, he fell asleep. - Acts 7:56-60

As Stephen died he saw heaven opened and Jesus standing at the right hand of God. Throughout the New Testament Jesus is ordinarily pictured as seated at the right hand of God. Evidently he stands to receive his bride, the Church, at the rapture. Thus all Christians get to heaven at the same moment. In one sense, then, heaven is now empty. There is no value in praying to the Virgin Mary or St. Jude since they aren't there yet! But as will be seen shortly, there is another sense in which all believers are already in heaven.

Who is Presently in Heaven?

Not only has Jesus Christ been raised from the dead, he is now seated in heaven at the right hand of God in a new resurrection body. All authority and power in the universe has been placed into his hands (Matthew 28:18). Therefore heaven is certainly not empty. The angels are there and the splendor and glory of God is unchanged and undiminished.

"As I looked,
    "thrones were set in place,
    and the Ancient of Days took his seat.
    His clothing was as white as snow;
    the hair of his head was white like wool.
    His throne was flaming with fire,
    and its wheels were all ablaze.
[10] A river of fire was flowing,
    coming out from before him.
    Thousands upon thousands attended him;
    ten thousand times ten thousand stood before him.
    The court was seated,
    and the books were opened.
[11] "Then I continued to watch because of the boastful words the horn was speaking. I kept looking until the beast was slain and its body destroyed and thrown into the blazing fire. [12] (The other beasts had been stripped of their authority, but were allowed to live for a period of time.)
[13] "In my vision at night I looked, and there before me was one like a son of man, coming with the clouds of heaven. He approached the Ancient of Days and was led into his presence.
[14] He was given authority, glory and sovereign power; all peoples, nations and men of every language worshiped him. His dominion is an everlasting dominion that will not pass away, and his kingdom is one that will never be destroyed."
- Daniel 7:9-14

When an individual enters into a personal relationship with Jesus Christ as Lord, he or she is immediately spiritually regenerated and becomes identified with Jesus Christ in his death, burial and resurrection. This is the meaning of baptism—being "placed into" Christ, into the Body of Christ (Romans 6:3-9).

Paul elaborates on this in Ephesians,

> As for you, you were dead in your transgressions and sins, [2]in which you used to live when you followed the ways of this world and of the ruler of the kingdom of the air, the spirit who is now at work in those who are disobedient. [3]All of us also lived among them at one time, gratifying the cravings of our sinful nature and following its desires and thoughts. Like the rest, we were by nature objects of wrath. [4]But because of his great love for us, God, who is rich in mercy, [5]made us alive with Christ even when we were dead in transgressions—it is by grace you have been saved. [6]And God raised us up with Christ and seated us with him in the heavenly realms in Christ Jesus,- Ephesians 2:1-6

Although our spirits and souls are made new if we know Jesus Christ personally, our bodies are not yet redeemed. It is our present mortal physical bodies (connecting us by the five senses), which link us to the "old creation." In spirit we already have been "raised" from the dead, we are dwelling in the heavenly places. We are already seated with Christ at the right hand of God. If we had our resurrection bodies "put on" instead of our old earth-tents, we would immediately perceive that we all had arrived in heaven together. Hebrews Chapter 12:18-29 describes our present dwelling in heaven.

So in one sense as all the above passages tell us, all believers are presently dwelling in the heavenly places in Christ Jesus. But in another sense the only man who is now in heaven is Jesus. Mary is not there yet, nor Jude the half-brother of Jesus, nor the Apostle Paul, nor my grandmother. The resurrection has not yet taken place. And there is no "waiting room" where our loved-ones are now in a holding pattern standing-by for heaven either.

When the resurrection does occur we shall all arrive there at exactly the same time. This is explained in more detail in a sermon on "Time and Eternity" by Ray C. Stedman.[139]

Rewards Beyond this Life

Eternal life—which is the free gift of God to all those who receive Jesus Christ as Lord—is a kind of time dimension characterized not only by endless duration, but by very high quality. God's time has richness, variety, freedom from boredom and endless diversity. Living in fellowship with him who is Life is not only liberating but exciting beyond the power of language to describe. Eternity does not mean timelessness, except perhaps for those in hell.

> Oh, the depth of the riches of the wisdom and knowledge of God!
> How unsearchable his judgments,

and his paths beyond tracing out!
[34]"Who has known the mind of the Lord?
   Or who has been his counselor?"
[35]"Who has ever given to God,
   that God should repay him?"
[36]For from him and through him and to him are all things.
   To him be the glory forever! Amen. - Romans 11:33-36

Appendix G
The Day of the Lord
By Lambert Dolphin

The Day of the LORD is a special term in the Bible used to refer to a period of time when God directly intervenes in human affairs—in judgment or in blessing. The Day of the Lord we are presently waiting for in our time frame will begin with the rapture (or "translation") of the Church and will continue through The Tribulation Period (seven years), and on through the thousand-year reign of Christ on earth until the time of the "new heavens and new earth" (Revelation 21).

In contrast to the coming Day of the Lord, we can think of the present age as "The Day of Man," because God has allowed human evil to run its full course in our time. God's interference with man's attempts to conduct his own affairs as he pleases is today minimal. Although there is restraint from God on man's attempts to run things, God is now allowing what is called "the mystery of lawlessness" to run its course. The culmination of "Man's Day" will be the appearance on the stage of history of a great world leader, a "lawless one," who will in actuality attempt to counterfeit God's Messiah and King, Jesus.

> For the secret power of lawlessness is already at work; but the one who now holds it back will continue to do so till he is taken out of the way. [8]And then the lawless one will be revealed whom the Lord Jesus will overthrow with the breath of his mouth and destroy by the splendor of his coming. [9]The coming of the lawless one will be in accordance with the work of Satan displayed in all kinds of counterfeit miracles, signs and wonders, [10]and in every sort of evil that deceives those who are perishing. They perish because they refused to love the truth and so be saved. [11]For this reason God sends them a powerful delusion so that they will believe the lie [12]and so that all will be condemned who have not believed the truth but have delighted in wickedness. - 2 Thessalonians 2:7-12

At the present time Jesus Christ the Lord is ruling over the earth (and indeed over the entire universe), however he is not yet reigning on the earth. It is God's will "that at the name of Jesus every knee should bow, in heaven and on earth and under the earth, [11]and every tongue confess that Jesus Christ is Lord, to the glory of God the Father" (Philippians 2:10-11). According to God's decree, all men will one day submit to the authority of Jesus willingly or by force—one way or the other. The above quotation is repeated also in Romans 14:11 and is derived from Isaiah Chapter 45 in the Old Testament.

Before departing from his disciples for the last time from the Mount of Olives Jesus instructed his disciples giving them what has been called "The Great Commission."

> Then Jesus came to them and said, "All authority in heaven and on earth has been given to me. [19]Therefore go and make disciples of all nations, baptizing them in[l] the name of the Father and of the Son and of the Holy Spirit, [20]and teaching them to obey everything I have commanded you. And surely I am with you always, to the very end of the age."- Matthew 28:18-20

The disciples and Christians of the First Century all expected Jesus to return very soon. Indeed this has been the hope of the true church in every generation.

> Come Thou long expected Jesus, born to set Thy people free,
> From our fears and sins release us; Let us find our rest in Thee.
> Israel's Strength and Consolation, Hope of all the earth Thou art;
> Dear Desire of every nation, Joy of every longing heart.
> Born Thy people to deliver, Born a child and yet a King.
> Born to reign is us forever, Now Thy gracious kingdom bring.
> By Thine eternal Spirit Rule in all our hearts alone;
> By Thine all sufficient merit, Raise us to Thy glorious throne.
> (Charles Wesley, 1707 - 1788)

The actual second coming of Christ to earth is described several places in the New Testament (as well as in the Old). Towards the very end of the First Century the aged apostle John saw the Second Advent in a great vision. Jesus descended from heaven on a white horse to fight the Battle of Armageddon. His title was King of kings and Lord of lords (Revelation 19:11-16).

For the unrepentant who reject Christ's rule over them now during the present Day of Grace, the fast-approaching Day of the Lord will be a time of terrible retribution, judgment and eternal destruction. For God's people it will mean final purifying, fulfillment, and reward. The Apostle Paul describes the *parousia* ("presence," or "appearing") and the *epiphaneia* ("shining-forth" or second coming) of the Lord as a single event in his First letter to the Thessalonians. In our earthly time frame these two events (the rapture of the

Church and the second coming in power and glory) are separated by the seven years of The Tribulation Period (2 Thessalonians 1:3-12).

The Old Testament is replete with vivid poetic descriptions of impending judgments on Israel, and/or the Gentile nations, which also will be more completely carried out by the Lord at the end of the age in which we now live (Isaiah 13:6-13).

God's judgments-both of men and Satan, "the god of this world (or, age)"—are especially directed at the root problem of sin—which is pride.

> [10] Go into the rocks,
>   hide in the ground
>   from dread of the LORD
>   and the splendor of his majesty!
> ...
> [19] Men will flee to caves in the rocks
>   and to holes in the ground
>   from dread of the LORD
>   and the splendor of his majesty,
>   when he rises to shake the earth.
> [20] In that day men will throw away
>   to the rodents and bats
>   their idols of silver and idols of gold,
>   which they made to worship. - Isaiah 2:10, 19-20

Today, the New Testament offers wonderful, complete forgiveness of all sin made possible by the death of God's own son, Jesus, on our behalf. The full power of his resurrection enables those who follow Jesus to live whole and godly lives. Furthermore, Christ promises that his bride, the true church, will escape from the wrath to come (1 Thessalonians 1:10).

The writer of the letter to the Hebrews warns that God will soon shake not only all the cities of the earth, the foundations of all human society, but also the heavens themselves, including the "principalities and powers in the heavenly places," the unseen angelic orders who presently control human affairs to a great extent. Only those things in heaven and on earth which God himself has built will survive! (Hebrews 12:25-29).

Zephaniah the prophet gives us an especially vivid view of the Day of the Lord. A partial fulfillment of this prophecy occurred about 30 years later in the Babylonian captivity. However it is clear that the full implications of this prophecy are yet future (Zephaniah chapter 1).

> [14] "The great day of the LORD is near—
>   near and coming quickly.
>   Listen! The cry on the day of the LORD will be bitter,

the shouting of the warrior there.
[15] That day will be a day of wrath,
a day of distress and anguish,
a day of trouble and ruin,
a day of darkness and gloom,
a day of clouds and blackness,
[16] a day of trumpet and battle cry
against the fortified cities
and against the corner towers.
[17] I will bring distress on the people
and they will walk like blind men,
because they have sinned against the LORD.
Their blood will be poured out like dust
and their entrails like filth.
[18] Neither their silver nor their gold
will be able to save them
on the day of the LORD's wrath.
In the fire of his jealousy
the whole world will be consumed,
for he will make a sudden end
of all who live in the earth." - Zephaniah 1:14-19

Zephaniah also writes of blessings upon Israel and all the nations in the days of Messiah's visible, earthly, thousand-year reign (Zephaniah 3:8-20).

Joel tells of disturbances in the heavens and great disruptions in nature associated with the Day of the Lord. These events are also described in the New Testament.

[30] I will show wonders in the heavens
and on the earth,
blood and fire and billows of smoke.
[31] The sun will be turned to darkness
and the moon to blood
before the coming of the great and dreadful day of the LORD.
[32] And everyone who calls
on the name of the LORD will be saved;
for on Mount Zion and in Jerusalem
there will be deliverance,
as the LORD has said,
among the survivors
whom the LORD calls. - Joel 2:30-32

And in the New Testament,

I watched as he opened the sixth seal. There was a great earthquake. The sun turned black like sackcloth made of goat hair, the whole moon turned blood red, [13]and the stars in the sky fell to earth, as late figs drop from a fig tree when shaken by a strong wind. [14]The sky receded like a scroll, rolling up, and every mountain and island was removed from its place.
[15]Then the kings of the earth, the princes, the generals, the rich, the mighty, and every slave and every free man hid in caves and among the rocks of the mountains. [16]They called to the mountains and the rocks, "Fall on us and hide us from the face of him who sits on the throne and from the wrath of the Lamb! [17]For the great day of their wrath has come, and who can stand?" - Revelation 6:12-17

God's ultimate purpose in judging evil is not the destruction of mankind but a new creation (Isaiah 65:17-25).

The Apostle Paul tells us that the Day of the Lord will approach and come upon the world silently and unannounced:

[1]Now, brothers, about times and dates we do not need to write to you, [2]for you know very well that the day of the Lord will come like a thief in the night. [3]While people are saying, "Peace and safety," destruction will come on them suddenly, as labor pains on a pregnant woman, and they will not escape.
[4]But you, brothers, are not in darkness so that this day should surprise you like a thief. [5]You are all sons of the light and sons of the day. We do not belong to the night or to the darkness. [6]So then, let us not be like others, who are asleep, but let us be alert and self-controlled. [7]For those who sleep, sleep at night, and those who get drunk, get drunk at night. [8]But since we belong to the day, let us be self-controlled, putting on faith and love as a breastplate, and the hope of salvation as a helmet. [9]For God did not appoint us to suffer wrath but to receive salvation through our Lord Jesus Christ. [10]He died for us so that, whether we are awake or asleep, we may live together with him. [11]Therefore encourage one another and build each other up, just as in fact you are doing. - 1 Thessalonians 5:1-11

References

For the term the **Day of the Lord** see Isaiah 13:6, Isaiah 13:9, Isaiah 58:13, Jeremiah 46:10, Ezekiel 13:5, Ezekiel 30:3, Joel 1:15, Joel 2:1, Joel 2:11, Joel 2:31, Joel 3:14, Amos 5:18, Amos 5:20, Obadiah 15, Zephaniah 1:7, Zephaniah 1:14, Zechariah 14:1, Malachi 4:5, Acts 2:20, 1 Corinthians 5:5, 2 Corinthians 1:14, 1 Thessalonians 5:2, 2 Thessalonians 2:2, 2 Peter 3:10.

For the term **that Day** (which refers either to an impending or a final judgment when God intervenes) see Deuteronomy 31:17, Deuteronomy 31:18, 1Samuel 8:18, Isaiah 2:11, Isaiah 2:17, Isaiah 2:20, Isaiah 3:7, Isaiah 3:18, Isaiah 4:1, Isaiah 4:2, Isaiah 7:18, Isaiah 7:20, Isaiah 7:21, Isaiah 7:23, Isaiah 10:20, Isaiah 10:27, Isaiah 11:10, Isaiah 11:11, Isaiah 12:1, Isaiah 12:4, Isaiah 17:4, Isaiah 17:7, Isaiah 17:9, Isaiah 19:16, Isaiah 19:18, Isaiah 19:19, Isaiah 19:21, Isaiah 19:23, Isaiah 19:24, Isaiah 20:6, Isaiah 22:8, Isaiah 22:12, Isaiah 22:20, Isaiah 22:25, Isaiah 23:15, Isaiah 26:1, Isaiah 27:1, Isaiah 27:2, Isaiah 27:12, Isaiah 27:13, Isaiah 28:5, Isaiah 29:18, Isaiah 30:23, Isaiah 31:7, Isaiah 52:6, Jeremiah 4:9, Jeremiah 30:8, Jeremiah 48:41, Jeremiah 49:22, Jeremiah 49:26, Hosea 2:16, Hosea 2:21, Joel 3:18, Amos 2:16, Amos 8:3, Amos 8:13, Amos 9:11, Micah 2:4, Micah 4:6, Micah 5:10, Micah 7:11, Micah 7:12, Zechariah 2:11, Zechariah 3:10, Mark 2:20, Luke 6:23, John 14:20, John 16:23, John 16:26.
Paul uses the term "the day of Christ" in 1 Corinthians 1:8, Philippians 1:10 and 2:16.

Especially recommended for a better understanding of this complex subject are Ray Stedman's commentary on the two letters to the Thessalonians[140], his Expository Study on the Olivet Discourse[141], and his commentary on the book of Revelation[142].

Appendix H
The History of Edom
Brief History and Final Destiny of Edom
By Lambert Dolphin

A longer version of this study, including full quotations
from the Scriptures may be read on the Internet at
http://ldolphin.org/edom.html

Immediate Family History

The immediate family history of Jacob and Esau, the twin sons of Isaac and Rebecca, begins in Genesis Chapter 25 and continues through the end of Genesis.

The Descendants of Jacob's Brother Esau (Edom):

Genesis 36, which records the family tree of Esau, lists many names still associated with the land of Edom in Southern Jordan, and also mentions individuals whose unfavorable interactions with the people of Israel are recorded for us elsewhere as the Old Testament unfolds. The chapter starts with "This is the account of Esau (that is, Edom)" (Genesis 36:1).

A further historical note is found in I Chronicles:
[43] These were the kings who reigned in Edom before any Israelite king reigned:
Bela son of Beor, whose city was named Dinhabah.
[44] When Bela died, Jobab son of Zerah from Bozrah succeeded him as king.
[45] When Jobab died, Husham from the land of the Temanites succeeded him as king.
[46] When Husham died, Hadad son of Bedad, who defeated Midian in the country of Moab, succeeded him as king. His city was named Avith.
[47] When Hadad died, Samlah from Masrekah succeeded him as king.

[48] When Samlah died, Shaul from Rehoboth on the river succeeded him as king.

[49] When Shaul died, Baal-Hanan son of Acbor succeeded him as king.

[50] When Baal-Hanan died, Hadad succeeded him as king. His city was named Pau, and his wife's name was Mehetabel daughter of Matred, the daughter of Me-Zahab. [51] Hadad also died.

The chiefs of Edom were:

Timna, Alvah, Jetheth, [52] Oholibamah, Elah, Pinon, [53] Kenaz, Teman, Mibzar, [54] Magdiel and Iram. These were the chiefs of Edom. - 1 Chronicles 1:43-54

Edom Denies Israel Passage Through Their Land During the Exodus

Moses sent messengers from Kadesh to the king of Edom, saying:

"This is what your brother Israel says: You know about all the hardships that have come upon us. [15] Our forefathers went down into Egypt, and we lived there many years. The Egyptians mistreated us and our fathers, [16] but when we cried out to the LORD, he heard our cry and sent an angel and brought us out of Egypt.

"Now we are here at Kadesh, a town on the edge of your territory. [17] Please let us pass through your country. We will not go through any field or vineyard, or drink water from any well. We will travel along the king's highway and not turn to the right or to the left until we have passed through your territory."

[18] But Edom answered:

"You may not pass through here; if you try, we will march out and attack you with the sword."

[19] The Israelites replied:

"We will go along the main road, and if we or our livestock drink any of your water, we will pay for it. We only want to pass through on foot—nothing else."

[20] Again they answered:

"You may not pass through."

Then Edom came out against them with a large and powerful army. [21] Since Edom refused to let them go through their territory, Israel turned away from them. - Numbers 20:14-21

God's Coming Slaughter of Nations; Edom to be a Perpetual Wasteland - Isaiah 34:1-17

Jeremiah Prophesies: Edom to Become a Wasteland." - Jeremiah 49:7-22

Some Reasons for Divine Judgment on Edom According to Ezekiel

This is what the Sovereign LORD says: "Because Edom took revenge on the house of Judah and became very guilty by doing so, [13] therefore this is what the Sovereign LORD says: I will stretch out my hand against Edom and kill its men and their animals. I will lay it waste, and from Teman to Dedan they will fall by the sword. [14] I will take vengeance on Edom by the hand of my people Israel, and they will deal with Edom in accordance with my anger and my wrath; they will know my vengeance, declares the Sovereign LORD." - Ezekiel 24:12-14 (See also Ezekiel 35:1-15.)

Obadiah's Prophecy against Edom

The entire book of Obadiah is a scathing prophecy against Edom. It begins with these verses:

The vision of Obadiah.
    This is what the Sovereign LORD says about Edom—
    We have heard a message from the LORD:
    An envoy was sent to the nations to say,
    "Rise, and let us go against her for battle"-
[2] "See, I will make you small among the nations;
    you will be utterly despised.
[3] The pride of your heart has deceived you,
    you who live in the clefts of the rocks
    and make your home on the heights,
    you who say to yourself,
    'Who can bring me down to the ground?'
[4] Though you soar like the eagle
    and make your nest among the stars,
    from there I will bring you down,"
    declares the LORD. - Obadiah 1:1-4

Malachi on God's Perpetual Enmity against Edom

An oracle: The word of the LORD to Israel through Malachi.
[2] "I have loved you," says the LORD.
    "But you ask, 'How have you loved us?'
    "Was not Esau Jacob's brother?" the LORD says. "Yet I have loved Jacob, [3] but Esau I have hated, and I have turned his mountains into a wasteland and left his inheritance to the desert jackals."
[4] Edom may say, "Though we have been crushed, we will rebuild the ruins."
    But this is what the LORD Almighty says: "They may build, but I will demolish. They will be called the Wicked Land, a people always under the wrath of the LORD." - Malachi 1:1-4

Esau: A Type of the Flesh

One of the most valuable lessons to be learned from the family history of the descendants of the brothers Jacob and Esau concerns the New Testament application. The New Testament views the conflict between the flesh and the spirit as typified by the conflict between Jacob and Esau (Galatians 5:13-26).

Jacob in many ways typifies the average believer. He was deceitful, manipulative, clever and bent on advancing his own causes for many years. After wrestling all night with The Angel of the Lord at the Brook Jabbok near Peniel, his name was finally changed to Israel (Genesis 32). Though he may have been somewhat slow to fully believe and trust God, Jacob's heart was inclined from his birth towards the things of the Lord.

Esau's heart and motives, on the other hand, were perpetually set on the goals and rewards of the world. He cared not at all about the things that were important to God.

See to it that no one misses the grace of God and that no bitter root grows up to cause trouble and defile many. [16]See that no one is sexually immoral, or is godless like Esau, who for a single meal sold his inheritance rights as the oldest son. [17]Afterward, as you know, when he wanted to inherit this blessing, he was rejected. He could bring about no change of mind, though he sought the blessing with tears. - Hebrews 12:15-17

When the people of Israel left Egypt under the leadership of Moses the first opposition they encountered was from a people known as the Amalekites. Genesis 36 tells us that Amalek was the grandson of Esau!

The Amalekites came and attacked the Israelites at Rephidim. [9] Moses said to Joshua, "Choose some of our men and go out to fight the Amalekites. Tomorrow I will stand on top of the hill with the staff of God in my hands."
[10] So Joshua fought the Amalekites as Moses had ordered, and Moses, Aaron and Hur went to the top of the hill. [11] As long as Moses held up his hands, the Israelites were winning, but whenever he lowered his hands, the Amalekites were winning. [12] When Moses' hands grew tired, they took a stone and put it under him and he sat on it. Aaron and Hur held his hands up—one on one side, one on the other—so that his hands remained steady till sunset. [13] So Joshua overcame the Amalekite army with the sword.
[14] Then the LORD said to Moses, "Write this on a scroll as something to be remembered and make sure that Joshua hears it, because I will completely blot out the memory of Amalek from under heaven."
[15] Moses built an altar and called it The LORD is my Banner. [16] He said, "For hands were lifted up to the throne of the LORD. The LORD will be at war against the Amalekites from generation to generation." - Exodus 17:8-16

Later King Saul was told by the prophet Samuel to completely eradicate the Amalekites (1 Samuel 15ff). Saul's incomplete obedience not only cost him his throne and his life, but reveals clearly how easy it is for us as believers to compromise with our own flesh—which God has said is utterly worthless. (See Ray Stedman's "First Samuel: The Death of the Flesh.").

In the book of Esther, the arch-fiend and enemy of the Jews is the infamous Haman, an Agagite. Sure enough, Agag's name is to be found listed as the king of the people of Amalek! (See Ray Stedman's commentary, "The Struggle for Power."[143])

Herod Antipas, before whom Jesus remained silent (Luke 23:9), was an Idumean, that is one of the last of the Edomites. God has nothing further to say to the flesh, nor to the descendants of Edom. Their fate was sealed long ago.

King David's successful military dealings with Edom are recorded in 2 Samuel 8. Solomon's compromises with his "many foreign wives" caused the Lord to raise up against him an adversary, Hadad, from the royal line of Edom (2 Kings 11). Thus there is a long history of antagonism between the descendants of Jacob and of Esau throughout Old Testament history.

King Amaziah's famous (but ill-fated) raid into Edom is recorded in 2 Chronicles 25,

All of this history serves to illustrate for us that no good ever comes from our best efforts, our self effort in the Christian life, which is the root source of what the Bible calls "the flesh." Only the works of God, the works of the Holy Spirit done through us when we are obedient and submissive to God—have any lasting worth. All else will, in the end, be destroyed.

Appendix L

The Return of Jesus Christ
In Power Glory and Splendor
(The *epiphaneia*)
By Lambert Dolphin

This is a shortened version of this study. View the full article at
http://ldolphin.org/Sadvent.html

Jesus of Nazareth was seen by his disciples and by groups as large as 500 persons (1 Corinthians 15:6) during the 40 days between his resurrection from the dead and his ascension to the "right hand of the Majesty on High." Then instructing his disciples to wait for the promised arrival of the Holy Spirit, he departed this earth from the summit of the Mount of Olives, just East of the Temple Mount in Jerusalem (Acts 1:4-12),

The Holy Spirit then descended, from the Father and the Lord Jesus, ten days later, on the day of Pentecost, a Sunday morning, while the believing community was gathered for prayer and fellowship. Thus began the era of the Church, which has been God's means of calling out the world "a people for his name" (Acts 15:14). The church is especially called the "body of Christ" with Jesus the Head of the body, Wherever Christians gather Jesus is with them by means of the Holy Spirit—but Jesus has been visibly absent from the earth was nearly 2000 years,

The return of Jesus to earth is in two stages, First, He arrives unannounced to call out the true church, his Bride, This event (described in 1 Thessalonians 4 and usually called "the rapture") is distinguished from his visible return in power and glory seven years later, Two different Greek words are used, parousia, meaning "presence" describes the coming of Jesus for his saints, and epiphaneia, meaning "appearing" describes his public unveiling (apokalupsis) in splendor, power and glory.

A number of passages in the Bible describe the glorious second coming of the Messiah Jesus to save our beleaguered planet from total destruction, and to set up his kingdom on earth, Zechariah tells us that the place of Jesus' return to earth will not be Zion, Illinois, but the Mount of Olives in Jerusalem, Israel (Zechariah 14:1-9).

When Jesus returns to the Mount of Olives he will arrive from the direction of Edom (Southern Jordan)—with the blood of his enemies spattering his garments, he will bring with him the remnant of believing Jews who fled earlier to Jordan at the midpoint of The Tribulation Period, And with him also will be his Bride, the Church, and great myriads of his holy angels (Isaiah 63:1-6).

During the Olivet Discourse, Jesus describes his future public return in these words,

"Immediately after the distress of those days
"'the sun will be darkened,
     and the moon will not give its light;
the stars will fall from the sky,
     and the heavenly bodies will be shaken.
[30]"At that time the sign of the Son of Man will appear in the sky, and all the nations of the earth will mourn. They will see the Son of Man coming on the clouds of the sky, with power and great glory. [31]And he will send his angels with a loud trumpet call, and they will gather his elect from the four winds, from one end of the heavens to the other. - Matthew 24:29-31 (See parallel passages in Luke 21:23-27; Mark 13:24-27.)

The Apostle Paul describes this event in his second letter to the Thessalonians (2 Thessalonians 1:3-2:8).

God is just: He will pay back trouble to those who trouble you [7]and give relief to you who are troubled, and to us as well. This will happen when the Lord Jesus is revealed [unveiled, that is *apokalupsis*] from heaven in blazing fire with his powerful angels. [8]He will punish those who do not know God and do not obey the gospel of our Lord Jesus. - 2 Thessalonians 1:6-8

The Apostle John also presents a full picture of the coming of the Lord Jesus with his saints (Revelation 19:11-21).
John's vision closes with an invitation and a final warning,

The Spirit and the bride say, "Come!" And let him who hears say, "Come!" Whoever is thirsty, let him come; and whoever wishes, let him take the free gift of the water of life. [18]I warn everyone who hears the words of the prophecy of this book: If anyone adds anything to them, God will add to him the plagues described in this book. [19]And if anyone

takes words away from this book of prophecy, God will take away from him his share in the tree of life and in the holy city, which are described in this book.
[20]He who testifies to these things says, "Yes, I am coming soon."
Amen. Come, Lord Jesus.
[21]The grace of the Lord Jesus be with God's people. Amen. - Revelation 22:17-21

The warning is equally clear: Don't change a word in this prophecy! The book of Revelation is God's truth, Don't add to it, Don't subtract from it, Certainly a book so rich in symbolism must be interpreted-but it must be interpreted carefully, Don't take away its meaning by emphasizing the symbolic at the expense of the literal, Do not destroy its intent by literalizing everything in it and ignoring the meaning of the symbols, Most important of all: Believe it, Ignore, reject, or distort God's truth and you risk missing out on God's plan; you risk having to endure the terrors described in the book; you risk losing out on your portion of the tree of life and the beautiful Holy City, Believe it—because Jesus is coming soon! He who testifies to these things says, "Yes, I am coming soon." Amen, Come, Lord Jesus, Doesn't your heart reverberate with that same poignant prayer! Amen! Come, Lord Jesus! The world is waiting, aching, crying for your return! The church is watching and expecting you! Amen! Come, Lord Jesus.

Appendix M
The Marriage Supper Of The Lamb
By Lambert Dolphin

This is a shortened version of this study. View the full article at
http://ldolphin.org/Msup.html

The church of Jesus Christ is described by at least seven symbols or figures in the New Testament. Jesus is the Great Shepherd and we are the sheep (John 10:1-18). He is the True Vine and we Christians are the branches (John 15:1). We are "living stones" being built into a house, which is a habitation for God—Christ Jesus is the cornerstone (1 Peter 2:4-7). The Lord is described as a merchant who finds and buys a single pearl of great price (Matthew 13:45). He is Great High Priest over the household of faith, and we are his servant-priests (Hebrews 4:14-16). The church is the Body of Christ, every one a member of every other, and all under the direction of Christ the Head of the Body (1 Corinthians 12:12-14). Finally the Church is the Bride of Christ and Jesus the waiting Bridegroom (Revelation 21:9).

The Apostle Paul wrote to the Corinthians:

> I am jealous for you with a godly jealousy. I promised you to one husband, to Christ, so that
> I might present you as a pure virgin to him. - 2 Corinthians 11:2

Although the Old Testament does not reveal God's purpose in calling out a church comprised of Jew and Gentile (Ephesians 3), a great feast prepared by God himself for his people was described by the Prophet Isaiah (Isaiah 25:6-9).

While the Church as the Bride of Christ is nowhere spoken of in the OT, Israel was called the "wife of Yahweh." The prophets eloquently describe God's nurture, courtship and betrothal of Israel (e.g. Ezekiel 16). They also dealt with the nation's spiritual adul-

291

tery-and finally divorce from the Lord—(e.g. the book of Hosea). In spite of this "divorce" under the Old Covenant God promises to restore his beloved wife at the close of the age in which we now live. This restoration of Israel under the New Covenant is clearly explained in Hosea, in Jeremiah 31, and Romans 9, 10, and 11 to cite only a few references.

When it came time for Isaac, Abraham's son, to be married (he was 40 years old), Abraham sent his eldest servant back to his native land to select a bride for his son. Chapter 24 of Genesis is a remarkable picture of the way God the Father would later send the Holy Spirit into the world to call out a bride for his beloved Son, our Lord Jesus that most commentators on Genesis take note of this.

Jesus suggested a great marriage feast would be part of his final return to earth to be with his own. He used a number of direct and indirect references to this festive meal. The marriage supper was anticipated when Jesus celebrated the "Last Supper" with his disciples:

> While they were eating, Jesus took bread, gave thanks and broke it, and gave it to his disciples, saying, "Take and eat; this is my body."
> [27]Then he took the cup, gave thanks and offered it to them, saying, "Drink from it, all of you. [28]This is my blood of the[a] covenant, which is poured out for many for the forgiveness of sins. [29]I tell you, I will not drink of this fruit of the vine from now on until that day when I drink it anew with you in my Father's kingdom."
> [30]When they had sung a hymn, they went out to the Mount of Olives. - Matthew 26:26-30

The universality of God's invitation for all men everywhere to come to the marriage supper is clearly implied by a famous parable related by Jesus in Matthew 22:1-14. The required wedding garment represents true righteousness imparted by faith, which replaces that normal self-righteous we all have as a result of the fall.

The wedding feast, celebration, and intimate union with the Lord of the universe—who is himself Love—will be so joyful, fulfilling and marvelous that all efforts should be focused on getting ready to attend (Luke 13:22-30).

In the parable of the Ten Virgins Jesus distinguished between professing and true believers. True believers have the endless resources of the indwelling Holy Spirit within them while those who have not yet enter a personal relationship with Jesus as Lord are merely enjoying temporary fringe benefits of associating with those who know Jesus personally:

> "At that time the kingdom of heaven will be like ten virgins who took their lamps and went out to meet the bridegroom. [2]Five of them were foolish and five were wise. [3]The foolish ones took their lamps but did not take any oil with them. [4]The wise, however, took oil in jars along with their lamps. [5]The bridegroom was a long time in coming, and they all became drowsy and fell asleep.

[6]"At midnight the cry rang out: 'Here's the bridegroom! Come out to meet him!'

[7]"Then all the virgins woke up and trimmed their lamps. [8]The foolish ones said to the wise, 'Give us some of your oil; our lamps are going out.'

[9]" 'No,' they replied, 'there may not be enough for both us and you. Instead, go to those who sell oil and buy some for yourselves.'

[10]"But while they were on their way to buy the oil, the bridegroom arrived. The virgins who were ready went in with him to the wedding banquet. And the door was shut.

[11]"Later the others also came. 'Sir! Sir!' they said. 'Open the door for us!'

[12]"But he replied, 'I tell you the truth, I don't know you.'

[13]"Therefore keep watch, because you do not know the day or the hour." - Matthew 25:1-13

The actual marriage supper of the Lamb itself is specifically announced in connection with the second coming (the *epiphaneia*) of the Lord Jesus:

Then I heard what sounded like a great multitude, like the roar of rushing waters and like loud peals of thunder, shouting:
"Hallelujah!
    For our Lord God Almighty reigns.
[7]Let us rejoice and be glad
    and give him glory!
For the wedding of the Lamb has come,
    and his bride has made herself ready.
[8]Fine linen, bright and clean,
    was given her to wear." (Fine linen stands for the righteous acts of the saints.)
[9]Then the angel said to me, "Write: 'Blessed are those who are invited to the wedding supper of the Lamb!'" And he added, "These are the true words of God." - Revelation 19:6-9

The Great Supper of God

The Marriage Supper of the Lamb is not to be confused with the Great Supper of God, which is an invitation for vultures and other carrion feeders to gorge themselves on the dead bodies of the wicked men of earth slain in battle during the campaign of Armageddon (Revelation 19:17-21).

:This same "sacrificial feast"—for the benefit of the birds of prey—is described in Ezekiel. The time is after the great Northern invasion of Syria and Russian satellite powers, which many Bible scholars believe is part of the campaign of Armageddon during the last half of The Tribulation Period just prior to the triumphant return of Jesus Christ to establish his kingdom on earth. The Ezekiel passage describes the destruction of the invading armies as due to the direct intervention of the hand of God (Ezekiel 39:17-29).

Appendix N
The Judgment Seat of Christ
By Lambert Dolphin

This is a shortened version of this study. View the full article at
http://ldolphin.org/Jseat.html

Whether a Christian dies before his time from an accident or tragedy, or whether he or she lives out a normal life span of 70 or 80 years, each and every one of us must, at death, pass a special reviewing stand of God known in Scripture as the "Judgment Seat of Christ." Even those who remain alive on earth until the rapture will experience this judgment as they pass from the earthly realm to the heavenly. The Greek word, (Bema), basically means a law tribunal where defendant and accuser stand in front of a magistrate in a court. Many Bible commentators use the analogy that the Bema is the evaluation of athletes in competition passing the judges' reviewing stand in order to win the rewards appropriate to how well they have run the race.

This "athletes' reward ceremony" aspect of the Judgment Seat of Christ is based upon such Scriptures as 1 Corinthians 9:24-27:

> Do you not know that in a race all the runners run, but only one gets the prize? Run in such a way as to get the prize.
> [25]Everyone who competes in the games goes into strict training. They do it to get a crown that will not last; but we do it to get a crown that will last forever. [26]Therefore I do not run like a man running aimlessly; I do not fight like a man beating the air. [27]No, I beat my body and make it my slave so that after I have preached to others, I myself will not be disqualified for the prize.

John's Gospel, and Romans 8, promises that Christians have passed out from under all condemnation and will not fail to pass the test of the Judgment Seat of the Christ. Without negating the notion that this judgment does involve the rewarding of all those running the race, the notion of a legal tribunal is also implied by key passages in Corinthians:

> By the grace God has given me, I laid a foundation as an expert builder, and someone else is building on it. But each one should be careful how he builds. [11]For no one can lay any foundation other than the one already laid, which is Jesus Christ. [12]If any man builds on this foundation using gold, silver, costly stones, wood, hay or straw, [13]his work will be shown for what it is, because the Day will bring it to light. It will be revealed with fire, and the fire will test the quality of each man's work. [14]If what he has built survives, he will receive his reward. [15]If it is burned up, he will suffer loss; he himself will be saved, but only as one escaping through the flames. - 1 Corinthians 3:10-15

> For we must all appear before the judgment seat of Christ, that each one may receive what is due him for the things done while in the body, whether good or bad.
> [11]Since, then, we know what it is to fear the Lord, we try to persuade men. What we are is plain to God, and I hope it is also plain to your conscience. - 2 Corinthians 5:10-11

Every Christian is given the opportunity of building a Christian life, like a house, upon the foundation of Jesus Christ. Hay, wood, and stubble are insubstantial building materials that are neither structurally sound nor fireproof. These materials represent all our self efforts—whether on behalf of our own interests or in the service of God. Gold, silver and precious stones—which do survive fire—are those permanent enduring things, which God is building in us and in others. The Lord has promised to shake our entire universe one day so that only what He has built will remain:

> "Once more I will shake not only the earth but also the heavens." [27]The words "once more" indicate the removing of what can be shaken—that is, created things—so that what cannot be shaken may remain.
> [28]Therefore, since we are receiving a kingdom that cannot be shaken, let us be thankful, and so worship God acceptably with reverence and awe, - Hebrews 12:26b-28

While the prospects of endless delights, joy, and freedom of sin forever when we all get to heaven are held before us in the Bible and vividly pictured for us by inspiring Christian writers such as C.S. Lewis in *The Great Divorce*, none of us shall reach the other side without passing through a process of seeing ourselves as we really always were and have finally become. This will be a time when God makes known "the thoughts and intentions of the heart." All those activities in our lives undertaken in the energy of self-effort will be burned up and lost to us forever. It is perhaps because he knew more than we do about the awesomeness of facing God and leaving our present world of darkness and illusion for the glorious light of holy reality, that the Apostle Peter urged his readers to look forward to, and count upon the "extra" grace that is coming to us at the revelation of Jesus Christ (1 Peter 1:13).

Our Lord himself spoke of the end of life, and the end of the age as carrying with it great agony like that of a woman in travail, but He said, "...your sorrow will be turned into joy...you have sorrow now, but I will see you again and your hearts will rejoice, and no one will take your joy from you" (John 16:20-22).

The Apostle Paul writes regarding the Apostolic calling to ministry and advises us to practice self-evaluation. Note that the judgment seat of Christ is one of rewards, approval and commendation,

> Therefore judge nothing before the appointed time; wait till the Lord comes. He will bring to light what is hidden in darkness and will expose the motives of men's hearts. At that time each will receive his praise from God. - 1 Corinthians 4:5

> You, then, why do you judge your brother? Or why do you look down on your brother? For we will all stand before God's judgment seat. [11]It is written:
> "'As surely as I live,' says the Lord,
> 'every knee will bow before me;
> every tongue will confess to God.'"
> [12]So then, each of us will give an account of himself to God. - Romans 14:10-13

It is better for us to grow more and more aware of our sins through diligent pursuit of holy living, through prayer and fellowship, through study of the Word of God and regular self-judgment that averts the judgment of God. Otherwise we may drift away with the crowd into compromises that leave us in the end no different from the pagans around us. If that occurs we are in jeopardy of losing our rewards, which God desires to give us.

> Whatever you do, work at it with all your heart, as working for the Lord, not for men, [24]since you know that you will receive an inheritance from the Lord as a reward. It is the Lord Christ you are serving. [25]Anyone who does wrong will be repaid for his wrong, and there is no favoritism. - Colossians 3:23-25.

This present life is not where our goals, hopes and dreams and fulfillment are to be found—God's purpose is for us to regain our lost humanity and become whole persons who will live forever in a new creation. It is not for this life only that God is preparing us, but for something far more glorious and splendid. This is all made possible not by our best efforts but by the grace and mercy he has already lavished upon us and is ready to supply anew if we will but ask.

Appendix O
The Great White Throne Judgment
By Lambert Dolphin

God is the Judge of All

Information about life after death and eternal judgment is sparse in the Old Testament. However, Daniel clearly describes a final resurrection of the dead divided into two classes:

> "At that time [the end-time] shall arise Michael, the great prince [archangel] who has charge of your people [Israel]. And there shall be a time of trouble, such as never has been since there was a nation till that time; but at that time your people shall be delivered, every one whose name shall be found written in the book. And many of those who sleep in the dust of the earth shall awake, some to everlasting life, and some to shame and everlasting contempt. And those who are wise shall shine like the brightness of the firmament; and those who turn many to righteousness, like the stars for ever and ever." - Daniel 12:1-3

Judgments in the Bible are of various types and kinds. Often they are temporal—we all suffer lost opportunities in life due to inappropriate choices that have displeased God. Discerning the will of God (for believers) is described in Romans 12:1, 2 as being three-tiered. We are to prove in experience what is the will of God,"...what is good, acceptable and perfect." Excessively carnal behavior after one becomes a Christian can result in what is called a "sin unto death". This is essentially a foreshortening of one's lifespan on this earth due to sin. Other temporal judgments of God in history can include the destruction of a city or a nation due to sin. For instance, God ordained the total destruction of the Canaanite peoples who inhabited the promised land in the time of Abraham, though God granted them a stay of execution amounting to some 400 years (Deuteronomy 10:16-18).

The entire Old Testament records temporal judgments on Israel and the surrounding nations as well as judgments upon individuals or cities. Temporal judgments differ from eternal judgments in that the death of an individual because of such a judgment may be unrelated to whether or not a person is eternally saved or lost. First Corinthians 10 describes the death of an entire generation of Israelites in the wilderness of Sinai after the Exodus from Egypt. Even Moses was denied entrance into the land because of disobedience. Yet great numbers of these covenant people knew the Lord in their hearts and so will enter the eternal kingdom of the Lord Jesus Christ. Lot's life in Sodom was hardly exemplary, yet he is described as a believer in the New Testament. Much more can be said on the general subject of judgment, but to end this introduction on a positive note, it can be said that repentance and a whole-hearted turning to God delays judgment pushing it further into the future.

Seven Special Judgments of God

Seven judgments described in Scripture have special significance. These are,
(1) The judgment of the cross, which includes the judgment of the believer's sins,

(2) The self-judgment of the believer whereby we avoid God's judgment for sins (1 Corinthians 11:31);

(3) The judgment seat of Christ immediately after the believer's death where the quality of a Christian's life is evaluated and rewarded (2 Corinthians 5:10);

(4) The "sheep and goat" judgment at the start of the Millennium determining which Gentiles may enter the kingdom;

(5) The judgment of Israel at the beginning of the Millennium. This is described in Ezekiel 20:33-44;

(6) The judgment of fallen angels (Jude 6, 1 Corinthians 6:3), and,

(7) The great white throne judgment (or "last judgment") of unbelievers at the end of the Millennium.

Judgments in Eternity are outside of Time

Although the last judgment follows 1000 years after the second coming of Christ to earth, as far as earth-time is concerned, when any individual dies he or she immediately leaves time and enters eternity—there is no intermediate state. In the experience of that individual, whether he is a believer or an non-believer, the next event experienced is one of two judgments. Unfortunately in our culture we are so accustomed to thinking of time as linear and everywhere the same in the universe. But, it is clear from the Bible that mortal man is trapped in a linear time frame, whereas heaven runs by different set of clocks. At physical death the individual time-travels in an instant to one of two judgments—either reward or eternal punishment.

This immediate judgment after death (as far as eternity is concerned), for both believers and unbelievers, is described for us in connection with the Second coming of Christ in glory (his epiphaneia) recorded in 2 Thess. 2:

> "...we ourselves boast of you in the churches of God for your steadfastness and faith in all your persecutions and in the afflictions which you are enduring. This is evidence of the righteous judgment of God, that you may be made worthy of the kingdom of God, for which you are suffering—since indeed God deems it just to repay with affliction those who afflict you, and to grant rest with us to you who are afflicted, when the Lord Jesus is revealed from heaven with his mighty angels in flaming fire, inflicting vengeance upon those who do not know God and upon those who do not obey the gospel of our Lord Jesus. They shall suffer the punishment of eternal destruction and exclusion from the presence of the Lord and from the glory of his might, when he comes on that day to be glorified in his saints, and to be marveled at in all who have believed, because our testimony to you was believed." -2 Thessalonians 2:4-10

All judgment of mankind is committed to the Lord Jesus Christ. One man, Christ Jesus, is now ruling our entire universe as the Lord of time and space, and nature, and history, and human affairs. Every person's life and destiny is in his hands. Jesus himself said this:

> "For as the Father raises the dead and gives them life, so also the Son gives life to whom he will. The Father judges no one, but has given all judgment to the Son, that all may honor the Son, even as they honor the Father. He who does not honor the Son does not honor the Father who sent him. Truly, truly, I say to you, he who hears my word and believes him who sent me, has eternal life; he does not come into judgment, but has passed from death to life. "Truly, truly, I say to you, the hour is coming, and now is, when the dead will hear the voice of the Son of God, and those who hear will live. For as the Father has life in himself, so he has granted the Son also to have life in himself, and has given him authority to execute judgment, because he is the Son of man. Do not marvel at this; for the hour is coming when all who are in the tombs will hear his voice and come forth, those who have done good, to the resurrection of life, and those who have done evil, to the resurrection of judgment. - John 5:21-29

The setting of the judgment of the great white throne is associated with an event in the Bible called the "second" resurrection. "The rest of the dead did not come to life until the thousand years were ended. This is the first resurrection. Blessed and holy is he who shares in the first resurrection! Over such the second death has no power, but they shall be priests of God and of Christ, and they shall reign with him a thousand years. And when the thousand years are ended...

> "...Then I saw a great white throne and him who sat upon it; from his presence earth and sky fled away, and no place was found for them. And I saw the dead, great and small, standing before the throne, and books were opened.
> Also another book was opened, which is the book of life. And the dead were judged by what was written in the books, by what they had done. And the sea gave up the dead in it, Death and Hades gave up the dead in them, and all were judged by what they had done. Then Death and Hades were thrown into the lake of fire. This is the second death, the lake of fire; and if any one's name was not found written in the book of life, he was thrown into the lake of fire." - Revelation. 20:5, 6; 11-15

Two different documents are presented at this awesome courtroom scene. Books recording the life-deeds of every individual are presented. These books are evidently the records kept by recording angels (see for example, Ezekiel and The Destruction of Jerusalem).

The second book is "the Lamb's Book of Life" where the names of all believers are written "before the foundation of the world" (Rev. 13:8, see also, Phil. 4:3, Rev. 3:5, Rev. 13:8, Rev. 17:8, Rev. 20:12, Rev. 21:27). Although eternal separation from God might seem to be in itself the most awful and terrible ultimate punishment in itself, the text strongly suggests that there are degrees of punishment in the lake of fire, for "all were judged by what they had done."

Ray C. Stedman, offers the following comments on the judgment of the great white throne:

> Here is a startling and terrifying scene. Imagine standing on a starship, watching the earth and the planets recede from view, the stars moving against the background of eternal night. That is the vision suggested by John's words, "Earth and sky fled from his presence, and there was no place for them." This suggests that all of humanity will be removed from earth, perhaps from the universe as we know it, to eternity itself, where there is no space and no time. That is where judgment will take place. The judge is Jesus, not God the Father. "The Father judges no one," said Jesus, "but has entrusted all judgment to the Son." It is Jesus who sits upon the Great White Throne of majesty and gathers all the dead before him.
> There will also be some living people from the Millennium, far it must be determined if their names are recorded in the book of life Judgment will be "according to what one had done." Deeds reveal the condition of the heart. Deeds reveal belief. All

the deeds of mankind are preserved in God's great library. Books are a symbol of the eternal record of our lives. If John were receiving this vision today, the symbol would probably be videotape or computer disks rather than books. The books are metaphors for the record of every life—and the final judgment of every life shall be made on the basis of that record. Only those whose names are in the book of life can do righteous deeds. Only the deeds of the righteous will survive the fire of judgment. All other deeds will be consumed to ashes. Only those acts that have been done by the power of the Spirit of God and done for the glory of God will remain. Even the noblest and most impressive accomplishments, even acts that have helped many people or changed the course of history—if they were done by the power of the self and for the glory of the self—will vanish without a trace.

If your name is not in the book of life, your evil deeds will be revealed. All the hidden corners of your life will be subjected to scrutiny. Nothing will go unnoticed. Today you may have a reputation for your devotion, your caring, your humility, your abilities—but in that day Jesus will judge the hidden motives behind your deeds. He will know if your real reason for service in the Church and the community was to glorify God—or if it was all tainted by selfishness, pride, and the lust for prominence, power, influence, and recognition...

When Jesus sent out the twelve disciples to minister to other cities and towns in Israel, they returned rejoicing that they had cast out demons with just a word of command. They were amazed at the power of God that was flowing through them, at the wonderful deeds that were being accomplished, at the fact that even the demons submitted to them in the name of Jesus. "Do not rejoice that the spirits submit to you," Jesus replied, "but rejoice that your names are written in heaven." That is the central question in life: Is your name written in the Lamb's book of life? Beside this one issue, everything else pales in comparison. Your name is written in that book when you commit your life to Jesus. No one needs to face the lake of fire. No one goes into the Abyss against his or her own will. It is a choice we all make in this life. If we refuse the Savior, God can only give us the fate we demand.

The issue of eternal punishment raises a problem in the minds of most thoughtful Christians: What about those who have never heard the gospel of Jesus Christ? Isn't it unfair that someone should be condemned to an eternity apart from God simply because he never had the opportunity to hear about Jesus? This is a difficult question, but it is addressed in Scripture. Hebrews 11:6 tells us, "Anyone who comes to [God] must believe that he exists and that he rewards those who earnestly seek him." God knows the intent and condition of every human being, and he will deal with every individual according to the great declaration of Scripture, "Far be it from [God] to...kill the righteous with the wicked, treating the righteous and the wicked alike...Will not the Judge of all the earth do right?" We know that God only holds us accountable for the light of understanding we have received. Those of us who have received more revelation are responsible for how we respond to that revelation. Scripture does not explicitly tell us the fate of those who have not heard of Jesus, of the cross and the empty tomb, of the grace of God and the forgiveness of sins. But the Bible does tell us that God will deal justly with them.

The question that confronts you and me, since we have received so much of the revelation of God's truth, is this: Have our names been written in the Lamb's book of life? Jesus knows our hearts. Nothing is hidden from his view. If we come to him, we belong to him and he to us. We need fear nothing from the final judgment and the second death." [144]

One final note: Believers are raised from the dead and given resurrection bodies. When unbelievers are raised at the Last Judgment they also stand before God with resurrection bodies. We are not told anything about these bodies, but they will evidently be imperishable. The Bible suggests that unbelievers suffer eternal torment separated from God—not as disembodied spirits, but as persons who have body, soul, and spirit and are forever conscious of where they are and why.

Appendix P
Outline of The Olivet Discourse
By Ron Graff

THE OLIVET DISCOURSE
Matthew 24 and 25

Introduction	24:1-3
1A. Jesus' Explanation of the Future	24:4-31
1B. Beginning of Birth Pains	24:4-8
2B. The Tribulation	24:9-14
3B. The Great Tribulation	24:15-28
4B. After the Tribulation	24:29-31
2A. Jesus' Examples about the Future	24-32-25:46
1B. Parable of the Fig Tree	24:32-35
2B. Days of Noah	24:36-51
3B. Illustrative Parables	25:1-46
1C. Parable of the Virgins	25:1-13
2C. Parable of the Talents	25:14-30
3C. Parable of the Sheep and Goats	25:31-46

Appendix Q
Outline of the Book of Revelation
By Ron Graff

THE REVELATION OF JESUS CHRIST

INTRODUCTION & SALUTATION   1:1-8
   1B. Introduction 1:1-3
   2B. Salutation 1:4-8
1A. THE PERSON OF JESUS CHRIST   1:9-18
(The things which you have seen)
   1B. Preparation for the vision 1:9-10
   2B. Presentation of the vision 1:11-18
      1C. The revelation to John 1:11-16
         1D. The Golden Stands 1:11-12
         2D. The Glorified Savior 1:13-16
      2C. The reaction of John 1:17-18
2A. THE PRESENCE OF JESUS CHRIST IN THIS AGE   1:19-3:22
   (The things which are)
   1B. Insight about the Church 1:19-20
   2B. Instruction to the Church 2:1-3:22
      1C. To Ephesus 2:1-7
      2C. To Smyrna 2:8-11
      3C. To Pergamum 2:12-17
      4C. To Thyatira 2:18-29
      5C. To Sardis 3:1-6
      6C. To Philadelphia 3:7-13
      7C. To Laodicea 3:14-22

3A. THE PROGRAM OF JESUS CHRIST FOR THE FUTURE   4:1-22:21
    (The things which will take place...)
  1B. The scene in Heaven 4:1-5:14
    1C. View of the Heavenly Majesty 4:1-11
      1D. The Throne 4:1-3
      2D. The Elders 4:4
      3D. The Surroundings 4:5-6b
      4D. The Four Creatures (living beings) 4:6c-8
      5D. The Worship 4:9-11
    2C. Vision of the Holy Mystery 5:1-14
      1D. The Scroll 5:1
      2D. The Search 5:2-4
      3D. The Savior 5:5-7
      4D. The Song 5:8-10
      5D. The Saying 5:11-14

  2B. The Scene on Earth 6:1-20:15
    1C. The Tribulation 6:1-19:21
      1D. Opening of the Seven Seals 6:1-8:1
        1E. First Seal - Antichrist 6:1-2
        2E. Second Seal - Arms 6:3-4
        3E. Third Seal - Agony (Famine) 6:5-6
        4E. Fourth Seal - Annihilation (Death) 6:7-8
        5E. Fifth Seal - Anticipation (Martyrs) 6:9-11
        6E. Sixth Seal - Agitation 6:12-17
        ( ) Tribulation Saints 7:1-17
          1F. The Sealed Ones 7:1-8
          2F. The Saved Ones 7:9-17
            1G. Enormity of the Multitude 7:9
            2G. Exultation by the Multitude 7:10-12
            3G. Explanation about the Multitude 7:13-17
        7E. Seventh Seal - Adjustment 8:1
      2D. Sounding of the Seven Trumpets 8:2-11:19
        1E. Expectation 8:2-6
        2E. Execution 8:7-11:19
          1F. First Trumpet - Scorching of the Earth 8:7
          2F. Second Trumpet - Slaughter in the Sea 8:8-9
          3F. Third Trumpet - Souring of the Water 8:10-11
          4F. Fourth Trumpet - Smiting of the Planets 8:12-13

5F. The Fifth Trumpet - Striking by Locusts 9:1-12
    1G. The Diabolical Pit 9:1-2
    2G. The Demonic Plague 9:3-10
        1H. Their Actions 9:3-6
        2H. Their Appearance 9:7-10
    3G. The Destructive Potentate 9:11-12
6F. The Sixth Trumpet - Slaying of One-third of the Population 9:13-21
    1G. The Command from Heaven 9:13-16
    2G. The Consuming Holocaust 9:17-19
    3G. The Conscious Hardness 9:20-21
( ) Parenthetical Explanations 10:1-11:14
    1G. About God's Program 10:1-7
    2G. About John's Prophecy 10:8-11
    3G. About Gentile Power 11:1-2
    4G. About Two Prophets 11:3-14
7F. The Seventh Trumpet - Sovereignty of God 11:15-19
3D. Important Considerations of the Period 12:1-19:21
  1E. The Role of Israel in the Tribulation 12:1-18
    1F. Birth of the Deliverer 12:1-6
      1G. Purpose for Israel 12:1-2
      2G. Plan of the devil 12:3-4
      3G. Protection of the Child 12:5-6
    2F. Battle with the devil 12:7-17
      1G. War in Heaven 12:7-12
      2G. War on Earth 12:13-17
  2E.. The Reign of the Unholy Trinity during The Tribulation 13:1-18
    1F. The Dragon (Satan) 13:2,4
    2F. The Despot (the Beast) 13:1-10
      1G. His Appearance 13:1-4
      2G. His Actions 13:5-10
    3F. The Deceiver (False Prophet) 13:11-18
      1G. His Person 13:11
        1H. Like a Lamb
        2H. Like a Dragon
      2G. His Power 13:12-13
      3G. His Purpose 13:14-18
  3E. The Redemption of the 144000 during The Tribulation 14:1-5
  4E. The Reports from Heaven during The Tribulation 14:6-13

1F. The First Message 14:6-7
2F. The Second Message 14:8
3F. The Third Message - 14:9-12
4F. The Fourth Message 14:13
5E. Reaping of Judgment during the Tribulation 14:14-19:21
   1F. Judgment of the Beast and False Prophet 14:14-20
      1G. The Conqueror 14:14
      2G. The Conquest 14:15-20
   2F. Judgment of the Earth 15:1-16:21
      1G. The Victorious Vision 15:1-8
         1H. Songs of Praise 15:1-4
         2H. Scene of Preparation 15:5-8
      2G. The Venomous Vials 16:1-21
         1H. The First Vial - Damaging Sores 16:1-2
         2H. Second Vial - Deadly Seas 16:3
         3H. Third Vial - Deplorable Springs 16:4-7
         4H. Fourth Vial - Dangerous Sunlight 16:8-9
         5H. Fifth Vial - Dark Seizure 16:10-11
         6H. Sixth Vial - Drying of the Strait 16:12
         ( ) Demonic Spirits 16:13-16
         7H. Seventh Vial - Destructive Scourge 16:17-21
   3F. Judgment of Babylon 17:1-19:6
      1G. Preface about the Woman 17:1-2
      2G. Perversity of the Woman 17:3-6
      3G. Position of the Woman 17:7-18
      4G. Punishment of the Woman 18:1-19:6
         1H. Ruin 18:1-8
         2H. Reaction 18:9-19:6
            1I. On Earth 18:9-19
            2I. In Heaven 18:20-19:6
   4F. Judgment at Armageddon 19:7-21
      1G. Heavenly Jubilation 19:7-10
      (The Marriage Supper of The Lamb)
      2G. Horrible Judgment 19:11-21
         1H. The Coming of Christ's Army 19:11-16
         2H. The Crumbling of the Beast's Army 19:17-21
2C. The Millennium 20:1-15
   1D. Preparation for the Period 20:1-3
   2D. Progress during the Period 20:4-6

3D. Postscript to the Period 20:7-15
   1E. Rebellion 20:7-9
   2E. Retribution 20:10-15
      1F. The devil 20:10
      2F. The Deceived 20:11-15
3B. The Scene on the New Earth 21:1-22:21

Appendix R
Expository Sermons on Daniel, by Ray C. Stedman
From the Ray Stedman Library

View at:
http://www.raystedman.org/old-testament/daniel/

Appendix S
Ancient Prophecies and Ancient Prayers for the End of the Age
By Lambert Dolphin

This is a shortened version of this study. View the full article at
http://www.ldolphin.org/kingdom/append.html

Chuck Missler has often noted that the world is now entering into a climactic time about which the Bible has more to say than any other period of history, including the time of the first Advent of Jesus.

The Old Testament speaks with clarity and new relevance of the end time events again and again. As we approach the time of the end we can expect the Spirit of God to illuminate many previously obscure passages in the Old Testament. We can also expect to see new light on passages we previously understood only in part.

For example, the deliverance of the godly remnant by Jesus, "the angel of the presence" from Petra at the close of The Tribulation Period is alluded to by Moses in his last words to his people before he died. All we need do is to change the past tense verbs to future in our English translations of the Hebrew text (Deuteronomy 33:1-5).

Earlier we saw that the imagery of the remnant being taken to Petra "on eagles' wings" was reminiscent of God's deliverance of his people under Moses. God will supernaturally protect his remnant in the wilderness of Petra and supernaturally rescue them from the pursuit of the devil's forces (Revelation 12:15, 16). Jesus will then lead the remnant to

Jerusalem where he will make his public appearance, his *epiphaneia*. Earth's rightful ruler will be publicly unveiled in Jerusalem. Jesus foretold of this event (Luke 21:22-28).

Moses at his death gave prophetic blessings upon the tribes of Israel, one by one. The final fulfillment of these promises will take place after Messiah returns to Jerusalem by way of Seir and Bozrah (Deuteronomy 33).

An enigmatic prophecy about Enoch (who was translated into heaven prior to the flood of Noah) is recorded in the book of Jude has a double-fulfillment: First, at the time of the Flood of Noah to judge the antediluvian world, destroying probably many billions of earth's inhabitants and delivering eight persons in the Ark. Then, at the end of the age in which we live Jesus will again appear "with his ten thousands of holy ones" (Jude 14-15).

Mystery-filled prophecies in Ezekiel and Isaiah clearly relate in part to the end time and God's judgment of his people Israel (Ezekiel 20:33-44; Isaiah 11).

Ezekiel says the following about God's mercy, grace and compassion coming on the nation of Israel at the close of the age we live in:

> For I will take you out of the nations; I will gather you from all the countries and bring you back into your own land. [25] I will sprinkle clean water on you, and you will be clean; I will cleanse you from all your impurities and from all your idols. [26] I will give you a new heart and put a new spirit in you; I will remove from you your heart of stone and give you a heart of flesh. [27] And I will put my Spirit in you and move you to follow my decrees and be careful to keep my laws. - Ezekiel 36:25-27

This is an announcement, similar to Jeremiah 30, of God's intention to bring the people of Israel into the New Covenant, which Jesus put into effect with his 11 disciples at the Last Supper.

Ezekiel then describes Messiah's reign over all the nations, from Jerusalem, and the millennial prosperity he will bring to all mankind, through Israel (Ezekiel 36:21-38).

The believing remnant is gathered under the care of the Great Shepherd of the Sheep at Bozrah,

"I will surely gather all of you, O Jacob;
    I will surely bring together the remnant of Israel.
    I will bring them together like sheep in a pen,
    like a flock in its pasture;
    the place will throng with people.
[13] One who breaks open the way will go up before them;
    they will break through the gate and go out.
    Their king will pass through before them,
    the LORD at their head." - Micah 2:12-13

The Lord's return (at the *parousia*) to care for his remnant at Petra and his leading them safely back to Jerusalem by way of Bozrah is then compared by Isaiah with God's care for the Jews through the wilderness in the Days of Moses. Then follows a prayer of the remnant for deliverance (Isaiah 63).

Prayers for Israel from Long Ago
The Hebrew Prophetic Future Verb Tense

Verb tenses are not as clearly specified in the Hebrew language as they are in English. In a number of prophetic passages of the Old Testament the verbs are commonly translated as past tense in our English Bibles. However, the prophetic future tense can equally well be used. (Note: When the Hebrew letter *waw* is added before a word it means "and." When added as a suffix it means "his." *Waw* before a verb indicates a change of the tense of the verb from past to future and vice versa (a verb in the past tense with a *waw* in front of it is to be understood as future tense).

Notice in the passage below how the words of the prophet Habakkuk take on new meaning for the end of the age if one switches the verb tenses from past tense to future. Habakkuk lived just before Nebuchadnezzar's siege and destruction of Jerusalem and the Second Temple so he was downhearted and grieved because God was bringing great Israel against the chosen people through a foreign people of even great wickedness. It was a dark hour for history similar to the hour that Israel faces in our own time, so Habakkuk's words and prayers applied to his immediate situation. Yet his prayer would seem to apply equally well to the end of the present age.

> A prayer of Habakkuk the prophet. On shigionoth .
> ² LORD, I have heard of your fame;
>> I stand in awe of your deeds, O LORD.
>> Renew them in our day,
>> in our time make them known;
>> in wrath remember mercy.
> ³ God came from Teman,
>> the Holy One from Mount Paran.
>> Selah
>> His glory covered the heavens
>> and his praise filled the earth.
> ⁴ His splendor was like the sunrise;
>> rays flashed from his hand,
>> where his power was hidden.
> ⁵ Plague went before him;
>> pestilence followed his steps.
> ⁶ He stood, and shook the earth;

he looked, and made the nations tremble.
The ancient mountains crumbled
and the age-old hills collapsed.
His ways are eternal.
[7] I saw the tents of Cushan in distress,
the dwellings of Midian in anguish.
[8] Were you angry with the rivers, O LORD?
Was your wrath against the streams?
Did you rage against the sea
when you rode with your horses
and your victorious chariots?
[9] You uncovered your bow,
you called for many arrows.
Selah
You split the earth with rivers;
[10] the mountains saw you and writhed.
Torrents of water swept by;
the deep roared
and lifted its waves on high.
[11] Sun and moon stood still in the heavens
at the glint of your flying arrows,
at the lightning of your flashing spear.
[12] In wrath you strode through the earth
and in anger you threshed the nations.
[13] You came out to deliver your people,
to save your anointed one.
You crushed the leader of the land of wickedness,
you stripped him from head to foot.
Selah
[14] With his own spear you pierced his head
when his warriors stormed out to scatter us,
gloating as though about to devour
the wretched who were in hiding.
[15] You trampled the sea with your horses,
churning the great waters.
[16] I heard and my heart pounded,
my lips quivered at the sound;
decay crept into my bones,
and my legs trembled.
Yet I will wait patiently for the day of calamity
to come on the nation invading us.
[17] Though the fig tree does not bud

and there are no grapes on the vines,
    though the olive crop fails
    and the fields produce no food,
    though there are no sheep in the pen
    and no cattle in the stalls,
[18] yet I will rejoice in the LORD,
    I will be joyful in God my Savior.
[19] The Sovereign LORD is my strength;
    he makes my feet like the feet of a deer,
    he enables me to go on the heights.
    For the director of music. On my stringed instruments. - Habakkuk 3:1-19

Isaiah Chapters 24 through 27 are often called "The Little Apocalypse" because of the prophet's description of this end-time period, "the time of Jacob's trouble" for Israel (Jeremiah 30).

The Final Conversion of Israel

Israel's national prayer for their Messiah to come and to forgive them is found in Hosea Chapter 5 beginning at verse 15. Most reputable scholars believe this prayer must be prayed by the nation as a precondition for their national salvation in the coming of Jesus the Messiah to save them:

Then I will go back to my place
    until they admit their guilt.
    And they will seek my face;
    in their misery they will earnestly seek me."
[1] "Come, let us return to the LORD.
    He has torn us to pieces
    but he will heal us;
    he has injured us
    but he will bind up our wounds.
[2] After two days he will revive us;
    on the third day he will restore us,
    that we may live in his presence.
[3] Let us acknowledge the LORD;
    let us press on to acknowledge him.
    As surely as the sun rises,
    he will appear;
    he will come to us like the winter rains,
    like the spring rains that water the earth." - Hosea 5:15-6:3

Earlier we traced the escape of a remnant of some thousands—perhaps tens of thousands—of believing Jews from Jerusalem to Petra, which will take at the time of the desecration of the Third Temple at the mid-point of the Tribulation period.

As the age comes to a full close many passages of Scripture speak of the national conversion of Israel. We have seen that the imagery of the trampling out of the vineyard and the blood like grape juice flowing as high as a horse's bridle up and down the length of Israel will be Jewish blood as God judges the apostate majority of Jews in the land of Israel. In this terrible time for Israel, millions of men from invading Gentile armies fighting World War III in Israel will also meet their violent end. All the while the terrible judgments from God depicted in the book of Revelation will devastate the entire earth. Most of mankind will perish and the great infrastructures of the past thousand of years of civilization will be destroyed.

Yet Paul argues in Romans 11 that in spite of all this, "all Israel will be saved" (Romans 11:25-36). Here is a portion of that passage:

> I do not want you to be ignorant of this mystery, brothers, so that you may not be conceited:
> Israel has experienced a hardening in part until the full number of the Gentiles has come in.
> [26]And so all Israel will be saved, as it is written:
> "The deliverer will come from Zion;
>   he will turn godlessness away from Jacob.
> [27]And this is my covenant with them
>   when I take away their sins." - Romans 11:25-27

Paul is careful to make clear that he is not speaking of each and every Jew being converted, but true Israel is limited to those who ultimately believe in Jesus within the nation. Just how many Jews will be saved at the very end of the age?

Though our own nation, the United States, contains a professing Christian population that appears to number many tens of millions of believers, it is more realistic to say that the "believing remnant" in America today is perhaps only 5 to 10% of those professing faith in Jesus Christ. Thus the future large-scale conversion of Jews to belief in Jesus at the close of the age will represent a very great work of grace by the God of Israel. A final conversion of one-third of the populace of Israel will surely be very large in percentage compared to the size of the fractional wheat harvest from among the Gentiles. The end result of Jesus' work in Israel at the end of the age will be a completely righteous nation of believers chosen to be the head of all the nations.

In the midst of Isaiah's description of the terrible judgments during the time of Jacob's trouble, the prophet gives a call for the remnant to hide themselves for a season (Isaiah chapters 24-27).

The post-exilic prophet Zechariah had much to say about the close of the age we live in as well as details about both the identity and character of both the true Messiah and the end-times imposter (Zechariah 12-14).

> I am going to make Jerusalem a cup that sends all the surrounding peoples reeling. Judah will be besieged as well as Jerusalem. ³ On that day, when all the nations of the earth are gathered against her, I will make Jerusalem an immovable rock for all the nations. All who try to move it will injure themselves. - Zechariah 12:2-3

The term "on that day" indicates that the passage is referring to the Day of the Lord, i.e. the Great Tribulation period:

The Wine Press of Wrath upon the Jews

> ¹⁴I looked, and there before me was a white cloud, and seated on the cloud was one "like a son of man" with a crown of gold on his head and a sharp sickle in his hand. ¹⁵Then another angel came out of the temple and called in a loud voice to him who was sitting on the cloud, "Take your sickle and reap, because the time to reap has come, for the harvest of the earth is ripe." ¹⁶So he who was seated on the cloud swung his sickle over the earth, and the earth was harvested.
> ¹⁷Another angel came out of the temple in heaven, and he too had a sharp sickle. ¹⁸Still another angel, who had charge of the fire, came from the altar and called in a loud voice to him who had the sharp sickle, "Take your sharp sickle and gather the clusters of grapes from the earth's vine, because its grapes are ripe." ¹⁹The angel swung his sickle on the earth, gathered its grapes and threw them into the great winepress of God's wrath. ²⁰They were trampled in the winepress outside the city, and blood flowed out of the press, rising as high as the horses' bridles for a distance of 1,600 stadia. - Revelation 14:14-20

The first sickle and the references to the reaping of the harvest of the earth indicates the reaping of the wheat and the tares from the nations (Matthew 13).This is a final separation of the believers in the nations other than Israel divided and differentiated from the unbelievers with whom they are co-mingled.

This series of events is also foretold by the prophet Joel (Joel 3). First Joel discusses the judgment of the nations on the basis of their treatment of the God's people the Jews. This is the same judgment we know as the "Judgment of the Sheep and the Goats" from Matthew 25:31-46.

Joel now announces the assembly of the nations to the Battle of Armageddon. It is God who draws these armies into his land.

Next, Joel invokes the Lord to come down with his armies of heaven to fight against the nations. Again, this is the sheep and goat judgment of Matthew 25:31-46. The Valley of

Jehoshaphat is most probably the Kidron Valley between the Temple Mount and the Mount of Olives.

Likewise, Israel is to be judged.

The Lord makes his open appearance upon the Mount of Olives in Jerusalem in the midst of the battle:

The return of the Lord leads at last into the conditions of peace on earth under Messiah's long-expected reign.

A clear description of this same event—the coming of Messiah to the Mount of Olives in power and glory—is described by the aged Apostle John (Revelation 19:11-20).

Notice that the armies of the world originally gather to battle at Megiddo—to fight one another. In the midst of that battle, ominous portents from outer space—visions and signs of the approach of Jesus—cause the armies of the world to turn and fight against God and his armies!

Isaiah's Prayer for the Soon-Coming of Messiah:

In Isaiah chapters 64 through 66, the prophet asks for the Lord to come down to deliver Israel, and Messiah answers him with great detail, announcing his return in judgment for sinners and blessing for believers.

Appendix T
Do You Know Christ Personally?

So what is the meaning of all of this? Why did God go to so much trouble to tell us what is going to happen in the future? Two thousand years ago the people who asked these very questions were the ones who were looking for the coming of Messiah. They recognized Jesus for who He was and they believed in him. They accepted the Gospel, or "Good News" about Christ. Today when you recognize these "Signs of the Times" it may cause you to ask the most important question of all: *What must I do to be saved?* (Acts 16:32) And the answer is: *Believe on the Lord Jesus Christ, and you shall be saved* (Acts 16:33). But what exactly does this mean?

First, you must admit that you have sinned: fallen short of God's expectations of you, and that the payment of sin is death. You could never pay for your own sin, but Jesus Christ paid for it by dying in your place.

For all have sinned and fall short of the glory of God... - Romans 3:23

For the wages of sin is death, but the gift of God is eternal life in Christ Jesus our Lord. - Romans 6:23

Then, you must ask Christ to be your Savior and your Lord. Here are several verses of Scripture that say the same thing in slightly different ways:

Yet to all who received him, to those who believed in his name, he gave the right to become children of God. - John 1:12

That if you confess with your mouth, "Jesus is Lord," and believe in your heart that God raised him from the dead, you will be saved. For it is with your heart that you believe and are justified, and it is with your mouth that you confess and are saved. - Romans 10:9-10

Here I am! I stand at the door and knock. If anyone hears my voice and opens the door, I will come in and eat with him, and he with me. - Revelation 3:20

You may ask Christ into your life by prayer. Prayer is simply talking to God. Tell him something like this: "Dear Lord, I know that I'm a sinner, and I need Jesus Christ to save me from my sin. Right now, I open the door of my life and ask Jesus to come in. Be my Savior and my Lord."

Did you pray? It isn't the exact words that count, but in your own way, if you confessed your sin and asked Christ to become your Savior, he kept his promise and entered your life. This is what the Bible means about being "born again." (John 3:3,5) You have been born into the family of God. Now, be sure to tell someone what you have done!

There is one other thing. The Bible teaches that all believers should be baptized (Matthew 28:18-20 and the example of all converts in the Book of Acts). Find a good Bible-teaching church in your area and ask to be baptized right away in order to be identified with Christ and to be obedient to him.

If you have made that decision and would like to have help to get started in your Christian life, contact either of the authors via their web sites (See Bibliography), and we will be happy to send you some simple follow-up materials.

NOTES

[1] Life in 2050: Amazing Science, Familiar Threats: Public Sees A Future Full of Promise and Peril, The Pew Research Center For The People & The Press,
http://people-press.org/reports/pdf/625.pdf (accessed July 17, 2010).

[2] C.G. Finney, "The Whole Counsel of God," The Gospel Truth,
http://www.gospeltruth.net/1849-51Penny_Pulpit/510402pp_counsel_of_god.htm (accessed July 18, 2010).

[3] Josh McDowell, Evidence That Demands a Verdict (San Bernardino, CA: Campus Crusade for Christ, 1972), 175; and Peter Stoner, Science Speaks (Chicago, IL, 1963).

[4] Joseph A. Seiss, The Gospel In The Stars (Philadelphia: The United Lutheran Publishing Company, 1884); and

E.W. Bullinger, The Witness of the Stars (Grand Rapids, MI: Kregel Publications, 1967). This theory has been endorsed today by such well known Bible teachers as Chuck Missler. Audio: Signs in the Heavens. (Coeur d'Alene, ID: Koinonia House); and

D. James Kennedy (Message televised from Coral Ridge Presbyterian Church, Jan. 7, 1996, and) The Real Meaning Of The Zodiac (Coral Ridge, FL: Coral Ridge Media Ministries); and by

Dr. Henry M. Morris in his book, The Long War against God (Grand Rapids, MI: Baker Book House, 1990), 265-269.

[5] Jewish, and Christian End-Times Prophecy Comparison, Contender Ministries,
http://www.contenderministries.org/prophecy/eschatology.phpMuslim (accessed September 20, 2010).

[6] Islamic Prophecies, Wikiislam.net, http://www.wikiislam.net/wiki/Islamic_Prophecies (accessed September 20, 2010).

[7] John von Heyking, Iran's President and the Politics of the Twelfth Imam, Ashbrook Center.com, http://www.ashbrook.org/publicat/guest/05/vonheyking/twelfthimam.html (accessed September 20, 2010).

[8] Palestine, Nelson's Illustrated Bible Dictionary, Copyright (c)1986, Thomas Nelson Publishers, PC Study Bible, v.3

[9] See Chapter 10 (online) of Sir Robert Anderson's "The Coming Prince." He calculated the duration of the first sixty-nine years of Gabriel's prophecy about the "Seventy Weeks." This prophecy is recorded in Daniel 9:20-27. The 69 weeks represent 483 years (69 X 7) beginning with the decree issued by Artaxerxes Longimanus in the twentieth year of his reign, authorizing Nehemiah to rebuild the fortifications of Jerusalem. It ends on the very day that Christ offered himself to be King of the Jews, but was rejected by his enemies.
http://philologos.org/__eb-tcp/chap10.htm (accessed July 17, 2010).

[10] Ray Stedman, "The New Earth," Ray Stedman.org

http://www.raystedman.org/thematic-studies/prophecy/the-new-earth (accessed July 11, 2010).

[11] Chuck Missler, "Revelation 17—19," Koinonia House,
http://www.khouse.org/6640/CD005-13/ (accessed July 11, 2010).

[12] Alexander Hislop, The Two Babylons, Chapter 6 - Section 1 - The Great Red Dragon, BibleBelievers.com
http://www.biblebelievers.com/babylon/sect71.htm (accessed July 11, 2010).

[13] Ibid.

[14] The phrase Finder, "Attributed to John Emerich Edward Dalberg Acton, first Baron Acton (1834–1902). The historian and moralist, who was otherwise known simply as Lord Acton, expressed this opinion in a letter to Bishop Mandell Creighton in 1887: 'Power tends to corrupt, and absolute power corrupts absolutely. Great men are almost always bad men.'" http://www.phrases.org.uk/meanings/288200.html (July 28,2010).

[15] The average age of the inhabitants of that first generation was approximately 900 years, and during that span they had very large families. Therefore the population of the earth during Cain's lifetime could have reached many thousands of people. They were, of course all related, but being so close to the origin of Adam and Eve's originally perfect gene pool, they did not suffer the birth defects that now accompany inbreeding.

[16] Jack Kinsella, "In The Days of These Kings," The Omega Letter, http://www.omegaletter.com/articles/articles.asp?ArticleID=4234 (accessed July 24, 2010).

[17] Wikipedia, "Western European Union," Wikipedia, http://en.wikipedia.org/wiki/Western_European_Union (accessed July 24, 2010).

[18] Alexander Hislop, "The Two Babylons," ...-ibid.
also online at http://philologos.org/__eb-ttb/ (accessed July 24, 2010).

[19] History of the Knights Templar, Wikipedia, http://en.wikipedia.org/wiki/History_of_the_Knights_Templar (accessed July 30,2010).

[20] Gary H. Kah, En Route to Global Occupation (Noblesville, IN: Hope for the World, 2008; originally published in Lafayette, LA: Huntington House Publishers, 1992), 107.
This book is our primary source for the information in this chapter and is recommended reading for gaining greater understanding of the historical influence of Freemasonry. (See www.garykah.org)

[21] Ibid.

[22] Ibid., 26-27.

[23] (From U.S. George Washington Bicentennial Commission, The Writings of George Washington, Vol. 20 (Washington D.C.: U.S. Government Printing Office, 1941), 518; and Ralph Epperson, The Conspiratorial View of History (Tucson, AZ: Epperson, 1986),2.

[24] Ibid., 113.

[25] Ibid., 111-114.

[26] Ibid.

[27] Ibid., 116-117.

[28] History of the Parliament, Council for the Parliament of World Religions, http://www.parliamentofreligions.org/index.cfm?n=1&sn=4 (accessed July 29,2010).

[29] Gary Allen with Larry Abraham, None Dare Call It Conspiracy, 1971, p. 48, Captain Canada's Crusade, http://www.captaincanadacrusades.ca/articles/none-dare-call-it-conspiracy%5B1%5D.pdf (accessed July 30, 2010).

[30] Ibid.

[31] European Union in 2010: Austria, Belgium, Bulgaria, Cyprus, Czech Republic, Denmark, Estonia, Finland, France, Germany, Greece, Hungary, Ireland, Italy, Latvia, Lithuania, Luxembourg, Malta, Netherlands, Poland, Portugal, Romania, Slovakia, Slovenia, Spain, Sweden, and UK. There are four candidate countries: Croatia, Iceland, Macedonia, and Turkey.

[32] Union For The Mediterranean: 27 from the EU, plus, Albania, Algeria, Bosnia Herzegovina, Croatia, Egypt, Israel, Jordan, Lebanon, Mauritania, Monaco, Montenegro, Morocco, the Palestinian Authority, Syria, Tunisia, and Turkey.

[33] Mediterranean Union To Be Launched, EUObserver, http://euobserver.com/9/26478 (accessed 8/2/2010).

[34] Crisis makes Europe the richest region in the world, study says, EUObserver, http://euobserver.com/9/28672, (accessed August 2, 2010).

[35] Muslim Demographics, You Tube, http://www.youtube.com/watch?v=6-3X5hIFXYU (accessed September 20, 2010).

[36] Leah Seppanen Anderson, Islam in Europe, Books and Culture, http://www.booksandculture.com/articles/2010/janfeb/islamineurope.html, (accessed August 2, 2010).

[37] Gary H. Kah, The New World Religion (Noblesville, Indiana: Hope International Publishing, Inc., 1999), 29.

[38] Ibid., 30.

[39] Barbara Curtis, What is 'New Age' Religion, and Why Can't Christians Get on Board?, Crosswalk.com, http://www.crosswalk.com/spirituallife/11573681/ (accessed August 6, 2010).

[40] The Omega Letter, Jan Markel, The Twisted World of Oprah and Friends, OmegaLetter.com, http://www.omegaletter.com/articles/articles.asp?ArticleID=6236 (accessed August 8, 2010).

[41] Top 25 Influential Women in the World Today, TotallyHer.com, http://www.totallyher.com/top-25-influential-women-in-the-world-today/ (accessed August 8, 2010).

[42] Chapter 8.5: The Club of Rome, The Modern History Project, http://www.modernhistoryproject.org/mhp/ArticleDisplay.php?Article=FinalWarn08-5 (accessed August 2, 2010).

[43] The Club of Rome, Organization, ClubOfRome.org, http://www.clubofrome.org/eng/about/3/ (accessed August 12, 2010).

[44] Wikipedia, United Religions Initiative, Wikipedia.org, http://en.wikipedia.org/wiki/United_Religions_Initiative#cite_note-2 (accessed August 8, 2010).

[45] United Religions Official Website, http://www.uri.org/cooperation_circles, (accessed August 8,2010).

[46] Joseph Farah, Out of chaos, a new world order, WorldNetDaily, http://www.wnd.com/index.php?fa=PAGE.view&pageId=91100 (accessed August 12, 2010).

[47] Brown sees 'new world order' after crisis, Google: AFP, http://www.google.com/hostednews/afp/article/ALeqM5i401zq4gx4DHyS97JTNbQmF_Hqbg (accessed August 16, 2010).

[48] Joseph Farah, The most chilling words since 'New World Order', WorldNetDaily, http://www.wnd.com/index.php?fa=PAGE.view&pageId=94301, (accessed Aug. 13, 2010).

[49] Ahmadinejad Stresses need for a new world order, PressTV, http://www.presstv.ir/detail/98260.htm?sectionid=351020101 (accessed August 12, 2010).

[50] Stephen C. Webster United Nations conference calls for new global currency, RawStory.com, http://rawstory.com/08/news/2009/09/07/united-nations-calls-for-new-world-currency/, (accessed august 13, 2010).

[51] Rabbi Yehudah Prero, "The Shofar: A Wake-Up Call," Torah.org, http://www.torah.org/learning/yomtov/roshhashanah/vol1no37.html (accessed July 23, 2010). Also: "The Last Trump," Philologos, http://philologos.org/bpr/files/002.htm (accessed July 23, 2010).

[52] Allah and the Temple Mount, Focus On Jerusalem, http://focusonjerusalem.com/allahandthetemplemount.html (accessed Aug. 18, 2010).

[53] Caliph is an Arabic word meaning successor (to Muhammad),

[54] Ilya/Jerusalem, InTheNameOf allah.org, http://www.inthenameofallah.org/Ilya%20Or%20Jerusalem.html (accessed August 18, 2010).

[55] Lambert Dolphin, Allah and the Temple Mount, TempleMount.org., http://www.templemount.org/allah.html (accessed August 18, 2010).

[56] Ibid.

[57] Ibid.

[58] This section is taken from author Lambert Dolphin's website: A Short Summary of Islamic Beliefs and Eschatology, Lambert Dolphin's Library, http://ldolphin.org/islam.shtml (accessed August 18, 2010).

[59] Lambert Dolphin, Allah and the Temple Mount, TempleMount.org., http://www.templemount.org/allah.html (accessed August 18, 2010)..

[60] Ibid.

[61] Ibid.

[62] Ibid.

[63] Third Temple, Wikipedia, http://en.wikipedia.org/wiki/Third_Temple (accessed September 22, 2010).

[64] How Strong Is The Jewish Connection To Its Homeland?, The Peace FAQ, http://www.peacefaq.com/zionism.html (accessed September 22, 2010).

[65] Lambert Dolphin, Ibid.

[66] Ibid.

[67] Ibid.

[68] Ibid.

[69] The Balfour Declaration November 2, 1917,Israeli Ministry of Foreign Affairs, ttp://www.mfa.gov.il/MFA/Peace%20Process/Guide%20to%20the%20Peace%20Process/The%20Balfour%20Declaration (accessed August 19, 2010).

[70] Article 22, The Covenant of the League of Nations, and "Mandate for Palestine," Encyclopedia Judaica, Vol. 11 (Jerusalem: Keter Publishing House, 1972), 862.

[71] Palestinian Liberation Organization, Wikipedia.org, http://en.wikipedia.org/wiki/Palestine_Liberation_Organization (accessed August 23, 2010).

[72] Palestinian Liberation Organization, Wikipedia.org, http://en.wikipedia.org/wiki/Palestine_Liberation_Organization (accessed August 23, 2010).

[73] Mosab Hassan Yousef with Ron Brackin, Son of Hamas (Carol Stream, Illinois: Tyndale House Publishers, Inc. 2010).

[74] Hamas accepts Israel's right to exist, Prophecy Central, http://www.bible-prophecy.com/2010/warmideast2010.htm#100122 (accessed August 23, 2010).

[75] Mosab Hassan Yousef with Ron Brackin, Son of Hamas (Carol Stream, Illinois: Tyndale House Publishers, Inc. 2010), Kindle, location 907.

[76] Ibid., location 921.

[77] Palestinians Get Saddam Charity Checks, CBS News, http://www.cbsnews.com/stories/2003/03/14/world/main543981.shtml (accessed August 23, 2010). And Saddam Pays $25K for Palestinian Bombers, Fox News, http://www.foxnews.com/story/0,2933,48822,00.html (accessed August 23, 2010).

[78] Mike Evans, The Final Move Beyond Iraq (Lake Mary, Florida: Frontline, 2007), 155.

[79] Ibid., 161.

[80] Muslim Conversions to Christianity, John Mark Ministries, http://jmm.aaa.net.au/articles/19621.htm (accessed September 4, 2010).

[81] Sir Robert Anderson, The Coming Prince, http://philologos.org/__eb-tcp/chap10.htm (accessed July 17, 2010).

[82] Ray C. Stedman, What on Earth is Happening, (Grand Rapids: Michigan, 2003) copyright by Elaine Stedman 2003. Grateful acknowledgement is made to the Stedman Family for permission to use quotations from Ray C. Stedman. Quotations remain the property of Ray Stedman Ministries; © 2007 by Elaine Stedman — www.raystedman.org.

[83] Ibid.

[84] Ray Stedman, Four Terrible Horsemen, RayStedman.org, http://www.raystedman.org/new-testament/revelation/four-terrible-horsemen. Used by permission.

[85] The Development and Proliferation of Nuclear Weapons, NobelPrize.org, http://nobelprize.org/educational/peace/nuclear_weapons/readmore.html (accessed August 25, 2010).

[86] Archive of Nuclear Data, Natural Resources Defense Council, http://www.nrdc.org/nuclear/nudb/datab19.asp (accessed August 25, 2010).

[87] Bruce Menzies, Studies in Eschatology, 128, BruceMenzies.com, http://brucemenzies.com/files/Studies_in_Eschatology.pdf (accessed August 25, 2010).

[88] Ibid.

[89] Chuck Missler, "The Magog Invasion" Briefing Package, (Coeur d'Alene, Idaho: Koinonia House, 1995), 1-2.

[90] Ray Stedman, Ibid.

[91] Ibid.

[92] Poll: Israelis want their temple back, IsraelToday.com, http://www.israeltoday.co.il/default.aspx?tabid=178&nid=21549 (accessed August 27, 2010).

[93] The Temple Mount In Jerusalem, TempleMount.org, http://templemount.org/ (accessed August 27, 2010).

[94] Tuvia Sagiv, The Hidden Secrets of the Temple Mount, TempleMount.com, http://www.templemount.org/tempmt.html (accessed August 27, 2010).

[95] Chuck Missler, The Coming Temple Briefing Package, (Coeur d'Alene, Idaho: Koinonia House, 1995).

[96] Arthur & Rosalind Eedie, The Ark of the Covenant, http://webhome.idirect.com/~birkej/ark/arcofcov.htm (accessed August 28, 2010).

[97] The Ark of the Covenant, CovenantKeepers.co.uk, http://www.wyattarchaeology.com/ (accessed August 28, 2010).

[98] Ark of the Covenant, Prophecy Central, http://www.bible-prophecy.com/ark.htm#ark (accessed August 28, 2010).

[99] Arnold Fruchtenbaum, The Modern State of Israel In Bible Prophecy, Ariel.org, http://www.arielm.org/dcs/pdf/mbs189m.pdf (accessed August 28, 2010). Also see:
Ateret Cohanim, Wikipedia, http://en.wikipedia.org/wiki/Ateret_Cohanim (accessed August 28, 2010).

[100] Tim LaHaye and Jerry B. Jenkins, Are We Living In The End Times? (Tyndale House Publishers, 1999) 125.

[101] Temple Mount and Eretz Israel Faithful Movement, http://www.templemountfaithful.org/ (accessed August 28, 2010).

[102] The Temple Institute in Jerusalem Has Spent Approximately 27 Million Dollars On Preparations For The Rebuilding Of The Jewish Temple, The Last Days, http://signsofthelastdays.com/archives/the-temple-institute-in-jerusalem-has-spent-approximately-27-million-dollars-to-make-preparations-for-the-rebuilding-of-the-jewish-temple (accessed August 28, 2010).

[103] Solomon's Temple in Brazil would put Christ the Redeemer in the shade, Guardian.co.uk, http://www.guardian.co.uk/world/2010/jul/21/solomon-temple-brazil-christ-redeemer (accessed August 28, 2010).

[104] The Temple Mount, http://www.templemount.org, and
The Temple, Prophecy Central, http://www.bible-prophecy.com/temple2.htm

[105] L. Gordon Crovitz, Technology Predictions Are Mostly Bunk, The Wall Street Journal, Dec. 27, 2009, http://online.wsj.com/article/SB10001424052748704039704574616401913653862.html?mod=rss_opinion_main (accessed August 29, 2010).

[106] Intel Core i7-980X processor, Intel.com, http://ark.intel.com/Product.aspx?id=47932 (accessed August 30, 2010).

[107] Intel Core i7-980X Extreme 6-Core Processor Review, HotHardware.com, Intel Core i7-980X Extreme 6-Core Processor Review (accessed August 30, 2010).

[108] Laptop for every pupil in Uruguay, BBC News, http://news.bbc.co.uk/2/hi/technology/8309583.stm (accessed August 30, 2010).

[109] Fastest Supercomputer Ever To Simulate Nuclear Blasts, Fox News, http://www.foxnews.com/story/0,2933,487324,00.html?sPage=fnc/scitech/innovation (accessed August 30, 2010).

[110] Quantum computer slips onto chips, BBD, http://news.bbc.co.uk/2/hi/science/nature/8236943.stm (accessed September 1, 2010).

[111] Biocomputers, Wikipedia, http://en.wikipedia.org/wiki/Biocomputers (accessed Sept. 1, 2010).

[112] China becomes biggest net nation, BBC, http://news.bbc.co.uk/2/hi/technology/7528396.stm (accessed September 1, 2010).

[113] "The Grid" Could Soon Make the Internet Obsolete, Fox, http://www.foxnews.com/story/0,2933,347212,00.html (accessed September 1, 2010).

[114] Ben Dominico, Get Connected! Achieving vIDD, the Next-Generation IDD, Unidata, http://www.unidata.ucar.edu/newsletter/1997sprsum/97sprsumel.html (accessed Sept. 1, 2010).

[115] Peter Eichenbaum and Margaret Collins, AT&T, Verizon to Target Visa, MasterCard With Smartphones, Bloomberg, http://www.bloomberg.com/news/2010-08-02/at-t-verizon-said-to-target-visa-mastercard-with-smartphones.html (accessed September 1, 2010).

[116] Gregory Daigle, Digital displays under the skin. display whatever, whenever, OhMyNews, http://english.ohmynews.com/articleview/article_view.asp?no=296497&rel_no=1 (accessed September 1, 2010).

[117] Tom Barlow, Your Social Security number may not be unique to you, Wallet Pop, http://www.walletpop.com/blog/2010/08/12/your-social-security-number-may-not-be-unique-to-you/?icid=main|htmlws-sb-wldl5|link1|http%3A%2F%2Fwww.walletpop.com%2Fblog%2F2010%2F08%2F12%2Fyour-social-security-number-may-not-be-unique-to-you%2F (accessed September 1, 2010).

[118] John W. Whitehead, The National Biometric ID Card: The Mark of the Beast?, The Rutherford Institute, http://www.rutherford.org/articles_db/commentary.asp?record_id=649 (accessed September 1, 2010).

[119] Germany to roll out ID cards with embedded RFID, International Business Times, http://www.ibtimes.com/articles/44536/20100821/identity-cards-with-rfid-chip-on-track-in-germany.htm (accessed September 1, 2010).

[120] MIT-developed 'Bokodes' could replace bar codes, RFIDNews, http://www.rfidnews.org/2009/07/28/mit-developed-%E2%80%9Cbokodes%E2%80%9D-could-replace-barcodes (accessed September 1, 2010).

[121] Ray C. Stedman, That Strange People, The Jews, PBC Library, http://www.pbc.org/files/messages/11447/0048.html (accessed Sept. 5, 2010).

[122] William Ewing, Bozrah, International Standard Bible Encyclopaedia, Electronic Database Copyright (c)1996 by Biblesoft.

[123] Ray Stedman, The Secret Presence, RayStedman.org, http://www.raystedman.org/new-testament/matthew/the-secret-presence (accessed Sept. 6, 2010).

[124] Asteroid, World Book at NASA, NASA.gov, http://www.nasa.gov/worldbook/asteroid_worldbook.html (accessed September 6, 2020).

[125] Russell Chandler, Doomsday (Ann Arbor, MI: Servant, 1993).

[126] Asteroid, World Book at NASA, NASA.gov, http://www.nasa.gov/worldbook/asteroid_worldbook.html (accessed September 6, 2020).

[127] What If a Comet Hits Earth? TIME Magazine, Aug. 1, 1994, http://www.time.com/time/magazine/article/0,9171,981200,00.html (accessed September 6, 2010).

[128] Spacecraft Observes Coronal Mass Ejection, NASA.org, http://www.nasa.gov/topics/solarsystem/sunearth-system/main/News080210-cme.html (accessed September 6, 2010).

[129] NASA: 2012 'space Katrina' may cripple U.S. for months, 1/20/09, WorldNetDaily, http://www.wnd.com/index.php?fa=PAGE.view&pageId=85819 (accessed September 6, 2010).

[130] Hal Lindsey, There's A New World Coming, (Harvest House Publishers: Eugene, Oregon, 1984) 117.

[131] Largest Star Ever Discovered, 7/21/2010, TGDaily.com, http://www.tgdaily.com/space-features/50747-largest-ever-star-discovered (accessed September 7, 2010).

[132] Ray C. Stedman, The Near East In Prophecy, RayStedman.org, http://www.raystedman.org/thematic-studies/prophecy/the-near-east-in-prophecy (accessed September 9, 1010).

[133] Thomas Ice and Timothy J. Demy, Fast Facts on Bible Prophecy From A to Z (Harvest House: Eugene, Oregon, 1997) 24. Online at http://books.google.com/books?id=ouYiaw7xlc0C&printsec=frontcover&dq=intitle:Fast+intitle:Facts+intitle:on+intitle:Bible+intitle:Prophecy+intitle:from+intitle:A+intitle:to+intitle:Z+inauthor:thomas+inauthor:ice&hl=en&ei=sL2JTOO0HIuasAOFlaXaBA&sa=X&oi=book_result&ct=result&resnum=1&ved=0CDMQ6AEwAA#v=onepage&q&f=false (accessed September 9, 2010).

[134] Campaign of Armageddon, Spirit and Truth, SpiritandTruth.com, http://www.spiritandtruth.org/teaching/Book_of_Revelation/commentary/htm/topics/campaign.html (accessed September 9, 2010).

[135] Basics on Covenants, Focus On Jerusalem, http://focusonjerusalem.com/basicsonbiblicalcovenants.html (accessed August 24, 2010).

[136] C. I. Scofield, Scofield Reference Notes, Various Covenants, BibleStudyTools.com, http://www.biblestudytools.com/search/?q=covenants&s=References&ps=10&rc=COM&p=8 (accessed August 25, 2010).

[137] See for instance, Charles B. Thaxton, Walter L. Bradley and Roger L. Olsen, The Mystery of Life's Origin (Philosophical Library: New York, 1984).

[138] Ray Stedman, Are These The Last Days, RayStedman.org, http://www.raystedman.org/thematic-studies/prophecy/are-these-the-last-days (accessed August 25, 2010).

[139] Ray Stedman, Ch. 9: Time and Eternity, Authentic Christianity, http://www.raystedman.org/authentic-christianity/time-and-eternity (accessed August 29, 2010).

[140] Ray Stedman, 1 Thessalonians, pbc.org, http://www.pbc.org/books/1Thessalonians, and 2 Thessalonians, pbc.org, Ray Stedman, 1 Thessalonians, pbc.org, http://www.pbc.org/books/1Thessalonians (accessed September 1, 2010).

[141] Ray Stedman, What On Earth's Going To Happen?, RayStedman.org, http://www.raystedman.org/new-testament/matthew (accessed September 1, 2010).

[142] Ray Stedman, Revelation, pbc.org, http://www.pbc.org/books/Revelation (accessed Sept. 1, 2010).

[143] Ray Stedman, The Struggle for Power, RayStedman.org, http://www.raystedman.org/old-testament/esther/the-struggle-for-power (accessed September 2, 2010).

[144] Ray C. Stedman, God's Final Word: Understanding the Revelation (Discovery House: Palo Alto, CA, 1991). Used by permission.

Bibliography

Books

Alnor, William M. *Soothsayers of the Second Advent*. Old Tappan, NJ: Fleming H. Revell Company, 1989.

Ankerberg, John and John Weldon. *One World: Bible Prophecy and the New World Order*. Chicago: Moody Press, 1991.

Baldwin, Joyce. *Haggai, Zechariah, Malachi*. Downers Grove, IL: Intervarsity Press, 1972.

Baron, David. *The Visions and Prophecies of Zechariah*. Grand Rapids: Kregel Publications, 1981.

Benware, *Paul N. Understanding the End Times: A Comprehensive Approach*. Chicago: Moody Press, 1995.

Biederwolf, William E. *The Prophecy Handbook*. World Bible Publishers, 1991, first published in 1924.

Browning, Ian. *Petra*. London: Chatto and Windus Ltd., 1995, Third Edition.

Chafer, Lewis Sperry. *Ecclesiology - Eschatology:* Volume IV of Systematic Theology. Dallas, TX: Dallas Seminary Press, 1948.

Donnan, Graeme. *The King's Highway*. Amman, Jordan: Al Kutba Publishers, 1994.

Dyer, Charles H. *The Rise of Babylon: Sign of the End Times*. Wheaton, IL: Tyndale House Publishers, 1991.

Evans, Mike. *Jerusalem Betrayed: Ancient Prophecy and Modern Conspiracy Collide in the Holy City*. Dallas: Word Publishing, 1997.

Feinberg, Charles Lee. *The Prophecy of Ezekiel: The Glory of the Lord*. Chicago: Moody Press, 1969.

Franciscan Fathers, *Guide to Jordan*. Jerusalem: Franciscan Fathers Press, 1978.

Fruchtenbaum, Arnold G. *The Footsteps of the Messiah: A Study of the Sequence of Prophetic Events*. Tustin, CA: Ariel Ministries Press, 1982.

Fruchtenbaum, Arnold G. *Israelogy: The Missing Link in Systematic Theology*. Tustin, CA: Ariel Ministries Press, 1992.

Graham, Billy. *Approaching Hoofbeats: The Four Horsemen of the Apocalypse*. Minneapolis: Grason, 1983.

Graham, Billy. *Storm Warning*. Dallas: Word Publishing, 1995.

Harding, G. Lankester, *The Antiquities of Jordan*. London: The Lutterworth Press, 1990.

Hislop, Alexander. *The Two Babylons*. Neptune, NJ: Loizeaux Brothers, 1959.

Hocking, David. *The Coming World Leader*. Portland: Multnomah Press, 1988.

Hutchings, Noah W. *Petra in History and Prophecy*. Oklahoma City: Hearthstone Publishing, 1991.

Ice, Thomas and Timothy Demy. *Prophecy Watch: What to Expect in the Days to Come*. Eugene, OR: Harvest House Publishers,1998.

Ice, Thomas and Timothy Demy, editors. *When the Trumpet Sounds: Today's Foremost Authorities Speak Out on End-Time Controversies*. Eugene, OR: Harvest House Publishers, 1995.

Ice, Thomas and Randall Price, *Ready to Rebuild: The Imminent Plan to Rebuild the Last Days Temple*. Eugene, OR: Harvest House Publishers, 1992.

Jefferies, James J. *America's Seal: Its End-Time Connection*. Mission Viejo, CA: Battleline Publications, 1994.

Grant, Jeffrey R. *Armageddon: Appointment with Destiny*. Toronto: Frontier Research Publications, 1988.

Hunt, Dave. *A Woman Rides the Beast*. Eugene, OR: Harvest House Publishers, 1994.

Kah, Gary H. *The Demonic Roots of Globalism*. Lafayette, LA: Huntington House Publishers, 1995.

Kah, Gary H. *En Route To Global Occupation*. Noblesville, IN: Hope for the World, 2008; originally published in Lafayette, LA: Huntington House Publishers, 1992.

Kah, Gary H. The New World Religion. Noblesville, IN: Hope International Publishing, Inc.,1998,

Kinsella, John. *The Eternal Generation*. Stevensville, Ontario: Calvary Baptist Publishing, 1996.

LaHaye, Tim and Thomas Ice. *Charting the End Times*. Eugene Oregon: Harvest House Publishers, 2001.

LaHaye, Tim. *No Fear of The Storm*. Sisters, OR: Multnomah Press, 1992.

LaHaye, Tim. Prophecy Study Bible. Chattanooga, TN: AMG Publishers, 2001.

Lalonde, Peter and Paul Lalonde. *The Mark of the Beast*. Eugene, OR: Harvest House Publishers, 1994.

Lewis, David Allen. *Signs of His Coming*. Green Forest, AR: New Leaf Press, 1997.

Lindsey, Hal. *Planet Earth-2000 AD*. Palos Verdes, CA: Western Front, Ltd., 1994.

Lindsey, Hal. *There's A New World Coming*. Santa Ana, CA: Vision House Publishers, 1973.

Lightner, Robert P. *The Last Days Handbook: A Comprehensive Guide to Understanding the Different Views of prophecy*. Nashville: Thomas Nelson Publishers, 1990.

MacDonald, Burton. *Ammon, Moab and Edom*, Amman, Jordan: Al Kutba Publishers, 1994.

McAlvany, Donald S. *Toward A New World Order: The Countdown to Armageddon*, 2nd. ed. Phoenix: Western Pacific Publishing Co., 1992.

McClain, Alva J. *Daniel's Prophecy of the 70 Weeks*. Grand Rapids, MI: Zondervan Publishing House, 1940.

McDowell, Josh. *Evidence That Demands A Verdict*, Vol. I. Nashville: Thomas Nelson Publishers, 1972, 1979.

Missler, Chuck. *The Magog Invasion*. Palos Verdes, CA: Western Front, 1995.

Missler, Chuck. Prophecy 20:20: *Bringing the Future into Focus through the Lens of Scripture*. Nashville, TN: Nelson Books division of Thomas A. Nelson Publishers, 2006.

Monteith, Stanley, *Brotherhood of Darkness*. Oklahoma City, OK; Stanley Monteith, 2000.

Pentecost, J. Dwight. *Things to Come: A Study in Biblical Eschatology*. Grand Rapids: Zondervan, 1958.

Perkins, Bill, ed. *Steeling the Mind of America*. Green Forest, AR: New Leaf Press, 1995.

Rosenberg, Joel C. *Epicenter 2.0: Why the Current Rumblings in the Middle East Will Change Your Future*. Carol Stream, IL: Tyndale House Publishers, 2008.

Rosenberg, Joel C. *Inside The Revolution*. Carol Stream, IL: Tyndale House Publishers, 2008.

Schmitt, John W. and J. Carl Laney. *Messiah's Coming Temple: Ezekiel's Prophetic Vision of the Future Temple*. Grand Rapids: Kregel Publications, 1997.

Seiss, Joseph A., *The Gospel In The Stars*. Philadelphia: The United Lutheran Publishing Company, 1884.

Stedman, Ray C. *God's Final Word: Understanding Revelation*. Grand Rapids: Discovery House Publishers, 1991.

Stedman, Ray C. *Waiting for The Second Coming: Studies in Thessalonians*. Grand Rapids: Discovery House Publishers, 1990.

Stewart, Don and Chuck Missler. *The Coming Temple: Center Stage for the Final Countdown*. Orange, CA: Dart Press, 1991.

Taylor, Jane. *Petra*. London: Aurum Press Ltd, 1993.

Van Impe, Jack. *2001: On the Edge of Eternity*. Dallas: Word Publishing, 1996.

Walvoord, John F. *Armageddon, Oil and the Middle East Crisis*. Grand Rapids: Zondervan Publishing House, 1990.

Walvoord, John F. *Major Bible Prophecies*. Grand Rapids: Zondervan Publishing House, 1991.

Young, Edward J. *The Book of Isaiah*, Grand Rapids: Wm. H. Eerdmans, 1992.

Electronic Literature

Graff, Ron. *The Prophecy Puzzle*. Rancho Cucamonga, CA: Foremost Packaging, 1996.

Matthew Henry's Commentary, part of *PC Study Bible*. (CD ROM) Seattle, WA: Biblesoft, 1994.

Nelson's Illustrated Bible Dictionary, Thomas Nelson Publishers, 1986, part of *PC Study Bible*. (CD ROM) Seattle, WA: Biblesoft, 1994.

New Grolier Multimedia Encyclopedia, CD-ROM, 1992.

Internet Sites
— Authors' Sites
Apologetics Central. http://www.apologetics-central.com
Lambert Dolphin's Resource Files. http://ldolphin.org
Prophecy Central (Ron Graff). http://www.Bible-prophecy.com
The Temple Mount in Jerusalem. http://templemount.org

— Recommended Sites
Hal Lindsey Report, http://www.hallindsey.com/
Hope for the World (Gary Kah), http://www.garykah.org/
Hope for Today (David Hocking), http://www.davidhocking.org/
Joel C. Rosenberg, http://joelrosenberg.com/
Koinonia House (Chuck Missler), http://www.khouse.org
Prophecy Update, http://www.prophecyupdate.com/
Prophezine, (Ray Gano), http://www.prophezine.com/
Rapture Ready (Todd Strandberg), http://www.raptureready.com/
The Ray C. Stedman Library. http://pbc.org/dp/stedman
Tim Lahaye Ministries, https://timlahaye.com/
World Watch Daily (Bill Koenig), http://www.watch.org/articles.html?mcat=1

— Extensive List of Prophecy Sites
About Prophecy. http://www.bible-prophecy.com/links.htm

Index

Breinigsville, PA USA
15 November 2010
249326BV00003B/2/P